The UK Anti-Bribery Handbook

Second Edition

Christopher Sallon QC
Formerly Head of the Finance and Regulatory Team,
Doughty Street Chambers

Sam Tate
Partner RPC LLP

Contributors

Nichola Higgins
Barrister, Matrix Law

Susan Scott
Leadership Coach and Financial Crime Consultant

Stephen Storey
Group Head of Ethics and Integrity, Compass Grc

Christopher Sykes
Barrister, Doughty Street Chambers

Bloomsbury Professional

LONDON • DUBLIN • EDINBURGH • NEW YORK • NEW DELHI • SYDNEY

BLOOMSBURY PROFESSIONAL
Bloomsbury Publishing Plc
50 Bedford Square, London, WC1B 3DP, UK
1385 Broadway, New York, NY 10018, USA
29 Earlsfort Terrace, Dublin 2, Ireland

British Library Cataloguing-in-Publication Data

A catalogue record for this book is available from the British Library.

ISBN: PB: 978-1-52651-720-3
ePDF: 978-1-52651-722-7
ePub: 978-1-52651-721-0

Typeset by Evolution Design & Digital Ltd (Kent)
Printed and bound by CPI Group (UK) Ltd, Croydon, CRO 4YY

MIX
Paper from responsible sources
FSC® C013604

To find out more about our authors and books visit www.bloomsburyprofessional.com. Here you will find extracts, author information, details of forthcoming events and the option to sign up for our newsletters

The UK Anti-Bribery Handbook

Foreword to the First Edition

As the authors of this book rightly recognise, the Bribery Act 2010 is a game changer. The reach of the Act, the strictness of some of the obligations, and the duties imposed on entities caught by its provisions signal a significant shift in the approach to the prosecution of bribery in the UK. Having played my part in developing the early guidance about the approach of the prosecutor under the Bribery Act, I am only too acutely aware that these changes are here to stay. The international impetus to tackle bribery worldwide is clear, the ramifications of a conviction are very significant and the approach of the prosecutor is more proactive than at any time in recent history. One of the great strengths of this book is the way the authors blend good practical legal advice, genuine insight about the attitude and approach of the authorities in the UK, and off-the-shelf policies to help corporate bodies navigate their way through these often difficult waters (the sample Code of Conduct for dealing with small bribes and/or facilitation payments set out at the end of Chapter 5 is an example of this and a model of its kind).

But to truly understand the impact of the Bribery Act 2010, it important to appreciate the conceptual thinking that lies behind it and the environment in which it is intended to work. After years of frustration in investigating and prosecuting corporate wrongdoing, the notion that the sole responsibility for enforcing the law lies with the relevant authorities has been ditched. There is now dual responsibility. The duties now placed on corporate bodies, some blunt, others more subtle, are intended to make these entities as responsible for policing their own conduct as the authorities. That is clear from the legislation itself, from the published guidance and from associated and all important back up measures such as deferred prosecution agreements (which are dealt with in Chapter 11 of the book). The message is crystal clear: corporate bodies which do not have an effective compliance regime, which do not self-police and which do not self-report are at greatest risk of prosecution. And, if prosecuted, they will face stiffer and stiffer sanctions (the sentencing guidelines also being dealt with in an informed and helpful way in the book).

This shift in conceptual thinking – putting a shared responsibility on the corporate body for policing their own patch – is what makes this book so useful. Sitting back and hoping that any corporate body will not be so unlucky as to be the subject of any interest from the relevant authorities in relation to bribery is a non-starter these days. Proactive measures are the best insurance – and that calls for proactive lawyering. As a practical handbook which guides the reader through the often complicated legislative provisions and at the same time offers practical advice, it is as valuable to the corporate body seeking to put in place an effective compliance regime as it is to the corporate body facing investigation or prosecution. It is a book perfectly pitched for directors, staff, agents, interested third parties and in house lawyers. It is also a first rate guide for all legal practitioners called upon to advise on any issue concerning bribery. The game has changed and those who ignore the practical advice offered in this book do so at their own peril.

Sir Keir Starmer KCB QC
Director of Public Prosecutions 2008–13

About the authors

Christopher Sallon QC specialises in cases involving financial services law, FSMA regulation,fraud, bribery and corruption. He advises individuals and companies across a range of sectors on compliance and in pre-charge negotiations. He also appears on behalf of those facing regulatory proceedings brought by the FCA in the UK, and by the DFSA in Dubai. Formerly the leader of Doughty Street Chambers' Regulatory and Financial Crime team, he has been listed in Legal 500 and Chambers UK Guide for over 10 years as a leading QC. He was Special Adviser to the House of Commons Public Administration Select Committee Enquiry into bribery and the honours system. He is an honorary member of the American Board of Criminal Lawyers, a Bencher of Gray's Inn, and was a Recorder of the Crown Court from 1996 to 2020.

Sam Tate is one of the leading financial crime solicitors in the UK specialising in anti-corruption law and related issues. Legal 500 (2020 edn) says 'Sam Tate is an outstanding lawyer in the field…' and 'is fantastic, he has the air of a man who is unflappable, having seen it all before, yet is patient in answering difficult questions and provides honest, helpful answers'.

Sam leads the white-collar crime practice at international law firm RPC LLP, working with states, corporates, insurers, banks and individuals. In 2021 he led the negotiations for two Deferred Prosecution Agreements with the SFO and he has previously held significant roles in global monitorships, including the HSBC monitorship which was the most complex and largest of its kind. Sam's practical experience also includes over four years as the subject matter expert in anti-corruption at BP Plc conducting investigations across a range of jurisdictions, and advising the current director of the SFO, Lisa Osofsky, during her time at Exiger LLP. Since 2009, Sam has been a visiting lecturer on the Durham University LLM. He is also a conference speaker (New Scotland Yard, ABA, C5, IBA and AMLP), provides input to government reviews, sat on TI's risk assessment expert panel, is an honorary member of the Institute for Commercial and Corporate Law and certified Lead Auditor for ISO37001. More recently in 2021, Sam became a member of RUSI's Taskforce on a Transatlantic Response to Illicit Finance.

Acknowledgments

We would like to give special acknowledgment and thanks to Nichola Higgins of Matrix Chambers, who wrote Chapter 10 with Anita Davies on Self-Reporting, advised on a number of other chapters, and carried out the unenviable task of co-ordination and communication between the authors and the editor with an impressive combination of perseverance, patience and determination. We would also like to thank Christopher Sykes, of Doughty Street Chambers, for his meticulous research when updating chapters 1, 3, 4, 6, 7, and 11. Also Stephen Storey, who kindly co-authored Chapter 9 of this book and who has an incredible depth of experience and is the Group Head of Ethics and Integrity at Compass Group Plc, and Sue Scott, formerly global head of Anti-bribery and Corruption at HSBC Plc, whose expertise is obvious from the contents of Chapter 13. It is also appropriate to thank the team at RPC including Kate Langley, Toby Lamarque, Emily Pica and Rob Semp who fact checked and added new ideas and practical examples to Chapters 2, 5, 8, 9 and 12 and acknowledge the team at US firm Miller & Chevalier LLP and specifically James Tillen and Virginia Newman for their critical and thoughtful input to the Chapter 2.

The authors would also like to thank Raj Chada, who appeared as an author of the first addition of this book and to whom much is owed, including in particular for chapters 1-9 and 11-12 that have been updated by Christopher Sallon and Sam Tate for this book.

We could not let this introduction pass without acknowledging the special skill of our editor Kiran Goss, our copy editor Chris Harrison, and all those at Bloomsbury Professional who made this book possible, and to all of whom we owe a great debt of gratitude.

We also wish to thank the following: Transparency International for their kind permission to reproduce extracts from their documents on Diagnosing Bribery Risk, as well as their highly useful Corruption Perceptions Index 2020, which is shown in Appendix 8; the UK Sentencing Council for allowing us early access to their Guideline on Fraud, Bribery and Money Laundering, shown in Appendix 4; and the Serious Fraud Office for providing the Code of Practice on Deferred Prosecution Agreements, shown in Appendix 7, as well as details of the number of self-reports it has received in recent years.

Special thanks are also due to Sir Keir Starmer for providing the foreword to this publication.

We would like to thank our families and friends for all their patience and support, including special heartfelt thanks to Christopher's wife, Jackie, and Sam Tate's mother, Miriam.

Despite the assistance we have had, any mistakes remain our own.

Lastly, the choice of content in this book, and any expressions of opinion therein are those of the authors alone.

The law is stated as at July 2021, although where it has been possible to include further developments, we have endeavoured to do so.

Although the authors have made reasonable efforts to ensure that the information in their chapters is correct at the time of printing, the authors and publishers do not assume and disclaim any liability to any party for any loss, damage, or disruption caused by errors or omissions; whether such errors or omissions result from negligence, accident, or any other cause other than fraud. This book is not intended as a substitute for obtaining specific legal advice. The reader should regularly consult an appropriately qualified lawyer in matters relating to their potential liabilities and compliance programs.

For the avoidance of doubt the contents of this book and any opinions it contains does not represent the views of the employers of the authors or in the case of a partnership, their partners.

Christopher Sallon QC, former Head of the Finance and Regulatory Team, Doughty Street Chambers.
Sam Tate, Partner RPC LLP and visiting lecturer, Durham University.

Contents

Table of Statutes

All references are to paragraph number

Table of Statutory Instruments

All references are to paragraph number

Table of Cases

All references are to paragraph number

S

T

U

1 Introduction

Developments in anti-corruption law

1.1

The Greek philosopher Heraclitus declared 'There is nothing permanent except change.' As the scourge of global bribery and corruption continues to grow in scale and complexity, there can be no doubt that the supranational reach posed by the UK Bribery Act 2010 ('UKBA') has permanently changed the landscape of corporate regulation. Initiatives by the UK and other governments to combat this phenomenon continue to be made, such as the active use of Deferred Prosecution Agreements and measures designed to encourage self-reporting, all of which demonstrate the continuing desire on the part of law makers and law enforcers for permanent change in this area. Furthermore, recent policy announcements by the SFO under Lisa Osofsky's leadership, coupled with an enhanced intelligence gathering team and a growing number of prosecutions, indicate that the authorities mean business. The House of Lords Select Committee Report on the Bribery Act 2010: post-legislative scrutiny noted that between 2011 and 2017, there were some 36 prosecutions under sections 1 and 2 of the UKBA.[1] Since then, a further eight successful prosecutions have been brought, most recently against David Lufkin, former Global Head of Sales at Petrofac, who in January 2021 pleaded guilty to three counts of bribery in relation to corrupt offers and payments made to influence the award of contracts in the UAE worth approximately US$3.3 billion. The SFO has also entered into twelve Deferred Prosecution Agreements since 2015,[2] and has used extensive civil powers to freeze property and recover the assets of international money launderers who choose the UK as a safe harbour for their corrupt funds.[3] The step-up in the enforcement of the law presents profound challenges to the integrity of international corporations, and poses increasing reputational and financial risks to organisations which remain ignorant of their regulatory obligations or wilfully chose to ignore them. Investigations resulting in criminal charges and conviction have resulted in large fines, disgorgement of profits, imposition of cost orders, and stringent conditions for targeted organisations. Loss of liberty for directors, staff and agents, where individually prosecuted, is now a reality.

---

1 House of Lords Select Committee on the Bribery Act 2010, Report of Session 2017–19 The Bribery Act 2010: post-legislative scrutiny.

2 Chapter 11.148.

3 *SFO v Julio Faerman*, 12 November 2020.

1.2

The number of UK organisations which have reported experiencing bribery and corruption has grown considerably. In 2016, the number stood at 6%. Between 2017 and 2018, the figure leapt to 23%.[4] Given the ever-greater risks of investigation by regulators and enforcement agencies, there is an increasing awareness amongst corporates and professionals of the need to invest in anti-bribery and due diligence programmes,[5] and many have now done so.

The aims of this book

1.3

This book is, first and foremost, a practical handbook which guides the reader through the background to and intricate provisions of the UKBA. It contrasts old legislation with the new; highlights the growing body of case law, offers practical advice to organisations wishing to put in place processes and adequate procedures for effective due diligence; assists companies who want to carry out internal investigations; explains the advantages and disadvantages of self-reporting, and provides guidance for companies under investigation, or facing prosecution, or looking to defer it. The need for simplicity and ease of reference, and the desire to convey the key day-to-day experience and expertise of the authors have determined the form and substance of this book.

1.4

As its title suggests, this book is primarily aimed at the directors and staff of companies, agents and interested third parties. It can also be used by in-house lawyers as a first port of call, as well as students and practitioners.

1.5

Among the practical difficulties addressed are:

- How to recognise bribery
- How to implement adequate procedures to guard against the risks of bribery
- How to conduct an internal investigation
- When, how and to whom to report suspected wrongdoing within a company
- How to co-operate with an external investigation
- When and how a prosecution may be deferred
- Corporate hospitality.

4 PwC Global Economic Crime Survey UK Findings 2018.
5 Transparency International Report by Ben Cowdock, 25 October 2019.

Scope and structure of the book

1.6

Whilst each chapter is self-contained and sets out the law and principles pertaining to the specific topic under discussion, the reader will benefit from cross-references throughout the book. It will enable those who wish, to familiarise themselves with a topic in its entirety. It will also enable the busy company director, in-house lawyer, independent practitioner or student to speedily locate the relevant part of a chapter or chapters. Where appropriate, some chapters contain charts, reference tables and case studies which illustrate how the law can be applied in practice.

1.7

Chapter 2 explains the global, economic and legal context which resulted in the UKBA, and examines the increased risks of corruption for many commercial organisations against a background of COVID-19, recession, globalisation and the emergence of new markets. It also compares and contrasts the UK's legislative regime in this area with that of the United States, in particular the Foreign Corrupt Practices Act 1977, and related guidance.

1.8

Chapter 3 recounts the common law and legislative history of bribery and corruption legislation before the UKBA, and in particular discusses the complexities and differences between the now superseded Public Bodies Corrupt Practices Act 1889, the Prevention of Corruption Acts of 1906 and 1916, the Honours (Prevention of Abuses) Act 1925, Part 12 of the Anti-terrorism, Crime and Security Act 2001, and the current legislation.

1.9

Chapter 4 dissects the essential elements of the two primary offences of UKBA, and the different ways in which they can be committed. These are contained in sections 1 and 2 respectively, namely the giving of bribes and the taking of bribes – otherwise known as active and passive bribery. It also identifies the relevant functions or activities, listed in section 3, to which a bribe must relate. Also set out are the penalties for such conduct.

1.10

Chapter 5 deals with the law and policy considerations relating specifically to small bribes and 'facilitation' payments. It includes practical ways for companies to mitigate the risk of small bribery.

1.11

Chapter 6 recognising the increasing risks which are inherent in global trade, deals with the section 6 offence of bribery of a foreign public official. We have also appended a flow chart of suggested checks that organisations should undertake when making payments or providing other advantages overseas.

1.12

The radical strict liability offence of failure of commercial organisations to prevent bribery in section 7, the extraterritorial breadth of its provisions and its relationship with section 14 (on the general criminal liability of organisations concerning bribery) are all discussed in Chapter 7. Chapter 8 then explains the practical compliance measures contained in Ministry of Justice Guidelines that are the only defence to the corporate failure to prevent offence. This includes detailed practical guidance on how to assess risk and implement an appropriate compliance programme.

1.13

Chapter 9 is designed to assist organisations in carrying out internal investigations, in their effort to prevent and respond to corruption. The chapter is essentially intended as an overview of measures which can be adopted by directors of small to medium sized enterprises, and identifies factors relevant to any decision as to what, when and how to investigate. Also included is a useful case study relating to the investigation launched by Wal-Mart into corrupt payments in Mexico.

1.14

One of the most difficult decisions for any company which discovers evidence of bribery is whether or not to self-report to a regulator or prosecuting authority. The advantages and disadvantages of self-reporting coupled with the vexed questions of when and to whom to self-report are dealt with in Chapter 10.

1.15

Deferred Prosecution Agreements ('DPAs') became operative in February 2014, and a DPA Code of Practice has been jointly issued by the Serious Fraud Office ('SFO') and the Crown Prosecution Service ('CPS') which provides guidance as to when and how DPAs will be utilised. DPAs represent a discretionary but well-established alternative measure to full scale prosecution. In Chapter 11, the nature of DPAs, to whom they can apply, the criteria for their application and the procedure for their implementation and discontinuance are all fully explained, and recent cases have been listed and summarised. Sentencing guidelines for bribery and corporate offenders, recently issued by the Sentencing Council for England and Wales, to be found in Appendix 4, are also considered in this context.

1.16

Chapter 12 provides important practical guidance for companies and individuals facing external investigation into allegations of bribery.

1.17

Chapter 13 brings together the elements of an Anti-Bribery programme discussed in previous chapters through the lens of the financial services sector. The chapter provides a brief context for the industry, a summary of the UK regulatory expectations found in the Financial Conduct Authority regulatory guidance, how aspects of the framework apply in a financial institutional setting, and key control challenges linked to recent prosecutions and enforcement actions. The chapter concludes with a brief look ahead to challenges and opportunities for the financial services industry, in supporting the fight against bribery and corruption.

1.18

Chapter 14 looks at the difficult issue of corporate hospitality in the public and private sector. A checklist of high and low risk factors helps to illustrate what are likely to be regarded as acceptable values of gifts and levels of entertainment, and what are not.

2 Global context including the FCPA

Introduction

2.1

This chapter explains the global, economic and legal context which led to the UK Bribery Act 2010 ('the UKBA') and continues to affect practice and priorities relating to anti-bribery compliance and enforcement.

2.2

The chapter includes the following: statistics relating to economic growth, employment and standards of living; information regarding prosecutions and fines; a synopsis of the Foreign Corrupt Practices Act 1977 ('FCPA'); three FCPA case studies; two UKBA case studies; a table showing the key legal components for bribery offences pursuant to the FCPA and section 1 of the UKBA; and a quick reference table comparing the UKBA and the FCPA.

Key points

2.3

- Recession, globalisation and the emergence of new markets has increased corruption risk for many commercial organisations subject to the UKBA.
- The FCPA is (and is likely to remain) the most potent global anti-corruption legislation, given its active enforcement by the US Securities Exchange Commission ('SEC') and Department of Justice ('DoJ').[1] However, the ground-breaking and sometimes controversial UKBA is also having a significant and increasing impact on international businesses and lawmakers.
- Outside the US, enforcement of anti-corruption laws against commercial organisations, including in the UK, remains below some parties'

1 Although the FCPA is principally enforced by the US DoJ and SEC, in recent years, the US Commodities Future Trading Commission ('CFTC') has also begun to pursue enforcement actions for violations of the US Commodities Exchange Act involving foreign corruption.

expectations or predictions.[2] However, no business can afford to be complacent, as: (a) influenced partly (but not solely) by the G20, OECD, US and UK, countries including Australia, Japan, South Korea, China and Peru have introduced new anti-corruption legislation and/or are more actively enforcing their laws; (b) internationally, prosecutors are continuing to co-operate; (c) prosecution in at least the US and UK is a real possibility for companies who allow the payment of bribes; and (d) bribery remains endemic in many countries.

- The scope and legal requirements of the UKBA and FCPA are materially different. Nevertheless, although the UKBA is broader or stricter than the FCPA in some important respects (eg in relation to 'facilitation payments'), when applying the two laws on a real-life, case-by-case basis, the application of the different legal tests to the bribery of public officials often leads to the same or similar outcomes.

Recession and business

2.4

The paragraphs immediately below, when read together with the paragraphs regarding 'globalisation' (from paragraph 2.11), summarise how the recession, which began in 2008, was one of the key causes of the introduction of more comprehensive anti-bribery laws in the UK and elsewhere and how the recession and globalisation contributed to a general increase in corporate corruption risk for many companies with part of their business in the UK.

2.5

Following the failure of Lehman Brothers Bank in September 2008, the Dow Jones Industrial Average fell in 2009 to less than half of its starting position, the FTSE crashed by over 10% in a day[3] and employment dropped markedly.[4] Many businesses struggled and as during the UK's recession of the late 1980s – but on a far larger scale – 'UK Plc' experienced insolvencies, state take-overs, corporate consolidations, the unwinding of banking transactions, and a material change in regulatory environment.

2.6

Quick change brought new corporate challenges. As regards financial crime, from at least 2008 to 2009,[5] when the 'high tide' of the boom went out and

---

2 Using a measure of successful corporate prosecutions. See Corporate Anti-corruption Compliance Drivers, Mechanisms and Ideas for Change (October 2020) www.oecd.org/daf/anti-bribery/Corporate-anti-corruption-compliance-drivers-mechanisms-and-ideas-for-change.pdf.

3 A larger drop than the drop that occurred on 'Black Monday' at the outset of the UK recession of 1987.

4 As at May 2013, youth unemployment in Greece was reportedly recorded at 64.9% (see www.telegraph.co.uk/finance/financialcrisis/10230653/Greek-youth-unemployment-soars-to-64.9pc.html).

5 For example, LIBOR and Forex related investigations.

companies 'hit the rocks', potential fraud, economic crime and unethical behaviours were identified, which were exemplified by a number of corporate scandals. For the public and press, who partly blamed 'big' business and particularly banks for causing the 'crash' through unethical (and short-sighted) cultures, the ensuing investigations at least appeared to vindicate their suspicions. In businesses and banks public opprobrium resulted in the questioning of prior behaviour and priorities.

2.7

Slightly later but within the same period, the 'Arab Spring' from December 2010 onwards (revolutions reportedly sparked by an anti-corruption demonstration in Tunisia) removed long established rulers in North Africa.[6] This kept the UK public, UK politicians, the international community and UK business focused on foreign corruption.

2.8

Meanwhile, as regards the UK legislature, legal commentators and prosecutors considered the UK's anti-bribery laws long overdue for reform given: (a) the near absence of corporate prosecutions; (b) the shortcomings of the 1889, 1906 and 1916 Acts highlighted as long ago as the Nolan Committee Report of 1994; (c) pressure from the OECD; and (d) criticism of the UK enforcement record from the US.[7]

2.9

As a result, three trends reached their height in and around 2010 and 2011:

(a) public pressure on UK politicians in light of corporate scandals exposed during the recession;

(b) tacit acceptance in the business community of the need to better regulate the conduct of some of its members; and

(c) international and internal legal pressure on the UK government to bring the UK's laws up to date.

This led to a situation in which the 'ground-breaking' and sometimes controversial new form of corporate liability and extra-territorial jurisdiction contained in the UKBA, explained in Chapter 4, could be passed into UK law (with all political parties' support). As importantly, it resulted in a window of time in which the wide 'principles based' guidance of the MoJ (published

6 The 'Arab Spring' is often cited as having begun in Tunisia in relation to alleged corruption (see www.huffingtonpost.com/cobus-de-swardt/a-year-after-corruption-i_b_1174219.html).

7 Also variously by the Maud Report, Salmon Commission Report and Law Commission Report of 2003 (see Chapter 3).

in March 2011), contained in Annex 3, could be debated and issued without serious legal challenge.[8]

2.10

Since the enactment of the UKBA, successful prosecutions have mainly involved large multi-national corporates. The relatively low level of enforcement has faced criticism from organisations such as Transparency International which have campaigned for increased enforcement.[9]

In 2018, the budget of the Serious Fraud Office (SFO) was increased by over 50%,[10] in response to criticism that it was over reliant on large matter specific funding to investigate big cases.

Globalisation

2.11

Although the recession of the late 2000's effects continue to provide lessons for business, the world was in 2008/2009 – and remains now – full of business opportunities. Specifically, even with COVID-19 we can predict that, tens of millions of people will in short order continue to bring themselves out of poverty each year and become consumers in new expanding markets and growing economies.[11]

2.12

As regards this expanding trade and the UK, at the time of writing post-Brexit, the UK entered into a free trade deal with the EU which came into force on 1 January 2021. The UK has made deals to continue to trade with 63 non-EU countries with further deals due to come into force with other nations including Mexico and Canada. The end of the transition period marks the opportunity for the UK to diverge and re-negotiate future deals, potentially increasing trade with non-EU countries.[12] The result is that UK companies are increasingly likely

8 In this regard there is in some ways a parallel to the FCPA 1977, which has been described a consequence of the Watergate scandal and the resignation of President Richard Nixon in 1974 and of course the investigations into Lockheed Aircraft Corporation, Exxon Corporation and Ashland Oil and their alleged payments to foreign government officials or political parties.

9 www.transparency.org.uk/post-brexit-strong-anti-bribery-legislation-more-important-ever.

10 www.ft.com/content/a5830aa8-43ec-11e8-803a-295c97e6fd0b; www.sfo.gov.uk/2020/10/09/future-challenges-in-economic-crime-a-view-from-the-sfo/.

11 The global extreme poverty rate fell to 9.2% in 2017, from 10.1% in 2015. That is equivalent to 689 million people living on less than US$1.90 a day. At higher poverty lines, 24.1% of the world lived on less than US$3.20 a day and 43.6% on less than US$5.50 a day in 2017. Global extreme poverty is expected to rise in 2020 for the first time in over 20 years as the disruption of the COVID-19 pandemic compounds the forces of conflict and climate change, which were already slowing poverty reduction progress (see create.kahoot.it/creator/c8023299-142a-46df-8f20-2837908bb117).

12 www.bbc.co.uk/news/uk-47213842.

to be engaging in global trade with exposure to more markets and their specific regulations, raising the risk of jurisdictional specific breaches.

2.13

This increased inherent risk of trading abroad has risen at the same time that the UK authorities (see the above paragraphs 2.5 and 2.6 relating to recession) are focused on both foreign corruption and corporate compliance, having passed legislation that makes it easier to prosecute bribery and worse to be found guilty.[13]

Pressure to tackle corruption abroad

2.14

Identifying which governments are seeking to prevent bribery, and particularly the demand for bribes, is an issue that companies now regularly consider as part of the risk-based decision to enter business in a new country.

2.15

In this context pressure for reform has grown as some countries' wealth has increased and, at least ostensibly steps in, for instance, BRIC countries have and continue to be made by their governments to increase the share of inward investment and respond to pressure from internal and external stakeholders to tackle corruption.[14]

2.16

By way of example, in amongst sobering reports and reviews from in-country commentators and NGO sources, examples of government-led and potentially positive anti-corruption initiatives include South Korea's Improper Solicitation and Graft Act 2016, Japan's amendment to its Criminal Code to widen territorial scope to include bribes to public officials and Australia's Combatting Corporate Crime Bill 2017. In Russia, since January 2019, companies can now be prosecuted under administrative law for providing unlawful remuneration.

2.17

In the rest of the world, although bribery also continues to be widespread and is a serious business and criminal risk, there are also changes in the anti-bribery landscape, partly owing to the UKBA/FCPA and partly to the recession and country specific circumstances, leading to new or amended legislation in

13 Law No. 12.846, also known as the 'Clean Company Law'.

14 The BRIC countries were ranked as follows by the annual TI corruption perception index 2020: Brazil ranked 94th of 179 with a rating of 38 out of 100, China ranked 78th with rating of 42, India ranked 86th with a rating of 40 and Russia ranked 129th with a rating of 30 (infobrics.org).

Australia,[15] Japan[16] and South Korea[17] amongst others. This chapter, of course, does not analyse each new law, or indeed the bribery risk in any country.[18] However, as regards local bribery law legislation, there is a global trend towards extra-territorial jurisdiction, longer custodial sentences, larger fines, defences of 'adequate procedure' or similar defences[19] and a general broadening of the definition of bribery.

2.18

Finally, the US has not been excluded from pressure to review its anti-bribery law, the FCPA. The FCPA's exception for facilitation payments has drawn criticism. In an effort to better deter corruption at its source, US legislators have also proposed expanding the law to cover 'demand-side' bribery – ie, to punish bribe recipients. These reform efforts have been unsuccessful.

2.19

Another criticism is that the FCPA does not include a defence to liability based on corporate compliance programmes akin to the 'adequate procedures' defence under the UKBA. Although the SEC and DoJ consider the existence and effectiveness of such programmes when deciding whether to prosecute corporations for perceived FCPA violations, the agencies have essentially unfettered discretion in making these determinations. As discussed further below at paragraphs 2.20 to 2.22, the DoJ and SEC have issued detailed FCPA guidance intended to incentivise corporations to establish effective compliance programmes and to voluntarily disclose violations, when discovered. However, this agency guidance is non-binding in nature, and corporations therefore have little assurance that (often costly) compliance programmes or voluntary disclosure will insulate them from liability in the event of a violation. Prosecutorial discretion and the lack of predictability in enforcement determinations may disincentivise corporations from voluntarily disclosing potential violations.

The FCPA

2.20

The primary subject of this book is UKBA compliance and as a result the FCPA, which: (a) has already been the subject of academic analysis; (b) has resulted in

15 See, eg: www.ashurst.com/en/news-and-insights/insights/australian-anti-bribery-and-corruption---key-developments-in-2020-and-what-to-expect-in-2021/.

16 See, eg: https://globalcompliancenews.com/anti-corruption/anti-corruption-in-japan/.

17 See, eg: www.legal500.com/developments/thought-leadership/sweeping-changes-to-the-korean-criminal-procedures-starting-in-the-new-year/.

18 For information regarding specific country risk or regional trends, the Transparency International website is helpful, as are other sources such as the country reports created by the OECD.

19 Such as the 'reasonable procedures' defence to the failure to prevent facilitation of tax evasion, pursuant to the Criminal Finances Act 2017.

numerous deferred prosecution agreements; and (c) has a reasonable amount of case law, can only be dealt with in a cursory way. However, given that the FCPA is arguably the most important piece of foreign criminal legislation for any UK company trading abroad, a synopsis of the FCPA is essential to understanding compliance practice,[20] and therefore this chapter reviews the following FCPA related matters, including two tables to help compare the FCPA and UKBA:

- Overview of the FCPA
- Largest US fines
- Jurisdiction
- Comparison table – FCPA 'active' bribery offence with the UKBA
- Corporate Liability, Voluntary Disclosure, and Compliance Programmes
- Position on small bribes/facilitation payments
- Accounting provisions
- FCPA penalties and risks in more detail
- FCPA case studies (Morgan Stanley, Total, Panalpina)
- UKBA case studies (Standard Bank and Rolls Royce)
- Quick reference general comparison table – UKBA/FCPA

Overview

2.21

Passed in 1977 following the Watergate scandal, the FCPA contains two key sets of provisions, which are explained below from paragraphs 2.27 and 2.39. First, the FCPA creates an 'active' bribery offence of bribing foreign public officials, (eg offering bribes to non-US public officials).[21] Secondly, in addition to prohibiting foreign bribery, the FCPA requires issuers of US securities to keep accurate books and records and to establish and maintain a system of internal controls adequate to ensure accountability for assets (the 'accounting

20 US Department of Justice and US Securities and Exchange Commission, A Resource Guide to the U.S. Foreign Corrupt Practices Act at 57 (2d edn, 2020), www.justice.gov/criminal-fraud/file/1292051/download [hereinafter 'Resource Guide']. Note: The Resource Guide contains a detailed explanation of the FCPA, as well as examples of violative conduct, from the view of the enforcing agencies.

21 The FCPA does not criminalise the actual receipt of a bribe (ie, 'demand-side' bribery). See *US v Castle*, 925 F 2d 831, 833-835 (5th Cir 1991) (finding that Congress chose in the FCPA to 'punish only one party to the agreement', and that 'the very individuals whose participation was required in every case — the foreign officials accepting the bribe — were excluded from prosecution for the substantive offense.'); see also *United States v Hoskins*, 902 F.3d 69, 101 (2d Cir. 2018). Nevertheless, the DoJ will consider prosecuting bribe recipients under other applicable US laws, such as US anti-money laundering laws. Demand-side bribery may also be illegal in the local jurisdiction in which the bribe was received.

provisions'). Specifically, the accounting provisions require issuers to make and keep books, records and accounts, which, in reasonable detail, accurately and fairly reflect the transactions and dispositions of the issuers' assets.[22]

2.22

To demonstrate the serious nature of the potential liabilities that arise under either set of provisions of the FCPA, the average FCPA corporate settlement was US$89,521,912 in 2016, which rose to US$189,496,373 in 2019 and US$294,488,085 in 2020.[23]

Largest US fines

2.23

Below are two tables setting out the ten largest FCPA penalties (all of which have arisen since 2008). The first table reflects the largest FCPA penalties paid to the DoJ and SEC only. However, when resolving FCPA matters, the DoJ and SEC often coordinate with enforcement authorities in other jurisdictions, in which case the fines paid to US authorities may be offset or reduced by amounts paid to authorities in other jurisdictions. The second table thus reflects the largest internationally-coordinated resolutions involving the FCPA.

Top Ten FCPA Fines [DoJ and SEC Only][24]	
1.	Goldman Sachs Group Inc., US: **US$1.6 billion** in 2020
2.	Telefonaktiebolaget LM Ericsson, Sweden: **US$1.06 billion** in 2019
3.	Mobile TeleSystems, Russia: **US$850 million** in 2019
4.	Siemens AG, Germany: **US$800 million** in 2008
5.	Alstom, France: **US$772 million** in 2014
6.	KBR/Halliburton, US: **US$579 million** in 2009
7.	Teva, Israel: **US$519** million in 2016
8.	Telia Company AB, Sweden: **US$483 million** in 2017
9.	Och-Ziff Capital Management Group LLC, US: **US$412 million** in 2016

22 15. U.S.C. § 78m.

23 Updated through to 23 March 2021. These statistics reflect only settlement agreements with the DoJ and SEC related to the FCPA and do not include parallel or coordinated settlements with foreign enforcement authorities. Where a matter involved more than one action brought by US authorities against a particular company and its subsidiaries and affiliates, those numbers are 'combined' and counted as one action. Calculations of total FCPA penalties are based on amounts paid to the US after any offsets or credits, including credits for amounts paid to authorities in foreign jurisdictions. Accordingly, these statistics may differ from those compiled by other sources that use different calculation methods or datasets.

24 See n 23 above.

10.	BAE Systems plc, UK: **US$400 million** in 2010
TOTAL: approximately **US$7.5 billion** (excluding legal fees and other penalties)	

Top Ten FCPA Fines [Internationally-Coordinated Resolutions][25]	
1.	Airbus SE, France: **US$3.92 billion** in 2020[26]
2.	Odebrecht SA and Braskem SA, Brazil: **US$3.56 billion** in 2016[27]
3.	Goldman Sachs Group Inc., US: **US$2.91 billion** in 2020[28]
4.	Petróleo Brasileiro S.A., Brazil: **US$1.79 billion** in 2018[29]
5.	Siemens AG, Germany: **US$1.67 billion** in 2007-2008[30]
6.	Telia Company AB, Sweden: **US$965 million** in 2017[31]
7.	Rolls-Royce plc, UK: **US$816 million** in 2016[32]
8.	VimpelCom Limited, the Netherlands: **US$795 million** in 2016[33]
9.	BAE Systems plc, UK: **US$447 million** in 2010[34]
10.	SBM Offshore NV, the Netherlands: **US$240 million** in 2014[35]
TOTAL: approximately **US$17.1 billion** (excluding legal fees and other penalties)	

25 Updated through to 23 March 2021.These statistics count the 10 largest FCPA-related resolutions in which US authorities, in resolving a matter, coordinated with a foreign authority's enforcement action. Where a matter involved more than one action brought by US authorities against a particular company and its subsidiaries and affiliates, those numbers are 'combined' and counted as one action. These statistics may differ from those compiled by other sources that use different calculation methods or datasets.

26 Resolutions with authorities in France, the UK, and the US. The US settlement amount of US$532.2 million includes a US$237.7 million penalty for conduct related to the US International Traffic in Arms Regulations ('ITAR') and US$294.5 million for FCPA-related conduct.

27 Resolutions with authorities in the US, Brazil, and Switzerland. The Odebrecht/Braskem amount reflects the reduced US fine amount following the inability-to-pay analysis by the DoJ that lowered the total from approximately US$5.56 billion to US$3.56 billion.

28 Resolutions with authorities in the US, the UK, Malaysia, Hong Kong, and Singapore. The US settlement amount of US$1,663,088,000 includes US$400 million civil penalty to SEC and credits against previously paid amounts and other enforcement authorities but does not include US$154 million to be paid to the United States Federal Reserve or US$150 million to be paid to New York's Department of Financial Services.

29 Resolutions with authorities in the US and Brazil.

30 Resolutions with authorities in the US and Germany.

31 Resolutions with authorities in the US and the Netherlands.

32 Resolutions with authorities in the US, the UK, and Brazil.

33 Resolutions with authorities in the US and the Netherlands.

34 Resolutions with authorities in the US and the UK.

35 Resolutions with authorities in the US and the Netherlands. The DoJ declination was contingent upon the Dutch settlement.

Jurisdiction

2.24

The anti-bribery provisions of the FCPA apply to: (1) issuers of US securities; (2) US 'domestic concerns' (US citizens, residents and nationals, together with US companies); and (3) any person who is *not* a US issuer or domestic concern, but who takes acts in furtherance of a violation while in the territory of the US.[36]

2.25

The FCPA's accounting provisions primarily concern the issuers of securities in the US. The term 'issuer' includes any business entity that is registered under section 78 of the US Securities Exchange Act of 1934, or that is required to file reports under section 78(d) of the Act.[37] Issuers may be headquartered outside the US, and in fact many of the largest FCPA resolutions have involved foreign companies listed on US exchanges.

Comparison of FCPA 'active' bribery offence with UKBA

2.26

Establishing liability for the anti-bribery provisions of the FCPA, ie relating to the payment of bribes to a foreign public official, requires consideration of *six basic elements/steps*. The table below compares the basic elements of an offence of the FCPA's anti-bribery provisions with the elements of the broadest active bribery offence in the UK (case 1, the active bribery offence contained in section 1 of the UKBA). Where appropriate, notes are also supplied to the UK offence that only targets bribes paid to a foreign public official.[38]

---

36 The Foreign Corrupt Practices Act of 1977 ('FCPA'), 15 U.S.C. §§78dd-1 et seq.

37 15 U.S.C. §§ 78dd-1(1), 78*l*(g), 78*o*(d). The FCPA's anti-bribery provisions apply, inter alia, to foreign issuers that have American Depository Receipts or American Depository Shares listed on a US exchange.

38 Section 6 of the UKBA. Case 2 for s 1 of the UKBA is not considered in this comparison but creates a criminal liability, for instance, where an offer is made of a gift where the offeror knows that receipt would breach the recipient's Code of Conduct or corporate gifts policy.

Element/ step	FCPA	UKBA
Intended transfer of value	a payment, offer, authorisation, or promise to pay money or anything of value	[person] offers, promises or gives a financial or other advantage
Intended recipient	to a foreign government official (including any employee of (1) a foreign government or a foreign government's 'instrumentality', such as a state-owned enterprise, and (2) a public international organisation); to any foreign political party, official, or candidate for foreign political office; or to any other person, knowing that the payment or promise will be passed on to a foreign official	to another person or (directly or indirectly)[39]
Intention	with a corrupt motive	and intends the advantage (a) to induce a person to perform improperly a relevant function or activity, or (b) to reward a person for the improper performance of such a function or activity[40]
Purpose	for the purpose of (a) influencing any act or decision of that person, (b) inducing such person to do or omit any action in violation of his lawful duty, (c) securing an improper advantage, or (d) inducing such person to use his influence to affect an official act or decision	
Business related	in order to assist in obtaining or retaining business for or with, or directing any business to, any person	N/A (except as regards the separate s 6 offence of bribing a foreign government official, where there must be an intention to obtain or retain a business advantage)

39 UKBA, s 6 creates a separate offence as regards foreign public officials.

40 Note that the improper performance criteria is not required in relation to the s 6 offence, (ie bribing a foreign public official.)

Element/ step	FCPA	UKBA
Defences	facilitation payment exception; affirmative defences for (1) reasonable and bona fide marketing expenses and (2) payments that are lawful under the written laws of the foreign official's country	no small bribe exception. No exception as regards marketing expenses.[41] Very limited local law defence for s 6 (public official offence) only, which requires a written law allowing official to be influenced by offered advantage.

Knowing

2.27

US enforcement authorities have, in practice, taken a broad view of the definitions of 'foreign government official',[42] 'anything of value' and other terms in the FCPA statute. However, for purposes of comparison with the UKBA, it is the definition under the FCPA of 'knowing' of a bribe that is the most relevant, as this is key to creating personal and corporate liability for violations of the FCPA's anti-bribery provisions.

2.28

'Knowing' does not mean only actual knowledge. It is also defined as having knowledge similar in nature to the English law meaning of 'wilful' or perhaps 'Nelsonian' blindness to a fact or situation that should be obvious from information known by a person and to which the person turns a 'blind eye'. In the FCPA the definition of knowledge is as follows:[43]

> '(3)(A) A person's state of mind is "knowing" with respect to conduct, a circumstance, or a result if –
>
> (i) such person is aware that such person is engaging in such conduct, that such circumstance exists, or that such result is substantially certain to occur; or

41 However, see Chapter 13, which explains the UK Ministry of Justice's Guidance in this area.

42 Resource Guide, n 20 above, at 19-20 (noting that 'the FCPA broadly applies to corrupt payments to 'any' officer or employee of a foreign government and to those acting on the foreign government's behalf,' and that employees of state-owned or state-controlled entities may be foreign government officials if the entity constitutes an 'instrumentality' under the FCPA. Whether an entity is an instrumentality of a foreign government is a fact-specific analysis.).

43 In the words of the 1988 Congress that amended the FCPA as regards facilitation payments, there was an intent to include actions that 'demonstrate evidence of a conscious disregard or deliberate ignorance of known circumstances that should reasonably alert one to high probabilities of violations of the Act'.

(ii) such person has a firm belief that such circumstance exists or that such result is substantially certain to occur.

(B) When knowledge of the existence of a particular circumstance is required for an offense, such knowledge is established if a person is aware of a high probability of the existence of such circumstance, unless the person actually believes that such circumstance does not exist.'

2.29

A person is deemed to 'know' that a third party will use money provided by that person to make an improper payment if he or she is aware of, but consciously disregards, a 'high probability' that such a payment or offer will be made. US enforcement authorities have identified a number of 'red flags' that, in their view, indicate a 'high probability' of corrupt third-party payments (see Appendix 1 of the Resource Guide). Third-party payments are a frequent basis for FCPA enforcement actions – often in instances where the subject of the enforcement action did not have *actual* knowledge of any corrupt payments.

Corporate liability[44]

2.30

As a preliminary matter, most corporate FCPA enforcement actions are resolved out of court. Corporations tend not to litigate alleged offences, instead resolving them via Deferred Prosecution Agreements ('DPAs') or Non-Prosecution Agreements ('NPAs') with the DoJ, and / or via settlement agreements with the SEC. In these circumstances, the DoJ and SEC have broad discretion to determine both whether a violation has occurred, and how to dispose of the perceived offence. Given the lack of case law and corporations' tendency not to challenge the agencies' determinations, DoJ and SEC enforcement practices provide the best guidance in terms of assessing what constitutes an FCPA violation and the likely consequences. US enforcement authorities have issued three significant pieces of non-binding guidance that shed light on their enforcement practices: (1) the DoJ and SEC jointly-issued comprehensive FCPA guidance, *A Resource Guide to the Foreign Corrupt Practices Act* ('Resource Guide', revised in July 2020);[45] (2) the DoJ's *Corporate Enforcement Policy*,[46]

44 Also see www.fcpablog.com/blog/2012/9/20/americas-view-of-corporate-criminal-liability-is-unique.html by Richard L Cassin.

45 Resource Guide, n 20 above, red flags include: excessive commissions to third-party agents or consultants; unreasonably large discounts to third-party distributors; third-party 'consulting agreements' that include only vaguely described services; the third-party consultant is in a different line of business than that for which it has been engaged; the third party is related to or closely associated with the foreign official; the third party became part of the transaction at the express request or insistence of the foreign official; the third party is merely a shell company incorporated in an offshore jurisdiction; and the third-party requests payment to offshore bank accounts. Citation: Resource Guide, n 20 above, at 23.

46 US Department of Justice, US Attorneys' Manual §9-47.120 (2019) ('FCPA Corporate Enforcement Policy'), www.justice.gov/jm/jm-9-47000-foreign-corrupt-practices-act-1977 [hereinafter 'Corporate Enforcement Policy'].

which provides guidelines for US prosecutors on enforcement determinations; and (3) *Evaluation of Corporate Compliance Programs*,[47] which provides guidance to prosecutors regarding how to assess corporate compliance programmes. These documents detail the agencies' views on the FCPA, circumstances in which corporations may incur FCPA liability, and the circumstances in which corporations may avoid prosecution or (in some instances) may avoid criminal liability altogether.

2.31

Unlike the UKBA, the FCPA does not create an automatic 'strict' liability where a 'service provider', which is presumed to include an employee, pays a bribe for a corporate's benefit. Instead, assuming an employee or other relevant person meets the 'knowledge' threshold above and is acting within the scope of their employment,[48] their acts can be 'imputed' to the company using traditional US legal principles of agency, which the DoJ describes in the Resource Guide at page 28 as follows:

> 'General principles of corporate liability apply to the FCPA. Thus, a company is liable when its directors, officers, employees, or agents, acting within the scope of their employment, commit FCPA violations intended, at least in part, to benefit the company.'[49]

A corporation may also be held liable for the misconduct of its subsidiary under traditional agency principles, if the parent exercises sufficient control over the subsidiary.[50] The DoJ and SEC have brought numerous enforcement actions on the agency theory of liability, holding corporations liable for the acts of both their employees and subsidiaries.

2.32

Thus, although the FCPA appears on its face to apply more narrowly to corporations than does the UKBA, in practice, corporations are often held liable for the acts of their employees, subsidiaries, and third-party agents – even without actual knowledge or direction of those entities' or individuals' corrupt conduct. In many cases, then, the same conduct that would trigger 'strict liability' under the UKBA for payment of bribes by an 'associated person' (explained in Chapter 7) to a government official will also effectively give rise to corporate liability under the FCPA.

---

47 US Department of Justice, Evaluation of Corporate Compliance Programs (Updated June 2020), www.justice.gov/criminal-fraud/page/file/937501/download.

48 Note that the general scope of an employee's assumed function, remit or role tends to be construed, in general, more narrowly than under English law.

49 Resource Guide, n 20 above, at 28.

50 ibid (noting that '[t]he fundamental characteristic of agency is control').

Voluntary Disclosure

2.33

The FCPA does not require companies to voluntarily disclose FCPA violations to the DoJ, SEC, or any other government authority. However, US enforcement authorities encourage self-disclosure and have publicly asserted that self-disclosure will influence the decision regarding whether to bring an enforcement action, as well as the extent of penalties imposed. Specifically, the DoJ's *Corporate Enforcement Policy* provides that, absent certain aggravating circumstances, there will be a 'presumption that the company will receive a declination' (ie, that the DoJ will decline to prosecute the company) when the company has 'voluntarily self-disclosed misconduct … fully cooperated, and timely and appropriately remediated' the misconduct.[51] Aggravating circumstances may include misconduct by senior executives, pervasive wrongdoing within the company, significant profits stemming from the corruption or criminal recidivism.[55] Even if the DoJ determines that aggravating circumstances exist such that criminal prosecution is warranted, the Corporate Enforcement Policy provides that the DoJ will 'accord, or recommend to a sentencing court, a 50% reduction' off of the low end of the fine range, and 'generally will not require appointment of a monitor if a company has, at the time of resolution, implemented an effective compliance program'.[52]

2.34

Importantly, the Corporate Enforcement Policy is non-binding in nature, and the benefits of voluntary disclosure are therefore not statutorily guaranteed. In addition – and notably – the Corporate Enforcement Policy is a DoJ policy only, and disclosure therefore does not insulate an issuer from a parallel enforcement action by the SEC. Indeed, the SEC has brought enforcement actions in matters in which the DoJ has issued declinations for the same violative conduct.[53] In addition to any separate SEC action, the DoJ may still require companies to disgorge profits obtained as a result of the misconduct,

51 FCPA Corporate Enforcement Policy.

52 ibid. Note that the DoJ may, in its discretion, require as part of DPAs or NPAs that a company install an independent corporate monitor to assess the company's adherence to certain compliance program requirements. Corporations can incur significant costs in connection with an independent monitor.

53 In a recent example, in August 2020, the DoJ issued a declination letter to World Acceptance Corporation ('WAC'), citing WAC's voluntary disclosure and cooperation among the factors contributing to the DoJ's decision not to prosecute the company for the alleged bribery of Mexican government officials. The day after the DoJ issued its declination letter, the SEC announced that WAC had settled charges of alleged violations of the FCPA's anti-bribery and accounting provisions. Without admitting or denying the findings of the SEC, WAC agreed to pay US$21.7 million in total, including US$17.826 million in disgorgement, US$1.9 million in prejudgment interest, and a US$2 million fine. See Letter from Robert Zink, Chief, Fraud Sec., Crim. Div., US Dep't of Justice to Mark E. Schamel et al., Womble Bond Dickinson LLP, (5 August 2020), www.justice.gov/criminal-fraud/file/1301826/download; Order Instituting Cease-and-Desist Proceedings, Exchange Act Release No. 89489, 1-2 (Aug. 6, 2020), www.sec.gov/litigation/admin/2020/34-89489.pdf.

in the event of declination.[54] However, voluntary disclosure can result in more lenient treatment than if the government were to learn of the violations from other sources.[55]

Corporate Compliance Programmes

2.35

As discussed, the FCPA contains no affirmative defence to corporate liability based on 'adequate procedures' or the establishment of an effective compliance programme. In practice, however, US enforcement authorities consider corporate compliance programmes (among other factors) when determining whether to bring an enforcement action, the amount of monetary penalties imposed, and whether to impose any ongoing compliance obligations on a corporate offender.

2.36

The DoJ and SEC's jointly-issued Resource Guide details the criteria used by enforcement authorities to assess the effectiveness of a company's compliance programme, and specifically states that the DoJ and SEC will 'consider the adequacy and effectiveness of a company's compliance program[me] at the time of the misconduct and at the time of the resolution' when deciding whether to bring an enforcement action.[56] Notably, enforcement authorities may also consider a corporation's compliance programme for purposes of determining *how* to resolve criminal FCPA violations; the DoJ may, rather than prosecute, enter into a Deferred Prosecution Agreement ('DPA') or Non-Prosecution Agreement ('NPA'), with a corporate offender. It is important to note that, although the Resource Guide provides helpful insight into the DoJ and SEC's expectations for and the potential benefits of establishing an effective compliance programme, the guidance is explicitly 'non-binding' and 'informal.' Establishing a corporate compliance programme does not guarantee leniency in enforcement, in the event of a perceived FCPA violation.

---

54 For example, in December 2018, the DoJ entered into a letter agreement with Polycom, Inc. ('Polycom') in which it declined to prosecute Polycom for bribery committed by employees of the company's subsidiaries in China and related violations of the FCPA's accounting provisions. Under the agreement, Polycom agreed to disgorge US$30,978,000 in profits obtained in connected with the illegal conduct. Later that month Polycom entered into a cease-and-desist order with the SEC, agreeing to pay disgorgement of US$10,672,926 and prejudgment interest of US$1,833,410. The SEC Order also imposed a civil monetary penalty of US$3.8 million. See US Department of Justice Letter from Sandra Moser to Caz Hashemi re: Polycom, Inc. (20 December 2018), www.justice.gov/criminal-fraud/file/1122966/download; Order Instituting Cease-and-Desist Proceedings, In the Matter of Polycom, Inc., Rel No. 84978, File No. 3-18964 (26 December 2018), www.sec.gov/litigation/admin/2018/34-84978.pdf.

55 Notably, these are DoJ policies, and issuers that may be subject to SEC enforcement actions … doesn't have as clear guidance regarding the benefits of voluntary disclosure – (and maybe – and in fact, the SEC has brought actions where the DoJ has issued declinations).

56 Resource Guide, n 20 above, at 57.

Facilitation payments

2.37

The FCPA contains a narrow exception for facilitation payments. Specifically, the statute provides an exception to the anti-bribery provisions for 'any facilitation or expediting payment to a foreign official, political party, or party official for the purpose of which is to expedite or to secure the performance of a routine governmental action by a foreign official, political party, or party official'.[57] The statute further defines 'routine governmental action' as 'only an action which is ordinarily and commonly performed by a foreign official,' such as actions in connection with obtaining permits or processing governmental papers.[58] Decisions as to whether – or on what terms – to award or continue business are not routine governmental actions, and are explicitly excluded from the facilitation payments exception.[59] Note also that the FCPA's accounting provisions (discussed in paragraphs 2.38 and 2.39 below) do not contain any exception for facilitation payments, and facilitation payments permissible under the anti-bribery provisions may therefore violate the FCPA if not properly recorded in an issuer's books and records.[60]

2.38

Although debated at length during the course of the Bribery Bill through the UK Parliament, no similar exemption arises either historically or currently in the UK.[61]

Given that this is an important area, facilitation payments are considered in depth within Chapter 5, which specifically covers the broader subject of small bribes.

Accounting Provisions

2.39

In addition to its anti-bribery provisions, the FCPA's 'accounting provisions' also require issuers of securities in the US[62] to: (1) make and maintain 'accurate' books, records, and accounts, in 'reasonable detail', which fairly reflect the issuer's transactions; and (2) 'devise and maintain a system of internal accounting

57 15 U.S.C. §§78dd-1(b), 78dd-2(b), 78dd-3(b).

58 15 U.S.C. § 78dd-1(f)(3)(A); 15 USC §§ 78dd-2(h)(4)(A), 78dd-3(f)(4)(A).

59 15 U.S.C. § 78dd-1(f)(3)(B); 15 USC §§ 78dd-2(h)(4)(B), 78dd-3(f)(4)(B). See Chapter 5 on Small Bribes for more on this topic.

60 See Resource Guide, n 20 above, at 26.

61 Chapter 5 on Small Bribes provides practical assistance in responding to the risks posed by small bribes. Note that the FCPA also includes a local law defence and an exemption for marketing expenses that are not considered in this book.

62 A company, US or foreign, that issues securities (including American Depositary Receipts (ADRs)) traded on a US exchange or where for another reason reports are required to be filed with the SEC.

controls sufficient to provide reasonable assurances that transactions are properly executed and recorded'.[63]

2.40

As a consequence, when issuers of US securities (or their agents) make bribe payments and conceal or otherwise do not accurately record these payments in their books and records (eg by recording a bribe payment in their accounts as a 'miscellaneous payment' or 'petty cash payment'), a violation of the FCPA occurs. Perhaps more significantly, as explained further in Chapter 9 on 'Adequate Procedures', US authorities broadly interpret the meaning of 'internal accounting controls'. The accounting provisions, like the anti-bribery provisions, do not explicitly require US issuers to implement compliance programmes designed to prevent and detect FCPA violations. However, when determining how to resolve a perceived offense, enforcement authorities will consider whether the company had established effective compliance procedures. Therefore, despite the lack of a statutory requirement to develop compliance programmes to prevent and detect corrupt payments, companies are significantly incentivised to establish corporate controls and procedures to comply with the FCPA similar to the adequate procedures set out in the UK MoJ Guidance.[64]

Penalties and consequences

2.41

Penalties for breaches of the FCPA are significant. Corporations can be fined up to US$2 million per anti-bribery violation; however, actual fines can exceed this maximum under alternative fine provisions of the US Sentencing Reform Act, which allow a court to impose a fine of up to twice the gross pecuniary gain that the corporation obtained from the transaction enabled by the bribe.[65] Individuals face fines of up to US$100,000 per anti-bribery violation or up to five years' imprisonment, or both.[66] Likewise, under the alternative fine provisions of the Sentencing Reform Act, individuals may also face increased fines of up to US$250,000 per anti-bribery violation or the greater of twice the gross pecuniary gain or loss the transaction enabled by the bribe.[67]

Violations of the FCPA's accounting provisions can result in fines of up to US$25 million for corporations and US$5 million for individuals, along with up to 20 years' imprisonment.[68]

63 15 USC § 78m.
64 See Evaluation of Corporate Compliance Programs, n 47 above. Chapter 8 contains further discussion of MoJ guidance on 'adequate procedures'.
65 15 U.S.C. §78dd-1 et seq.; 18 U.S.C. §3571.
66 15 U.S.C. §78dd-1 et seq.
67 18 U.S.C. §3571(d).
68 15 U.S.C §78ff(a).

2.42

In practice, FCPA violations often result in higher losses than the amount of the criminal fine itself. The SEC, via settlement agreements, frequently requires corporate offenders to disgorge illegally obtained profits that result from the bribery. FCPA enforcement actions may also form the basis of follow-on civil litigation in the US, such as shareholder derivative lawsuits, securities fraud class actions or victim restitution claims. Depending on the anti-corruption laws of the local jurisdiction(s) in which the misconduct occurred, FCPA enforcement actions could also lead to fines by non-US authorities and other related consequences.

The highest US fine levied against any company under the FCPA to date is the US$1.66 billion imposed by the DoJ and SEC on Goldman Sachs Group in October 2020 relating to violations involving US$1.6 billion in bribes to government officials in Malaysia and Abu Dhabi.[69]

2.43

Legal fees associated with FCPA investigations and resolutions can also themselves be effectively punitive, in some cases running into hundreds of millions of dollars. By way of example, in June 2019, Walmart agreed to pay the DoJ and SEC approximately US$283 million to resolve violations of the FCPA's accounting provisions.[70] The resolution followed a nearly decade-long investigation by US authorities into widespread bribery by third-party agents of Walmart's subsidiaries in Brazil, China, Mexico, and India. In addition to monetary fines and disgorgement amounts that Walmart agreed to pay US authorities, Walmart reportedly spent over US$900 million in legal fees and compliance programme improvements over the course of the lengthy investigation.[71]

2.44

In comparison, the UKBA provides for unlimited fines/a maximum sentence for individuals of ten years. A few large 'US style' sentences (similar to those referred to in this chapter) have been awarded by UK courts more recently,

---

69 Deferred Prosecution Agreement, *United States v The Goldman Sachs Group, Inc.*, No. 20-CR-437 (E.D.N.Y. 22 October 2020), www.justice.gov/criminal-fraud/file/1329926/download; Order, *In re The Goldman Sachs Group, Inc.*, Securities Exchange Act Rel. No. 90243 (Oct. 22, 2020), www.sec.gov/litigation/admin/2020/34-90243.pdf. Note Goldman's resolutions with the DoJ and SEC included an aggregate US$2.3 billion in penalties and fines and US$606 million in disgorgement; however, the amount paid to the DoJ and SEC was reduced to US$1.663 billion after allowing offsets for amounts paid to other (domestic and foreign) regulators in connection with the misconduct.

70 US Department of Justice Non-Prosecution Agreement with Walmart, Inc. (20 June 2019), www.justice.gov/opa/press-release/file/1175791/download; Order Instituting Cease-and-Desist Proceedings, In the Matter of Walmart, Inc., Securities Exchange Act Rel. No. 86159 (20 June 2019), www.sec.gov/litigation/admin/2019/34-86159.pdf.

71 See Press Release, Walmart, Inc., Walmart Reaches Agreements with the DoJ and the SEC to Resolve Their FCPA Investigations (20 June 2019), https://corporate.walmart.com/newsroom/2019/06/20/walmart-reaches-agreements-with-the-doj-and-the-sec-to-resolve-their-fcpa-investigations.

such as £497.25 million to Rolls Royce in January 2017 and €991 million to Airbus SE in January 2020. Such fines are a 'sea change' from earlier cases.[72] Chapter 11 provides more detailed information in this regard.[73]

2.45

Assuming UK fines continue to increase in line with US fines, the unfortunate likelihood is that legal costs defending actions will also significantly rise.

FCPA Case Studies[74]

2.46

FCPA enforcement actions are most often resolved without a trial through plea agreements, civil administrative actions and settlement agreements (such as DPAs or NPAs). Below are three recent case studies which demonstrate how US authorities apply the FCPA to real-world scenarios.

Cognizant – Voluntary Disclosure, Civil but no Criminal Action against Company, Multiple Executives Charged

2.47

COGNIZANT

Reported by the SEC on 15 February 2019 and by the DoJ on 13 February 2019

Cognizant Technology Solutions Corporation ('Cognizant'), a publicly traded, US-based technology services company, agreed to pay US$28.14 million to resolve FCPA violations related to bribery of Indian government officials.[75] The DoJ declined to prosecute the company; however, both the DoJ and SEC brought actions against senior Cognizant executives involved in the misconduct.

72 See *Lissack and Horlick on Bribery* (Lexis Nexis, 2011) at paras 3.53 to 3.80.

73 See Chapter 11.

74 Note that all case studies are based on publicly available information and that every reader should conduct their own investigations as regards information relating to these studies, given the complex nature of the investigations and number of parties involved. No criticism is intended of any person, company or other entity – or should be inferred.

75 See Order Instituting Cease-and-Desist Proceedings, *In re Cognizant Technology Solutions Corporation*, SEC Exch. Act Release No. 85,149 (15 February 2019), www.sec.gov/litigation/admin/2019/34-85149.pdf; DoJ Declination Letter, Cognizant Technology Solutions Corp. (13 February 2019), www.justice.gov/criminalfraud/file/1132666/download.

From 2014 to 2015, Cognizant allegedly authorised and reimbursed a third-party construction company for approximately US$2 million in bribe payments to one or more Indian government officials for their assistance with securing permits to construct an office park in India for Cognizant's India subsidiary ('Cognizant India'). In order to hide the payments to officials, Cognizant employees allegedly used construction invoices and fictitious 'change orders' to reimburse the construction company. US authorities further alleged that Cognizant employees in the United States and India allegedly falsified the company's books and records to conceal the payments. Senior US-based Cognizant executives, including its former president and former chief legal officer, reportedly approved both the bribe payments and efforts to conceal the payments.

Cognizant agreed to pay the SEC approximately US$25 million to resolve civil charges for violations of the FCPA's anti-bribery and accounting provisions. The SEC settlement amount included disgorgement of US$16,394,351, prejudgment interest of US$2,773,017, and a civil monetary penalty of US$6,000,000. Cognizant additionally agreed to report to the SEC for a period of two years on the company's remediation and implementation of compliance measures, as well as on any credible evidence of questionable or corrupt payments or false books and records.

Cognizant agreed to disgorge an additional US$3 million to the DoJ. Notably, however, the DoJ declined to prosecute the company for criminal violations of the FCPA's anti-bribery provisions – *despite* aggravating circumstances created by the involvement of senior management in the misconduct. The DoJ cited Cognizant's prompt and voluntary self-disclosure of the misconduct and the effectiveness of the company's pre-existing compliance program as among the factors contributing to its decision not to prosecute.

Although Cognizant avoided criminal prosecution, both the DoJ and SEC commenced actions against Cognizant's former president and former chief legal officer. The SEC additionally brought civil charges against a third executive: Cognizant's former chief operating officer. These actions are significant as a demonstration of US enforcement authorities' pursuit of individuals at corporations alleged to have violated the FCPA. In its declination letter, the DoJ specifically noted that Cognizant's timely and voluntary disclosure allowed the Department to identify culpable individuals at the company.

Sargeant Marine – Failure to Disclose, Criminal Actions against (Private) Company and Numerous Individuals

2.48

SARGEANT MARINE

Reported by the DoJ on 22 September 2020

Florida-based asphalt company Sargeant Marine, Inc. ('Sargeant Marine') pleaded guilty to conspiracy to violate the anti-bribery provisions of the FCPA and agreed to pay a criminal fine of US$16.6 million to resolve charges related bribery of foreign officials in multiple South American countries.[76]

Between 2010 and 2018, Sargeant Marine allegedly paid millions of dollars in bribes to officials at state-owned and state-controlled oil companies in Brazil, Venezuela, and Ecuador in order to obtain contracts for asphalt purchases or sales. The DoJ alleged that the company executed sham consulting contracts, making bribe payments to government officials through offshore shell companies controlled by intermediaries engaged under the fake contracts. Sargeant Marine allegedly earned over US$38 million in profits as a direct result of the bribery scheme.

Sargeant Marine did not self-report, and the conduct was serious, pervasive, and included the involvement of high-level executives. Despite the presence of these aggravating factors, the DoJ recommended a criminal fine of only US$16.6 million, reduced from the 'appropriate criminal penalty' of US$90 million. Sargeant Marine's inability to pay a heftier fine factored into the DoJ's decision, as did several mitigating factors, including the company's full cooperation with the investigation; discipline of employees involved; the fact that the company had ceased operations in the countries in which bribe payments were made; and its pledge to continue cooperating with related investigations. Sargeant Marine also agreed to implement an FCPA compliance program and to self-report on the status of the program's implementation for three years.

The DoJ charged numerous Sargeant Marine employees with conspiracy to violate the FCPA's anti-bribery provisions. Also of note, the DoJ charged two of the bribe *recipients* – foreign government officials – with conspiracy to commit money laundering for their respective roles in the scheme.

76 See Plea Agreement, *United States v Sargeant Marine, Inc.*, Cr. No. 20-CR-363 (E.D.N.Y. 21 September 2020).

Novartis – Failure to Timely Disclose, Cooperation with Investigations

2.49

NOVARTIS

Reported by DoJ and SEC on 25 June 2020

Novartis AG (Novartis), a Switzerland-based pharmaceutical company, and certain of its current and former subsidiaries agreed to pay US authorities a combined total of US$346.7 million for committing numerous FCPA violations.

Novartis and two subsidiaries resolved the investigations via settlement agreements with both the DoJ and the SEC, agreeing to pay US$225 million to the DoJ and US$112.8 million to the SEC. A former Novartis subsidiary based in Singapore agreed to pay US$8.9 million in a separate resolution with the DoJ for conduct that occurred while it was still controlled by Novartis.[77]

The SEC resolution with Novartis centered around evidence that the companies had offered inappropriate economic benefits to healthcare professionals in Greece, Vietnam, and South Korea (and without internal controls for a program in China), while the DoJ resolutions with the subsidiaries involved the same conduct in Greece and Vietnam. The conduct under investigation allegedly spanned from 2009 to 2016. The DoJ determined that the relevant subsidiaries profited from the bribery of medical professionals, hospitals, and clinics and then falsified their books and records to conceal the improper conduct. Novartis and its subsidiaries admitted to violating both the anti-bribery and the accounting provisions of the FCPA and undertook three-year-long obligations to self-report back to the agencies once a year on the companies' progress in enhancing their compliance programs and internal controls.

Prior to these investigations, Novartis reached a separate resolution with the SEC in 2016. Under the 2016 resolution, Novartis paid US$25 million for violating the FCPA when its China-based subsidiaries implemented a pay-to-prescribe scheme. The 2016 Cease and Desist Order required Novartis to periodically report to the SEC regarding its remediation and compliance measures over a two-year term, including the discovery of any additional misconduct.

77 See www.justice.gov/usao-nj/pr/novartis-ag-and-subsidiaries-pay-345-million-resolve-foreign-corrupt-practices-act-cases.

The companies failed to timely disclose the conduct at issue in the investigations. However, Novartis, as well as all relevant subsidiaries, cooperated with both the DoJ and SEC investigations, and the companies therefore received credit for their cooperation. The companies also engaged in remedial measures, such as terminating the individuals who orchestrated the misconduct, adopting heightened controls and compliance mechanisms, and devoting increased resources to these issues. Notably, the DoJ resolution did not require that Novartis or its subsidiaries install an independent corporate compliance monitor.

Standard Bank[78] – inducement to Government of Tanzania

2.50

STANDARD BANK

Reported by SFO on 30 November 2015

Leveson LJ agreed to the first UK Deferred Prosecution Agreement (DPA) brought by the SFO and ICBC Standard Bank Plc (Standard Bank).

The SFO investigated a US$6 million payment made in March 2013 by a related company of Standard Bank, Stanbic Bank Tanzania, to a Tanzanian partner, Enterprise Growth Market Advisors (EGMA). It was alleged that the payment was to induce members of the government of Tanzania to give preferential treatment to Standard Bank and Stanbic Tanzania. Standard Bank was to carry out a US$600 million private placement on behalf of the government of Tanzania.

The government of Tanzania needed the funds to support the country's infrastructure developments. Standard Bank and Stanbic Tanzania stood to gain millions of dollars in fees through their proposals. EGMA's role was to induce senior representatives of the government of Tanzania to favour Standard Bank's bid, in exchange for a 1% fee.

Standard Bank self-reported to the SFO in April 2013. Under the terms of the DPA, Standard Bank agreed to pay financial orders of US$25.2 million and it was agreed that US$8.4 million of this sum was to disgorge the profits made by Standard Bank. It would also pay the government

78 www.sfo.gov.uk/cases/standard-bank-plc/.

of Tanzania US$7 million in compensation and to pay the SFO's costs of £330,000.

Of note is that Standard Bank agreed to commission an independent report on its anti-bribery and corruption policies. This report included advice or recommendations on situations where third-party intermediaries are involved in Standard Bank's transactions.

With the SFO's co-operation, the DoJ and the SEC also investigated Standard Bank, concerning separate but related conduct and Standard Bank agreed to a penalty of US$4.2 million.

Rolls Royce – corrupt payments to agents[79]

2.51

ROLLS ROYCE

Reported by SFO on 17 January 2017

Rolls-Royce agrees with SFO to pay over £497 million by way of settlement.

In a multi-jurisdictional investigation, carried out with the aid of the US DoJ and Brazil's Ministério Público Federal, the prosecutors agreed that Rolls-Royce had committed 12 counts of conspiracy to corrupt, false accountancy and failure to prevent bribery. The SFO's UK DPA covered conduct involving seven jurisdictions: Indonesia, Thailand, India, Russia, Nigeria, China and Malaysia.

It was identified that there were various agreements to make corrupt payments to agents for the sale of engines in civil aircrafts in Indonesia and Thailand; concealing the use of intermediaries to facilitate its Indian Defence business; making a corrupt payment to recover a list of intermediaries; agreeing to make corrupt payments in Russia; along with failing to prevent bribery contrary to s 7 of the UKBA. The offending conduct was carried out over three decades and involved Rolls-Royce's Civil Aerospace and Defence Aerospace businesses.

Under the DPA, Rolls-Royce agreed to pay a total sum in the UK settlement of £497 million plus interest and the SFO's substantial costs

79 www.sfo.gov.uk/2017/01/17/sfo-completes-497-25m-deferred-prosecution-agreement-rolls-royce-plc/; www.sfo.gov.uk/download/deferred-prosecution-agreement-statement-facts-sfo-v-rolls-royce-plc/.

of £13 million incurred during a four-year investigation. There was a separate criminal investigation into the conduct of relevant individuals relating to this conduct.

The SFO's investigation involved co-operation with the DoJ and Brazil's Ministério Público Federal. Under the agreements with these authorities, Rolls-Royce agreed to pay US$170 million in the US and US$25 million in Brazil.

Quick Reference UKBA/FCPA Comparison Table

2.52

A quick reference guide setting out the main similarities and differences between the FCPA and UKBA is set out below. When reading the table, it is important keep in mind that despite the material differences between the UKBA and FCPA as reflected in the text of the statutes, the statutes align more in practice than on paper given the following:

- The reported breadth of US enforcement agencies' interpretation of 'internal … controls';
- DoJ statements on 'the hallmarks of an effective compliance programme'[80] (contained in the Resource Guide, referred to in paragraph 2.38 above), which includes by way of example references to (a) compliance policies and procedures, (b) risk assessment; and (c) training of employees and business partners;
- the reported narrowness of the US 'facilitation payment' exemption.[81]

2.53

In practice, therefore, the FCPA is interpreted by US prosecutors in a way that often makes the outcome of FCPA analysis, in cases related to public officials, the same or similar to the analysis using the UKBA alone.

80 See Evaluation of Corporate Compliance Programs, above n 47.

81 For the DoJ's view, see Resource Guide, above n 20, at 28 (fn 170) and 111 (fn 171)

FCPA/UKBA QUICK COMPARISON TABLE		
	FCPA	**UKBA**
Scope: public officials	Relates to bribes intended for non-US government officials	Relates to bribes intended for anyone with an obligation of trust – whether a government official or not
Active and passive bribery	Relates to the givers of bribes. Widely defines 'knowledge' of violative conduct	Relates to the givers of bribes and where there is jurisdiction the recipients of bribes (s 2, ie non-government officials only)
Active bribery offence re offeror's knowing breach of recipient's policies	No separate offence	A separate active bribery offence where a offeror knows or believes that what is offered, if received, would breach the obligations of the recipient to his employer – eg offeror knows that overnight accommodation in an invitation would breach the intended recipient's entertainment policy (s 1 case 2 of the UKBA)
Corporate liability	Yes, for relevant acts: a) in which the corporation directly participated; b) by subsidiaries, employees, or agents under traditional theories of agency; or c) by third party agents undertaken with the corporation's knowledge (including wilful blindness)	Yes, for active bribery where bribes offered by 'associated parties', ie 'service providers' with a presumption in favour of 'associated party' status for employees
Small bribes	A limited exception for facilitating payments that are for non-discretionary/ routine services, (ie to expedite or to secure the performance of a routine governmental action by a foreign official)	No exception or exemption but prosecutor may use discretion – (eg where enforcement would not be 'in the public interest')

FCPA/UKBA QUICK COMPARISON TABLE		
	FCPA	**UKBA**
Corporate defence: having procedures in place to prevent bribery by others	No 'adequate procedures' defence but compliance programme is relevant to decision to prosecute, assessment of fines, and imposition of additional compliance obligations in connection with settlements	Yes, 'adequate procedures' a complete defence but onus on the company to prove that adequate procedures are in place. Extent of compliance programme likely to be relevant to decision to prosecute and to any fine
Deferred Prosecution Agreements available	Yes (subject to prosecutorial discretion)	Yes – since 2015
Non-Prosecution Agreements possible	Yes (subject to prosecutorial discretion)	No, but prosecutor may use discretion not to prosecute
Corporate fines	Can effectively be unlimited. Calculated using established formula	Unlimited but now clarified by the Sentencing Guidelines Council
Jurisdiction	For anti-bribery provisions, jurisdiction lies over US issuers, persons, and where any act in furtherance of the corrupt payment is taken in the territory of the US – including the use of US bank accounts. For accounting provisions, jurisdiction applies to US 'issuers' only	For active bribery (UKBA ss 1 and 6) and passive bribery (s 2) normal English law principles of jurisdiction apply according to public international law. The jurisdiction is therefore narrower than for the FCPA. As regards the corporate offence (UKBA, s 7), a commercial organisation must be incorporated in or have part of its business in the UK, ie there is a broad jurisdiction
Accounting offence	Yes – a separate offence for 'issuers'	No separate offence but failures in keeping risk based and proportionate books and records may prevent an 'adequate procedures' defence. Separate company laws also apply which create positive obligations

Trends

2.54

Corruption risk is likely to remain high on the agenda of many companies and in the future, as now, each day and week will bring legal and compliance developments. In that context, new legislation will keep coming forward in countries that have not recently reviewed their laws. Post UKBA, that legislation will be more likely to feature broad extra-territorial reach, stricter sentences, no exception for facilitation payments (per the OECD position on such payments) and is likely to incentivise the implementation of procedures in corporates to prevent bribery.

2.55

Within industry and banking, there is a 'trickle down' effect, as smaller and medium sized companies and smaller banks ('SMEs') adopt adequate procedures. This is particularly expected where SMEs are engaged by larger businesses to provide a service, given that those larger businesses will not want their 'service provider' to create a vicarious criminal liability. Various recent natural disasters have shone a spotlight on the environmental, social and corporate governance (ESG) agenda has further added to this movement, with increased acceptance that smaller companies should adhere to financial crime policy and procedures. For example, many organisations now require all third parties to be onboarded via platforms which generate a specific risk rating for each business relationship.

2.56

In the UK, we expect to see continued growth and 'deepening' of anti-compliance programs as the result of 'speak up' telephone lines, internal investigations and monitoring, which have the capacity to create a 'virtuous circle' – keeping anti-bribery risks and mitigations on the senior management agenda.

Cross-border cooperation

2.57

This chapter would not be complete without referring to the continued trend of cross-border co-operation between governments, prosecutors and regulators. In addition to well publicised joint enforcement actions such as Rolls Royce (UK/US/Brazil) and Airbus SE (France/UK/US)[82] international information sharing on an informal basis between prosecutors without the use

82 January 2020 (www.sfo.gov.uk/2020/01/31/sfo-enters-into-e991m-deferred-prosecution-agreement-with-airbus-as-part-of-a-e3-6bn-global-resolution/).

of formal mutual legal assistance treaties is a daily occurrence and has continued following Brexit.

2.58

As a result, even where one prosecutor becomes aware of a matter through its intelligence network and does not wish to proceed with it, there may be other foreign prosecutors with whom the information is shared and who take an active interest in investigating. In other situations that touch on numerous jurisdictions, companies may well find themselves responding to requests from regulators or prosecutors in their home state, the US, and the state in which most of the wrongdoing occurred, eg China. In addition to this, they could be investigated by authorities in any other state in which they have part of their business, provided that state has laws similar to the UKBA, (ie laws with wide extra-territorial reach).

2.59

In other words, despite issues of jurisdiction (as well as double jeopardy and *res judicata*[83]), the likelihood of multi-authority interest in any publicised corruption matters is only increasing as governments adopt new anti-bribery laws, extend the sharing of information to prevent other forms of financial crime (such as tax evasion) and agree closer co-operation between authorities.[84] This of course means that investigation costs for larger matters could continue to rise, and that managing larger investigations could become more complex, creating another incentive to prevent bribery issues arising through the use of adequate procedures.

83 A common law rule that a final judgment on the merits by a court having jurisdiction is conclusive between the parties to a suit as to all matters that were litigated or that could have been litigated in that suit and cannot be relitigated.

84 See, for example www.antibriberyguidance.org/sites/default/files/pdf/publications/GlobalAntiBriberyGuidance_TIUK_Small.pdf.

3 Background to British bribery legislation

Introduction

3.1

'Every man has his price'; so observed Sir Robert Walpole,[1] a political survivor of the notorious South Sea Bubble, who was himself briefly imprisoned on allegations of corruption[2] before becoming the first Prime Minister of England under George I. Just as in eighteenth century England, corruption today is sometimes justified as a necessary evil, succinctly termed by some commentators as 'the Prisoner's Dilemma: If we don't pay bribes our competitors will'.[3] Those who continue to claim that success in business or politics is an end which justifies the means delude themselves. Corruption is now recognised as a global problem, with a wide ranging and corrosive impact on commerce, investor confidence and political stability, particularly in developing countries with fragile democracies.

3.2

As Kofi Annan, former UN Secretary General stated in 2004:

> 'Corruption is an insidious plague that has a wide range of corrosive effects on societies. It undermines democracy and the rule of law, leads to violations of human rights, distorts markets, erodes the quality of life and allows organised crime, terrorism and other threats to human society to flourish. This evil phenomenon is found in all countries – big and small, rich and poor – but it is in the developing world that its effects are most destructive. Corruption hurts the poor disproportionately by diverting funds intended for development, undermining a government's ability to provide basic services, feeding inequality and injustice and discouraging foreign aid and foreign investment. Corruption is a key element in economic underperformance and a major obstacle to poverty alleviation and development.'

---

1 1676–1745.

2 1712.

3 Nick Kochan and Robin Goodyear, *Corruption: The New Corporate Challenge* (Macmillan, 2011).

3.3

The Bribery Act 2010 ('UKBA'), which came into force on 1 July 2011, has been a strong and timely response by the United Kingdom to the problems of domestic and international corruption. First, it abolished and replaced the confusing patchwork of anti-corruption common law and statutes which have developed piecemeal in England and Wales over the last two centuries.[4] Secondly it was intended as a co-ordinated response to the way in which international law on transnational bribery had developed, particularly the 1997 OECD Convention on Bribery, which was ratified by the UK in 1998. At that time, although conspiracy to engage in corrupt conduct together with a foreign public official was an offence,[5] questions were raised as to whether the existing UK laws of bribery and corruption directly covered bribery of foreign public officials. It was considered that this potential lacuna breached the UK's obligations under the Convention. As we will see, although section 108 of the Anti-Terrorism, Crime and Security Act 2001 attempted to shore up this deficiency by extending the existing law to acts taking place outside the UK, the OECD Working Group on Bribery nonetheless characterised the legal situation as 'uncertain and complex'.[6] The position has been clarified by section 6 of the UKBA, which for the first time created a specific offence of bribery of public officials.[7]

3.4

The increasingly transactional nature of serious economic crime, and the comparative ease and speed with which money is moved around the globe, ensure that global corruption continues to grow and thrive. Although debate persists about its impact, the efficacy of the Bribery Act 2010 in securing convictions, particularly against companies, and in shoring up lacunas in the UK's bribery regime, is generally well recognised. The Act has been declared 'an excellent piece of legislation which has created offences which are clear and all-embracing.'[8]

3.5

Since July 2011, there have been over 100 convictions under the Act. Moreover, following the introduction of the Crime and Courts Act 2013, a statutory mechanism has been introduced which permits investigations into fraud, corruption and other crimes committed by corporate organisations to be concluded without prosecution. Such agreements, known as Deferred Prosecution Agreements ('DPAs') can now be made between an organisation

---

4 Section 17 and Schedule 2.

5 *R v Raud* [1989] Crim LR 809 (CA).

6 UK Phase 11 Report (www.oecd.org/dataoecd/43/13/38962457.pdf).

7 See Chapter 6.

8 House of Lords Select Committee Report on the Bribery Act 2010: post-legislative scrutiny, published 14 March 2019.

and the relevant prosecuting authority, and supervised by the courts. Between 2015 and 2020 some nine DPAs have taken place, and generated large sums of money for the Treasury.[9]

3.6

The current Director of the SFO, Lisa Orsofsky, has recognised the new challenges of law enforcement on tackling fraud and corruption, particularly during a pandemic, and has announced her intention to continue to bring strong cases to court, and to negotiate 'airtight' DPAs to ensure good corporate citizenship and protect the UK's national reputation.[10] Citing, amongst others, a recent €3.6 billion global DPA with Airbus SE which covered conduct in five jurisdictions and involved concerted engagement with impacted countries round the world[11] and the *Unaoil* case, which involved corrupt oil contracts in Iraq and resulted in the conviction of three defendants,[12] the Director asserted the unique role played by the SFO in the UK's wider law enforcement and prosecution agenda. She also acknowledged the success of the SFO's collaboration with the Joint Money Laundering Intelligence Taskforce which links law enforcement with the private sector, and the NCA-led Foreign Bribery and Corruption Clearing House.

3.7

While the SFO and CPS still retain a wide discretion to enter into civil settlements or DPAs[13] where it is in the public interest to do so, the message is clear: the SFO will prosecute to the full extent of the law. It is submitted that the concept of what is or is not in the public interest continues to be vague, and guidance on DPAs issued by the SFO, and reproduced elsewhere in this book, still leaves an element of uncertainty which will be unwelcome to those in the commercial world.[14]

3.8

Despite the more pro-active prosecutorial stance currently adopted by prosecuting authorities, timely and full self-reporting by a commercial organisation and whether or not the organisation had adequate procedures in place to prevent bribery will be considered in the light of new guidelines, and will remain two of a number of important factors in the decision whether or not to prosecute under section 7 of the Act. These are discussed fully in Chapter 7.

---

9 Chapter 11.148.
10 Speech at the Royal United Services Institute on 8 October 2020.
11 *SFO v Airbus SE* 31 January 2020, Case no. 20200108.
12 March 2021.
13 See Chapter 11 on deferred prosecution agreements.
14 Bribery Act 2010: Joint Prosecution Guidance of the Director of the SFO and the DPP.

3.9

Failure to report wrongdoing within a reasonable time of the offending coming to light is a public interest factor *in favour* of prosecution. According to the guidance, 'for a self-report to be taken into account as a public interest factor tending against prosecution it must form part of a genuinely proactive approach adopted by the corporate management team when the offending is brought to their notice, involving self-reporting and remedial actions, including the compensation of victims'. However, no corporate should expect to receive wholesale assurances that if it self-reports, it will not be prosecuted. Such an instance occurred in February 2018, when the CPS secured its first conviction *R v Skansen Interiors Ltd.*[15] Despite measures taken by the company's CEO, including a report to the police, and submission of a suspicious activity report to the National Crime Agency, the company was nonetheless charged with an offence under section 7 related to a bribe paid by the managing director of Skansen Interiors Ltd to the project manager of a property company, to award Skansen refurbishment contracts with £6 million. The jury considered and rejected an 'adequate procedures' defence, and the company was convicted after a contested trial.

3.10

Facilitation payments, unofficial payments made to public officials in order to secure or expedite the performance of a routine or necessary action, continue to remain illegal in the United Kingdom.[16] This contrasts with the position in the United States where the Foreign Corrupt Practices Act 1977 ('FCPA')[17] exempts modest payments to foreign, political party, or party officials for 'routine governmental action', such as processing papers and issuing permits in order to expedite performance of duties of a non-discretionary nature. Such payments are not intended to influence the outcome of the official's action, only its timing.

3.11

The introduction of DPAs[18] has undoubtedly added to the armoury of prosecuting authorities. In addition, the SFO's current Director has argued that the UK's system for prosecuting corporate fraud is 'antiquated', fuelling the debate over the test for corporate criminal liability, including whether the strict liability offence of failure of commercial organisations to prevent bribery (UKBA, section 7) could be extended to other fraud offences. These matters were raised in a consultation paper issued by the government in early 2017. A response from the Ministry of Justice is still awaited.

---

15 21 February 2018 Southwark Crown Court Case no. T2017024.

16 See paragraphs 2.35–37 for the US context, and Chapter 5 for small bribes under the UKBA regime.

17 As clarified in the 1988 amendments.

18 See Chapter 11.

History of the law on bribery and corruption

3.12

The common-law offences of *bribery* developed organically with the advancement of common law in England and Scotland. There were also a series of statutes which created specific offences and aimed at specific forms of *corruption*; namely:

- The Public Bodies Corrupt Practices Act 1889
- The Prevention of Corruption Act 1906
- The Prevention of Corruption Act 1916
- The Honours (Prevention of Abuses) Act 1925
- Part 12 of the Anti-terrorism, Crime and Security Act 2001

Each of these statutes is discussed below.

3.13

The term 'bribery' is found in common law offences and civil law, whereas the statutes of 1889, 1906 and 1916 employ the term 'corruption'. As we will see, these terms are largely synonymous and are often used interchangeably.

Bribery at common law

3.14

The offence of bribery at common law was classically defined by the editors of *Russell on Crime* as:

> '[The] receiving or offering [of] any undue reward by or to any person whatsoever, in a public office, in order to influence his behaviour in office, and incline him to act contrary to the known rules of honesty and integrity.'[19]

3.15

Separate offences of common law bribery tended to capture specific offices or functions and were charged in a variety of situations. So for instance, the bribery of jurors (also known as the now defunct common law offence of embracery),[20] the bribery of privy councillors, the bribery of justices, and the bribery of others who discharged any duty in which the public had an interest,

19 Turner, *Russell on Crime* (12th edn, Sweet & Maxwell, 1964), p 364.

20 This offence, now repealed by the UKBA, is defined by *Russell on Crime* as '[any] attempt whatsoever to corrupt or influence or instruct a jury … or in any way to incline them to be more favourable to the one side than to the other, by money, promises, letters, threats, or persuasions, except only by the strength of the evidence and the arguments of counsel in open court …'.

irrespective of whether or not such persons held judicial or ministerial office,[21] are all forms of offences known to the common law. They are very broad in scope. Provided that the briber intended to influence the decision by the person discharging the duty, however minor, such offences would have been committed.[22]

3.16

The concept of 'undue reward' has not been defined and will depend on the facts of an individual case, but as a matter of common sense, it suggests a reward to which the recipient would not in other circumstances be entitled.

3.17

The amount of the award may be very small. A practical difficulty often arises with gifts or entertainment by way of corporate hospitality. The matter is usually determined by the nature, value and purpose of the gift or entertainment, and the context in which it is offered or given. Whilst there is no minimum limit on the value of an award at common law, UKBA guidelines, issued by the Ministry of Justice to assist commercial organisations,[23] suggest that the offer or provision of proportionate and reasonable hospitality by a company 'in order to get to know' a client would be unlikely to be caught by the Act. In this respect, statutory guidance reflects the likely position at common law.

Misconduct in public office

3.18

The offence of misconduct in public office, which continues to survive, involves either wilful and improper act or omission by someone acting as a public officer, such as a magistrate, judge, registrar, council official, minister, civil servant or police officer. Wilful misconduct requires the commission of a deliberate and wrongful act by an individual, knowing it to be wrong, or with reckless indifference as to whether it is wrong or not. The threshold is high, and 'a mistake, even a serious one, will not suffice.'[24] Where the nature of the misconduct alleged involved theft or fraud, then dishonesty must be proved.[25]

---

21 *R v Whitaker* [1914] 3 KB 1283 where the person bribed was a colonel, indicted for taking bribes from a catering company wishing to provide services to the army.

22 *R v Gurney* (1867) 10 Cox CC 550.

23 Discussed in Chapter 13.

24 *A-G Ref (No 3 of 2003)* [2004] EWCA Crim 868.

25 *R v W* [2010] EWCA Crim 372.

Statutory corruption

3.19

The late nineteenth and early twentieth century was an era of growing commercial activity, and several statutes were introduced by Parliament to fight a corresponding increase in corruption. The main statutory offences, and those under which most prosecutions were brought, were the Public Bodies Corrupt Practices Act 1889 ('the 1889 Act'), the Prevention of Corruption Act 1906 ('the 1906 Act') and the Prevention of Corruption Act 1916 ('the 1916 Act') and the Honours (Prevention of Abuses) Act 1925. Despite the repeal of all but the Act of 1925 and the common law offence of misconduct in public office, the UKBA is not retrospective in nature. This means that offences of bribery and corruption committed or partly committed before 1 July 2011 will continue to be prosecuted under the old law. It is possible that some overlap remains, so that in cases where A offered a bribe to B *before* the commencement date of the new Act, but B accepted the bribe *after* the Act came into force, A would be liable under the old law, and B under the new.[26]

The Public Bodies Corrupt Practices Act 1889

3.20

This Act was passed exclusively to deal with bribery of local government employees and those who worked in certain other public bodies following exposure of widespread misconduct within the Metropolitan Board of Works, London's governing body at the time. No prosecution can be commenced without the consent of the Attorney-General. Section 1 provides:

> '(1) Every person who shall by himself or by or in conjunction with any other person, corruptly solicit or receive, or agree to receive, for himself, or for any other person, any gift, loan, fee, reward, or advantage whatever as an inducement to, or reward for, or otherwise on account of any member, officer, or servant of a public body as in this Act defined, doing or forbearing to do anything in respect of any matter or transaction whatsoever, actual or proposed, in which the said public body is concerned, shall be guilty of a misdemeanour.
>
> (2) Every person who shall by himself or by or in conjunction with any other person corruptly give, promise, or offer any gift, loan, fee, reward, or advantage whatsoever to any person, whether for the benefit of that person or of any other person, as an inducement to or reward for or otherwise on account of any member, officer, or servant of any public body as in this Act defined, doing or

26 See s 19(5) and (6) for the transitional provisions of the Act.

> forbearing to do anything in respect of any matter or transaction whatsoever, actual or proposed, in which such public body as aforesaid is concerned, shall be guilty of [an offence].'

Definitions

3.21

'Public body' was narrowly defined by section 7 as:

> '… any council of a county or city or town, any council of a municipal borough, also any board, commissioners, select vestry, or other body which has power to act under and for the purposes of any Act relating to local government, money, raised by rates in pursuance of any public general Act, and includes any body which exists in a county or territory outside the United Kingdom and is equivalent to any body described above.'

3.22

'Public office' was defined to mean any office or employment of a person as a member, officer or servant of such a public body.

3.23

The expression *'person'* includes a body of persons, corporate or unincorporate.

3.24

The expression *'advantage'* includes any office or dignity, and any forbearance to demand any money or money's worth or valuable thing, and includes any or any pretended aid, vote, consent or influence, as well as 'any promise or procurement of or agreement or endeavour to procure, or the holding out of any expectation of any gift, loan, fee, reward, or advantage, as before defined.'

3.25

The definition of a public body in section 7 proved to be somewhat restrictive, and the definition of 'public body' did not extend to the problem of growing corruption in the private sector, which was increasingly undermining confidence in trade. As a result, a Special Committee of Secret Commissions of the London Chamber of Commerce was appointed. Its recommendations led first to the Secret Commissions Bill in 1889, and then to the 1906 Act. However, it was not until 1916 that the definition of 'public body' was extended by section 4(2) of the Prevention of Corruption Act 1916, so as to include local and public authorities of all descriptions, in addition to the bodies specified in the 1889 Act.[27] Despite the broadening of the definition, members of the civil service

---

27 *DPP v Holly* (1977) 64 Cr App R 143.

and those working under the Crown, such as immigration officers, continued to be excluded.[28]

Meaning of 'corruptly'

3.26

The word 'corruptly' is not defined in either the 1889 Act, or the 1906 Act. It has been left to the courts to clarify its meaning. *R v Wellburn,* decided in 1979, remains the leading authority.[29] In that case, the Court of Criminal Appeal, relying on a statement by the court in *Cooper v Slade* made more than 120 years earlier,[30] ruled somewhat tautologically that 'corruptly means purposefully doing an act which the law forbids as tending to corrupt', and that the word 'corruptly' should be given its ordinary meaning, and should cause a jury little difficulty. Unsurprisingly the definition has proved troublesome in practice, particularly for juries asked, for example, to distinguish corrupt conduct from mere corporate hospitality.

3.27

Any improper and unauthorised gift, payment or other form of inducement made to a councillor is likely to be corrupt. Dishonesty on the part of the giver is not required, so long as he knew that the gift or bribe was a reward for the past or future performance of public duties.[31] The offence can be committed even where no agreement is reached between the parties,[32] and the fact that the recipient was not influenced by the gift or reward is no defence.[33] On the other hand, where the recipient accepts a gift, unaware that it was intended as an award or inducement, then the offence will have been committed only by the giver.[34]

The Prevention of Corruption Act 1906

3.28

The 1889 Act failed to stem the growing tide of corruption in the 1890's and paved the way for the introduction of the more effective and more frequently used Prevention of Corruption Act 1906, which came into force in 1907. The measure was wider in scope, and directed at corruption between two or more private parties, as well as to officials beyond the reach of the 1889 Act. The legislation gained considerable public and judicial support at the time,

28 *R v Natji* [2002] EWCA Crim 271.
29 (1979) 69 Cr App R 254.
30 *Cooper v Slade* (1858) 6 HL 746.
31 *R v Harvey* [1999] Crim LR 70.
32 *Andrews-Weatherfoil Ltd* [1972] 1 WLR 118.
33 *R v Parker* (1986) 82 Cr App R 69.
34 *Millray Window Cleaning Co Ltd* [1962] Crim LR 99.

including one judge whose observations about the scourge of corruption could have been uttered today:

> 'It is obviously a dangerous and seductive form of immorality: it is difficult to detect, for it is in the interest alike of the giver and the receiver of the corrupt gift to keep the thing secret; its ugliness can easily be disguised under the mask of generosity or gratitude; and it had become at the time of the passing of this Act so notoriously common practice that I verily believe that not infrequently both the guilty parties have persuaded themselves, or almost persuaded themselves, that they were not doing anything which was really deserving of serious reproach.'[35]

3.29

The 1906 Act was intended to be considerably broader in its application, and extends to corruption between private individuals and those working in the public, including a wider range of officials than those in the Act of 1889. Section 1 defines the offence as follows:

> **'1 Punishment of corrupting transactions with agents**
>
> (1) If any agent corruptly accepts or obtains, or agrees to accept or attempts to obtain, from any person, for himself or for any other person, any gift or consideration as an inducement or reward for doing or forbearing to do, or for having after the passing of this Act done or forborne to do, any act in relation to his principal's affairs or business, or for showing or forbearing to show favour or disfavour to any person in relation to his principal's affairs or business; or
>
> If any person corruptly gives or agrees to give or offers any gift or consideration to any agent as an inducement or reward for doing or forbearing to do, or for having after the passing of this Act done or forborne to do, any act in relation to his principal's affairs or business, or for showing or forbearing to show favour or disfavour to any person in relation to his principal's affairs or business; or
>
> If any person knowingly gives to any agent, or if any agent knowingly uses with intent to deceive his principal, any receipt, account, or other document in respect of which the principal is interested, and which contains any statement which is false or erroneous or defective in any

35 Kennedy LJ speaking in October 1907.

material particular, and which to his knowledge is intended to mislead the principal:

He shall be guilty of a misdemeanour and shall be liable—

(a) on summary conviction, to imprisonment for a term not exceeding 6 months or a fine not exceeding the statutory maximum, or to both; and

(b) on conviction on indictment, to imprisonment for a term not exceeding 7 years or to a fine, or to both.

(2) For the purpose of this Act the expression "consideration" includes valuable consideration of any kind; the expression "agent" includes any person employed by or acting for another and the expression "principal" includes an employer.

(3) A person serving under the Crown or under any corporation or any … borough, county, or district council, or any board of guardians, is an agent within the meaning of the Act.

(4) For the purposes of this Act it is immaterial if—

(a) the principal's affairs or business have no connection with the United Kingdom and are carried out in a country or territory outside the United Kingdom.

(b) the agent's functions have no connection with the United Kingdom and are carried out in a country or territory outside the United Kingdom.'

Similarities between the Acts of 1889 and 1906

3.30

There are obvious similarities and cross-over between the 1889 and 1906 Acts. As with the 1889 Act, the consent of the A-G is required before a prosecution can be commenced. Although the 1889 Act prohibits a corrupt 'gift, loan, fee, reward or other advantage', and the 1906 Act speaks of a corrupt 'gift or consideration', the difference is one of terminology rather than of substance. Whereas the 1906 Act refers to 'attempts' to obtain gifts, the 1889 Act refers to the 'soliciting' of such gifts, which amounts to broadly the same thing, unless the act of solicitation is merely preparatory and falls short of an attempt. The concept of corruption is identical in both Acts, and an element of dishonesty is not required under either.[36]

36 *R v Harvey* [1999] Crim LR 70.

Differences

3.31

The main distinction between the two Acts is that for an offence to be committed under the 1906 Act, the recipient must be the 'agent' of a 'principal', and the object of the bribe must be to influence the agent's actions in relation to his principal's affairs. The Act does not confine itself to agents of public bodies. Bribes to private persons such as employees, directors, and trustees and to private enterprises are also caught within the definition of 'agent'. The meaning of 'agent' was further supplemented by section 4(3) of the Prevention of Corruption Act 1916, which provides that a person serving under any public body[37] 'is an agent within the meaning of the 1906 Act'.

3.32

Another distinction is that councillors in local government are not agents, so the 1906 Act will not apply with regard to them. The converse is also true. Since the Crown is not a public body, the corruption of Crown servants can be dealt with under the 1906 Act, but not under the 1889 Act.[38]

3.33

Where agents of public bodies are alleged to have behaved corruptly, the provisions of both the 1889 Act and the 1906 Act overlap. Under both statutes, an offence can be committed by the potential giver of a bribe even if the intended recipient was unaware that such a bribe was to be made, provided that the apparent purpose of the transaction was to affect the conduct of such a person corruptly.[39] It does not follow that both the giver and the recipient are guilty of the offence if a bribe is received. Where, for instance, a payment intended as a corrupt gift by A is accepted innocently by B, ie without B understanding it to be a reward or inducement, only A would be guilty of corruption.[40] Guilt depends on each party having a corrupt intent at the relevant time.

The Prevention of Corruption Act 1916

3.34

The implementation of the 1906 Act, effective though it was, failed to prevent a number of public scandals, which contributed significantly to the enactment of the Prevention of Corruption Act 1916. One such incident, the 'Marconi Scandal 1911–1913' was an early example of insider trading. Several senior government officials were involved in the purchase of shares in the British

---

37 The Prevention of Corruption Act 1916, s 4(2) defines 'public body'.
38 *R v Natji* [2002] 1 WLR 2337.
39 *Jagdeo Singh v The State of Trinidad and Tobago* [1960] 1 WLR 146.
40 *R v Millray Window Cleaning Co* [1962] Crim LR 99.

communications and engineering company Marconi before they went on sale to the public. They did so in the knowledge that the government had recently signed a large and profitable contract with the company.

3.35

As already discussed, the 1916 Act amended the definition of 'public body' for the purposes of the 1889 Act, and for the purposes of the 1906 Act, it also extended the definition of agent to include persons serving under a public body.[41]

3.36

The most important measure to be introduced by the 1916 Act was to create a statutory presumption of corruption where payments, gifts etc were made to public officials by those seeking to obtain a contract from a public body. Section 2 provides:

> 'Where in any proceedings against a person for an offence under the Prevention of Corruption Act 1906, or the Public Bodies Corrupt Practices Act 1889, it is proved that any money, gift, or other consideration has been paid or given to or received by a person in the employment of His Majesty or any government department or a public body by or from a person, or agent of a person, holding or seeking to obtain a contract from His Majesty or any government department or public body, the money, gift, or consideration shall be deemed to have been paid or given and received corruptly as such inducement or reward as is mentioned in such Act unless the contrary is proved.'

3.37

The presumption of corruption applies only to money paid or gifts etc given to employees as defined by the Act, in relation to a relevant contract, ie the one which is sought to be obtained. There is no presumption in relation to intermediaries, unless they are acting as agents or as part of a joint enterprise.[42] Nor can a presumption be made where a conspiracy is charged, or where the offence was committed abroad.[43]

Application of the Human Rights Act 1998

3.38

Article 6(2) of the Convention on Human Rights, enshrined by the Human Rights Act 1998, incorporates the presumption of innocence, and section

41 Paragraphs 3.29 and 3.30 above.
42 *R v A* [2007] EWCA Crim 2868.
43 *R v Rockall* [2000] 1 WLR 882.

3 of the Act requires UK courts to interpret statutory legislation so that its provisions are compatible with the articles of the European Convention of Human Rights. When making a statutory presumption of corruption, section 2 of the 1916 Act should be read down as imposing no more than an evidential burden on the defendant to raise an issue as to whether a gift was corruptly made, with the ultimate legal burden of proving it was so made resting with the prosecution.[44]

The Honours (Prevention of Abuses) Act 1925

3.39

The Honours (Prevention of Abuses) Act 1925 makes the sale of peerages or any other honours illegal, and survives the introduction of the UKBA. It was brought in after the Liberal Party government of David Lloyd George was embroiled in a widespread and long-term sale of honours, to help shore up the party's dwindling finances. Only one person has ever been convicted under the Act – Maundy Gregory, Lloyd George's 'honours broker', who around 1918 approached the Prime Minister to offer payments to the party in exchange for the sale of a range of honours. These ranged from £10,000 for a knighthood to £40,000 for a baronetcy.

3.40

Section 1 provides that:

> 'If any person accepts or obtains or agrees to accept or attempts to obtain from any person, for himself or for any other person, or for any purpose, any gift, money or valuable consideration as an inducement or reward for procuring or assisting or endeavouring to procure the grant of a dignity or title of honour to any person, or otherwise in connection with such a grant, he shall be guilty of a misdemeanour.'

3.41

Section 2 states that:

> 'If any person gives, or agrees or proposes to give, or offers to any person any gift, money or valuable consideration as an inducement or reward for procuring or assisting or endeavouring to procure the grant of a dignity or title of honour to any person, or otherwise in connection with such a grant, he shall be guilty of a misdemeanour.'

44 *R v Webster* [2010] EWCA Crim 2819.

Reports

3.42

Renewed impetus for reform of the law of bribery and corruption began most recently in the mid-seventies with a reports triggered by a highly publicised scandal in the North East of England, leading in 1974, to the establishment of the Royal Commission on Standards in Public Life.

The Redcliffe Maud Commission Report

3.43

A Commission of Inquiry was set up in 1974 under the chairmanship of the distinguished civil servant and diplomat Lord Redcliffe Maud, to examine a serious example of local government corruption better known as the 'Poulson Affair'.[45] In that context, his committee considered the limitations of the Prevention of Corruption Act 1916. It recommended that the presumption of corruption should extend further than local authority employees in contract cases so as to cover elected officials who exercised discretion in areas such as housing and planning.

The Salmon Commission Report

3.44

Lord Redcliffe Maud's recommendations were ultimately eclipsed by the Report of the Royal Commission on Standards of Conduct in Public Life under a Law Lord, Lord Salmon. His committee reviewed anti-corruption measures in the Acts of 1889–1916, and identified the conflicts between and the shortcomings of the legislation. Its recommendations, which were limited to the public sector and included ways in which 'whistleblowers' could be protected, were debated in Parliament but not acted on.

The Nolan Report

3.45

A further Commission of Inquiry was set up in 1994 by John Major under another much respected senior judge, Lord Nolan, to examine standards

45 John Poulson was an architect working in the North East of England who entered into a corrupt relationship with T Dan Smith, chairman of the planning and housing committees of Newcastle City Council, to win local authority building contracts.

of conduct of 'all holders of public office'.[46] The Prime Minister had been prompted to act following what had become known as the 'Cash for Questions Affair'. The scandal had been sparked by allegations in the Guardian newspaper that a well known parliamentary lobbyist had bribed two Conservative members of Parliament in exchange for asking parliamentary questions and performing other tasks on behalf of Mohamed Al-Fayed, who was at that time the owner of Harrods department store.

3.46

The Committee's First Report established the 'Seven Principles of Public Life', also known as the 'Nolan principles'. These principles are now included in the Ministerial Code.[47] They are:

- *Selflessness* – Holders of public office should act solely in terms of the public interest. They should not do so in order to gain financial or other benefits for themselves, their family or their friends.
- *Integrity* – Holders of public office should not place themselves under any financial or other obligation to outside individuals or organisations that might seek to influence them in the performance of their official duties.
- *Objectivity* – In carrying out public business, including making public appointments, awarding contracts, or recommending individuals for rewards and benefits, holders of public office should make choices on merit.
- *Accountability* – Holders of public office are accountable for their decisions and actions to the public and must submit themselves to whatever scrutiny is appropriate to their office.
- *Openness* – Holders of public office should be as open as possible about all the decisions and actions they take. They should give reasons for their decisions and restrict information only when the wider public interest clearly demands.
- *Honesty* – Holders of public office have a duty to declare any private interests relating to their public duties and to take steps to resolve any conflicts arising in a way that protects the public interest.
- *Leadership* – Holders of public office should promote and support these principles by leadership and example.

---

46 The term 'public office' includes ministers, civil servants, Members of Parliament, UK members of the European Parliament, members and senior officers of all non-departmental public bodies and National Health Service bodies, non-ministerial office holders, members and other senior officers of other bodies discharging publicly funded functions, and elected members and senior officers of local authorities.

47 The Ministerial Code for Conduct and Guidance was originally published in 2011.

Anti-Terrorism Crime and Security Act 2001

3.47

Part 12 of the Anti-Terrorism Crime and Security Act 2001 ('the 2001 Act') came into force on 14 February 2002, but has since been repealed by the far broader provisions of the UKBA. It was an attempt to comply with Article 1 of the OECD (see below), and to broaden the jurisdiction of the existing law to cover allegations of corruption of persons abroad. It extended the laws against bribery to cases in which:

> 'functions of the person who receives or is offered a reward have no connection with the United Kingdom and are carried out in a country or territory outside the United Kingdom'.

3.48

It also widened the laws against corruption so to make prosecutions possible for:

> 'act[s that] would, if done in the United Kingdom, constitute a corruption offence'.

3.49

The 2001 Act was in large part in reaction to the murderous terrorist attacks on New York, Washington DC and Pennsylvania on 11 September 2001, in which almost 3,000 people were killed. It represented merely one of a package of measures in that statute designed to combat terrorism, with which corruption is often indirectly linked.

3.50

The relevant sections are sections 108 and 109. Section 108 inserts the following into the 1906 Act:

> '(4) For the purposes of this Act it is immaterial if—
>
> (a) the principal's affairs or business have no connection with the United Kingdom and are conducted in a country or territory outside the United Kingdom;
>
> (b) the agent's functions have no connection with the United Kingdom and are carried out in a country or territory outside the United Kingdom'

and provides:

> '(3) In section 7 of the Public Bodies Corrupt Practices Act 1889 (c. 69) (interpretation relating to corruption in office) in the definition of "public body" for "but does not include any public body as above defined existing elsewhere than in the United Kingdom"

substitute "and includes any body which exists in a country or territory outside the United Kingdom and is equivalent to any body described above".

(4) In section 4(2) of the Prevention of Corruption Act 1916 (c. 64) (in the 1889 and 1916 Acts public body includes local and public authorities of all descriptions) after "descriptions" insert "(including authorities existing in a country or territory outside the United Kingdom)".'

Section 109 states:

'(1) This section applies if—

(a) a national of the United Kingdom or a body incorporated under the law of any part of the United Kingdom does anything in a country or territory outside the United Kingdom, and

(b) the act would, if done in the United Kingdom, constitute a corruption offence (as defined below).

(2) In such a case—

(a) the act constitutes the offence concerned, and

(b) proceedings for the offence may be taken in the United Kingdom.

(3) These are corruption offences—

(a) any common law offence of bribery;

(b) the offences under section 1 of the Public Bodies Corrupt Practices Act 1889 (c. 69) (corruption in office);

(c) the first two offences under section 1 of the Prevention of Corruption Act 1906 (c. 34) (bribes obtained by or given to agents).

(4) A national of the United Kingdom is an individual who is—

(a) a British citizen, a British Dependent Territories citizen, a British National (Overseas) or a British Overseas citizen,

(b) a person who under the British Nationality Act 1981 (c. 61) is a British subject, or

(c) a British protected person within the meaning of that Act.'

3.51

The 2001 Act was intended, however, only as a temporary measure whilst Parliament considered and consulted on a Corruption Bill which promised to be a comprehensive clarification of the law, and which removed its inconsistencies and uncertainties. Although some progress was made to meet the Working Group's recommendations, the process was slow. Sustained and justified criticism followed from many quarters, and included a call from the OECD in 2003 for the UK to enact 'a comprehensive anti-corruption statute'. As recently as 2008, the OECD reported that the UK had signally failed to successfully prosecute any company for bribery.

Law Commission Reports and Draft Bill

3.52

In 2003, partly in response to an earlier Law Commission Report entitled 'Legislating the Criminal Code: Corruption',[48] and partly in acknowledgement of the requirements of the OECD Convention, a draft bill aimed at reforming bribery was published by the government for pre-legislative scrutiny. Reaction was mixed. It was heavily criticised by a Parliamentary Joint Commission; not least because of what was felt to be an inadequate definition of corruption. As a result, the bill was withdrawn.

3.53

A period of consultation then followed, in which Gordon Brown's Government invited the Law Commission to report again. This was ultimately to result, in 2008, in the publication of the Law Commission Final Report: 'Reforming Bribery'.[49]

3.54

In early 2009, the government invited the OECD Working Group to London to discuss the UK Law Commission's proposals for the reform of bribery law, and confirmed that a new Bribery Act would be introduced and approved by Parliament before June 2010. The draft bill was introduced on 25 March 2009, broadly reflecting the Law Commission's report, and garnering sufficient support to make its way through Parliament largely without amendment. The bill received Royal Assent on 8 April 2010, and guidance on the new Act was issued on 14 September of that year, with further guidance provided on 30 March 2011. The Act came into force on 1 July 2011.

3.55

Initial reaction to the new Act was mixed. It has since become widely regarded as a highly successful legislative measure.[50] Significantly, Transparency International acknowledges the Act as 'one of the toughest anti-bribery laws

48 Law Commission Report: 'Legislating the Criminal Code: Corruption' (1998).

49 'Reforming Bribery' (19 November 2008), Law Com No 313.

50 House of Lords Select Committee Report of Session 2017-19 Bribery Act 2010: post legislative scrutiny.

in the world'. Nonetheless, the burdens of compliance, the difficulties in distinguishing between active bribery and legitimate business hospitality, and the problems of ensuring that corporate procedures are sufficiently 'adequate' so as to avoid prosecution for a section 7 offence, continue to be the subject of criticism within the business community.

The international context

3.56

The development of the UK's anti-bribery and corruption laws must be seen in the context of the world's changing political and economic landscape, shifting patterns of migration, the development of international business, a global pandemic, the impact of Brexit, and the proliferation of international crime. Many countries, recognising the way in which corruption undermines global trade and wrecks communities, wish to join common cause in defeating it. There has been wide support for the initiatives of international bodies such as the United Nations, the European Union, the Council of Europe and the Organisation for Economic Co-operation and Development in the establishment and harmonisation of legally binding standards amongst member states to criminalise corruption and to cooperate in efforts to eliminate it. Such measures have incentivised the UK to update and simplify laws to prevent bribery and corruption in business.

The United Nations

3.57

The United Nations can be credited for leading the global response to corruption. A series of resolutions, declarations and conventions, and the launch of the Global Programme against Corruption,[51] culminated in 2003 in the Convention against Corruption which was ratified by the UK in 2006. The eight part Convention includes a number of mandatory obligations on Member States including the adoption of legislative measures:

(1) to promote and strengthen measures to prevent and combat corruption more efficiently and effectively;

(2) to promote, facilitate and support international cooperation and technical assistance in the prevention of and fight against corruption, including in asset recovery;

(3) to promote integrity, accountability and proper management of public affairs and public property.

---

51 This programme commenced in 1999 in order to help Member States to co-ordinate their efforts against corruption.

The European Union

3.58

Combating corruption and fraud is a vital part of the EU's mission to create security, freedom and justice amongst its Member States.[52] There are a number of protocols and other measures which oblige Member States take active measures to root out and punish public and private sector bribery and eliminate corruption, and which seek to harmonise different legal regimes.[53] Convictions against companies and individuals for corruption in the European Union may lead to exclusion from tendering for contracts for the award of public work contracts, public supply contracts and public service contracts. Although debarment is not mandatory and the process does not have the force of law, Article 45 of an EU Procurement Directive dated 31 March 2004 provides for such a regime. The practical effect of these protocols and measures, and the level of cooperation between the UK and Europe following the UK's departure from the European Union on 31 December 2020, have yet to be determined.

The Council of Europe

3.59

The UK has been and continues to be a Member State of the Council of Europe since the organisation's inception in 1949. The Council's Multidisciplinary Group on Corruption has been responsible for drafting the Criminal Law Convention on Corruption to which the UK is a signatory. It requires Member States to criminalise active and passive bribery, and potential recipients include both domestic and public foreign officials.[54]

3.60

A Civil Law Convention on Corruption, which the UK signed in 2000 but has not yet ratified, requires Member States to provide victims of corruption with legal mechanisms to sue for damages.

3.61

In 1999, the Council established the Group of States against Corruption (GRECO) to monitor states' compliance with the organisation's anti-corruption standards by means of evaluation, peer pressure, and to provide guidance on best practice.

---

52 Article 29 of the EU Treaty.

53 These include the First and Second Protocols to the Convention on the Protection of the European Communities' Financial Interests, and the Convention on the Fight against Corruption involving Officials of the European Communities or Officials of Member States of the European Union Framework Decision of 22 July 2003.

54 Articles 1, 2, and 5. This category of persons was extended by an Additional Protocol, effective from February 2005, to include domestic or foreign jurors or arbitrators.

Organisation for Economic Cooperation and Development ('OECD')

3.62

The reasons which have underpinned and driven reform of the law relating to bribery and corruption in the UK, cannot be fully understood without also considering the role of the Organisation for Economic Cooperation and Development ('OECD') in deterring and monitoring such activities, and bringing political pressure to bear.

3.63

The Convention on the Organisation for Economic Cooperation and Development was signed in December 1960, and ratified by the UK on 2 May 1961. It currently consists of 34 Member States, including the US and Canada. In 1989, OECD set up a Working Group to compare and review the law and its application in each member state. It became apparent that only the US criminalised bribery and corruption of foreign public officials.[55]

3.64

So far as the UK was concerned, the Working Group discovered that extra-territorial jurisdiction in English criminal law generally had a statutory basis, which reflected the general rule that our courts only have power to try offences committed in the UK. Although there were exceptions, the Acts of 1889, 1906, 1916 and 1925 did not extend the jurisdiction of courts in the UK to deal with cases of bribery or corruption committed abroad.

3.65

The OECD recognised that in order to achieve its objectives of sustainable economic growth and development, a rising standard of living, and financial stability for its members, consistent and effective criminal sanctions were required by all Member States to 'detect, prevent and combat bribery of foreign public officials in international business.'[56]

The OECD Convention

3.66

In 1994, the OECD adopted the Recommendation of the Council on Bribery in International Business Transactions, which suggested that 'effective measures' should be taken 'to detect, prevent and combat bribery of foreign public

---

55 United States' Foreign Corrupt Practices Act 1977.

56 In 1994, the OECD adopted a recommendation of the Council on Bribery in International Business Transactions in these terms.

officials in international business.' A revised recommendation to this effect, limited to those who actively bribe foreign public officials, was enshrined in Article 1 of the OECD Convention which was signed in 1997 and came into force in 1999. The Convention also required Member States, amongst other things, to impose appropriate criminal penalties and to consider additional civil sanctions[57] to ensure international co-operation in matters of mutual legal assistance, extradition, and to establish effective communication through the OECD.[58] The Convention also added a degree of political pressure by providing for periodical reviews and visits by the Working Group to check for deficiencies and compliance in a Member State's anti-corruption measures.

Conclusion

3.67

Historically, the legal concept of 'corruptly' has proved difficult to define. We can paraphrase the famous words of Supreme Court Justice Steward Potter, who said when struggling to find the threshold test for obscenity: 'I shall not … attempt to define it. Perhaps I could never succeed in intelligibly doing so … but I'll know it when I see it'.[59] The UKBA provides in concise and clear form a series of measures in language which juries will understand. The indistinct differences between the concepts of bribery and corruption have been removed, the circularity and complexity of the old definitions of corruption have been replaced, and new offences such as bribery of a foreign official and failure of a commercial organisation to prevent bribery have filled in the gaps in our law and fulfilled our international legal obligations.

57 Article 3.
58 Articles 9–11.
59 *Jacobellis v Ohio* 378 US 184 (1964).

4 Giving and taking of bribes

Introduction

4.1

This chapter considers the offences set out in sections 1 and 2 of the Bribery Act 2010 – namely the giving and taking of bribes respectively. These are two of the 'primary' offences in the Act. They can be committed by individuals and corporations. This chapter also covers offences committed by senior officers consenting to, or conniving in, the primary bribery offences. It sets out who may be liable for these offences.

4.2

The relevant provisions are set out in full and then consideration is given to each offence in detail. Worked examples are provided to illustrate how the law could apply in different circumstances. The offeror of the bribe is referred to as 'P' and the recipient as 'R'.

4.3

Offences under section 7 (failure of commercial organisations to prevent bribery) are dealt with in Chapter 7. The aim of any organisation is to prevent offences under sections 1, 2 or 6 from occurring in the first place. It should also be noted that for an offence under section 7 to be made out, the 'associated person' must commit an offence under section 1 or section 6.

To whom does the Act apply?

4.4

The sections 1 and 2 offences (and the section 7 offence of bribing foreign public officials) apply to UK citizens and those ordinarily resident in the UK *irrespective of where the relevant act takes place.* This is also the position for companies or partnerships formed in the UK. The key concern is whether the person, company or partnership in question has a 'close connection' with the UK as defined by section 12 of the Act. Under section 12(4), a person has this close connection if they are a British citizen, an individual ordinarily resident in the UK, or a body incorporated under the law of any part of the UK.

4.5

For example, P is a British citizen resident in Russia. P bribes a Russian official in Moscow to grant him an export licence to China. No part of the transaction occurs in the UK. P is, however, a British citizen and so has a close connection to the UK under section12(4)(a). P can therefore be prosecuted in the UK.[1]

4.6

Furthermore, if any part of the act or omission forming the offences takes place in the UK, then an offence under sections 1, 2 or 6 will have been committed. This will be the position even if the offence is committed by non-British citizens, companies or partnerships.

Bribery Act: section 1

4.7

1. Offences of bribing another person

(1) A person ('P') is guilty of an offence if either of the following cases applies.

(2) Case 1 is where –

  (a) P offers, promises or gives a financial or other advantage to another person, and

  (b) P intends the advantage –

    (i) to induce a person to perform improperly a relevant function or activity, or

    (ii) to reward a person for the improper performance of such a function or activity.

(3) Case 2 is where –

  (a) P offers, promises or gives a financial or other advantage to another person, and

  (b) P knows or believes that the acceptance of the advantage would itself constitute the improper performance of a relevant function or activity.

1 Section 12(4) defines someone with a 'close connection with the UK'.

> (4) In Case 1 it does not matter whether the person to whom the advantage is offered, promised or given is the same person who is to perform, or has performed, the function or activity concerned.
>
> (5) In Cases 1 and 2 it does not matter whether the advantage is offered, promised or given by P directly or through a third party.

Essential elements

4.8

Cases 1 and 2 involve the making or offering of a bribe or 'advantage'. Although the offence can be committed in two different ways, it is useful to consider its essential elements whether committed under Case 1 or 2. The essential elements are:

- P offers, promises or gives a financial or other advantage.
- That advantage must relate to a relevant function or duty of R.
- The advantage is intended to induce or reward improper performance of the relevant function, or in the knowledge or belief that the acceptance is itself improper.

4.9

The offence is established whether the bribe succeeds or not. It is the conduct of P that is prohibited, not whether or not R accepted the bribe. Of course, evidence of improper performance will be powerful and would lead to a situation akin to Case 1(b)(ii) above.

4.10

Under section 10, any prosecution under the Act requires the consent of the Director of Public Prosecutions or the Director of the Serious Fraud Office.

4.11

Each of the above elements of the section 1 offence is considered in more detail below.

Offers, promises or gives a financial or other advantage

4.12

The advantage can be offered, promised or given directly to R, or via a third party. There is no requirement that the 'offer or promise' be made in explicit terms. The language is wide enough to include cases where an offer, promise or request can be inferred from the circumstances.[2] The Law Commission used the example of an interview held over an open briefcase full of money, which could be seen as an implied offer.[3] It is for the court to decide whether an inference can be drawn in each case.

4.13

The common perception of bribery is of a brown envelope stuffed with cash being passed from one individual to another. This is clearly caught by the Act, but a range of other behaviour is also *potentially* caught. For example, offers of gifts or corporate hospitality could also be caught (see Chapter 14). The bribe or advantage could also be non-monetary or intangible. For example, it could entail the supply of confidential information to advantage R.

4.14

In terms of payments, consideration should be given to the level of any payments and whether they are proportionate to R's general resources or appropriate in the industry/sector. Much will depend upon the context of the case and the sector involved.

Bribe must relate to a relevant function or activity

4.15

Under section 3 of the Act, the activity that P is attempting to influence must be a relevant function. A relevant function is defined as:

(i) any function of a public nature;

(ii) any activity connected with a business;

(iii) any activity performed in the course of a person's employment; or

(iv) any activity performed by or on behalf of a body of persons (whether corporate or unincorporated).

4.16

Under section 3(3)–(5), as well as being a type of activity referred to above, the person performing the activity (ie R) must also satisfy one of the conditions below:

(i) they must be expected to perform the function or activity in good faith;

(ii) expected to perform the function or activity impartially; or

2 Bribery Act 2010: Joint Prosecution Guidance of the Director of the Serious Fraud Office and the Director of Public Prosecutions.

3 Law Commission No 313, para 3.43.

(iii) in a position of trust by virtue of performing the function or activity.

4.17

For example, P is a supplier of goods who offers cash to R who is a procurement manager for a business. This may be seen as an attempt by P to influence R in making procurement decisions to the advantage of P. If so, then the bribe relates to an activity being performed by R in the course of his employment. R would be expected to exercise that activity in good faith, impartially and as befits his position of trust. In this scenario, the cash bribe would 'relate to a relevant function or activity'.

4.18

R might, however, also be a consultant who provides advice to P. The cash payment could be for consulting services that are unrelated to his procurement role. If so, and if the payment was of appropriate value, then it becomes less likely that it 'related to a relevant function or activity' under section 3. In each scenario evidence will need to be presented as to the nature of the payments. Any payment arrangements (whether for 'consulting' or otherwise) should be probed to see if they are bona fide or are merely a front for bribery[4] [5]

Intention to induce/reward improper performance of the function, or knowledge or belief that acceptance of offer would be improper in itself

4.19

The final element shows that there are two ways of committing a section 1 offence:

Case 1: Intention to induce/reward improper performance.

Case 2: P knows or believes that acceptance of offer would be improper performance in itself.

Case 1: Intention to induce/reward improper performance

4.20

The first question to address is what is meant by 'improper performance'. Under section 4, improper performance is defined in the following terms:

4 See the case of *Alexander Brothers Ltd (Hong Kong SAR) v Alstom Transport SA* [2020] EWHC 1584 (Comm).

5 See, by way of comparison under the FCPA, *United States v Giffen* 379 F Supp 2d 337 (SDNY) where a consultancy (and loan) agreement were mere shams for the payment of bribes.

'(1) For the purposes of this Act, a relevant function or activity

(a) is performed improperly if it is performed in breach of a relevant expectation, and

(b) is to be treated as being performed improperly if there is a failure to perform the function or activity and that failure is itself a breach of a relevant expectation'.

4.21

Under section 4, a 'relevant expectation' is an expectation that the activity/function will be performed in good faith or impartially,[6] or in a manner consistent with the duties required of a person in a position of trust.[7]

4.22

The essence of the test above is what a reasonable person in the UK would expect in relation to the performance of the function or activity concerned.[8] This is not further defined by the Act. The Law Commission noted that:

> 'the expectation in question is that which would be had, in the circumstances by people of moral integrity … it would be for the tribunal of fact to decide what that expectation amounted to, in the circumstances'.[9]

It is therefore for the jury to reach decisions based on the ordinary meaning of words such as "moral integrity".

4.23

The issue of what a reasonable person would expect in relation to the performance of a function or activity may be complicated in circumstances where the performance is not subject to the law of any part of the UK. This may occur, for example, where performance occurs in a different jurisdiction with different norms. The law and guidance is clear that local custom or practice is immaterial to liability under the Act. It is not a defence to claim that the giving or receiving of bribes is an 'unwritten rule' or otherwise customary or unavoidable in a certain country. The only exception is if that local custom or practice is permitted by the written law of the jurisdiction concerned.[10]

4.24

In respect of hospitality allegedly serving as a bribe, the Ministry of Justice ('MoJ') Guidance explains that the prosecution would need to show that the

---

6 Section 4(2)(a).
7 Section 4(2)(b).
8 Section 5(1).
9 Law Commission No 313, para 3.176.
10 Section 5(2).

hospitality was intended to induce conduct that amounted to a breach of the 'relevant expectation'. The MoJ Guidance gives as an example the invitation of clients to a prestigious sporting event as part of a public relations exercise. This is 'extremely unlikely to engage section 1 as there is unlikely to be evidence of an intention to induce performance of a relevant function.'[11]

4.25

However, if the same invitation was made by a developer to the planning officers of the local council, at a point when a contentious application was pending, then an intention to induce improper performance might be inferred. This highlights that the same act can fall foul of the legislation depending upon its context. The key point is how the ordinary person would view that act. Perhaps the best advice to companies and individuals is to assume that the payment/hospitality is public knowledge and examine how it would be perceived by the general public in the context of the sector in which they are working.

Case 2: P knows or believes that acceptance of offer would itself be improper performance

4.26

Case 2 involves P offering an advantage or bribe to R, and P knows or believes that mere acceptance of it would amount to the improper performance of a relevant function or activity. In this case, R does not need to intend to perform the relevant function or activity improperly for P's offence to be established. This particular case may often arise where R is in a position of trust.

4.27

The example given by the Law Commission is that R, a government official, issues a Visa to P. P is very grateful and offers £1,000 to R.[12] This offer could fall under Case 2.

4.28

In respect of Case 2, attention would need to be given as to the circumstances and value of the payment. In other words, each case would turn on its own facts. This is a subject for later chapters.

11 MoJ Guidance, para 20 (see Appendix 3).
12 Law Commission, para 3.73.

Bribery Act: section 2

4.29

2. Offences relating to being bribed

(1) A person ('R') is guilty of an offence if any of the following cases applies.

(2) Case 3 is where R requests, agrees to receive or accepts a financial or other advantage intending that, in consequence, a relevant function or activity should be performed improperly (whether by R or another person).

(3) Case 4 is where –

(a) R requests, agrees to receive or accepts a financial or other advantage, and

(b) The request, agreement or acceptance itself constitutes the improper performance by R of a relevant function or activity.

(4) Case 5 is where R requests, agrees to receive or accepts a financial or other advantage as a reward for the improper performance (whether by R or another person) of a relevant function or activity.

(5) Case 6 is where, in anticipation of or in consequence of R requesting, agreeing to receive or accepting a financial or other advantage, a relevant function is performed improperly –

(a) by R or

(b) by another person at R's request or with R's assent or acquiescence.

(6) in Cases 3 to 6 it does not matter –

(a) whether R requests, agrees to receive or accepts (or is to request, agree to receive or accept) the advantage directly or through a third party,

(b) whether the advantage is (or is to be) for the benefit of R or another person.

(7) In Cases 4 to 6, it does not matter whether R knows or believes that the performance of the function or activity is improper.

(8) In Case 6, where a person other than R is performing the function or activity, it also does not matter whether that person knows or believes that the performance of the function or activity is improper.

4.30

It does not matter if the advantage is requested or accepted by R, or by someone else through whom R acts. Furthermore, the offence can be established whether the benefit is for R or for another person.

4.31

The essential elements of the offence are that:

- R requests, agrees to receive, or accepts a financial or other advantage (or does so through a third party).
- The advantage relates to a relevant function.
- As a reward for, or in anticipation of, or as a consequence of the advantage, someone improperly performs a relevant function or the request, agreement or acceptance itself is the improper performance.

Requested, agreed to receive or accepted

4.32

As with section 1, explicit words need not be used to indicate a bribe being offered or accepted. Instead, the conduct of R can be considered as a whole. The request can be express or implied. Indeed, this element can be satisfied by mere acceptance of the advantage.

4.33

This may be particularly important to Case 4, where acceptance of the advantage itself constitutes the improper performance. For example, R might be a financial adviser expected to provide independent advice to clients about investment opportunities in companies. If R receives a valuable and unsolicited gift from one such company (and R keeps it without telling his clients), then R is arguably committing an offence under the Case 4 example. R has accepted an advantage, it appears to relate to a relevant function, and mere acceptance could establish the section 2 offence. Criminal liability could attach to R even though the gift was unsolicited. In such situations, R should return the gift immediately and register this incident with his managers.

Bribe must relate to a relevant function

4.34

This is covered in paragraphs 4.15–4.18 above and must be similarly satisfied.

As a reward for, or in anticipation of, or as a consequence of the advantage, someone improperly performs a relevant function or the request, agreement or acceptance itself is the improper performance

4.35

The third element of the offence shows that the 'receiving' offence can be committed in four different ways (Cases 3 to 6), where:

- there is intent to perform improperly as a consequence of a bribe (Case 3);
- the request, agreement, or acceptance is itself improper (Case 4);
- there is reward for improper performance (Case 5); or
- improper performance is in anticipation of bribe (Case 6).

There is intent to perform improperly as a consequence of a bribe (Case 3)

4.36

- Request, agreement, or acceptance must be made.
- Improper performance of a relevant function or activity must be intended as the consequence.
- It does not matter if the improper performance has not occurred yet or does not in fact occur. What matters is the intention of R.
- It does not matter if the improper performance is to be performed by R or by another.

4.37

For example, R is a footballer who is asked by P to persuade a team mate to miss a penalty at a designated point in the match. P pays R to persuade him to do this. If R accepts the payment, then he is guilty of the offence at the time he receives the payment. This is the case even though the match is in the future and R will not commit the 'improper performance' himself.

Request/agreement/acceptance is itself an improper performance (Case 4)

4.38

- The request, agreement, or acceptance is made by R himself.
- The request, agreement, or acceptance is itself improper.
- No past or further improper performance is required.

- It is immaterial whether R knows or believes that the performance is improper.

4.39

For example, R is a referee in a football match and makes a decision in favour of P. P later sends R a cheque for £50,000 as a token of his appreciation. R banks the cheque. In this scenario, R has committed an offence under section 2. Receiving payment as a referee would be improper, irrespective of whether the decision during the match had been proper or not.

Reward for improper performance (Case 5)

4.40

- Improper performance, by R or another, will tend to have already occurred.
- The offer/acceptance/receipt is a reward for that performance.
- It is immaterial whether R knows or believes that the performance is improper.

For example, R is a footballer who gives confidential information about the health of a team mate to P (a bookmaker). P arranges for R an all-expenses paid holiday as a reward for this information. When questioned about this, R says he was unaware that his action was improper since it would not affect the outcome of the match. Nevertheless, acceptance of the all-expenses paid trip makes R guilty of an offence under section 2 (the improper performance being the provision of confidential information to a bookmaker, which would be a breach of good faith). Whether R was aware that this was improper is immaterial.

Improper performance in anticipation (Case 6)

4.41

- Improper performance, by R or another, has occurred.
- There has been no offer/acceptance/receipt as yet – but one is anticipated.
- It is immaterial whether R or another knows that performance is improper.

For example, having heard rumours of corrupt payments from P to other players, R provides more confidential information to P in the hope that P will make a similar payment to him in due course.

4.42

Each of the above cases constitutes an offence under section 2 of the Act. Individuals and corporations must review any advantages that they receive, accept or offer in order to ensure that their actions are not improper in themselves, or linked to improper performance.

Liability for company officers

4.43

As indicated above, sections 1 and 2 (and 6) offences can be committed by corporations. Chapter 7 deals with an offence under section 7, whereby the corporation fails to prevent bribery. Furthermore, under section 14, if an offence is committed under section 1, 2 or 6 by the company/partnership and it is proven that it was committed with the connivance or consent of a senior officer, then that senior officer can be prosecuted as well.

Elements of offence

4.44

A corporation can be guilty of the offence of receiving a bribe (section 7 gives criminal liability to a company for failing to prevent the giving of bribes rather than the taking). This means that:

- The offence under section 1, 2 or 6 is committed by a body corporate.
- It is conducted with the consent or connivance of a senior officer, or a person who purports to act in such a capacity.

Offence is committed under section 1, 2 or 6 by a body corporate

4.45

The offence must have been committed by the company/corporate under section 1 (see paragraph 4.7), section 2 (paragraph 4.29) or section 6 (paragraph 6.2. 'Body corporate' includes a company, partnership or LLP.

4.46

For the offence to be committed under the body corporate, the acts and state of mind of those managers and directors who represent the corporation's 'directing mind and will'[13] can be attributed to the corporation itself. This normally applies to the Board of Directors, the Managing Director and other

13 *Tesco Supermarket v Natrass* [1972] AC 153.

superior officers who carry out the functions of management. These officers are the 'embodiment' of the company.[14]

Consent or connivance

4.47

Consent will require some sort of agreement to the unlawful conduct. The agreement does not need to be explicit. Instead, the existence of an agreement can be inferred from all of the circumstances.

4.48

Connivance appears to be something less than consent. It is more likely to involve an awareness of the offence being committed. This might fall short of expressly encouraging it, but could involve knowingly allowing it to continue.

Senior officer or someone who purports to act in such a capacity

4.49

Senior officer means a director, secretary or other similar officer. The phrase 'purports to act in such a capacity' will likely be interpreted in line with how that phrase is used in other legislation. The key would appear to be the function of the officer concerned rather than their job title, and whether they are a real decision-maker or someone junior simply carrying out day to day operations.[15]

Example

4.50

R is the senior partner in the legal practice 'R & Co'. In the partnership agreement, R has a final say on whether cases and clients are taken on by R & Co. P offers R a bribe to persuade him to advise against litigation in a potential suit against P. The bribe offered is that P (a wealthy businessperson) will begin exclusively using the services of R & Co. R discusses this offer with his partners: A, B and C. A and B agree to the proposal. C initially disagrees but is aware that the proposal goes ahead. P begins using the services of R & Co. All of the partners subsequently draw a profit from their new and exclusive dealings with P.

---

14 CPS Guidance on Corporate Prosecutions, para 19.
15 *R v Boal* [1992] QB 591.

4.51

In this example, R has committed an offence under section 2. Furthermore, it is likely that R & Co will have committed an offence due to R's position. By virtue of section 14 of the Act, A and B will have committed an offence by 'consent' and C will have committed the offence by 'connivance'.

Penalties and sentencing

Sentencing

4.52

On 31 January 2014, the Sentencing Council for England and Wales published its definitive guidelines on the sentencing of corporates found guilty of fraud, bribery and money laundering. The detail is set out in paragraph 11.80 as to how these matters would apply in bribery cases.

4.53

For a section 1 or 2 offence, or an offence under section 14, the maximum penalty is ten years' imprisonment on conviction in the Crown Court or six months' imprisonment on conviction in the magistrates' court. Either court may impose a fine (amounting to a percentage of the offender's income) in addition to custody, or as an alternative to it. The penalties are detailed by section 11 of the Act. Under section 11(1)(a), the maximum penalty on conviction in the magistrates' court is 12 months' custody. The magistrates' court may impose a maximum custodial sentence of six months for a single offence, or a total of 12 months at most for two or more offences.

4.54

In addition, a court can order convicted defendants to pay compensation. The court can take into account losses and damages caused to third parties by the offence, but must also consider the means of the defendant and their ability to pay. There is no right of third parties to make representations for compensation. It would be expected that the prosecution would liaise with such third parties and put appropriate information before the court.

Confiscation orders

4.55

The courts may also make 'confiscation' orders against defendants after conviction. The legislation is meant to deprive defendants of the benefit gained from relevant criminal conduct. The confiscation provisions are complex and require more detailed explanation than is possible here. Nevertheless, there are some important factors to bear in mind.

4.56

To make a confiscation order, the court must consider whether the defendant has benefitted from 'general or particular' criminal conduct, and the value of that 'benefit'. After the benefit figure is calculated, consideration is next given to the 'realisable assets' of the defendant. The confiscation order will be the value of the benefit up to the amount of realisable assets that the defendant has.

4.57

For bribery cases, the challenge lies in calculating the benefit from the corruption. Benefit tends not to be calculated as the net benefit or profit of the defendant. It could be the value of the contract rather than the bribe itself.[16]

4.58

For example, R manages procurement for a government department. P is a supplier who pays a bribe of £10,000 to R in return for a contract worth £5 million. The benefit in this case is the value of the contract. The benefit is not the value of the bribe. A confiscation order of up to £5 million could subsequently be awarded against P, depending upon his assets.[17]

4.59

Courts have, however, indicated that confiscation orders need to be 'proportionate'. This may protect defendants from receiving crushing orders in cases where the value of their benefit far outweighs the value of the bribe.[18]

Being barred from public contracts

4.60

As more commercial organisations provide services to the public sector, the risk of being barred from such contracts is a significant threat for many firms. The Public Contract Regulations 2006 state that a contracting authority shall treat as ineligible and shall not select an economic operator if the contracting authority has actual knowledge that the economic operator, its director or any other person who has power of representation, decision or control of the economic operator has been convicted of bribery.[19]

16 In *R v Innospec* [2010] Crim LR 665, Thomas LJ stated that the 'benefit' in a corruption case was not the value of the bribe but the value of the contract.
17 A similar example was given in the Joint Committee Report on the Bribery Bill.
18 *R v Waya* [2012] UKSC 51, *R v Mahmood* [2013] EWCA Crim 325.
19 Public Contract Regulations 2006, reg 23(1).

4.61

It should be noted that this bar is mandatory since 'the public authority *shall* not select'. There is an exception under Regulation 23(2) if there is an 'overriding requirement in the general interest which justify doing so in relation to that economic operator'. This is a high hurdle and shows that the starting point is that a conviction will bar the organisation from public contracts.

Directors' disqualification

4.62

A conviction of a director for a bribery offence can lead to a director being disqualified from acting as a director or shadow director for up to 15 years.

5 Small bribes and facilitation payments

Introduction

5.1

Small bribes, of which 'facilitation' payments, also known as 'grease' payments,[1] are a subset, are pervasive in many higher-risk jurisdictions[2] and exposure to requests for such bribes is inescapable for any commercial organisation, whatever its business or size, that seeks to take full advantage of globalisation and the markets in high growth economies.[3] Furthermore, ever growing volumes of international trade, increasing reliance on 'just-in-time' supply chain models, trade disputes between the West and China and disruption caused by Brexit and the Covid-19 pandemic all also increase the small bribe risk.

5.2

The chapter explains: (a) the special features of small bribes, including facilitation payments; and (b) the laws relating to these types of bribes in the UK and US.[4] This chapter also includes inexpensive practical steps to help reduce the risks that small bribes and 'facilitation' payments present (including specific 'adequate procedures' that can be adopted to help meet the UK's Bribery Act 2010 ('UKBA') standards).

Key points

5.3

Small bribes of any kind are illegal under the UKBA and only exempt in very limited circumstances pursuant to the US Foreign Corrupt Practices Act 1977

1 A term used primarily in the US, limited to payments to foreign public officials for routine and non-discretionary acts. This exemption to the US Foreign Corrupt Practice Act 1977 is explained further below. Facilitation payments are most appropriately thought of as a subset of small bribes, given that they are intended to decriminalise some small improper payments, but (a) only relate to benefits intended for non-US government officials and (b) have a narrow definition.

2 According to Transparency International ('TI'), more than two thirds of the 180 countries in the Corruption Perceptions Index ('CPI') in 2020 scored below 50, on a scale from 100 (highly clean) to 0 (highly corrupt), suggesting a perception of widespread corruption globally, with the average country score being 43 out of 100. Source: Transparency International, CPI 2020.

3 See Chapter 2 on Global Context. Note that 2020 CPI rankings for the 'BRICS' economies show South Africa at 69th place, China at 78th, India at 86th and Brazil at 94th. Russia appears at 129th place.

4 Only the US federal law is summarised, ie the FCPA.

('FCPA') – so called 'facilitation payments'. All such improper payments are almost invariably illegal in the countries in which they are paid.

5.4

For companies subject to the UKBA, not implementing adequate procedures to prevent all types of small bribes is an unattractive option, given that this will almost certainly create an immediate corporate criminal liability if small bribes are paid by employees or broader 'service providers'.

5.5

For companies beyond the scope of the UKBA, a zero-tolerance approach to small bribes is an approach which any company might seriously consider given the apparent ethical, commercial and legal benefits and the US corporate trend towards zero tolerance of all bribes.

5.6

There are a growing number of resources available to assist companies in putting in place low cost and practical procedures to reduce the payment of small bribes, many of which are either provided or referred to in this chapter.

Why are small bribes special?

5.7

The difficulty in preventing the payment of small bribes arises because when paid on a 'one-off' basis small bribes can seem harmless, but in aggregate small bribes significantly increase business costs, cause delays and uncertainty, disadvantage the communities of those receiving bribes and give rise to prosecutions.[5] Although similar damage is true of other forms of bribery, small bribes are considered in this book separately, not just because in a minority of national jurisdictions, such as the US, certain small bribes can fall into their own category legally, but because they pose a unique set of issues:

- First, small bribery is a highly adaptable form of bribery, hindering efforts to identify and prevent it, eg bribes can be characterised at the point of request as unofficial fines, gratuities or processing fees.

5 Note that the Index of Corruption and Good Governance for Mexico indicates that Mexicans paid the equivalent of €1.9 billion in bribes to access basic services in 2010 and that a 1999 survey conducted by the European Bank for Reconstruction and Development found that bribes paid by smaller firms (with less than 49 employees) amounted to 5% of their annual revenues (see TI's helpful document www.transparency.org/files/content/corruptionqas/The_impact_of_facilitation_payments.pdf). Also see the matter of Panalpina World Transport (Holdings) Limited and Panalpina Inc deferred prosecution agreements, which is summarised in Chapter 2.

- Secondly, the low value of the bribes means it may feel disproportionate to investigate individual breaches, if indeed potential breaches are escalated at all – allowing practices to continue and expand.[6]
- Thirdly, if a company develops a reputation for paying small bribes, it will almost certainly face greater requests for them in the future. This can make it difficult to 'break the cycle' once small bribe payments have commenced, as employees will have to explain why a payment that was made yesterday is no longer permitted today.
- Fourthly, the payment of some small bribes, eg facilitation payments, can be a potent corrosive to ethically based anti-corruption programs because 'if you can pay some small bribes, why can't you pay large bribes?' As a result, if any exceptions to compliance policies which allow payments (for instance where there is a threat to personal safety) are not clear and properly explained to employees, they may struggle to understand the principle of zero-tolerance.[7]
- Fifthly, it requires significant courage and support for employees to 'speak up' and challenge frequent requests for small bribes, when they are in unfamiliar territory and fear that to do so could lead to repeated confrontations that may ultimately put them or others in danger. This problem may be particularly acute for local employees who, unlike ex-pats, cannot simply relocate their families if there are difficulties and who may also face regular requests for small bribes in their personal lives.
- Finally, because of their size, each small bribe creates a moral dilemma, which places in conflict the perceived larger harm in not making payments, eg damage to career/business/jobs/relationships and the unpredictability of 'rocking the boat', against the perceived lesser harm of making a small payment to often relatively lowly paid state employees.

5.8

The combination of the issues above can cause otherwise principled employees to pay small bribes, creating not only criminal liabilities for themselves and for their employer but also harming the society that many employees would hope their business will help and support.

---

6 Reappearing, for instance, as requests for undocumented fines, unreceipted processing charges or unspecified 'agency' fees.

7 See helpful article by Trace, 'Business Case Against Corruption Case Studies and Examples', at pp 69 onwards (www.pnud.or.cr/dmdocuments/Business%20Against%20Corrruption%20Case%20Studies.pdf).

What is a small bribe?

5.9

There is no separate definition in English law of what constitutes a small bribe, in the same way that there is no definition of a small fraud.[8] The issue of including an exemption for small bribes or a lesser offence was debated at length in the run up to the Bribery Act[9] but as enacted there are no exceptions, carve outs or *de minimis* values placing any type of small bribes in a different category to larger bribes in UK law.

Duress and other defences

5.10

Although the UKBA creates no exemption for small bribes or facilitation payments, at common law *duress, extortion and necessity* are all potential defences to UK bribery offences, including the payment of small bribes. Indeed, it is this area of bribery in which these defences are most likely to arise given that many small bribes are paid to low-level government officials who administer monopolies, with significant discretion and power but little transparency or oversight in the form of a quick and effective appeal process. In terms of these defences, the UK Ministry of Justice Guidance (the 'MoJ Guidance') on the corporate offence states:

> 'It is recognised that there are circumstances in which individuals are left with no alternative but to make payments in order to protect against loss of life, limb or liberty. The common law defence of duress is very likely to be available in such circumstances'.[10]

5.11

This means that where employees have a genuine and reasonable fear for their safety or liberty, they may make a small payment without fear of prosecution. However, such a payment would then have to be properly recorded in the company's accounts to comply with legislation such as the Companies Act 2006, Part 15 and the FCPA's provisions as regards books and records for any company which is subject to the FCPA.[11]

---

8 There is perhaps more likelihood however that one off payments made by an individual in breach of UKBA ss 1 and 6 would be prosecuted as summary offences with a maximum 12 (currently 6) month sentence or £5,000 fine.

9 *Lissack and Horlick on Bribery* (Lexis Nexis, 2011), paras 5.104 to 5.122.

10 The Guidance is reproduced in Appendix 3. As useful as the Guidance is, it is not binding on a court and only strictly relevant to the s 7 corporate offence and not to the s 1 or s 6 active bribery offences under the Bribery Act 2010.

11 See The Foreign Corrupt Practices Act of 1977, 15 USC § 78dd-1, 15 USC §§ 78m(b)(2)(A) and (B).

5.12

What is likely not to amount to a defence under English law is where a defendant simply finds it more expeditious to make an improper payment, for instance where not making such a payment would result in a delay or financial loss. Given the revised test for active bribery this appears to be the case even where the loss would be very high as against the cost of the bribe and could amount to extortion.[12] Put simply, financial loss cannot be relied on as a significant enough issue to give rise to a defence at common law in England and Wales to paying even a small bribe.

UKBA – corporates with service providers

5.13

Any company operating globally will usually require external service providers who assist in areas in which small bribes are more likely to be requested, eg freight forwarding companies, visa/travel companies and port agents.

5.14

The effect of section 7 of the UKBA, the corporate offence triggered by bribes paid by third parties, is dealt with in depth in Chapter 7 of this book. However, in summary, if a service provider for X co pays a bribe for X co's benefit, then X co itself commits a bribery offence and could be liable to an unlimited fine. It does not matter if X co was not aware of the bribe, did not authorise it or could not reasonably have known about it. It also does not matter where the bribe was paid, or whether the bribe paid by the service provider was small or large, repeated or a one-off. The only defence for X co is that at the time the bribe was paid it had in place 'adequate procedures' to prevent the service provider paying bribes (see Chapter 4).

5.15

As applied to small bribes, this means that a where a company subject to the UKBA has an employee (or by way of example only, retains a service provider such as a freight forwarder, visa/travel agent or port agent) anywhere in the world, and that party pays a small bribe for the benefit of the company, the

12 Lord Simon in *DPP for Northern Ireland v Lynch* [1975] AC 653, [1975] 2 WLR 641, HL. Also note the arguments suggested by Professor Sullivan in *Modern Bribery Law Comparative Perspectives* (Cambridge University Press, 2013). In summary, the pre-UKBA legislation required a jury to find a 'corrupt' intent and a jury may not have been minded to do so where extortion arose because this could be capable of negating the corrupt nature of the intent. In contrast the more structured and restrictive nature of the formation of active bribery offences under s 1 of the UKBA, which does not include the word 'corrupt' but only require a defendant to 'intend' to induce 'improper' performance of duties is perhaps less open to defences based on extortion. It is something of a moot point as to whether, to the extent they arise at all, a party can frequently rely on defences of extortion, ie continue to put themselves in a position where extortion would arise. However, it is suggested that a defendant who repeatedly placed themselves in a situation where extortion was expected would at the very least weaken any defence available.

company has committed a criminal offence in the UK unless the company has in place adequate procedures to prevent bribery by the third party.

Where small bribes commonly arise

5.16

There is no available research in relation to the absolute numbers of small bribes paid and little statistical research into the circumstances in which small bribes most commonly arise.[13] However, it seems generally accepted that small bribes are most likely to arise in the following types of situations:[14]

- entry and exit across a border by a person;
- customs payments on goods entering a country;
- the provision by the state of information;
- the provision by the state of an official stamp / seal of approval; and
- the provision of state amenities or essential services, eg access to utilities such as electricity and telecommunications.

5.17

All of the above activities will often involve contact with public officials, particularly in higher-risk countries that often have greater state involvement in what other societies would consider to be essentially 'business/commercial' activities.[15]

5.18

The monopoly that the state often controls in such areas provides an environment in which an individual or company has no option but to deal with the part of the government that the public official represents. By way of contrast (but still relevant for the UKBA which cover bribes paid to anyone), it will less frequently be the case that a private business will have a monopoly, meaning if such a business were to request a small bribe, the target of the request could simply turn to one of the business's competitors as an alternative.

---

13 As the SFO states 'The secret nature of the [corrupt] agreement means that it is difficult for anyone other than those involved to know what is going on' – SFO website as at March 2020.

14 Certain industries may also be more vulnerable to requests for small bribes than others. For example, the House of Lords Select Committee on the Bribery Act 2010's report cited anecdotal evidence from the shipping industry that 'while large-scale bribes to secure business have been significantly reduced in recent years, facilitation payments remain an issue in various parts of the word.'

15 Over 12 months, one in four people paid a bribe when they came into contact with one of nine institutions and services, from health to education to tax authorities. Source: Transparency International, GCB (2010), surveying 91,500 people across 86 countries.

5.19

However, the lack of a government monopoly does not itself eradicate the potential for small bribes and below there are three case studies to illustrate how small bribes could be paid in a purely commercial context:

- A security guard in a private car park requests a bribe to allow a car to remain in the car park over-night at 'no charge'. The bribe is less than the charge, which would otherwise be paid to the car park's owner.
- A junior salesman of a privately owned hedge fund requests a small 'unreceipted fee' in order for a representative of a potential purchaser to be included in a meeting to discuss a new project. The potential purchaser would not have been included because it is new to the market and has not registered in the appropriate way.
- A procurement manager accepts a series of 'light lunches' from a supplier on the joint explicit understanding that in return the supplier will be placed on the bid list for any upcoming projects.[16]

When the SFO prosecutes small bribes

5.20

Both England's Crown Prosecution Service and Serious Fraud Office are competent authorities to prosecute cases brought under the UKBA in England and Wales,[17] but it is the SFO which in its own words is 'the lead agency for enforcement of the Bribery Act 2010'.[18]

5.21

In July 2012, the SFO provided the following guidance as regards facilitation payments, which – by extrapolation – is likely to be the position of the SFO as regards all small bribes:

> 'A facilitation payment is a type of bribe and should be seen as such. A common example is where a government official is given money or goods to perform (or speed up the performance of) an existing duty. Facilitation payments were illegal before the Bribery Act came into force and they *are illegal under the Bribery Act, regardless of their size or frequency.*
>
> Whether or not the SFO will prosecute in respect of a facilitation payment (or payments) will be governed by the Full Code Test in the Code for Crown Prosecutors and the Joint Prosecution Guidance of

16 Also see Chapter 13 on gifts, entertainment and corporate hospitality.

17 In Scotland the SFO and CPS function is conducted by the Crown Office and Procurator Fiscal Service.

18 SFO statement entitled 'Enforcement of United Kingdom's Bribery Act – Facilitation Payments' dated 6 December 2012.

the Director of the SFO and the Director of Public Prosecutions on the Bribery Act 2010. Where relevant, the Joint Guidance on Corporate Prosecutions will also be applied.

If on the evidence there is a realistic prospect of conviction, the SFO will prosecute if it is in the public interest to do so. In appropriate cases the SFO may use its powers under proceeds of crime legislation as an alternative (or in addition) to prosecution; see the Attorney General's guidance to prosecuting bodies on their asset recovery powers under the Proceeds of Crime Act 2002.'[19] (emphasis added)

A further open letter was provided by David Green, the then Director of the SFO, on 6 December 2012, which stated as follows:

'Individuals and companies that use facilitation payments in the course of their business are at risk of criminal prosecution in the UK … the Serious Fraud Office stands ready to take effective actions against facilitation payments, regardless of where they are requested.'

5.22

Had there been any doubt that small bribes would be treated as a serious matter by the SFO, the above guidance and open letter have removed it.[20] However, for small bribes, including the subset of facilitation payments, it is still likely to be the case that in some circumstances it will not be in the public interest to prosecute small improper payments under the Full Code Test for prosecutors, for instance where the payments were very limited in time, number or scope, the company had already taken a number of proportionate steps to prevent bribery and the company can give assurances that it will improve its controls to make them 'adequate' under the UKBA.[21]

Risk of investigations or prosecution

5.23

At the time of publication of the second edition of this handbook, the SFO has entered into twelve deferred prosecution agreements with corporates

19 SFO 'Bribery Act guidance', section on Facilitation Payments, online at: www.sfo.gov.uk/publications/guidance-policy-and-protocols/bribery-act-guidance.

20 There is general consensus that businesses should not place reliance on the potentially more regulatory and to some more sympathetic approach of the now redundant SFO guidance published by previous SFO Director Richard Alderman. The old guidance was reportedly anomalous with the broader approach to prosecutions in England and Wales and has now been brought back into line with published SFO and CPS practice, ie to prosecute where: (a) there is sufficient evidence to provide a realistic prospect of conviction against each suspect on each charge; and (b) it is in the public interest to proceed, having regard to, amongst other factors, the seriousness of the offence and its impact on the community.

21 See also the joint guidance on prosecutions issued by the SFO and Director of Public Prosecutions, which at page 10 lists factors tending in favour of and against prosecution. Note that factors in favour include 'payments that are planned for or accepted as part of a standard way of conducting business'.

that included offences under the UKBA.[22] While none of these DPAs are specifically related to the payment of facilitation payments by the relevant corporates, it is clear that the SFO are taking an increasingly assertive stance on UKBA prosecution and enforcement. Given the SFO's stated position on the illegality of facilitation payments described above, it appears to be only a matter of time until they pursue a test case against a corporate making regular or egregious use of small bribes. In this respect, it is important to bear in mind the pressure on the SFO and government in general from organisations such as the Organisation for Economic Co-operation and Development (OECD) to take enforcement action as regards small bribes.[23] Furthermore, as discussed below, a company that permits facilitation payments is unlikely to be able to avail itself of the 'adequate procedures' defence against a charge of failure to prevent bribery of any kind, and not just payment of small bribes.

Contrast with US federal position for small bribes

5.24

When the issue of small bribes (of whatever type) arises in business discussions it is still common to hear statements such as 'these sort of payments are allowed under American law' or 'facilitation payments are allowed as part of our policy'. To contribute to such discussions knowledgeably, it is therefore helpful – particularly for any company subject to both the UKBA and the FCPA – to (a) understand the meaning of 'facilitation payments'; (b) be able to compare the US and UK legal positions; and (c) consider the general legal/compliance context surrounding small improper payments.

5.25

As set out in Chapter 2 on Global Context, the American federal legislation that criminalises improper payments offered or promised to non-US government officials and which is actively enforced, the FCPA 1977, contains an exemption for facilitation payments, ie payments 'facilitating or expediting payment to a foreign official, political party, or party official the purpose of which is to expedite or to secure the performance of a routine governmental action by a foreign official, political party, or party official.'[24]

5.26

The exemption was introduced or at least made more explicit in 1988 so as not to disproportionately prevent US businesses from trading abroad. Nevertheless, although the exemption still features in some policies on bribery

22 Standard Bank (2015), Sarclad Ltd (2016), Rolls-Royce (2017), Güralp Systems Ltd (2019), Airbus SE (2020) and Airline Services Ltd (2020).

23 See OECD phase 3 report for UK dated March 2012, www.oecd.org/daf/anti-bribery/UnitedKingdomphase3reportEN.pdf.

24 See Chapter 2 on Global Context and the FCPA.

for US companies, the following issues mean that it is receding in both use and importance:

- The nature of a 'facilitation payment' remains difficult to explain to employees. There is for instance no monetary limit, and an employee who makes what they might think of as a facilitation payment may in fact find they have breached the FCPA.[25]
- The payment of small bribes, of which facilitation payments are a subset, will nearly invariably be illegal in the country in which they are paid.[26] In addition to which, where a US or other company making a facilitation payment has part of its business in the UK, that company would breach the UKBA corporate offence and be unlikely to be able to rely on the adequate procedures defence if it had a global corporate policy to allow facilitation payments.
- Where improper payments genuinely fall into the definition of a facilitating payment, they must still be recorded accurately and as bribes/facilitation payments or otherwise will breach the books and records offence of the FCPA. However, the DOJ stress in their Resource Guide to the FCPA that 'labelling a bribe as a "facilitating payment" in a company's books and records does not make it one.'[27] Companies that allow facilitating payments therefore face the dilemma of either recording these openly in their accounts and risking the DOJ disagreeing with their interpretation of the payment or not recording them accurately and thereby violating the FCPA's books and records provisions.
- The trend in international anti-bribery law is moving away from allowing exceptions for facilitation payments. Other countries that previously permitted such exceptions have either removed them (eg South Korea in 2014 and Canada in 2017), have them under active review (eg Australia) or have the exception drawn so narrowly as to have very limited applicability in practice (eg New Zealand[28]).
- Civil society in the form of NGOs is also firmly against allowing exceptions for facilitation payments. For example, in their 2014 guidance on 'Countering Small Bribes', Transparency International write that: 'The artificiality of differentiating facilitation payments from other forms

25 Larger sums are less likely to be facilitation payments given that the value is less commensurate with an intent only to speed up a routine act. Also see commentary at www.iflr.com/Article/3030225/Facilitating-payments-why-best-practice-prevails-over-law.html.

26 Unless allowed for under local law, eg with a genuine 'fast track' entry fee.

27 Criminal Division of the US Department of Justice and the Enforcement Division of the US Securities and Exchange Commission, 'A Resource Guide to the U.S. Foreign Corrupt Practices Act: Second Edition', p26.

28 Under New Zealand's Organised Crime Bill, the exception for facilitation payments does not cover instances where the payment provides an undue material benefit to the person who makes the payment. As facilitation payments are illegal in almost all countries where they will be made, they will almost inevitably provide an undue material benefit to the payer and therefore fall outside the scope of the exception.

of bribery leads to uncertainties and inconsistencies for companies trying to reconcile their legal obligations and anti-bribery programmes across multiple jurisdictions. Codifying and permitting facilitation payments leads to anomalies and mixed messages, as well as perpetuating bribery in country.'[29]

- The exemption in the FCPA for facilitation payments is interpreted narrowly by the Department of Justice and Securities Exchange Commission, meaning that there is in effect only a small 'safe harbour'. By way of example, if small improper payments were made for a visa application to a non-US government official, it would always be an issue as to whether a true facilitation payment was made or whether in fact a non-discretionary service was paid for – such as allowing a person into the country who should not have been allowed, failing to conduct required checks or moving a person ahead of others in the visa queue.[30]

5.27

Furthermore, the hardening US attitude towards facilitation payments can be seen in the United States-Mexico-Canada Agreement (USMCA) that was negotiated to replace the North American Free Trade Agreement (NAFTA) and which entered into force on 1 July 2020. This agreement contains a dedicated chapter on Anti-Corruption, which includes the following wording:

> 'The Parties recognize the harmful effects of facilitation payments. Each Party shall, in accordance with its laws and regulations:
>
> a) encourage enterprises to prohibit or discourage the use of facilitation payments; and
>
> b) take steps to raise awareness among its public officials of its bribery laws, with a view to stopping the solicitation and the acceptance of facilitation payments.'[31]

5.28

If the US is to meet its obligations under this section, it is likely that the DOJ will seek to discourage the use of facilitation payments by applying a narrow interpretation of the exception under the FCPA and continuing to aggressively pursue companies that fall outside of this interpretation.

29 Transparency International, 'Countering Small Bribes: Principles and good practice guidance for dealing with small bribes including facilitation payments', published June 2014, p36.

30 In the words of the FCPA Resources Guide, at page 25: 'Examples of "routine governmental action" include processing visas, providing police protection or mail service, and supplying utilities like phone service, power, and water. Routine government action does not include … acts that are within an official's discretion or that would constitute misuse of an official's office …'.

31 United States-Mexico-Canada Agreement, Chapter 27: Anticorruption, p27-4, para 8.

A zero-tolerance to small bribes, including facilitation payments?

5.29

In terms of current business practice in the UK, although some organisations apparently continue to do little to mitigate the increasing risk of requests for small bribes,[32] others have or are in the process of taking robust steps to assess their risk from this type of bribery and to clarify, strengthen and support policies and controls dealing specifically with small bribes.

5.30

Benchmarking against their competitors, the central question for many companies is whether to adopt and implement a policy of zero tolerance to small bribes, which as we have seen are, in limited cases, allowed by the FCPA as 'facilitation payments'.

5.31

As for companies with part of their business in the UK, ie companies subject to the UKBA, we have seen in Chapter 4 of this book that a zero-tolerance approach to all small bribes, including facilitation payments, is effectively required by the UKBA and MoJ Guidance and that a company without this policy and relevant processes would be unlikely to able to rely on the 'adequate procedures' defence if a small bribe was paid on its behalf.

5.32

The House of Lords post-legislative scrutiny of the Bribery Act further reinforced the UK's strict prohibition on small bribes, stating in its report that '…it would be a retrograde step to legalise facilitation payments. All trends in the law in other jurisdictions are towards abolishing a facilitation defence. We do not recommend any change in the law.'[33] This position clearly indicates the position in UK law that a company which tolerates or turns a blind eye to small bribes is unlikely to receive any sympathy in the courts.

---

32 The accountancy firm E&Y's Global Integrity Report 2020 (online at: https://assets.ey.com/content/dam/ey-sites/ey-com/en_gl/topics/assurance/assurance-pdfs/ey-is-this-the-moment-of-truth-for-corporate-integrity.pdf) found that only 34% of companies surveyed were very confident that their third parties, including suppliers, vendors, partners or consultants, abide by relevant laws, codes of conduct and industry requirements. 13% of all respondents also indicated that they would be prepared to ignore unethical conduct by third parties in order to boost their career or pay.

33 Select Committee on the Bribery Act 2010, Report of Session 2017 – 19 'The Bribery Act 2010: post-legislative scrutiny', published 14 March 2019, p46.

5.33

As regards companies not subject to the UKBA that are reviewing whether they ought to assume a zero-tolerance policy, they may begin their review by considering both 'best practice' and 'industry practice'.

5.34

'Best practice' in business, based on TI, OECD and UN Global Compact publications amongst others, is not to include in compliance policies and controls an exception for small bribes, including facilitation payments. As set out above, countries that previously allowed for facilitation payments under their bribery laws are also increasingly removing or limiting these.

5.35

In relation to 'industry standard' practice, recent changes in the US indicate that, although of course genuine facilitation payments remain legal under the FCPA, the movement is away from exceptions for facilitation payments in corporate policy documents and towards a complete ban. Anecdotal evidence is supported by research in the US,[34] which suggests that in 2012 approximately a third of the Fortune 500 companies updated their codes of conduct and that the number of companies that prohibited facilitation payments more than doubled (19 to 44).

5.36

In any event, whether looking at best practice or the trend in current American industry practice, a company reviewing its policy in this area might also consider (in addition to those items listed as limitations on the FCPA at para 5.26 above) the following:

- Commercial counterparties are insisting on clauses that require the non-payment of all bribes and frequently on clauses requiring adequate procedures to prevent bribes.[35]
- The ethical standpoint taken by many companies as regards their policies and controls is incompatible with turning a 'blind eye' to this prolific but difficult issue.
- Facilitation payments in many cases do not 'expedite' or speed up the transfer of goods, services or people – quite the reverse. They act as reason for officials to create delays or complicated or needlessly bureaucratic procedures in which delays can easily occur.

---

34 Ryan McConnell and Charlotte Simon, 'Fashion Week FCPA: Are expediting payments the new black' (February 2013).

35 For example, larger companies are requiring smaller contracting counterparties to implement anti-bribery provisions as part of the larger company's risk mitigation/ adequate procedures.

- A company that does not implement a practical and accessible series of controls in this area, and 'hopes for the best', will be taking unnecessary risks as regards the FCPA.
- Recent history shows that a number of companies that were late in complying with the FCPA were eventually prosecuted or entered a deferred prosecution agreement when the statute became more actively enforced from 2004 onwards; the same may become true of companies that fail to meet UKBA standards.
- The jurisdiction of the UKBA corporate offence is so wide, given that it covers any business that conducts 'part of' its business in the UK, that few larger companies will be absolutely sure that they are not subject to the UKBA and its stricter position on small bribes.

5.37

In other words, ethical issues aside, if it has ever been sufficient not to adopt a policy and implement controls as regards small bribes for commercial or legal reasons, it appears a less attractive option now. A prudent company subject to the UKBA may, therefore, wish to take steps to implement a zero-tolerance approach to small bribes, and even a company not subject to the UKBA could also benefit from this approach.

Processes and controls

5.38

There is no one 'right way' to mitigate small bribery risk, including facilitation payments, and the following part of the chapter is not intended to be exhaustive or prescriptive as regards how commercial organisations manage their risk. Nevertheless, whether looking at complete zero-tolerance, an approach allowing a number of exceptions or a hybrid, no effective anti-corruption program can: (a) ignore small bribes, including facilitation payments; (b) fail to engage at senior management level with the special ethical and practical issues relating to small bribes; or (c) deal with the issue of small bribes without empathy and clear, practical and relevant guidance for employees.

5.39

The MoJ Guidance states that 'The Government does … recognise the problems that commercial organisations face in some parts of the world and in certain sectors', but is almost without practical advice for small bribes specifically (other than referring to facilitation payments in one of the case studies in Annex A to the Guidance, which does not form part of the statutory guidance). As a result, for small bribes more than other areas subject to the UKBA, until case law arises the practitioner is particularly reliant on knowledge of best practice, industry practice and a logical application of the MoJ Guidance and UKBA.[36]

5.40

It is clear from the MoJ Guidance generally that there is no legal requirement to put in place procedures to prevent small bribes that are more than proportionate to the risk and the size/resources of the company. However, given the role that appears to be envisaged for businesses in the MoJ Guidance above and the principles in the Guidance, regarding adequate procedures for small bribes in particular, companies operating in medium or high risk environments may wish to consider the following actions that are particularly relevant to reducing small bribery risk:

- a clear statement in the Code of Conduct that small bribes are prohibited, explaining any limited exceptions (eg in cases of genuine duress);
- a clear statement in the Code of Conduct or policy document regarding where to escalate questions or concerns; and
- a requirement that all payments are properly and accurately reported and recorded.[37]

5.41

An illustration, showing how the issue of small bribes, including facilitation payments, might be addressed in a policy document follows:

Sample Code Of Conduct (Small Bribes/Facilitation Payments)

We do not engage in bribery or corruption in any form, whether in the private or public sector. This means:

- Our employees or anyone acting for us must never offer, solicit, promise, give or accept a bribe, kickback or any other improper payment.

36 The MoJ Guidance notes as follows: 'As was the case under the old law, the Bribery Act does not (unlike US foreign bribery law) provide any exemption for such payments ... Exemptions in this context create artificial distinctions that are difficult to enforce ... The Government does, however, recognise the problems that commercial organisations face in some parts of the world and in certain sectors ... and the guidance below offers an indication of how the problem may be addressed through the selection of bribery prevention procedures by commercial organisations.'

37 To conform with normal accounting rules, the books and records requirements of the FCPA and to facilitate monitoring (principle 6 of the MoJ Guidance).

- We comply with all relevant laws and regulations that prohibit bribery and corruption.
- We *never* allow small bribes, including 'facilitation' or 'grease' payments (ie payments made to a government official to secure or speed up routine, non-discretionary, legal government actions, such as issuing permits or releasing goods held in customs) by anyone who works for the company or anyone acting for us. This applies no matter how small the amounts are. We also prohibit commercial or private sector bribery in all of its forms.
- As regards books and records, we require our employees to help us keep accurate books and records – and maintain adequate internal controls – so that payments are honestly described and company funds are not used for unlawful purposes.
- You can get more detailed information by referring to the [insert policy document] available at [insert] – or by talking with members of [Legal/Compliance or for smaller companies insert name of program manager]. You will also find more information [insert as appropriate].

5.42

Further measures relating to implementation of the above statements could potentially include the following:

- a **hotline/speak up** line to report, perhaps anonymously, questions relating to bribes, including small bribes;
- **training** for those on the hotline as regards what to do in the event that an employee calls because he or she is being requested to pay a small bribe or has made a payment;[38]
- **business cards** or letters carried by (or offered to) high risk employees explaining in English and/or the local language that the employee may be disciplined for paying even small bribes and would be committing an offence in their own country by doing so, eg:

38 Examples of lifelike case studies can be found in Resist's materials and the Transparency International 'Countering Small Bribes' publication. The UN Global Compact has produced video training that may also be of help. In addition, this chapter includes a proposed 'triage checklist' for phone-calls reporting small bribes.

[company logo]

STRICT NO BRIBES POLICY

- At [company name] we have a zero-tolerance towards both giving and receiving bribes and improper payments, including paying small bribes and facilitation payments.
- We require that all employees and service providers globally comply with relevant laws and make no unofficial or unreceipted payments.
- Failure to comply with the policy could lead to termination of employment or contract and may lead to a criminal prosecution in the UK or U.S.A.

Employee and service provider reporting/advice telephone number [insert].

- **training for employees** (either face to face or by electronic means) in relation to small bribes, perhaps as part of wider training, examples of which include those provided by TI, Trace and also the Resist training sponsored by the UN Global Compact (available free of charge in seven languages);[39]
- **engagement** with industry bodies trying to prevent small bribes and locally with industry groups facing common problems;[40] and
- **due diligence questionnaires** for higher-risk service providers that seek to identify 'red flags' relating to small bribes, eg questions relating to whether the counterparty will be moving goods or people across borders (see Appendix 2 to this book).

External service providers

5.43

General information regarding proportionate risk mitigations relating to higher risk external service providers is provided in Chapter 8 from paragraph 8.63.[41] However, for specific service provider relationships that are identified as high

39 It is suggested that specific advice is taken on training programs but that training will often make relevant employees aware of the company's policy and exceptions and that such employees understand how to escalate concerns/issues and to record any payment made.

40 Eg local business forums and anti-corruption industry groups, and related groups such as the Madison group for banks, the energy and extractive industry group (see www.ibe.org.uk/userfiles/exten_anti-corruptionprinciples_2011.pdf), the UN Global Compact, Transparency International UK's Business Integrity Forum and the Institute of Business Ethics.

41 The Transparency International 'Countering Small Bribes' publication previously cited in this chapter also provides suggestions as regards practical steps to respond to small bribes.

risk, the following additional measures could be considered on a case by case basis for small bribes:[42]

- communication of the company's policy of non-payment of facilitation payments and bribes in general to the counterparty and its staff;
- asking for and reviewing receipts from the counterparty to look for 'red flags' such as miscellaneous expenses or poor descriptions of services;
- building realistic timescales into the planning of the project so that shipping, importation and delivery schedules allow for resisting and testing demands for facilitation payments where feasible;
- requesting that the relevant counterparties train their staff in relation to resisting demands for facilitation payments and the relevant local law, perhaps adding comparisons to the UKBA;
- trying to avoid paying 'inspection fees' or 'processing fees' (if not properly due) in cash directly to an official;
- informing those demanding improper payments that compliance with the demand may mean that an offence is committed under UK law; and
- informing those demanding improper payments that the requests may be escalated, including to the UK embassy or other authorities.

Management response to employee in difficulty

5.44

No specific assistance is provided in the MoJ Guidance in relation to managing the situation in which an employee seeks advice in relation to a 'real time' request to pay a small bribe. However, a possible checklist is provided below:[43]

42 These items are based primarily on Case Study 1, appended to the MoJ Guidance. In addition to the items listed, an option is presented to 'Proposing or including as part of any contractual arrangement certain procedures for the counterparties and its staff, which may include one or more of the following, if appropriate:

- questioning of legitimacy of demands
- requesting receipts and identification details of the official making the demand
- requests to consult with superior officials'.

It is suggested that this would only be appropriate in unusual cases and could in practice be difficult to secure in a bilateral negotiation. Similarly the suggestions to (a) '[Maintain] close liaison with the counterparty so as to keep abreast of any local developments that may provide solutions and encouraging the counterparty to develop its own strategies based on local knowledge' and (b) 'procure advice on the law of the country in which the business activity occurs relating to fees that have to be paid by the agent e.g. certificates of inspection and fees for these to differentiate between properly payable fees and disguised requests for facilitation payments' would also only unusually seem proportionate. To be proportionate, there would presumably be red flags in these areas, eg where these were good reasons to doubt the legitimacy of local law charges or where there were known to be significant likely changes in the country in relation to the levying of local charges. The size and complexity of organisation, eg proportionality, would also be relevant.

43 The Institute of Business Ethics at the time of writing provides a free electronic tool aimed at employees that is developed with Serco, the 'Say No Toolkit' (see www.saynotoolkit.net).

Management Response Triage Checklist

DURING CALL

- Clarify if there was/is a threat to safety or liberty. What is the basis for this?
- Identify amount of payment and overall factual situation.
- If safe to do so, suggest identifying whether a receipt will be provided for any payment; and/or
- Suggest requesting a written copy of the relevant law or ordinance under which the charge is being required; and/or
- Suggest asking to speak to a more senior official; and/or
- Suggest re-stating company policy and indicating to the requester of the bribe that the employee could be disciplined for making the requested payment.
- Contact the UK or US (or other relevant) embassy or indicate that this might happen.
- Advise bribe requester that no payment can be made – even if this means loss of time/additional cost to the business – unless there are genuine reasons to think there will be an injury or unlawful detention.
- Reassure the employee and make certain they know that you and the company appreciate and are grateful for the escalation of the issue. At a later date consider further recognition, eg a bonus.
- If a payment occurs or has occurred, ensure that an accurate record of the payment is made.

POST CALL

- Consider writing to the relevant company/agency informing them that a bribe was requested, whether the bribe was paid or not. The authority may be grateful for assistance.
- If the company is a service provider, consider notifying the client company of the issue. Can they or their legal advisors assist or provide support?
- Consider discussing any continuing issues with sympathetic industry groups in country and/or raising the matter with the UK embassy – perhaps with a request that the embassy make representations to the relevant government.

- Post call (or ideally during the call), take an accurate note and consider seeking immediate compliance or legal advice.

5.45

The above steps, whilst only indicative, in the right situation could potentially help persuade the relevant person demanding a bribe that for the amount requested it is simply too time consuming or difficult to continue making the request and show the relevant employee that their decision to report the issue was appropriate and welcomed by their employer.

Trends

5.46

It is always appropriate to be cautious when identifying emerging issues. However, the following trends are of note:

- the risk of small bribes is set to increase as trade friction increases; and
- as knowledge and practice in this area expands and deepens, the effectiveness of resources aimed at preventing small bribes payments will increase and become more widely and cheaply available.

Demand for small bribes

5.47

Finally, in relation to that part of the bribery equation which is largely outside of any corporate's control, the question continues to be posed as to whether sufficient efforts are being made to reduce 'demand' for small bribes and particularly demand for 'facilitation' payments.

5.48

In this regard, the MoJ Guidance in 2011 stated that 'eradication of facilitation payments is recognised at the national and international level as a long term objective that will require economic and social progress and sustained commitment to the rule of law in those parts of the world where the problem is most prevalent'.

5.49

This 'long term objective' of removing or reducing demand appears materially no closer today than it was in 2011, as despite a number of attempts by governments and NGOs to reduce demands for small bribes, there appears to be little if any current evidence of a general reduction globally.[44] Ultimately perhaps either growing economic prosperity or candid and practical government to government talks (assisted by NGOs) will eventually help normalise conditions for lower paid state workers and so remove one of the key reasons for requests for bribes from foreign companies.[45]

44 However, it is noted that on 2 August 2019 the 'Foreign Extortion Prevention Act' (FEPA) was introduced to the US House of Representatives, which specifically targets foreign public officials who solicit bribes and does not include any exception for facilitation payments. While it is unlikely that the DOJ will regularly pursue overseas border agents or customs officials for requesting small bribes, their potential ability to do so may nevertheless have a deterrent effect on the 'demand side' of small bribery. If nothing else, it could also provide an additional tool for resisting requests for small bribes, through explaining to the requestor that if the payment is not legitimate they may be liable to prosecution both domestically and in the US.

45 Governments and NGOs may be best placed to have these discussions where they themselves implement and monitor anti-bribery controls in their own departments, set out in the manner of a successful compliance program as described by the DoJ Resource Guide or by adequate procedures (as defined in the MoJ Guidance to section 7 of the UKBA). In the UK, this might also assist government departments minded to provide advice to business as regards implementation of adequate procedures.

6 Bribery of a foreign public official

Introduction

6.1

Much media attention is given to revelations involving the corruption of foreign public officials by domestic companies. Such conduct is prohibited by the 'general offences' under the Bribery Act 2010, particularly the sections 1 and 2 offences. The corruption of foreign public officials is, however, specifically targeted by the discrete offence under section 6. Key to understanding this offence are two guidance documents issued by British authorities. The first is the guidance issued in March 2011 by the Ministry of Justice (MoJ) shortly before the Act came into force on 1 July 2011 ('the MoJ Guidance'[1]). The second is the more recent 'Joint Prosecution Guidance of the Director of the SFO and the DPP' reviewed in September 2019 ('the SFO Guidance'[2]).

Section 6 – Bribery of a Foreign Public Official

6.2

> (1) A person ('P') who bribes a foreign public official ('F') is guilty of an offence if P's intention is to influence F in F's capacity as a foreign public official.
>
> (2) P must also intend to obtain or retain –
>
> (a) business, or
>
> (b) an advantage in the conduct of business.
>
> (3) P bribes F if, and only if –
>
> (a) directly or through a third party, P offers, promises or gives any financial or other advantage –

1 www.justice.gov.uk/downloads/legislation/bribery-act-2010-guidance.pdf.

2 www.cps.gov.uk/legal-guidance/bribery-act-2010-joint-prosecution-guidance-director-serious-fraud-office-and.

> (i) to F, or
>
> (ii) to another person at F's request or with F's assent or acquiescence, and
>
> (b) F is neither permitted nor required by the written law applicable to F to be influenced in F's capacity as a foreign public official by the offer, promise or gift.

Essential elements

6.3

- P (or a third party acting for P) offers, promises or gives a financial or other advantage.
- To F (or another person at the request, acquiescence or assent of F).
- P intends to obtain or retain business/advantage in business.
- P intends to influence F in his capacity as a foreign public official.

Each of these elements is considered in detail below.

P offers, promises or gives a financial or other advantage

6.4

This is the same wording that as in the general offence of bribery in section 1, and readers should refer to paragraphs 4.15–18.

To a foreign public official (or to another person at his request, acquiescence or assent)

6.5

Foreign public official is defined under the legislation in subsection 5.

> '"Foreign Public Official" means an individual who:
>
> (a) holds a legislative, administrative or judicial position of any kind, whether appointed or elected, of a country or territory outside the United Kingdom (or any subdivision of such a country or territory);
>
> (b) exercises a public function:

(i) for or on behalf of a country or territory outside the United Kingdom (or any subdivision of such a country or territory), or

(ii) for any public agency or public enterprise of that country or territory (or subdivision); or

(c) is an official or agent of a public international organisation.'

6.6

Public function, public agency or public enterprise is not defined in the Act. The old common law offence of bribery may assist, in which a public officer was 'an officer who discharged any duty in the discharge of which the public are interested, more clearly so if he is paid out of a fund provided by the public'. The terms are also defined in the 'Commentaries on the OECD Convention'[3] as follows:

'Public function' includes any activity in the public interest, delegated by a foreign country, such as performance of a task delegated by it in connection with public procurement.

A 'public agency' is an entity constituted under public law to carry out specific task in the public interest.

A 'public enterprise' is any enterprise, regardless of its legal form, over which a government or governments may directly or indirectly exercise a dominant influence. This is deemed to the case when the government or governments hold the majority of the enterprise's subscribed capital, control the majority of votes attaching to shares issued by the enterprise, or can appoint a majority of the members of the enterprise's administrative or managerial body or supervisory body.

6.7

There was discussion in the Law Commission Paper[4] about whether to criminalise the bribery of foreign *private* individuals. The Commission rejected this approach and that is reflected in the Act. The distinction between public and private persons has, however, become blurred as many state-owned businesses have been privatised. Nevertheless, and using the definitions above, it appears that most such ventures would fall within the ambit of section 6. Even if there is doubt about whether someone is a foreign public official, it is possible that a payment to them would be caught by the section 1 offence in any case. A potential difficulty for the prosecutor is that the 'improper performance element' is required by section 1 whereas the section 6 offence requires only an

3 'OECD Commentaries on Convention on Combating Bribery of Foreign Officials in International Business Transactions' DAFFE/IME/BR(97)/REV 1, paras 11-14.

4 Law Commission Paper No 313, para 5.20.

intention to 'influence' the foreign public official in their capacity as such (as per section 6(1)).

6.8

To understand the risks, corporations should consider the *nature* of the function that the individual is performing and whether the *payment* for that function is ultimately via the public purse of the foreign jurisdiction in question.

6.9

A foreign public official can also work for, or be an agent of, a public international organisation. A public international organisation is defined by section 6(6) as follows:

> '(6) Public International Organisation means an organisation whose members are any of the following:
>
> (a) countries or territories,
>
> (b) governments of countries or territories,
>
> (c) other public international organisations,
>
> (d) a mixture of any of the above.'

6.10

It should be noted that the section 6 offence may be established by F requesting, acquiescing or assenting to the bribing of another person. As with section 1 offences (see Chapter 4), payment to a third party at the direction of the official will still be caught by section 6.

6.11

As already stated above, the key difference between a section 1 and a section 6 offence is that the latter does not require the intention that the FPO will perform his duties improperly.

6.12

As explained in Chapter 4, offering a bribe to an individual overseas could give rise to criminal liability under section 1 whether or not that person has any public responsibilities. Extra care should nevertheless be taken since, as the Court observed in *R. (on the application of Soma Gas and Oil*[5]*)*, companies face a 'very high hurdle' to overcome when challenging the 'wide discretion' of the SFO to open an investigation into such payments. This remains the position even for companies that cooperate with the SFO. Companies forced to defend

5 [2016] EWHC 2471 (Admin).

themselves against lengthy investigations for section 6 offences will incur severe legal expenses and loss of business, as occurred in the case cited above.

P intends to obtain/retain a business advantage

6.13

This phrase is used in a number of jurisdictions and interpreted widely. It includes not only situations where the payment is for an official who can directly assist in the obtaining/retention of business (for example, payments to officials who make procurement decisions), but also where payment to the official indirectly assists in the obtaining/retention of the business advantage.

6.14

For example in the FCPA-related case *US v Kay*,[6] money was paid to customs and tax officials in Haiti in order to obtain a reduction of import duties and taxes. This was held to 'assist in obtaining or retaining business'. It is likely that UK courts will follow this interpretation. Companies should therefore enforce policies to reduce potential liability for bribery not only in the procurement processes but also in the general facilitation of their business overseas.

P intends to influence F in his capacity as a foreign public official

6.15

This element is not satisfied where the official ('F') is permitted or required by the applicable written law (including case law) to be influenced by the advantage. Liability for section 6 will, however, arise even if the bribery arose from local custom, or was tolerated in the locality, or was practically necessary in order to conduct business.[7] The SFO Guidance is clear that facilitation payments (or 'speed' or 'grease' payments) are also not exempt from section 6.

6.16

Paragraph 25 of the MoJ Guidance states that when seeking publicly funded contracts, governments often permit or require those tendering for the contract to offer, in addition to the principal tender, some kind of additional investment in the local economy. The MoJ Guidance acknowledges that such arrangements could amount to a financial or other advantage to a foreign public official or another person at the official's request, assent or acquiescence. Where, however, relevant 'written law' permits or requires the official to be influenced by such arrangements then section 6 will not be engaged.

---

6 359 F. 3d 738, 6 A.L.R. Fed 2nd 711.

7 Paragraphs 7 and 8 of Commentaries as reviewed in para 5.81 of the Law Commission Paper.

6.17

It may be that the additional investment would amount to an advantage to an official but the local law is silent as to whether the official is permitted or required to be influenced by it. Should this arise, prosecutors will consider the public interest in prosecuting. This, according to the MoJ Guidance, will provide the 'appropriate backstop' in circumstances where the evidence suggests that the offer of additional investment is a legitimate part of the tender exercise. The SFO Guidance has elaborated on the public interest factors tending in favour of section 6 prosecutions such as large or repeated payments, and those against (for example, the payer being in a 'vulnerable position') These factors include those relevant to the decision to bring a prosecution under section 1.

6.18

Corporate hospitality is dealt with in Chapter 14. However, the provisions of section 6 are not meant to ban hospitality for foreign officials. The SFO Guidance is clear that reasonable, proportionate, and bona fide hospitality is an 'established and important part of doing business' which the Act 'does not seek to penalise'. It does emphasise however, that 'the more lavish the hospitality or expenditure (beyond what may be reasonable standards in the particular circumstances) the greater the inference that it is intended to encourage or reward improper performance or influence an official'. This is because it is 'clear that hospitality can be employed as bribes'.

6.19

There is plainly some ambiguity in how the SFO Guidance interprets the Act, which suggests that prosecutors will be required to assess 'hospitality cases' on their individual facts. That same ambiguity means that those dealing with foreign public officials must do so cautiously when considering whether any payment or advantage offered could be misinterpreted as a bribe.

Flowchart showing checks that organisations should undertake when giving payments/other advantages overseas

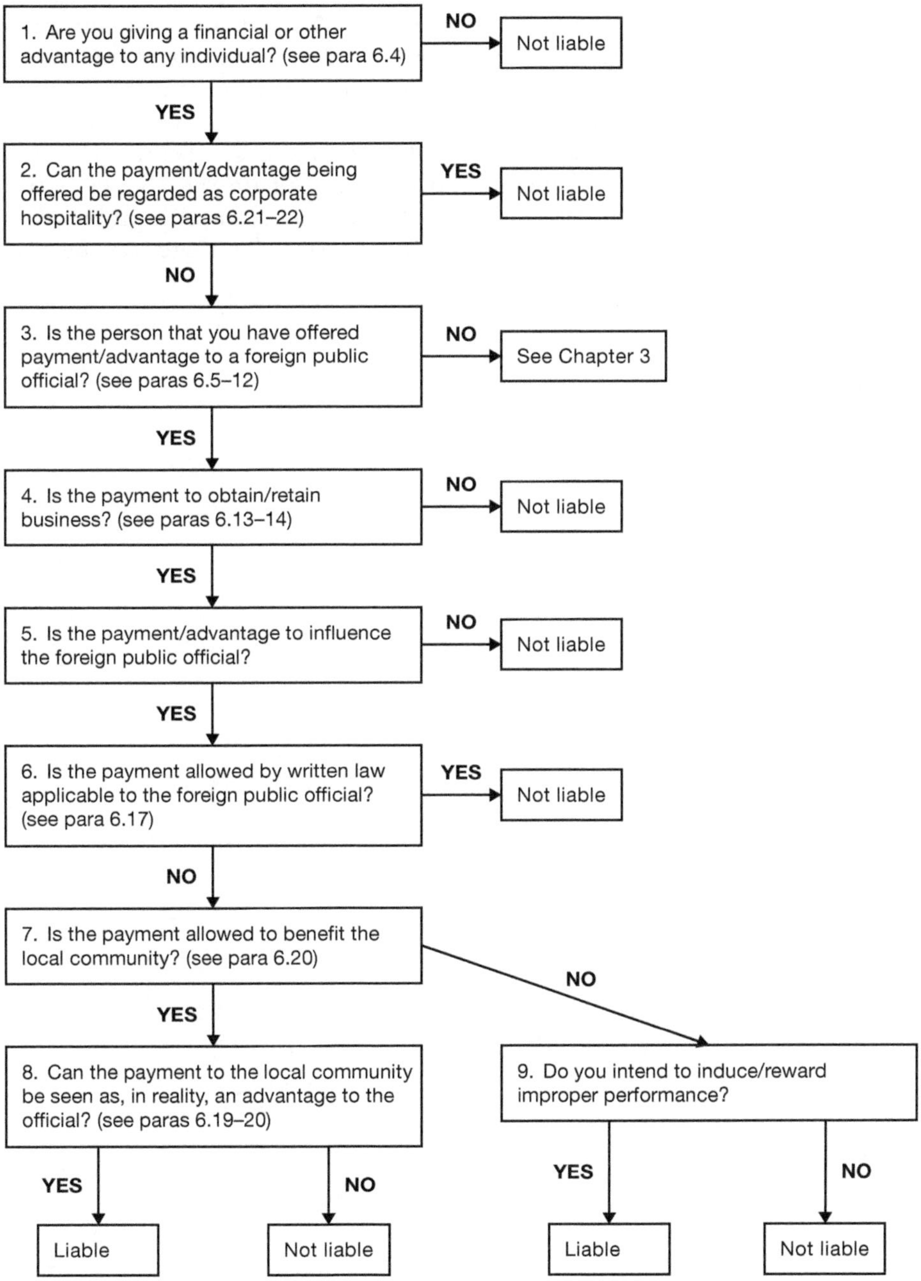

Conclusion

6.20

There is overlap between sections 1 and 6. The two offences may capture the same conduct. Section 6 exists to prohibit the influencing of decisions concerning publicly funded business opportunities overseas through the bribery of foreign public officials or their associates. Such activity is likely to induce 'improper performance' of an official function, even if section 6 does not require proof of this element. The justification for this is that the definition of such official functions is difficult, and often reliant on the cooperation of the state involved. Section 6 is drafted widely to overcome this problem and facilitate prosecutions. With this in mind, it is striking that there have been no convictions under section 6 since the Act became law.

7 Failure of commercial organisations to prevent bribery

Introduction

7.1

Section 7 of the Bribery Act 2010 ('UKBA') created a radical and now well-established offence which, for the first time in English law made it possible to prosecute a commercial organisation for its failure to prevent bribery. Although section 14 enables commercial organisations to be held criminally liable for offences committed under sections 1, 2, or 6, the prosecution needs to demonstrate consent or connivance of senior officers in the wrongdoing. As will be seen, section 7 makes no reference to the accused company's knowledge or authorisation of the bribes, for this is a strict liability offence which makes awareness or participation irrelevant. It also stretches deep into business relationships, since bribery by third parties, local suppliers or even their suppliers and contractors could all engage section 7. Importantly, section 7(2) gives the company a defence of 'adequate procedures' and shifts responsibility onto the shoulders of directors and senior management, who now have the burden of proving that the company had adequate procedures in place to prevent the bribery in question.

7.2

This chapter sets out and then considers the section 7 offence in detail, as well as the definition of 'associated person' in section 8. Principles governing the complex question of 'adequate procedures' are set out in Chapter 8, along with recent government guidance.

Bribery Act 2010: sections 7 and 8

7 Failure of commercial organisations to prevent bribery

(1) A relevant commercial organisation ('C') is guilty of an offence under this section if a person ('A') associated with C bribes another person intending –

(a) to obtain or retain business for C, or

(b) to obtain or retain an advantage in the conduct of business for C.

(2) But it is a defence for C to prove that C had in place adequate procedures designed to prevent persons associated with C from undertaking such conduct.

(3) For the purposes of this section, A bribes another person if, and only if, A –

(a) is, or would be guilty of an offence under section 1 or 6 (whether or not A has been prosecuted for such an offence), or

(b) would be guilty of such an offence if section 12(2)(c) and (4) were omitted.

(4) See section 8 for the meaning of a person associated with C and see section 9 for a duty on the Secretary of State to publish guidance.

(5) In this section –

'partnership' means –

(a) a partnership within the Partnership Act 1890. Or

(b) a limited partnership registered under the Limited Partnerships Act 1907,

or a firm or entity of a similar character formed under the law of a country outside the United Kingdom,

'relevant commercial organisation' means –

(a) a body which is incorporated under the law of any part of the United Kingdom and which carries on a business, or part of a business, (whether there or elsewhere),

(b) any other body corporate (wherever incorporated) which carries on a business, or part of a business, in any part of the United Kingdom,

(c) a partnership which is formed under the law of any part of the United Kingdom and which carries on a business (whether there or elsewhere), or

(d) any other partnership (wherever formed) which carries on a business, or part of a business, in any part of the United Kingdom,

and, for the purposes of this section, a trade or profession is a business.

8 Meaning of associated person

(1) For the purposes of section 7, a *person* ('A') is associated with C if (disregarding the bribe under consideration) A is a person who performs services for or on behalf of C.

(2) The capacity in which A performs services for or on behalf of C does not matter.

(3) Accordingly, A may (for example) be C's employee, agent or subsidiary.

(4) Whether or not A is a person who performs services for or on behalf of C is to be determined by reference to all the relevant circumstances and not merely by reference to the nature of the relationship between A and C.

(5) But if A is an employee of C, it is to be presumed unless the contrary is shown that A is a person who performs services for or on behalf of C.

Criminal liability of corporations under section 7

7.3

The common law regards a company as an individual entity, separate and distinct from its directors, managers and employees. Since a company, unlike an individual, has no mind of its own, it cannot be guilty of an offence such as those under sections 1, 2, and 6 of the UKBA, which require a mental element (*mens rea*) or, in other words, an intention to commit the crime. This has made it difficult but, depending on the circumstances, still possible to prosecute companies for corruption under the old law.[1]

1 The UKBA 2010 was brought into force on 1 July 2011. Section 17 and Sch 2 abolished the common-law offences of bribery and embracery, and repealed the Public Bodies Corrupt Practices Act 1889 and the Prevention of Corruption Acts 1889-1916, but not the Honours (Prevention of Abuses) Act 1925, or the common-law offence of misconduct in public office. The new offences created by ss 1,2,6, and 7 of the 2010 Act are subject to transitional provisions set out in s 19(5) and (6). See also *R v Mabey & Johnson Ltd* (2010) unreported, 25 September 2009; *R v Innospec Ltd* [2010] Crim LR 665.

7.4

One way around this problem has been the development of 'the identification principle' whereby a company can be held criminally liable by the identification of a 'directing mind', ie an individual within the company as opposed to its servant or agent, who knowingly directed the company to commit the crime. If such an individual can be said to have acted 'as the company',[2] then the company may be regarded as criminally liable. The identification principle acknowledges the existence of corporate officers who are to be treated in law as the embodiment of the company. Their acts and states of mind are deemed to be those of the company, and they are considered to be 'controlling officers' of the company. Criminal acts by such officers will not only be offences for which they can be prosecuted as individuals, but also, because of their status within the company, offences for which the company can be prosecuted.[3] Determining who those officers are is a matter of fact which may be difficult to prove.

7.5

This problem has been overcome by sections 7 and 8 which, in relation to bribery, create a strict liability offence which can be committed without a company or an individual within it having any intention or knowledge of the events at all. Corporate liability may now be proved merely by showing that a person 'associated with' the company committed offences under sections 1 or 6 of the Act, intending to retain or obtain business or a business advantage for the company. The company's guilt, on the other hand, may be established even though its directors, officers or management did not approve or were entirely ignorant of the bribery in question.[4]

7.6

The overarching purpose of section 7 is to create a culture of intolerance towards bribery, and to incentivise directors and senior management to retain overall supervision and control over the way in which the company does business.

7.7

Corporate liability for those 'associated' with the company under section 7 is broadly defined, and wide-ranging, as can be seen from the case of *Sweett Group PLC* ('Sweett Group'), the first company to be convicted and sentenced for an offence under section 7.[5] Sweett Group is a UK listed provider of professional services for the construction sector whose subsidiary company, Cyril Sweett International, made corrupt payments to a senior Emirati official at Al Ain

---

2 In *Tesco Supermarkets Ltd v Nattrass* [1972] AC 153, Lord Diplock formulated the 'identification' or 'attribution' test. Yet not every responsible individual, by his actions, can be said to make the company responsible. *R v Andrews Weatherfoil Ltd* (1972) 56 Cr App Rep 31.

3 Corporate Prosecutions CPS Legal Guidance.

4 Subject to the section 7(2) defence of adequate procedures.

5 Southwark Crown Court 19 February 2016.

Ahlia Insurance Company, in order to secure a contract to consult on the development of an hotel based in Abu Dhabi. Sweett Group pleaded guilty on the basis that it had failed to detect and prevent the payment of bribes by its subsidiary, and that its procedures for overseeing its operations in the Middle East were inadequate. The court imposed on the company a total penalty of £2.25 million.

When is an offence under section 7 committed?

7.8

The following elements must be present before an offence under section 7 can be proved.

(1) The commercial organisation 'C' must be a 'relevant commercial organisation' as defined by section 7(5)

At the time that the offence is alleged to have been committed, C must be:

(a) Incorporated under the law of any part of the UK and which carries on a business, or part of a business there or elsewhere;

(b) Incorporated anywhere else in the world and carries on a business, or part of a business, in the UK;

(c) A partnership which is formed under the law of any part of the UK and which carries on a business in the UK or elsewhere, or

(d) A partnership formed anywhere else in the world, which carries on a business, or part of a business, in the UK.

7.9

Commercial organisations which are incorporated or which are in the form of a partnership[6] fall within the definition. So too, do limited partnerships.[7] Sole traders, trusts, and unincorporated associations fall outside the definition, although individual trainers and trustees can be prosecuted under sections 1–6 of the Act.

7.10

If a section 7 offence is alleged against a partnership, section 15 of the Act provides that proceedings must be brought against the partnership, and not the partners, and that any fines are paid from partnership assets.

---

6 Section 1(1) of the Partnership Act 1890 defines partnership as 'the relation which subsists between persons carrying on a business in common with a view of profit.

7 As defined by section 4 of the Limited Partnerships Act 1907.

7.11

Whether C can be said to be 'carrying out a business or part of a business', although not defined by the UKBA, is a matter of fact and degree in every case. This can usually be determined by looking at the activities of the business as well as business records such as objects and memoranda of association, partnership agreements, accounts, annual returns, and the like. Business includes a trade or profession.

7.12

A foreign company or partnership with an accommodation address and bank account in the UK, which conducts even a small part of its business in the UK, will fall within the section, although in the view of the present government 'the mere fact that a company's securities have been admitted to the UK Listing Authority's Official List, and therefore admitted to trading on the London Stock Exchange [will not] in itself … qualify that company as carrying on a business or part of a business in the UK, and therefore falling within the definition of a 'relevant commercial organisation' for the purposes of section 7.'[8]

7.13

Liability under the UKBA does not appear to extend to the UK based subsidiaries of large foreign-based international parent companies, where the alleged acts of bribery are committed by the parent company and are otherwise entirely unconnected with the activities of the subsidiary. This reflects what is known as the 'corporate veil' principle, well established in UK company law, whereby wholly owned companies and their owners are regarded as entirely separate entities, in which the liabilities of the one are not the liabilities of the other.[9] On the other hand, the corporate veil may be pierced, and the Act engaged, if it is suspected that the corporate structure was merely a sham to facilitate bribery. This principle also exists in very limited circumstances 'when a person is under an existing legal obligation or liability or subject to an existing legal restriction which he deliberately evades or whose enforcement he deliberately frustrates by interposing a company under his control'.[10] Should this issue arise, the court may deviate from the principle, and lift the veil in order to deprive the company or its controller of the advantage which they would have obtained due to the company's separate legal personality.

(2) There must be a person 'A', associated with C

7.14

As we have seen above, section 8(1) provides that for the purposes of section 7, a person ('A') is associated with C if (disregarding the bribe under

8 MoJ Guidance issued in 2011 under section 9 of the UKBA (adequate procedures).

9 *Salomon v Salomon* [1897] AC 22.

10 *Prest v Petrodel Resources Ltd* [2013] UKSC 34.

consideration) A is a person who performs services *for or on behalf* of C. Thus, those who supply goods or services *to* C are unlikely to qualify, unless they also perform services for or on behalf of C. The question of whether or not A does perform services for or on behalf of C is a factual issue which will have to be resolved in each case. An individual who provides services *to* C is not associated with it.[11]

7.15

A must not only intend the offences of bribery under sections 1 or 6, but also intend by the bribery to obtain or retain business or an advantage in the conduct of business *for* C. The offence will be made out against A, whether or not the intended business or advantage was successfully obtained.

7.16

Section 8(2) is to be broadly construed since 'the capacity in which A performs services for or on behalf of C does not matter.' So A could be a director, a manager, an employee, an external agent or sub-contractor or subsidiary of C, or in another and less formal relationship with C. Agents, whether individual or corporate, can include financial advisers, consultants, and intermediaries instructed to represent the company abroad. The list provided by section 8(3) contains mere examples, and is not intended to be exhaustive. For the avoidance of doubt, section 8(4) states that the question of whether or not A in fact performs services 'is to be determined by reference to all the relevant circumstances and not merely by reference to the nature of the relationship between A and C.' It is the nature and substance of the service provided by A and of his relationship with C, rather than his official status, which is determinative.[12]

7.17

In the case of a supply chain involving several entities, or a project to be performed by a prime contractor and a series of sub-contractors, C may only be said to know and control the activities of main contractor. Recent MoJ guidance suggests that it is unlikely that C could find itself liable for sub-contractors further down the chain,[13] although technically this remains possible. Issues such as C's knowledge and control, or its lack of knowledge and control, are merely relevant factors to be considered when deciding whether A can truly be said to be associated with C.

11 For further interpretation on the meaning of 'associated person' see MoJ: Bribery Act 2010: Post Legislative Scrutiny Memorandum (June 2018) paras 61–65.

12 Explanatory Notes p 8.

13 MoJ Guidance, p 16 para 39.

7.18

Section 8(5) provides that if A is an employee of C, he will be presumed to be associated with C unless the contrary is proved. Occasionally a director of C or a partner of a partnership may also be an employee of C. Where the presumption is made, the burden shifts to A to prove on a balance of probabilities that he is not.

(3) A must have bribed another person, intending to obtain or retain business or an advantage in the conduct of business for C within the meaning of s 7(1) and (3)

7.19

First, it is essential that what A did amounted to an offence under either section 1 or 6, although section 7(3)(a) makes clear that there is no need for the prosecution to show that A has already been prosecuted or convicted, merely that he 'would be' guilty if prosecuted.

7.20

As discussed in Chapter 4, a person commits a section 1 offence by:

(1) Offering, promising or giving a financial or other advantage to another person, intending the advantage either to induce improper performance of a relevant function or activity or to reward such improper performance; or

(2) Offering or promising or giving a financial or other advantage to a person knowing or believing that the acceptance would itself constitute improper performance of a relevant function or activity.

7.21

Section 6 is concerned with bribery of a foreign public official 'F', and, amongst other things, requires that A intended to influence 'F' in his capacity as such an official, or another person at F's request or with F's consent or acquiescence, for a business purpose (see Chapter 6).

7.22

For the purposes of section 6, the payer (A) must intend to influence F in his capacity as a foreign public official, and must intend to obtain or retain business or an advantage in the conduct of business. Unlike section 1, A does not have to intend to induce F to act improperly.

7.23

Secondly, before C can be held liable under section 7(1) an additional mental element is required. A must intend the bribery either to obtain or retain business for C, or obtain or retain an advantage in the conduct of business for C, rather than wholly for himself.

7.24

What amounts to 'business' or 'an advantage in the conduct of business' will depend on the circumstances of the case, but it is likely that these words will be construed widely.

Extraterritoriality

7.25

Section 7 has a wide extraterritorial reach. It is broader than that of the Foreign Corrupt Practices Act 1977 ('FCPA') in the US, which, if the offence takes place outside US territory, requires the prosecution to establish that C was a US domestic concern, issuer or agent. Section 12(5) of the UKBA provides that a section 7 offence is committed 'irrespective of whether the acts or omissions which form part of the offence take place in the United Kingdom or elsewhere.' Those charged with offences under sections 1, 2 and 6 must be shown to have a 'close connection' with the UK, but, for the purposes of a corporate offence under section 7, there is no need for A to have a close connection with the UK as defined in section 12.[14] A UK court will have jurisdiction, provided the organisation is a 'relevant commercial organisation' within the meaning of section 7(5)(a)–(d) of the Act (see paras 7.7–7.12 above).[15]

(4) C has failed to establish a defence under s 7(2) that it had 'adequate procedures' to prevent bribery by persons associated with C, on C's behalf

7.26

A defence under section 7 relies upon an organisation having adequate, ie effective, procedures in place, aimed at preventing (rather than merely discouraging) those such as A from engaging in bribery. In this instance, the burden shifts to C, which must prove that it had such procedures on a balance of probabilities, ie that it was more likely than not that it did. Of course, no system is perfect, and, providing the procedures are found to be 'adequate' C will not be deprived of a defence under section 7 simply because they failed on this occasion. Adequate procedures, and the principles on which they are judged, are discussed in detail in the next chapter.

14 Section 7(3)(b).
15 See MoJ Bribery Act 2010: Post Legislative Scrutiny Memorandum (June 2018) para 58.

Self-reporting

7.27

The Serious Fraud Office ('SFO') operates a policy in England and Wales and Northern Ireland of co-operation with commercial organisations that self-refer incidents of bribery (see 'Approach of the SFO to dealing with overseas corruption' on the SFO website – www.sfo.gov.uk). C's willingness to co-operate with an investigation under the Bribery Act and to make a full disclosure by no means guarantees that charges will be avoided. The fact that C has self-reported is however a matter to be taken into account in any decision as to whether it is, in all the circumstances, in the public interest to commence criminal proceedings.

Place of trial and penalty

7.28

Unlike offences under section 1, 2, and 6, which can be tried summarily (in the magistrates' court) or on indictment (by judge and jury in the Crown Court), section 11(3) provides that an offence under section 7 may be tried only on indictment.

7.29

On conviction, C will face an unlimited fine.

7.30

An offence under section 7 has not been designated as a 'serious crime' for the purposes of the Serious Crimes Act 2007, which limits the court's power to impose serious crime prevention orders.

8 Adequate procedures

Introduction

8.1

This chapter provides an introduction to adequate procedures, including a practical and easy to follow overview of the compliance standards that are 'effectively required' of most commercial organisations incorporated in or with 'part of their business in' the UK as a result of section 7 of the Bribery Act 2010 ('UKBA').[1]

8.2

Examples, checklists and cross-references to further resources and materials are contained in this chapter. In addition, the primary source of the Ministry of Justice Guidance on Adequate Procedures ('MoJ Guidance') is reproduced with the consent of the Ministry at Appendix 3.

Key Points

8.3

- Adequate Procedures are 'effectively required' to safeguard against prosecution and to help mitigate both fines and reputational damage for most commercial organisations subject to the UKBA.
- The emphasis on meeting the standard is on actual implementation of controls and not on 'paper compliance'.
- A commercial organisation is expected to assess the risk that service providers, including employees, may pay bribes for the organisation's benefit.
- Based on that risk assessment, a commercial organisation is expected to apply a proportionate and risk-based approach to mitigate the identified risks by putting in place further procedures proportionate to the size

1 See Chapter 7 for an explanation of the meaning of 'commercial organisation' and the jurisdiction rule applying to s 7 of the UKBA, as well as detailed review of the s 7 offence to which having 'adequate procedures' is a complete defence. Note that nothing in this chapter or book should be considered as legal advice or is intended to suggest industry or other standards that may be higher than the non-prescriptive adequate procedures contained in the MoJ Guidance to the UKBA 2010.

and nature of the risk and the size, complexity and resources of the organisation.

- Although there is no 'one size fits all' approach, proportionate compliance programmes for even small to medium sized enterprises ('SMEs') operating in higher risk areas have common features and will usually include indicative elements such as a zero tolerance anti-bribery commitment communicated by senior management, training, risk assessment, monitoring, due diligence of relationships with service providers, financial controls and other mitigation of risk such as appropriate contract terms and accurate record keeping.
- While the compliance programme of companies of any size should always be guided by the level of risk encountered, generally, larger companies are expected to have more extensive procedures. In larger companies for example, the board or its delegate should be ultimately responsible for setting bribery prevention policies and procedures, tasking management to design, operate and monitor these procedures and keeping them under regular review. However, nothing in the UKBA requires even large companies to act disproportionately to the risk as it would have presented itself to a reasonable person at the time it arose.
- Compliance with the UKBA for those starting to do part of their business in UK may mean making significant changes for some companies but given available resources, compliance need not be expensive or 'alien' to an organisation's existing procedures or culture. Simple, thoughtful, incremental and inexpensive steps are sufficient for many companies to meet the standard needed or at least to improve their position and reduce the exposure to risk.
- For companies that adopt adequate procedures, an ethically based and coordinated compliance programme, which includes but is not limited to anti-corruption controls relating to corporate liability created by the UKBA, can be the most effective way to engage employees and manage anti-corruption compliance without creating 'compliance overload'. As a result, where a compliance programme is needed to meet UKBA standards, the programme can be designed to attain overall cost savings by incorporating environmental, social and governance (ESG) principles and combined controls to prevent passive bribery, fraud, sanctions breaches, modern slavery, anti-competitive behaviour, money laundering and breaches of the US Foreign Corrupt Practices Act 1977 ('FCPA').[2]

2 See Chapter 2 for further information relating to the FCPA, including a comparison table to key aspects of the UKBA.

Why adequate procedures are 'effectively' a requirement

8.4

Chapter 7 has explained the nature and jurisdiction of the corporate offence contained in section 7 of the UKBA.

8.5

In summary, the section 7 offence creates corporate criminal liability (with a potentially unlimited fine)[3] where a commercial organisation's service providers (its 'associated persons'), including its employees, pay a bribe for the organisation's benefit *and* where the organisation does not have 'adequate procedures' in place to prevent the service providers' payment of bribes.

8.6

At the time it was enacted, the UKBA was seen by many commentators as the strictest legislation of its type in the world. This is primarily because, although the UKBA (unlike the newer equivalent French law) did not introduce a positive regulatory obligation requiring companies to adopt adequate procedures, that was its practical effect, given that implementing adequate procedures is the only defence to the section 7 corporate criminal offence and bearing in mind that:

- all trading companies or banks will have employees and service providers; and
- a commercial organisation in even a low to medium risk area could not justify to its shareholders and broader stakeholders a failure to adopt procedures where an unlimited fine, debarment from government contracts and material reputational damage might be just some of the consequences should bribery take place.

In other words, adequate procedures became, on a commercial level, effectively required as part of good corporate governance for any organisations that is subject to section 7 of the UKBA and has anything greater than a very low intrinsic risk that bribes will be paid on the organisation's behalf.[4]

---

3 The Sentencing Guidelines Council has consulted on the level of fines appropriate for breaches of the section 7 offence, and the onus is currently on US sized fines based a multiplier of gross profit from the illegal activity. For larger activity or activity over a long period, this will potentially lead to fines of hundreds of millions of pounds for some commercial organisations. The levying of fines that would place a company into insolvency are suggested by the sentencing council as appropriate in some cases. In such circumstances, this would usually result in a total loss of value to shareholders in affected UK companies, ie companies subject to the Insolvency Act 1986 (as revised). For further information please the Council's website and Chapter 11.

4 Note that although this is true generally, there are some enterprises that are so small and inherently low risk, eg a family owned corner shop or a small local UK charity, that adequate procedures may arguably not be required. For further arguments in favour of adopting procedures to combat corruption, see also Chapter 5.

What is 'in scope'

8.7

Although section 7 has a wide scope that is likely to impact on all areas of a commercial organisation's function, there are areas in which 'adequate procedures' are not required by the UKBA given the following five components of the main active bribery offences:

- a commercial organisation with a
- service provider, which
- offers
- bribes[5]
- for the commercial organisation's benefit.

8.8

Specifically, the requirement to embed adequate procedures as specified by the MoJ Guidance, do not extend to the following:

- Entities that are not commercial organisations, eg government instrumentalities or public authorities.[6]
- Sales contracts without a service element, eg the simple buying and selling of goods.
- The acts of subsidiaries, where the subsidiaries are not themselves subject to the UKBA, are not performing services on behalf of the relevant parent company, or do not intend to obtain or retain business on their parent company's behalf.[7]
- The *receipt* of bribes by an employee of a commercial organisation, ie in relation to passive bribery (eg procurement fraud where the company is in essence the victim of its employee).
- Managing other legal and compliance risks including but not limited to environment risks, international trade rules, sanctions, money laundering or anti-trust/competition law risks.

---

5 Ie commits what would be an offence under ss 1 or 6 of the UKBA. Also note that no successful prosecution is required for this underlying bribery.

6 In the unusual situation where a government body is contracted to perform a service for a commercial organisation, it is not a defence under s 7 for the commercial organisation that the government body is not required to have adequate procedures

7 Note that joint ventures are not considered in this chapter given their complexity and that they will be relevant to only a minority of companies.

8.9

Nevertheless, there are commercial benefits, as well as legal and ethical reasons for a company to adopt a holistic or 'joined-up' approach in relation to many or all of these risk areas, for the reasons set out immediately below.

Adopting a 'joined-up' approach

8.10

Commercial organisations, whether large or small, now operate in a global environment and under a number of criminal codes and regulations – as diverse as from heath and safety to international trade rules and human rights to money laundering.

8.11

Concentrating on managing active bribery risk alone, whilst also likely to disproportionately use scarce compliance resources, can run the additional risk of blinding company employees to other important hazards. The temptation may be at first to implement only an anti-corruption programme or to oversee separate programs for each risk. However, few if any companies will find that attractive in the long run given the proliferation of compliance risks and given that managers have a preference for a simple, combined approach to risk that as far as is possible reduces duplication and time spent in meetings and form-filling.

8.12

As regards those non-corruption risks, many commercial organisations will be subject to money laundering laws requiring due diligence or 'to know your client'. Likewise, US, EU and UN sanctions, often actively pursued by prosecutors, can lead to large fines.[8] Where companies are exposed to such risks, the best compliance programmes in companies work in unison across similar subject matter areas, for instance conducting due diligence for sanctions and anti-money laundering purposes at the same time as for UKBA purposes. In addition, as well as efficiently combining compliance related activities, effective programmes usually incorporate ESG principles through implementing combined policies on issues such as climate change, modern slavery and more recent risks relating to Covid-19.

There is much to be said from a management perspective to a combined approach to compliance – both by using common measurements for risk, and

8 In April 2019, Standard Chartered Bank admitted to illegally processing transactions in violation of Iranian Sanctions and agreed to pay over US$1 billion under its deferred prosecution agreement with the US Justice Department.

by supporting better decision making through collating timely, accurate and useful management information across all material compliance risks.

8.13

As regards bribery risk (eg active and passive bribery), it has already been noted that adequate procedures under the UKBA only relate to active bribery – the paying of bribes by associated persons – and not to employees *receiving* bribes. However, passive bribery, which is often procurement fraud, is in many respects a form of theft from the company. As a result, commercial organisations typically create anti-corruption programmes that aim to prevent active (the offering of) and passive (the receiving of) bribes. Similarly, given the position of the US economy globally and the enforcement of relevant US legislation (see Chapter 2 on Global Context and the FCPA), companies also often seek to meet the high standards expected of companies subject to the US FCPA 1977 to prevent the bribery of non-US public officials summarised in Chapter 2.[9]

Cementing and explaining the 'joined-up' approach: ethics

8.14

A commercial organisation of any size can take a 'legalistic' approach to not paying bribes, eg 'we do not allow service providers to pay bribes as they may be caught and we may have to pay a large fine'. It can take a similar approach to sanctions risk, anti-trust risk and money laundering risk. However, such an approach can sit badly with the company ethos and can also result in employees seeking legal loop-holes, which may well be unreliable when tested. At a basic business level, a purely legalistic approach may also fail to show to employees the company's 'emotional' commitment to preventing corruption that a company's leadership will be showing to creating employment and growth. Employees in such an environment may prioritise short term profits over mere 'legal compliance' ie value over values, for instance where not paying a small bribe will result in an immediate larger financial loss but in the longer term will only lead to more requests for bribes.

8.15

The data on compliance programmes across the world shows the benefits of adopting an ethical approach for long term gain. In particular, studies have shown that corrupt working environments have a material effect on staff morale and productivity and Ethisphere Institute's research on the 135 companies identified

9 Note that other risks will still require proper resourcing, and that as this chapter relates to UKBA compliance it is not possible to explore in anything other than a cursory way non-corruption compliance risks.

as the 'World's Most Ethical Companies' showed that they outperformed the US large cap sector by more than 10% over a five year period.[10]

Consequences of the burden and standard of proof

8.16

As set out in more detail in Chapter 7,[11] in the event of prosecution it is for the commercial organisation that is charged to prove that it had adequate procedures in place at the time the bribery was committed, ie the burden of proof is on the organisation and not with the prosecutor.

8.17

As a result, it will be for a relevant commercial organisation to show that its programme was 'adequate' when it has already failed because a bribe or bribes has been paid. In practice this is likely to mean the company adducing evidence to prove that its adequate procedures were reasonable and proportionate to the risk assessed by the company and the reasonable resources available to it.

8.18

The standard of proof, ie the evidentiary standard that the company must meet in arguing such a case, is 'on the balance of probabilities',[12] or 'more likely than not', which is the usual test for non-criminal matters. Although this standard is lower than proving a case 'beyond all reasonable doubt' it is the same burden as the successful party would have reached in any contractual dispute or claim for nuisance or trespass. Therefore, the test is much more likely to be met where there is documented contemporaneous evidence of implemented adequate procedures at the date the bribe or bribes were paid.

8.19

As a company will often not know when bribes are paid for its benefit by service providers, the result of the standard of proof is that companies will find it prudent to continually maintain records that evidence not only the polices they have in place but also the fact that those policies have been implemented, used and monitored.[13]

---

10 For more on this interesting area see Steare, *Ethicability* (5th edn, Roger Steare Consulting Ltd, 2019).

11 See also UKBA, s 7(2).

12 See explanatory footnotes to the UKBA and specifically those relating to s 7.

13 Although corporate records will usually go back for some time (and frequently six years), evidence in the form of documentation showing implementation of adequate procedures need only be available for the period after the UKBA came into force, ie from 1 July 2011 onwards. The UKBA is not retroactive.

Document preservation

8.20

With no US-style five-year statute of limitations on the bringing of prosecutions after the date of the illegal activity,[14] the period for retaining records and other documentary evidence of adequate procedures presents something of a problem for companies subject to the UKBA. Specifically, standard corporate document destruction policies result in the periodic deletion or destruction of the evidence a company may otherwise have had available to meet its burden of proof under section 7. Nevertheless, although the MoJ Guidance[15] is silent on the issue, it is hoped that provided a destruction policy was not intended to pervert the course of justice and was within industry normal practice either prosecutors[16] would use their discretion not to prosecute (given that it would not be in the interests of justice to require companies to keep records in perpetuity) or, alternatively, that the broad MoJ Guidance on procedures being 'proportionate' would suffice to justify destruction of documents on the usual basis.[17]

Adequate procedures: a quantum leap?

8.21

During the consultation process leading to the MoJ Guidance, the UK government stressed that the adequate procedures defence would mean little change for most UK based companies, which they considered would already meet the requirements of the UKBA in any event. This was stated perhaps most clearly in the foreword to the MoJ Guidance itself, in which the then Secretary of State for Justice, Kenneth Clark QC, wrote as follows:

> 'These are certainly tough rules. But readers should understand too that they are directed at making life difficult for the mavericks responsible for corruption, not unduly burdening the vast majority of decent, law-abiding firms.'
>
> 'I have listened carefully to business representatives to ensure the Act is implemented in a workable way – especially for small firms that have limited resources. And, as I hope this guidance shows, combating

---

14 Pursuant to US federal law there is a statute of limitations of five years for corporate criminal liability, which can be extended in certain circumstances – see 18 USC 3282 (for criminal actions) and 28 USC 2462 (for civil actions).

15 Appendix 3 to this book.

16 Eg in England and Wales the Serious Fraud Office, the City of London Police/the Crown Prosecution Service and in Scotland the Crown Office and Procurator Fiscal Service.

17 Page 7 of the MoJ Guidance 'As the principles make clear commercial organisations should adopt a risk-based approach to managing bribery risks. Procedures should be proportionate to the risks faced by an organisation. No policies or procedures are capable of detecting and preventing all bribery. A risk-based approach will, however, serve to focus the effort where it is needed and will have most impact. A risk-based approach recognises that the bribery threat to organisations varies across jurisdictions, business sectors, business partners and transactions.'

the risks of bribery is largely about common sense, not burdensome procedures. The core principle it sets out is proportionality'.[18]

8.22

There appears to be little empirical evidence of the extent of commercial organisations' anti-corruption programmes at the date of the MoJ Guidance, and therefore the basis on which the MoJ was able to introduce in some cases detailed guidance at the same time as claiming the 'tough new rules' were directed at 'mavericks' and not expected to introduce 'burdensome procedures'. In relation to the potential divergence, a survey conducted by FTI Consulting in 2012[19] and also a House of Lords committee report from 2013 suggested that even three years after the UKBA was passed there remained 'some way to go' for many corporates to meet the standards of the MoJ Guidance and, although there has since then been mass adoption of adequate procedures by larger companies, there was still a question about levels of compliance in small to medium business by the time a Select Committee of the UK parliament again considered these issues again in 2019.[20]

8.23

Leaving aside the question of whether adequate procedures were adopted at similar rates across all sizes and types of business, it is in any event noteworthy that for the most part the MoJ Guidance sets out expectations similar to the principles found in the FCPA Sentencing Guideline[21] and the relevant collective works of the United Nations, Transparency International ('TI') and the OECD,[22] to which larger companies had reference for some time before the UKBA and which still remain relevant.[23] As a result, although the UK government was perhaps optimistic as regards the extent of corporate compliance within companies, and particularly small to medium companies, when it introduced the UKBA, the MoJ Guidance itself would not appear to

18 Some caution is appropriate when placing reliance on these statements, which do not appear to form part of the main statutory guidance itself and which were not part of the consultation.

19 On 3 October 2012, FTI Consulting reported on a survey of 571 board-level and senior and middle management respondents in UK companies, in which 40% of respondents believed the current economic climate is encouraging organisations to risk breaching the UK Bribery Act in order to win business, while just over a quarter (27%) did not believe the government will encourage regulators to pursue prosecutions in the current economic environment. A further one in five (21%) believe they will not be prosecuted for a breach of the Bribery Act, and a third (31%) believe the act exists mainly for appearance's sake and ethical guidelines.

20 2019 Select Committee report – 'The Ministry of Justice Guidance is less successful in providing small and medium enterprises with the information and advice they need to enable them to decide on a formal anti-bribery policy' https://publications.parliament.uk/pa/ld201719/ldselect/ldbribact/303/303.pdf

21 Now found in the US DoJ and SEC resource guide, 'U.S. Department of Justice and U.S. Securities and Exchange Commission, A Resource Guide to the U.S. Foreign Corrupt Practices Act at 57 (2nd edn, 2020), www.justice.gov/criminal-fraud/file/1292051/download/.

22 By way of examples only, see www.transparency.org/en/publications, as well as the work of the UN Global Compact.

23 Eg the anti-corruption section of the OECD website –www.oecd.org/corruption/keyoecdanti-corruptiondocuments.htm.

have been a 'quantum leap' for many larger companies and the international community.

Principles underpinning adequate procedures

8.24

In March 2011, the MoJ published statutory guidance regarding adequate procedures as required by section 9 of the UKBA.[24] The Guidance, which is 31 pages in total excluding its annex and 11 pages long in its explanation of the six key 'Principles',[25] sets out, at a high level, what is expected of commercial organisations wishing to rely on the adequate procedures defence. Throughout both the related Quick Start Guide and MoJ Guidance there is heavy emphasis on proportionality, a risk based approach and on actual implementation – as opposed to simply having policy documents 'on file', ie 'paper compliance'.[26]

8.25

The MoJ Guidance is 'not prescriptive' and does not create an exhaustive list of 'do's and do not's'. Specifically, it explains at page 6 as follows:

> '[T]he guidance is designed to be of general application and is formulated around six guiding principles, each followed by commentary and examples. The guidance is not prescriptive and is not a one-size-fits-all document. The question of whether an organisation had adequate procedures in place to prevent bribery in the context of a particular prosecution is a matter that can only be resolved by the *courts* taking into account the particular facts and circumstances of the case.' (emphasis added)

8.26

Despite the lack of clarity[27] on the precise requirements of the MoJ Guidance for any particular commercial organisation, set out below is an explanation of the overall approach that a company might consider taking to understand its risks and to implement appropriate adequate procedures.

---

24 See Appendix 3. The UKBA itself received Royal Assent on 8 April 2010. Its entry into force was originally set for April 2011 but was postponed to allow for further consultation on the MoJ Guidance required by s 9 of the Act.

25 Seven pages for the Quick Start Guide, which can be found at www.justice.gov.uk/downloads/legislation/bribery-act-2010-quick-start-guide.pdf.

26 See Lissack and Horlick on Bribery for an explanation of the progress of the 'proportionate' requirement prior to the Bribery Bill, and particularly the Joint Committee Report of 28 July 2009 which considered that 'guidance on 'adequate procedures' defence would be crucial, and must show that it would be interpreted in a flexible and proportionate manner'.

27 There is at the time of writing only a single piece of case law (*R v Skansen Interiors Limited*) as regards the interpretation of adequate procedures, although there is a growing amount of commentary.

Management approach to introducing anti-corruption compliance

8.27

Management approaches to introducing a programme to meet the challenges of anti-corruption compliance within the framework of the MoJ Guidance are explored below, but they often seem to have some or all of the following components:

(a) committing management to ethical behaviour and implementing adequate procedures;

(b) reviewing the existing corporate programme/culture against the MoJ (and perhaps additionally Transparency International) Guidance;

(c) making alterations to that programme's controls and policies using a risk based and proportionate approach;

(d) recording actions;

(e) recognising and communicating within all management levels of the company that 'paper compliance', ie issuing the policies, is necessary but not sufficient without active implementation; and

(f) monitoring progress over time/periodically benchmarking against companies with both similar commitments to anti-bribery and a similar risk profile/size.[28]

Methodology – planning your programme

8.28

There is no one single right or authorised way to plan a compliance programme. Truly, one size does not fit all. However, by way of example, a small to medium sized company operating in medium risk areas, without the complication of subsidiaries or joint ventures and concerned with higher risk issues, might consider following this simple three stage checklist:

---

28 Benchmarking and certification can be helpful for many companies. Often companies are willing and interested in such matters – some working through industry specific groups such as the Madison Group for banks, Transparency International's Business Integrity Forum UK (see www.transparency.org.uk/business-integrity-forum). ISO 37001 an anti-bribery management system (ABMS) standard for organisations published in October 2016 is also a consideration as is Trace Certification (www.traceinternational.org). The MOJ Guidance supports this sharing of information and industry standard setting by stating: '6.4 In addition, organisations might wish to consider seeking some form of external verification or assurance of the effectiveness of anti-bribery procedures. Some organisations may be able to apply for certified compliance with one of the independently-verified anti-bribery standards maintained by industrial sector associations or multilateral bodies. However, such certification may not necessarily mean that a commercial organisation's bribery prevention procedures are "adequate" for all purposes...'

- Stage 1
  - Consider what types of compliance risk will be included in the programme[29]
  - Read the MoJ Guidance and Quick Start Guide
  - Consider reading the US DoJ's Resource Guide[30] and related resources[31] and also the TI Checklist on Adequate Procedures[32]
  - Consider generally how the guidance applies to the businesses of the company and support functions
  - Conduct a risk assessment[33] led or supported by senior management, which engages with stakeholders in the process such as audit, legal, human resources and procurement.
- Stage 2
  - Decide on and communicate to a wide audience 'tone from the top' – including a zero tolerance to bribery and corruption[34]
  - Appoint/select a program manager(s)
  - Create a plan to implement and monitor the anti-corruption programme prioritising those more material risks identified in the risk assessment
  - Consider as part of the implementation programme the following:
    - Revised Code of Conduct/Anti-bribery Policy
    - Gifts and entertainment ('G&E') register and rules
    - Training of staff (including through e-learning)
    - Review of recording mechanisms and conflict rules to check they are fit for purpose
    - Code/contractual terms for higher risk service providers
    - Standard contractual terms
    - Due diligence of third parties and audit and monitoring of third parties using a risk-based approach

29 Non-bribery risks and not considered in any depth in this book, but a greater amount of compliance related guidance/commentary is often available than in the newer area of the UKBA.

30 US Department of Justice and U.S. Securities and Exchange Commission, A Resource Guide to the U.S. Foreign Corrupt Practices Act at 57 (2nd edn, 2020), www.justice.gov/criminal-fraud/file/1292051/download

31 US Department of Justice, U.S. Attorneys' Manual §9-47.120 (2019) ('FCPA Corporate Enforcement Policy'), www.justice.gov/jm/jm-9-47000-foreign-corrupt-practices-act-1977.

32 www.transparency.org.uk/sites/default/files/Adequate_Procedures_Checklist_PDF.pdf.

33 Risk assessments are considered in more depth within the chapter.

34 TI suggests a list of nine simple principles for SMEs, repeated in the Annex to 'Business Principles for Countering Bribery', SME Edition.

    - Speak up procedures allowing staff and others to raise concerns and questions without retaliation
  - Benchmark plans against companies of similar size and risk who have implemented adequate procedures
  - Consider seeking external advice on the adequacy of the programme from an experienced law firm, accountancy practice or suitable consultancy.
- Stage 3
  - Monitor of progress at regular intervals, with the oversight and input of senior management
  - Renew the risk assessment regularly (eg every two years or when business significantly changes)
  - Make recommendations to the board or relevant sub-committee regarding improvement, expansion or removal or relaxation of controls as appropriate to the identified risk and resources.

8.29

As regards external resources to assist with compliance programmes, unlike in the period immediately after the UKBA when there was only a small number of lawyers and compliance professionals working in this area in the UK (primarily on FCPA related matters given that there was one UK corporate prosecution for foreign corruption before 2010),[35] there are now many more experienced professionals, including law firms, accountancy practices and risk advisory firms. In addition, resources that might assist in planning or enhancing an adequate procedures programme are now readily available, including free resources such as the short Business Principles for Countering Bribery SME Edition published by TI[36] and Transparency International's compliance portal that collates helpful documents, check lists and analysis.[37]

---

35 After over 100 years of the 1906 Prevention of Corruption Act, *Mabey & Johnson* (September 2009) was the first conviction of a company for overseas corruption, and *Innospec* (March 2010) was the first joint corruption related settlement of a company with US and UK prosecuting authorities.

36 This free resource concludes as follows: 'the key to developing an effective Programme for countering bribery lies in: Recognising the benefits to your business; Identifying the risks; Agreeing a process to lower the risks, e.g. by having rules on gifts and entertainment; Communicating your Programme to your business partners; Keeping clear, accurate records, not only financial, but also of your decision to adopt your Programme and all your processes for countering bribery; Giving practical training on your Programme, Dealing effectively with incidents and concerns raised, Encouraging open discussion on issues arising, Continually reviewing your Programme for effectiveness.' – https://images.transparencycdn.org/images/2008_BusinessPrinciplesSME_EN.pdf.

37 www.antibriberyguidance.org/.

The starting point

8.30

Companies with a good corporate environment and governance will find new clear, practical and accessible anti-corruption processes straightforward and an extension of usual working practice. However, where internal processes are confusing, change is frequent and corporate governance is improving but not at industry best practice, introducing an anti-corruption programme can be much more problematic. In other words, good anti-corruption compliance relies on good corporate governance.

8.31

As regards that governance, for companies that have 'further to travel', it will be particularly important to have 'top-level commitment', adequate resource, an inclusive and informed planning stage and realistic timeframes/measurable objectives for implementation of the changes being adopted.

The MoJ Guidance on Adequate Procedures

8.32

Whatever an organisation's starting point in terms of capacity to create a working compliance programme, the primary resource for UKBA compliance remains the MoJ Guidance and its six principles, which are listed below and examined in the following paragraphs.

- Principle 1: proportionate procedures (paragraph 8.34 onwards)
- Principle 2: top-level commitment (paragraph 8.82 onwards)
- Principle 3: risk assessment (paragraph 8.84 onwards)
- Principle 4: due diligence (paragraph 8.107 onwards)
- Principle 5: communication (including training) (paragraph 8.114 onwards)
- Principle 6: monitoring and review (paragraph 8.125 onwards)

8.33

In this chapter, where it seems appropriate, there are suggested ways of combining the adequate procedures envisioned by the UKBA with other controls to prevent the company itself becoming a victim of passive bribery, mitigate US FCPA risk and reduce other regulatory compliance risks.

Principle 1: policies and procedures, including record keeping

8.34

Principle 1 of the MoJ Guidance provides a high-level description of a number of areas that comprise 'proportionate procedures'. However, given that Principle 1 contains a mix of aims, many of which themselves form part of separate principles (eg top-level commitment and risk assessment), this section considers only those issues that appear mainly or solely within Principle 1.

8.35

The MoJ Guidance summarises Principle 1 as follows:

> 'Principle 1
>
> **Proportionate procedures**
>
> A commercial organisation's procedures to prevent bribery by persons associated with it are proportionate to the bribery risks it faces and to the nature, scale and complexity of the commercial organisation's activities. They are also clear, practical, accessible, effectively implemented and enforced.'

Proportionality is at the heart of the MoJ Guidance. However, understanding the meaning in practical terms is a continuing difficulty as it has different meanings in different situations and there is currently no particularly helpful case law clarification of the definition. The most helpful advice is contained in the MoJ Guidance itself, which states as follows:

> '1.2 Adequate bribery prevention procedures ought to be proportionate to the bribery risks that the organisation faces. An initial assessment of risk across the organisation is therefore a necessary first step. To a certain extent the level of risk will be linked to the size of the organisation and the nature and complexity of its business, but size will not be the only determining factor. Some small organisations can face quite significant risks, and will need more extensive procedures than their counterparts facing limited risks. However, *small organisations are unlikely to need procedures that are as extensive as those of a large multi-national organisation.* For example, *a very* small business may be able to rely heavily on periodic oral briefings to communicate its policies while a large one may need to rely on extensive written communication.
>
> 1.3 The level of risk that organisations face will also vary with the type and nature of the persons associated with it. For example, a commercial organisation that properly assesses that there is no risk of bribery on the part of one of its associated persons will accordingly require nothing in the way of procedures to prevent bribery in the context of

that relationship. By the same token the bribery risks associated with reliance on a third party agent representing a commercial organisation in negotiations with foreign public officials may be assessed as significant and accordingly require much more in the way of procedures to mitigate those risks. Organisations are likely to need to select procedures to cover a broad range of risks but any consideration by a court in an individual case of the adequacy of procedures is likely necessarily to focus on those procedures designed to prevent bribery on the part of the associated person committing the offence in question.' (emphasis added)

8.36

On the basis of the above, and emphasising the benefit clear industry standards and case law will bring in due course, the guidance on proportionality asks companies to identify risk and apportion resources against the risk. It is perhaps vague in relation to the proper proportion of resources to use against risks, but for small, low-risk companies (eg those which trade in the UK and only trade rarely in higher risk areas) it appears to indicate in this and other passages that it is proportionate for the purposes of Principle 1 for such companies to have few formal anti-corruption specific procedures, but nevertheless to have a risk assessment, a clear, accessible and practical code of conduct and some type of training and periodic communication of the compliance programme, even if done orally.

8.37

In contrast, where a commercial organisation, either small or medium in size, is dealing in higher-risk areas (as defined by its risk assessment), it seems it will be proportionate or at least prudent to apply many or all of the policies and procedures suggested by the MoJ Guidance as 'indicative'. These include, for instance, managing contracts, creating financial controls and taking mitigating steps when hiring employees (see paragraph 1.7 of the MoJ Guidance). All such steps essentially flow from the following overview of the requirement contained in Principle 1 at paragraph 1.6:

'Procedures

1.6 Commercial organisations' bribery prevention policies are likely to include certain common elements. As an indicative and not exhaustive list, an organisation may wish to cover in its policies:

- its commitment to bribery prevention (see Principle 2)
- its general approach to mitigation of specific bribery risks, such as those arising from the conduct of intermediaries and agents, or those associated with hospitality and promotional expenditure,

facilitation payments or political and charitable donations or contributions; (see Principle 3 on risk assessment)

- an overview of its strategy to implement its bribery prevention policies.'

8.38

For larger companies in higher-risk areas, it appears even more is required, as they may be expected to consider, for instance, more detailed controls, more access to expert advice, investigative tools and additional monitoring. For such companies this would be likely to include investments in relevant technology, for instance in relation to third party management systems that apply due diligence consistently. Nevertheless, it does not appear from the MoJ Guidance that even the largest companies are expected to take a 'gold plated approach' and spend considerable sums on risks that (even if they eventuate) would have seemed unlikely or very unlikely to any reasonable person at the time the relevant risks arose. By way of example, it would be inappropriate to commission potentially expensive bespoke external due diligence reports on low risk and low value counterparties.

Clear, practical and accessible policies and procedures

8.39

Principle 1 encourages the use of plain language and easy to use controls. In practice this means, for instance, guarding against the overuse of acronyms, setting out policies clearly and logically, seeking to build anti-corruption controls into business processes and indicating to employees and others where further guidance can be obtained.[38] Simplicity and efficiency are key, and when creating anti-bribery documents, a programme manager should keep in mind that the organisation may eventually have to persuade a jury of twelve ordinary people, who may not be familiar with 'corporate' language or bureaucracy, that its anti-corruption programme was 'clear, practical and accessible' at the time bribes were paid.

8.40

In terms of accessibility, companies may choose to provide compliance documents electronically, eg by email or better still make documents available on-line through intranet pages and to allow access to hard copies at larger offices.

38 See also Lissack and Horlick on Bribery, para 6.49

8.41

Where intranet web links are used, they should of course ideally be easy to search for and find, so that in just a few clicks it is possible for employees to locate all the primary resources they need. Email communication can also be particularly helpful in targeting more specific groups, although in many companies and countries only a minority of employees may have access to computers at work. As a consequence, it may not be appropriate to use email or an intranet as the sole means of communication. Likewise, where a company operates across borders, thought should also be given to whether compliance documents – particularly key documents such as a code of conduct or anti-corruption policy – can be provided in different languages. Applying a risk-based approach, these translations are particularly important for employees in higher risk activities or working in higher risk jurisdictions.

What does 'practical' mean?

8.42

'Practicality' is a key concept for Principle 1 and has a number of meanings depending on the sense in which it is used. From its overall context in the MoJ Guidance, in one sense 'practical' appears to have a meaning which is closely associated with the concept of implementation and integrity, eg 'having those controls and processes you say you have and doing the things you say you do in your Code of Conduct'. In another connected sense 'practical' appears to mean creating a system which is both cogent and easy to use, eg providing sufficient guidance and support and process for employees and service providers to operate and efficiently abide by the controls put in place. By way of example, for medium sized businesses this could for instance result in amending certain job scopes to include an anti-corruption remit or a key performance indicator for compliant behaviour. It might also result in amending procurement processes to include anti-corruption controls as required steps before final authorisation and providing sufficient guidance for relevant employees on 'red flags' that they feel able to either escalate material issues or take mitigating steps.

Audit and financial controls

8.43

The MoJ Guidance in Principle 1 dedicates few words to internal accounting controls and record keeping;[39] which of course is, for UK commercial entities,

39 '1.7 The procedures put in place to implement an organisation's bribery prevention policies should be designed to mitigate identified risks as well as to prevent deliberate unethical conduct on the part of associated persons. The following is an indicative and not exhaustive list of the topics that bribery prevention procedures might embrace depending on the particular risks faced: … Financial and commercial controls such as adequate bookkeeping, auditing and approval of expenditure.'

dealt with primarily in separate company- and partnership-related legislation.[40] However, in addition to the above, and arguments made in support of retaining evidence given the standard and burden of proof (see para 8.20 above), internal financial controls can also be prudent in any event given their importance to the US FCPA.[41]

8.44

This is, therefore, one of the areas where a joined-up approach with the FCPA is particularly helpful, as the FCPA has and continues to put record keeping 'front and centre' in its investigations and prosecutions, examples of which are provided in Chapter 2.[42]

8.45

Given the US approach, any company with links to the US on which jurisdiction could be founded may want to give particular consideration when adopting adequate procedures to reviewing its internal accounting provisions, in particular to gauge whether they are fit for purpose from a UKBA and FCPA anti-corruption perspective. Here, particular focus and training on review of invoices to spot dubious claims for 'miscellaneous expenses', unsupported 'commissions' or other such payments may be particularly useful.[43] Likewise, controls over payments in cash and funds associated with marketing and charitable donations could help to ensure all payments are not only ethical and commercial but also properly recorded.[44] For more on this area, the 2020 Department of Justice and the Securities and Exchange Commission resource guide '*A Resource Guide to the U.S. Foreign Corrupt Practices Act Second Edition*', which is available on-line, provides helpful assistance.[45]

Employment contracts and recruitment processes

8.46

Employees of relevant commercial organisations pursuant to section 8(5) of the UKBA[46] are specifically presumed, unless proven otherwise, to be 'associated

40 See also *Lissack and Horlick on Bribery*, para 6.50.
41 See Chapter 2, for more information on the accounting provisions in the FCPA
42 See Chapter 2 Case Study on Novartis who admitted to violating both the anti-bribery and the accounting provisions of the FCPA and undertook three-year-long obligations to self-report back to the agencies once a year on the companies' progress in enhancing their compliance programs and internal controls.
43 See Panalpina settlement (www.sec.gov/litigation/litreleases/2010/lr21727.htm).
44 Schering Plough case: see *Securities and Exchange Commission v Schering-Plough Corporation*, United States District Court for the District of Columbia, Civil Action No. 1:04CV00945 (PLF) and www.sec.gov/litigation/litreleases/lr18740.htm.
45 US Department of Justice and U.S. Securities and Exchange Commission, A Resource Guide to the U.S. Foreign Corrupt Practices Act at 57 (2nd edn, 2020), www.justice.gov/criminal-fraud/file/1292051/download [hereinafter 'Resource Guide'].
46 www.legislation.gov.uk/ukpga/2010/23/section/8.

persons', and therefore their payment of bribes for the organisation's benefit creates an immediate potential section 7 corporate liability. Training, dealt with below under a separate heading, is one mitigation of this risk. However, pre-contract, recruitment processes are also helpful given that employees may present particular corruption risks because of previous unethical behaviour.

8.47

The MoJ Guidance within Principle 1 states as follows:

> 'The procedures put in place to implement an organisation's bribery prevention policies should be designed to mitigate identified risks as well as to prevent deliberate unethical conduct on the part of associated persons. The following is an indicative and not exhaustive list of the topics that bribery prevention procedures might embrace depending on the particular risks faced:
>
> - Direct and indirect employment, including recruitment, terms and conditions.'
>
> And in relation to Principle 4, Due Diligence:
>
> '4.6 A commercial organisation's employees are presumed to be persons 'associated' with the organisation for the purposes of the Bribery Act. The organisation may wish, therefore, to incorporate in its recruitment and human resources procedures an appropriate level of due diligence to mitigate the risks of bribery being undertaken by employees which is proportionate to the risk associated with the post in question. *Due diligence is unlikely to be needed in relation to lower risk posts.*' (emphasis added)

8.48

As a result, in addition to taking steps to appropriately discipline rogue employees when an issue arises, making enquires around employees' backgrounds, other than in low risk posts (such as taking up references for, at least, key positions) is envisaged. Where red flags arise, further investigation is suggested, perhaps including for high or very high risk employees some kind of external desk top or third party provider due diligence (such as obtaining a relatively inexpensive desk top report, either internally or from providers, which include amongst others Exiger and Dow Jones.

8.49

In addition (although not referred to in the MoJ Guidance), to help mitigate risk further, it may well also be sensible (in order to mitigate FCPA risk and reduce UKBA risk) to ask as part of the standard recruitment process whether candidates are close relations of government officials.

8.50

The aim of the above question is of course not to put an applicant with government connections at an advantage or disadvantage (as employment should be on the basis of merit alone). The aim is to allow corporate mitigations to be put in place if a successful candidate is closely connected with relevant government decision makers – mitigations that protect the applicant, the company and the relevant public official from allegations of conflicts of interest.

8.51

Although this may seem intrusive, particularly in countries with a high proportion of government officials, from a practical perspective most future employees closely connected with government officials will not be connected with officials relevant to a company's business and therefore will not present a higher corruption risk, eg a relative who is a policeman or traffic warden will rarely be high risk. However, there are situations where it is important to capture, understand and mitigate risk, eg where the future employee is the son of a public official who has decision making rights over licenses required by the company to operate in a particular country.

8.52

Whilst there is no one 'right way' of mitigating this risk, mitigations can potentially include the following: (i) asking or requiring the employee to recuse/remove themselves from dealing with their relatives on business matters and assigning such matters to other employees; (ii) 'flagging' the relationship in writing with the relevant third party or government department to create transparency; (iii) introducing further oversight over the application process and remuneration to make sure both are recorded and are commercial and fair; (iv) including in the employee's contract further relevant anti-corruption language; (v) putting the employee through anti-corruption training soon after joining the organisation; and (vi) entering the relationship on any relevant conflict register or otherwise making relevant management aware of the potential risk.

8.53

The US position and practice may be more developed in this area (although limited to concerns relating to non-US public officials) but the risks and attention it receives are clear given amongst other matters the US Securities and Exchange Commission-led investigation of investment banks as regards alleged systematic attempts to recruit the children of high ranking public officials.[47]

---

47 www.bloomberg.com/news/articles/2019-08-22/deutsche-bank-to-pay-16-8-million-to-settle-sec-bribery-claims.

Further mitigating risk within Principle 1

8.54

Risk assessment and due diligence are explained under paragraphs 8.84 onwards and 8.107 onwards respectively as they fall under their own Principles within the MoJ Guidance. However, both Principles are essentially concerned with gathering data and information on the basis of which a company can make informed decisions –in particular to take steps that mitigate risk in relation to Principle 1 (proportionate policies and procedures).

8.55

In relation to often difficult decisions on how to mitigate risk, eg whether to proceed with a transaction, whether to do so with mitigations in place or whether simply to walk away, the MoJ Guidance provides little practical advice, perhaps leading some companies to act as if due diligence is an end in itself.[48] However, the MoJ Guidance suggests within Principle 1 that a company of any size embrace within its controls '[g]overnance of business relationships with all other [ie non employee] associated persons including pre and post contractual agreements.' The governance of business relationships post-due diligence and practical management of risk in the context of Principle 1 is, therefore, explored below as regards contract terms, certifications, dealing with new higher risk counterparties and review of risk in current relationships, whistleblowing and 'speak up lines', gifts and entertainment and other related matters.

Contract terms

8.56

Assuming that due diligence leads to an assessment that business can potentially be undertaken with a counterparty, it is often the case that contract terms are an important early risk mitigation.

8.57

Contract terms even in low risk contracts with service providers often show the principal parties' intent to conduct business with zero-tolerance to bribery, and should benefit from specifically defining the scope of work as well as being entered into on a commercial basis, ie at a fair price for the work being completed.[49] The MoJ Guidance does not include or prescribe contract provisions but, by way of example, they could include an obligation to comply with relevant anti-corruption laws (eg the UKBA and the FCPA), a clause explaining what a bribe is and that all bribes are prohibited in both passive and

48 Although it does provide, for reference, some case studies as illustrations of potential practical steps.
49 A transparent and fair tender process can be of assistance in this regard.

active form, including as regards small bribes or facilitation payments,[50] and a termination or termination/suspension provision. On occasion they may also include an obligation on the service provider to allow an audit of books for compliance with the clause and/or an obligation on the service provider to report breaches to the principal.

8.58

The more risk associated with the contract, the more likely additional terms are, such as contract terms that no public official will indirectly benefit from the contract, broader audit provisions or warrantees that the company is not under investigation to its knowledge for breaches of anti-corruption law. Variations on the clauses, some of which can be complicated and lengthy depending on the risk and matter involved, are reportedly available from bodies such as the International Chamber of Commerce and through other trade organisations. Law firms also typically have standard low, medium and high-risk clauses that they can provide and tailor, at relatively small cost, to individual commercial organisations or transactions.[51]

Certification

8.59

Contractual certification by third parties to periodically confirm in writing that they are compliant with their contractual anti-corruption obligations, a practice reportedly widely used in the US, is not referred to in the MoJ Guidance, either within Principle 1 or elsewhere. However, certification can be said to fit within the ethos of Principle 1.

8.60

There is anecdotal evidence that requests for third-party certification are a growing trend in the UK, and that often these comprise the following: a request for the service provider to confirm that they have met their contractual obligations as regards anti-bribery in the relevant contractual period (often one year); confirmation that they are not under investigation by a regulator or prosecutor, and confirmation that notice has been provided to the principal of any material breaches of anti-corruption contract terms.

8.61

Although certificates are potentially a helpful tool for mitigating risk and meeting UKBA standards, particularly for high risk service providers, companies

50 For a discussion of adequate procedures as applied to small bribes and so called 'facilitation payments', see Chapter 5.

51 Certain types of contracts have more developed or industry specific clauses, eg the AIPN and OGUK standard anti-corruption clauses for joint ventures in the oil and gas sector.

subject to the UKBA would be prudent not to overly rely on certificates given, as stated above, that they are not referred to in the MoJ Guidance. In addition to this, although certificates provide comfort, that comfort is based on trust. Such trust is unlikely to extend to third parties that show clear indications of not acting in accordance with their anti-corruption obligations, eg where they state in meetings that they 'still have to make necessary local payments, even if illegal, for cultural reasons'.

Dealing with new higher risk counterparties

8.62

Due diligence programmes and related electronic third party management systems will often screen and then separate low, medium and high-risk counterparts using risk matrices. For high risk service providers in particular, eg those most likely to be in positions to bribe for a company's benefit, it will then be helpful for a company to develop bespoke processes and controls to mark these providers out for special treatment and monitoring. Suitable controls to manage the potentially increased risk can be either built into existing technology, policies and procedures such as those relating to account opening, finance and procurement or be organised in stand alone form relying more on specialist advisors.

8.63

A checklist containing practical potential measures that could help mitigate the risk of a high risk service providers might include some of the following non-exhaustive list of mitigations:

- requiring more restrictions on the scope of the work being undertaken;
- conducting repeat due diligence more frequently (eg once every two rather than three years) and using daily so called negative news monitoring software to find 'red flags';
- requiring training for relevant staff prior to or soon after a contract is place;[52]
- arranging regular in person or on-line monitoring and meetings to assess compliance aims;
- encouraging the third party company to adopt a suitable Code of Conduct or abide by the principal's Code or a statement of ethics;
- requiring the company to conduct due diligence on its contractors conducting work in relation to the principal;

52 See also Principle 5: Communication (including training) from paragraph 8.115.

- requiring the third party to include anti-corruption contract language in contracts with any contractors it retains in relation to the principal;
- obtaining further appropriate anti-corruption contractual obligations;
- periodic and proportionate use of supplier audit provisions;
- allowing break clauses in the contract (ie no 'evergreen contracts') and allowing termination on reasonable good faith suspicion of bribery or for material breach of the bribery clause;
- meeting or talking with senior management to reinforce the zero-tolerance message; or
- requiring periodic certifications that work is being undertaken in accordance with anti-corruption contractual language or, where appropriate, the Code of Conduct of the principal.

8.64

A further step could involve informing the third party company that the principal company's own whistleblowing/speak up service is available to any employees of the service provider who want to raise issues or questions regarding bribery and corruption.

Reviewing risk associated with historic counterparties

8.65

As regards service providers with which the commercial organisation is already in a historic relationship, the MoJ Guidance makes the following statement:

> '1.5 The Government recognises that applying these procedures retrospectively to existing associated persons is more difficult, but this should be done over time, adopting a risk-based approach and with due allowance for what is practicable and the level of control over existing arrangements.'

8.66

At the time the MoJ Guidance was published in 2011, this statement was intended to allow a 'breathing space' whilst companies reviewed the existing contract parties, of which in some cases there would be many hundreds or even thousands. However, that 'breathing space' has certainly come to an end and any company coming to this area or the UK for the first time would be prudent to start assessing current and historic relationships sooner rather than later. As the passage from the MoJ Guidance suggests, identifying parties for review can be done using a risk-based approach, eg prioritising high risk service providers and perhaps only reviewing other contracts as they come up naturally for renegotiation or renewal.

Speak up

8.67

Whistle blowing procedures or 'speak-up lines' are referred to within Principle 1 of the MoJ Guidance as follows:

> '1.7 The procedures put in place to implement an organisation's bribery prevention policies should be designed to mitigate identified risks as well as to prevent deliberate unethical conduct on the part of associated persons. The following is an indicative and not exhaustive list of the topics that bribery prevention procedures might embrace depending on the particular risks faced:
>
> - The reporting of bribery including 'speak up' or 'whistle blowing' procedures.'

And later in the MoJ Guidance under Principle 5, Communication, as follows:

> 'Another important aspect of internal communications is the establishment of a secure, confidential and accessible means for internal or external parties to raise concerns about bribery on the part of associated persons, to provide suggestions for improvement of bribery prevention procedures and controls and for requesting advice. These so called 'speak up' procedures can amount to a very helpful management tool for commercial organisations with diverse operations that may be in many countries. If these procedures are to be effective there must be adequate protection for those reporting concerns.'

8.68

Given the emphasis on 'speak up' facilities, it seems that even a company of medium size and medium risk should seriously consider implementing a 'speak up process' and 'speak up' recording.

8.69

In addition to the MoJ Guidance, speak up lines could help a company internally manage whistleblowers without involvement of prosecutors. In this regard, the SFO maintains a reporting line online,[53] but it is the US that has perhaps done the most to influence the adoption of internal speak up procedures through the Dodd-Frank Act,[54] which has further incentivised international companies (including those incorporated in the UK but with links to the US) to adopt or improve internal reporting processes. Specifically, the Dodd-Frank Act requires

53 The on-line reporting remains active through the SFO website, although the dedicated phone line has been removed some time ago. (www.sfo.gov.uk/contact-us/reporting-serious-fraud-bribery-corruption/).

54 Dodd-Frank Wall Street Reform and Consumer Protection Act 2010.

US authorities to pay rewards to those who speak up of up to 30% of recovered fines (with no maximum).[55]

8.70

With 5,200 reports in the 2019 fiscal year covering 70 countries, some significant rewards already paid and with the largest number of reports outside the US coming from Canada, Germany, and the United Kingdom,[56] the argument in favour of encouraging internal reporting rather than encouraging, by default, external reporting is relatively clear – even without the advantages of being able to monitor and improve internal governance that also arise.[57]

8.71

In practice there are a number of methods for a company to introduce speak up systems. These range from dedicated phone numbers and/or emails staffed by an external agency or independent internal company group who guarantee anonymity for employees to, for smaller and perhaps less resourced companies, simply providing the name and telephone number of the company secretary, legal officer, or other trusted person.

8.72

The well-known charity Protect (previously Public Concern at Work) is one UK-based group able to provide an anonymous 'speak up' line for employees, but it seems many different routes are potentially acceptable in relation to the MoJ Guidance. Crucial to a 'speak up' line's success is its ability to engender trust in employees that they will be listened to and that action will be taken where appropriate. Put simply, employees will not keep on risking reporting issues to the potential detriment of colleagues where nothing will be done. Whatever system used will therefore often be run with the intention of keeping recipients' information and name as confidential as reasonably possible, listening to and recording issues raised and escalating (and investigating) any material concerns. Furthermore, sometimes anonymous reporting will also be

---

55 The US Dodd-Frank Act provides for a reward of 10 to 30% to a whistleblower with appropriate evidence if the fine levied by the SEC relates to a 'covered action', which is defined as one that results in monetary sanctions exceeding US$1 million. As recently as 22 October 2020, the SEC announced that it was issuing a record whistleblower award of over US$114 million to a whistleblower consisting of an approximately US$52 million award in connection with the SEC case and an approximately US$62 million award arising out of the related actions by another agency. The SEC has awarded approximately US$676 million to 108 individuals since issuing its first award in 2012.

56 2019 Annual Report to Congress on the Dodd-Frank Whistleblower Program (www.sec.gov/files/sec-2019-annual%20report-whistleblower%20program.pdf).

57 Note that the majority of respondents to Public Concern at Work's consultation in 2013 reportedly were not in favour of introducing US style large financial incentives for reporting in the UK for reasons including that it was 'inconsistent with the culture or philosophy of the UK' and 'could undermine the credibility of witnesses in future criminal or civil proceedings'. As regards the first of these points, the cultural issue is perhaps more acute in countries such as France and Germany, which have long and primarily negative memories of 'informants' or the 'dénuncer' during and in the years following World War II.

possible, particularly where a third-party vendor is used to collate reports and add another layer of independence to the process. Where possible it can also be appropriate to give the person making the report at least basic information regarding the progress of any follow-up work – having regard to the need not to prejudice any investigation, lose 'privilege' over legal documentation or negatively affect others' rights and reasonable expectations.[58]

8.73

It should go without saying that although an employee may not be given an amnesty (or complete amnesty) for his or her active wrongdoing in any corruption, no retaliation should occur against the employee for making a report. Retaliation, as well as being unethical, is legally counter-productive as it would be likely to hinder further whistleblowing and a company's opportunity to 'monitor' its compliance programme pursuant to Principle 6 of the MoJ Guidance.[59]

Gifts and entertainment

8.74

Chapter 14 considers in detail the area of corporate hospitality and broader gifts and entertainment, including a sample policy. These matters are therefore dealt with only briefly below to put into further context the procedures commonly associated with the authorising and recording of gifts and entertainment.

8.75

The MoJ Guidance states as follows:

> 'Bona fide hospitality and promotional, or other business expenditure which seeks to improve the image of a commercial organisation, better to present products and services, or establish cordial relations, is recognised as an established and important part of doing business and it is not the intention of the Act to criminalise such behaviour. The Government does not intend for the Act to prohibit reasonable and proportionate hospitality and promotional or other similar business expenditure intended for these purposes. It is, however, clear that hospitality and promotional or other similar business expenditure can be employed as bribes.
>
> In order to amount to a bribe under section 6 there must be an intention for a financial or other advantage to influence the official in his or her

58 Companies may also wish to have reference to the Protect (formerly Public Concern at Work) Code of Practice published on 26 November 2018 – https://s3-eu-west-1.amazonaws.com/public-concern-at-work/wp-content/uploads/images/2018/11/26145923/PCaW_COP_FINAL.pdf

59 Also note the Public Interest Disclosure Act 1988 and that a qualifying disclosure includes where 'a criminal offence has been committed, is being committed or is likely to be committed'.

official role and thereby secure business or a business advantage. In this regard, it may be in some circumstances that hospitality or promotional expenditure in the form of travel and accommodation costs does not even amount to "a financial or other advantage" to the relevant official because it is a cost that would otherwise be borne by the relevant foreign Government rather than the official him or herself.'

8.76

Per Chapter 14 of this book, for most companies compliance with the MoJ Guidance above does not translate to a ban on entertainment or gifts or to considerable reduction in genuine business entertainment. It is misnomer that the UKBA or the FCPA prevent all types of entertainment and gifts. Care should be taken, but provided that entertainment or gifts are not lavish or in aggregate disproportionate and they are not given (a) when knowing that receipt would breach the recipient's entertainment policy or (b) with the intent to improperly influence, normal reasonable business relationship building and technical showcasing is allowable.

8.77

The UK Guidance has already been set out above[60] but a similar position in the US can be illustrated through the DoJ Resource Guide example below:

> 'Q. At the trade show, Company A invites a dozen current and prospective customers out for drinks, and pays the moderate bar tab. Some of the current and prospective customers are foreign officials under the FCPA. Is Company A in violation of the FCPA?
>
> A. No. Again, the FCPA was not designed to prohibit all forms of hospitality to foreign officials. While the cost here may be more substantial than the beverages, snacks, and promotional items provided at the booth [a previous example], and the invitees specifically selected, there is still nothing to suggest corrupt intent.'

8.78

As regards procedure relating to gifts and entertainment, the following is a non-exhaustive list of relevant basic information often retained on an electronic register:

- Date of entertainment/gift
- Person entertained/recipient (name and role) by whom (name and role)
- Reason for entertaining/gift (eg maintenance of the relationship)

60 The forward to the MoJ Guidance is apparently perhaps even more permissive, stating 'Rest assured – no one wants to stop firms getting to know their clients by taking them to events like Wimbledon or the Grand Prix.'

- Amount
- Form of gift or entertainment.

8.79

This information can both be used as part of an authorisation process, requiring line manager approval or even perhaps over certain thresholds compliance or legal review/advice, as part of record keeping and to help to meet the monitoring obligation.

Political donations

8.80

Political donations are identified in the MoJ Guidance as an area to be covered in anti-bribery controls. However, little change is usually necessary for UK companies as many of them in any event adopt a restrictive approach to political donations, being sensitive to potential reputational damage, shareholder actions and lobbying concerns. Commonly, UK companies per the UK Companies Act 2006 (and its predecessor) require donations to a political party to be authorised by a prior ordinary resolution of the shareholders in the required form.[61]

8.81

Material regarding UK law on this complicated area is limited, but notably includes Smyth CBE, Barratt and Campbell, *The Law of Political Donations* by (Wildy Simmonds & Hill, 2012).

Principle 2: top level commitment

8.82

The MoJ Guidance defines and explains top level commitment, also sometimes called 'tone from the top' as follows:

> '*Top-level commitment*
>
> The top-level management of a commercial organisation (be it a board of directors, the owners or any other equivalent body or person) are committed to preventing bribery by persons associated with it. They foster a culture within the organisation in which bribery is never acceptable.'

61 The 2006 Act, Part 14, regarding control of political donations and expenditure, applies to political expenditure and contributions within the EU or donations to EU political organisations as well as political donations to independent election candidates. Note further that in a number of other jurisdictions political donations by companies are prohibited or severely restricted.

…

'2.2 *Whatever the size, structure or market of a commercial organisation,* top-level management commitment to bribery prevention is likely to include:

(1) communication of the organisation's anti-bribery stance, and

(2) an appropriate degree of involvement in developing bribery prevention procedures.' (emphasis added)

'… whatever the appropriate model, top-level engagement is likely to reflect the following elements:

- Selection and training of senior managers to lead anti-bribery work where appropriate.
- Leadership on key measures such as a code of conduct.
- Endorsement of all bribery prevention related publications.
- Leadership in awareness raising and encouraging transparent dialogue throughout the organisation so as to seek to ensure effective dissemination of anti-bribery policies and procedures to employees, subsidiaries, and associated persons, etc.
- Engagement with relevant associated persons and external bodies, such as sectoral organisations and the media, to help articulate the organisation's policies.
- Specific involvement in high profile and critical decision making where appropriate.
- Assurance of risk assessment.
- General oversight of breaches of procedures and the provision of feedback to the board or equivalent, where appropriate, on levels of compliance.'

8.83

Although approaches will vary between companies, the above and the remainder of the MoJ Guidance in this area could for many companies at least partly be translated into the following practical steps:

- Inclusion in the Code of Conduct of a clear 'zero-tolerance approach' to bribery and reference to related policies and procedures endorsed by the CEO. A selection can be found online but TI provides the following example:

  'The company has a zero tolerance of bribery and corruption. This policy extends to all the company's business dealings and transactions in all countries in which it or its subsidiaries and associates operate.

This policy is given force in a detailed anti-bribery programme which is regularly revised to capture changes in law, reputation demands and changes in the business. All directors and employees are required to comply with this policy.'[62]

- Periodic re-enforcement (eg every one or two years) of a personal and public 'zero-tolerance message' from the CEO or similar leadership figures to employees through the use of meetings, email or hard copy correspondence.
- Optionally, messages from the CEO or directors at the start of e-learning or presentation based anti-corruption training.
- Board items relating to corruption issues or, for higher-risk companies, board sub-committees or ethics committees engaged more specifically with ethics/corruption issues, monitoring, approval of policies and receipt/review of risk assessments (for medium sized companies this may fall within the audit or finance committee).
- As regards senior to middle management and implementation, the appointment of programme manager or single points of accountability for the adequate procedures programme, reporting to the board, CEO or a relevant high-profile committee.

Principle 3: risk assessment

8.84

The MoJ Guidance relating to Principle 3 concerning risk assessment is a central tenet of anti-corruption practice, and is essentially the basis for most if not all activity and planning related to UKBA anti-corruption programmes as well as the allocation of resources and expenditure. Although not prescriptive, the MoJ Guidance, repeated below, suggests the process will be 'informed' and that the assessment will be 'documented':

> 'Risk Assessment
>
> The commercial organisation assesses the nature and extent of its exposure to potential external *and internal* risks of bribery on its behalf by persons associated with it. The assessment is periodic, informed *and documented*.' (emphasis added)
>
> '3.3 Risk assessment procedures that enable the commercial organisation accurately to identify and prioritise the risks it faces will, whatever its size, activities, customers or markets, usually reflect a few basic characteristics. These are:

62 TI, 'The 2010 UK Bribery Act Adequate Procedures', first published July 2010.

- Oversight of the risk assessment by top level management.
- Appropriate resourcing – this should reflect the scale of the organisation's business and the need to identify and prioritise all relevant risks.
- Identification of the internal and external information sources that will enable risk to be assessed and reviewed.
- Due diligence enquiries (see Principle 4).
- Accurate and appropriate documentation of the risk assessment and its conclusions.'

8.85

Given, as indicated above, that the risk assessment is a cornerstone of adequate procedures, and informs all other decisions, it is helpful at the outset of an assessment to create a realistic, inclusive and data/due diligence based process to ensure as far as reasonably possible that the risk assessment is robust and defensible. Where possible and assessment should also use and build upon already existing compliance related management information that could for instance be taken directly from compliance registers and due diligence systems.

8.86

There is little guidance for SMEs, but for very small companies with low or even medium risk, it is suggested that their risk assessment may involve discussing with relevant staff how they see the risks arising given their experience and information available to them, considering the TI Corruption Perceptions Index[63] or similar index, considering where corruption has arisen before in their business, looking at the strength/availability of their own resources and controls and recording where they consider the risks are most likely to arise. The outcome would usually be documented and could be repeated on an annual basis or every two years (perhaps longer) and updated as and when the nature of the risk materially changes, eg on a small company deciding to move its business into a new higher-risk country.[64]

8.87

For small or medium companies often operating in high-risk areas, or indeed for larger companies in a similar situation, a more formal and in depth approach is more likely to be prudent.

---

63 www.transparency.org/en/cpi/2020.

64 MoJ Guidance '3.4 As a commercial organisation's business evolves, so will the bribery risks it faces and hence so should its risk assessment. For example, the risk assessment that applies to a commercial organisation's domestic operations might not apply when it enters a new market in a part of the world in which it has not done business before (see Principle 6 for more on this).'

8.88

Whatever their size, companies with higher-risk profiles could save time and money by considering during their planning phase either or both of the main free resources in how to structure a risk assessment: TI's 'Diagnosing Bribery Risk',[65] the UN Global Compact's 'A Guide for Anti-Corruption Risk Assessment 2013'[66] and UNDOC's guide 'An Anti-Corruption Ethics and Compliance Programme for Business: A Practical Guide[67]'

8.89

Recognising the unusual depth of freely available resources, and given that TI's and the UN's documents run to hundreds of pages, this Chapter will not seek to develop or explore each of the many themes relevant to the area but will outline central principles and key practical issues for the practitioner embarking on, or updating, a corruption risk assessment.

Risk types

8.90

The MoJ Guidance sets out five risk categories for assessing risk, which are '*country risk*', '*sectoral risk*', '*transaction risk*', '*business opportunity risk*' and '*business partnership risk*'. As these divisions of risks may be unfamiliar, each type is summarised below.

8.91

Country risk relates to risks derived from the country in which business activities occur. The risk for some countries is higher because, for instance, there is lower enforcement of bribery laws, bribery is more accepted within business, small bribes are often part of day to day transactions, or bribery laws are either unclear, too narrow or are otherwise not a sufficient deterrent.

8.92

Most companies will operate in only a few countries, but whether an organisation operates across one or one hundred countries, the starting point for many in considering country risk is the TI's ubiquitous and freely available

65 The guide authored by Will Kenyon of PwC was published in July 2013 and was created with reference to an expert committee of financial and economic crime lawyers working in-house, including this author. The guide contains: (a) ten good practice principles for bribery risk assessment; (b) a risk assessment template – with an illustrated documented example; and (c) a bribery risk assessment process check list.

66 www.unglobalcompact.org/resources/411 published with Deloitte and also including practical examples and checklists.

67 www.unodc.org/documents/corruption/Publications/2013/13-84498_Ebook.pdf.

Corruption Perceptions Index ('TI CPI'), reproduced as at December 2020 in Appendix 8.[68]

8.93

The TI CPI, first produced in 1995, is updated in the autumn of each year and in 2020 covered 180 countries or territories around the world. It is by no means a perfect instrument, which is inevitable given the challenges of collecting data. However, its wide use suggests that it remains a well respected benchmarking tool.

8.94

In terms of country risk generally, the TI CPI reflects continuing high risks in numerous countries, and as at January 2021 approximately 66% of relevant countries scored less than 50 out of 100 (usually taken as meaning high risk) and the average country score was also below 50 out of 100.[69]

8.95

The 'BRIC' countries that have been identified as growing economies of particular relevance to commercial development globally, were ranked as follows in January 2021: Brazil ranked 94th with a rating of 38, China ranked 78th with rating of 42, India ranked 86th with a rating of 40 and Russia was ranked 129th with a rating of 30. Of the 'MINT' countries identified as quickly expanding economies, Mexico ranked 124th, Indonesia ranked 102nd, Nigeria ranked 149th and Turkey ranked 86th. By contrast, the UK was ranked 11th and France 23rd with the US 25th.

8.96

Although it is possible to draw some conclusions, for example, there are lower risks on average in Western Europe, especially when compared with overall poorly performing regions such as Africa and South America, these results do not paint the complete picture. First, it is not accurate to conclude that even in low risk countries, corruption is not an issue. You need only read the UK newspapers for a week to see how often corruption allegations arise and a 2016 study published by the European Parliamentary Research Service suggested that the cost to the European economy of corruption is between €179 billion and €990 billion in GDP terms on an annual basis. Additionally, from enforcement actions we can see that it is often companies in the lower risk countries taking part in international bribery (see the US enforcement actions

68 Also available with yearly updates from www.transparency.org/research/cpi/overview.

69 The top ten lowest risk countries on the list were Denmark, New Zealand (both of which had a joint rating of 88 out of 100), Finland, Singapore, Sweden, Switzerland, Norway, the Netherlands, Germany and Luxembourg. The UK ranked number 11 with a rating of 77, the US 25 with a rating of 67, France was ranked 24 with a rating of 69. The bottom ten countries were Somalia, and South Sudan (with a joint rating of 12), Syria, Yemen, Venezuela, Sudan, Equatorial Guinea, Libya, Korea (north) and Haiti.

reported in Chapter 2).[70] Secondly, received wisdom or over-generalisation tends to place insufficient weight on TI CPI data reviewed in 2020 which placed Italy lower than Rwanda, Georgia and Costa Rica. Thirdly an over-reliance on individual yearly surveys by country tends to obscure trends showing movement up and down the rankings (whoever they are produced by), and therefore tends not recognise (a) that all countries and territories are changing, with some becoming more corrupt and others less so, and (b) that regions within countries can and do vary in the risk that they present.[71]

8.97

As well as companies specialising in bringing risk tables/analysis together for the purposes of risk assessment,[72] primary reference materials other than the TI CPI also include TI's 'Global Corruption Barometer',[73] Global Integrity's 'The Global Integrity Report'[74] and the, also eponymous, World Bank's 'World Bank Worldwide Governance Indicators';[75] World Bank's 'Country Policy And Institutional Assessment on transparency, accountability and corruption in the public sector'[76] and the to which examples we could also add many others – for instance, for OECD member countries, the OECD country-specific reports on implementation of the OECD Anti-bribery Convention.[77]

8.98

Sectoral risk relates to sectors of the economy that are typically associated with higher levels of bribery risk than others. The MoJ Guidance refers to the extractive industries and also large-scale construction projects, but other sources also include industries such as pharmaceutical companies and defence companies. Few commentators have been willing, particularly given investigations relating to retailers such as Wal-Mart and enforcement actions relating to publishers such as Macmillan,[78] to identify lower risk industries or professions. However, in creating criteria for an in-house compliance programme, it might be sensible to start with criteria relating to smaller industries that conduct business primarily

70 See www.europarl.europa.eu/RegData/etudes/STUD/2016/579319/EPRS_STU(2016)579319_EN.pdf.

71 Although only one of many factors, it should be noted that many countries governments are apparently seeking to improve their environment eg the joining of Russia in February 2012 of the OECD anti-corruption convention (see www.oecd.org/newsroom/russiajoinsoecdanti-briberyconvention.htm), the signing of an agreement on combatting corruption between the UN and China in 2019 and the introduction of anti-corruption legislation in Brazil Law no. 12.846/2013, popularly called the 'clean company law').

72 There are a number of providers of specialist services, including Verisk Maplecroft.

73 www.transparency.org/research/gcb/overview.

74 www.globalintegrity.org.

75 http://info.worldbank.org/governance/wgi/index.aspx#home.

76 https://data.worldbank.org/indicator/IQ.CPA.TRAN.XQ.

77 www.oecd.org/daf/anti-bribery/countryreportsontheimplementationoftheoecdanti-briberyconvention.htm.

78 Wal-Mart (see www.nytimes.com/2012/04/22/business/at-wal-mart-in-mexico-a-bribe-inquiry-silenced.html?pagewanted=all&_r=0), Macmillan (see https://fcpablog.com/2011/07/22/macmillan-in-11-million-uk-civil-settlement/).

in lower risk regions and have less need for licenses or other contact with public officials and little history of commission based payments for sales.

8.99

Transactional risk relates to actual business activities and is therefore broad in nature. The helpful description used in the TI Diagnosing Corruption Risk guide is as follows:

> 'any activity involving some form of economic exchange between counterparties … Transactions may be more or less risky, depending on matters including: The subject matter of the transaction; The identity and nature of counterparties, for example whether they are connected to government in some way; The degree of transparency of the transaction or related dealings; How critical a particular service or supply is to the procuring party – for instance, its importance to the business and/or the level of urgency required'.

Risk factors relating to transactions would therefore include transactions where material commissions are payable or where public officials will inevitably be encountered and have to take discretionary decisions important to the business being undertaken.

8.100

Business opportunity risk is defined in the MoJ Guidance as 'Such risks [as] might arise in high value projects or with projects involving many contractors or intermediaries; or with projects which are not apparently undertaken at market prices, or which do not have a clear legitimate objective.' Essentially, this is risk closely related to transaction risk but focused on the broader value, complexity and commercial reason for a project; ie the bigger, more expensive and complex a project, or business function, the bigger risk rating it may receive.

8.101

Business partnership risk relates specifically to the section 7 risk that a commercial organisation will be held criminally liable for the acts of its 'associated persons' where they act on the organisation's behalf. At the risk of over simplifying, the risk here essentially reflects the extent that the organisation can reasonably place trust in its service providers not to pay bribes on its behalf, for example because they are of good character, they have a history of compliance, they have reliable processes in place to prevent bribery (eg an adequate compliance programme), and/or there is little risk of them being able to pay a bribe because of the nature of their role (eg they have a narrow in-house facing remit).

Additional risk – the 'control environment'

8.102

Although this risk is not captured in the description above, the control environment is also recognised (eg within the TI Diagnosing Corruption Risk) as a helpful element in risk assessment[79] and reflects the risk within the company or parts of the company that do not have the capacity to implement adequate procedures. Put simply, it encapsulates the risk that a company will not be capable of implementing all or parts of its compliance programme.[80]

8.103

There is no one approach to assessing control risk but a company could ask itself the following questions: whether (and why) its management's strength and ability in different parts of the company are appropriate, how similar projects are performing across the company, whether appropriate personnel have been trained, whether resources in the form of advisors are available and, if relevant, if information technology resources and documents are likely to be available to support the programme. In addition to which, as procedures do not operate in a corporate vacuum, it might be helpful to consider whether significant change (perhaps also caused by new compliance programmes or acquisitions) or other uncertainty in the business would be likely to mean that procedures would not be implemented or could be delayed.

Planning a risk assessment

8.104

A risk assessment will develop as it is produced and be reviewed periodically. As with risk assessment generally, there is of course no one right way to start, but a process that includes significant stakeholders, has senior management support, and is properly resourced and planned is much more likely to be successful. The following chart reproduced with kind permission of TI from their publication 'Diagnosing Bribery Risk' sets out a helpful and relatively detailed illustration of how a company might plan a risk assessment:[81]

---

79 The MOJ Guidance also suggests that '*The commercial organisation assesses the nature and extent of its exposure to potential external and internal risks of bribery*'.

80 It is axiomatic that, particularly for larger and higher risk companies, adequate procedures will struggle without good corporate governance and management of change.

81 www.transparency.org.uk/sites/default/files/pdf/publications/Diagnosing_Bribery_Risk.pdf.

Phase	Objectives	Actions
Planning, scoping and mobilisation	• Determine overall scope and approach • Obtain Board/senior management buy-in • Allocate appropriate resources • Establish a realistic work plan	• Obtain Board level buy-in • Appoint project lead • Define stakeholders, team, responsibilities and reporting lines • Identify potential information sources including management information • Establish risk assessment framework • Draft risk assessment plan • Design any information capture templates required • Obtain necessary approval for the plan • Communicate appropriate context and instructions to contributors
Information gathering and analysis	Obtain sufficient relevant information to form the basis of a comprehensive bribery risk assessment	Review of internal and external documents and data • Workshops/interviews • Distribution and return of questionnaires, risk assessment templates, etc • Collate and review information gathered from the above sources • Follow-up and challenge incomplete, inaccurate or inconsistent information
Risk identification	Use information gathered to identify a comprehensive set of potential bribery risks	• Consider key risk areas: country risk; sectoral risk; transaction risk; business opportunity risk; business partnership risk; other risk considerations
Risk evaluation	Use information gathered to evaluate and prioritise risks	• Consider key risk factors affecting likelihood and impact

Phase	Objectives	Actions
Documentation[82]	Record the risk assessment process in a way that will support communication of risks and the identification or design of effective mitigating controls	• Record results in the agreed format and validate with stakeholders • Communicate findings as required with practical recommendations

'Inherent' risk, 'residual' risk and recording a risk assessment

8.105

Once the completion of the risk assessment has identified and prioritised risks, there are any number of ways in which a risk assessment might be expressed, and ways in which bribery risks could be compared against other areas of compliance. Often a table or chart for the most senior management in the organisation is the result of the assessment, with a key showing risks ranked perhaps as a percentage, number or letter (or some combination indicating for instance seriousness and likelihood). The exact methodology and measures of risk will vary.

8.106

In the example assessment contained in the UN Global Compact Risk Assessment guidance, the overall risk rating provides a rating for 'inherent risk' (essentially the risk that bribes will be paid and the relative seriousness of the bribery[83]) and a reduced risk rating for 'residual risk', sometimes called exposure risk (the risk of bribery that arises in any particular area where relevant 'mitigations' are taken into account, such as for corporate hospitality a company operating a gifts and entertainment register). Of course, even effective compliance programmes may not significantly reduce the compliance risk in all risk areas. However, this approach of separately considering inherent and residual risk is also adopted by TI and now used by many multi-national companies.

82 For the reasons set out earlier in this chapter documenting the risk assessment, referred to immediately above is all but essential and the Guidance itself refers to '*accurate and appropriate documentation of the risk assessment and its conclusions*'.

83 This is of course different to the risk that a bribe will lead to a fine or a prosecution. Whereas a company may wish to look at the likelihood of a fine actually arising for other valid risk purposes, a commercial organisation would, it is suggested, under the UKBA find it difficult to argue in court that it had not utilised any resources to prevent bribery in country Y because country Y had weak laws or enforcement authorities and therefore the likelihood of a fine or other liability was very low.

Principle 4: due diligence[84]

8.107

As regards Principle 4 on due diligence, the MoJ Guidance states as follows:

> 'The commercial organisation applies due diligence procedures, taking a proportionate and risk based approach, in respect of persons who perform or will perform services for or on behalf of the organisation, in order to mitigate identified bribery risks.
>
> **Commentary**
>
> 4.5 'Due diligence' for the purposes of Principle 4 should be conducted using a risk-based approach (as referred to on page 27). For example, in lower risk situations, commercial organisations may decide that there is no need to conduct much in the way of due diligence. In higher risk situations, due diligence may include conducting direct interrogative enquiries, indirect investigations, or general research on proposed associated persons.'

Many companies take different approaches when translating these passages into practice and there is a considerable amount of variation between organisations given the risk-based approach. However, by way of a high-level summary, processes often seem to include the following: (a) identifying whether the third party is in scope (eg are they a service provider, should we in any event conduct due diligence on them, do they fall below any de minimus spending limitations), (b) a 'triage' or normal due diligence process to place the third party in into an initial low, medium or high risk category, perhaps based on reasonable assumptions relating to amongst other matters country, transaction risk, sectoral risk (explained in relation to risk assessment at para 8.91 above) and/or basic due diligence such as a counterparty questionnaire or short electronic third party vendor report,[85] and (c) applying a further or expanded due diligence regime for higher risk counterparties (medium or high).

8.108

For the usually relatively small number of higher risk service providers or counterparties, due diligence may build on the lower risk information and process but go further to incorporate enhanced information gathering such as further questions to explore identified 'red flags' (see para 8.105 below for explanation of red flags). Such information can be gathered through

---

84 On buying a company, the purchasing company assumes the risk that its new subsidiary will be prosecuted for a section 7 offence that arose under the old ownership. As a result both pre-acquisition of the company and post acquisition review of the procedures and liabilities in place (post acquisition due diligence) are prudent, and at least as regards pre-acquisition due diligence steps are envisioned by the MoJ Guidance. However, for the sake of brevity and given SME companies will usually wish to receive bespoke legal advice on these rare occurrences in a company's life, the issues are not covered in this chapter.

85 There are a number of vendors including MK Denial, World Check and Dow Jones.

meetings, telephone calls, questionnaires and in some limited circumstances the instruction of an enhanced due diligence provider to conduct more in-depth investigations. Such investigations could include visits to the country in which the services are being provided and/or where the company is located. There would then be consideration of the available information and a decision as to whether to proceed, proceed with specific mitigations or not to proceed at all. Where a company proceeds in a higher risk scenario with mitigations these will often be case specific, but by way of example they could include some of the following mitigations: more closely monitoring invoices, reducing the period in which due diligence is repeated, reducing the standard contract length, providing training, instigating periodic audits, and agreeing on the wording of annual anti-corruption certifications.

8.109

An example outline of a five stage due diligence process is set out below:

- **Stage 1**

  Consider if counterparty falls within the process. It may not be proportionate to conduct any due diligence on very small counterparties such as flower sellers, window cleaners or private retail customers.

- **Stage 2**

  Counterparty is triaged into low, medium or high risk categories based on risk assumptions (possibly including – but not limited to – the size of the contract) and potentially a short due diligence questionnaire or electronic third party vendor report.

- **Stage 3**

  Thought is given to information available and the risk that arises. Counterparty is rejected, proceeds (perhaps with mitigations to risk) or because of red flags is moved to a higher risk category and therefore further due diligence.

- **Stage 4**

  Further due diligence is completed. Further thought is given to information and the risk that arises. Counterparty is rejected or proceeds (perhaps with mitigations to risk).

- **Stage 5**

  Possibility of a 'repeat' of Stage 4 with more senior involvement and more due diligence, possibly including the use of an enhanced due diligence provider.[86] Counterparty is rejected or proceeds (often with mitigations).

86 There are a significant number, including in no particular order TRAG, FRA, FTI, Control Risks, Risk Analysis, Diligence, Billiter and Kroll to name only a small number of the larger companies who have expertise in creating in-depth due diligence reports on individuals or companies. It should however be axiomatic that only legal means can be used to obtain information, and that even with a report provided by a sophisticated provider there may be relatively little available information.

Red flags

8.110

'Red flags' are those pieces of information, which suggest that a counterpart company or individual may be more prone to be engaged in corrupt activity. Red flags are unlikely to include actual evidence that shows with certainty that bribery has occurred or is occurring. However, when taken individually or more likely together, they raise the overall risk that a bribe may be paid.

8.111

Through proportionate investigation and common sense analysis, red flags may be removed or downgraded. Two common examples are as follows: (a) a false positive or 'red herring' where, for instance, a name appears as a red flag that relates to an entity known to have paid bribes but also to the innocent party seeking to enter a business relationship; or (b) a historic or mitigated red flag, which could for instance be a compliance incident that is historic and reasonably appears to have been dealt with properly by the counterparty. Many red flags are also capable of being mitigated, ie reduced in risk to an acceptable level. An example could be where a party is reported to have poor compliance in respect of an aspect of its business but agrees to improve its procedures and controls as part of entering into a contractual relationship.

Identifying 'red flags'

8.112

Given that red flags arise from a mixture of fact, common sense and experience in the area they can be difficult to define, and there is not an approved list. Nevertheless, Appendix 2 sets out an extensive example checklist – which given that the UKBA relates to companies with part of their business in the UK, includes red flags relating to both active bribery and money laundering.

Responding to red flags/mitigation

8.113

The MoJ Guidance envisages that due diligence is not an end in itself but the beginning point to understand the risks that arise through red flags, undertake mitigation action where possible or take a decision not proceed with a relationship or transaction because of the risk that bribes will be paid. Assuming a transaction or relationship does proceed, the MoJ Guidance states as follows: 'Appraisal and continued monitoring of recruited or engaged "associated" persons may also be required, proportionate to the identified risks …'. These steps and other practical steps, including practical steps, are explained above from para 8.55, and also for small bribes in Chapter 5.

Principle 5: communication (including training)

8.114

As regards Principle 5 regarding communication (including training), the MoJ Guidance emphasises the need for effective internal and external communications and the benefits of training, stating specifically as follows:

> 'The commercial organisation seeks to ensure that its bribery prevention policies and procedures *are embedded and understood* throughout the organisation through internal and external communication, including training, that is proportionate to the risks it faces.' (emphasis added)

8.115

Communication has been considered earlier in this chapter.[87] However, it is perhaps worth reiterating the continuing nature of the implementation of this principle generally, ie that anti-corruption compliance is not a project that can be launched and left with minimal attention. For adequate procedures to remain a defence, a commercial organisation will usually provide periodic anti-corruption internal communication and training. By way of example, very large companies, or companies with greater risk, may be likely to be communicating on a frequent basis and may therefore engage stakeholders more effectively by using a variety of media (posters, emails, events, internal webpages, blogs) and creating a structured programme for communication of compliance issues – potentially incorporating within materials new topical case studies, industry news and compliance successes.

8.116

Furthermore, as regards training specifically, the MoJ Guidance states as follows:

> '5.5 Like all procedures training should be proportionate to risk but some training is likely to be effective in firmly establishing an anti-bribery culture whatever the level of risk. Training may take the form of education and awareness raising about the threats posed by bribery in general and in the sector or areas in which the organisation operates in particular, and the various ways it is being addressed.
>
> 5.6 General training could be mandatory for new employees or for agents (on a weighted risk basis) as part of an induction process, but it should also be tailored to the specific risks associated with specific posts. Consideration should also be given to tailoring training to the special needs of those involved in any 'speak up' procedures, and higher risk functions such as purchasing, contracting, distribution and marketing, and working in high risk countries. Effective training is continuous, and regularly monitored and evaluated.

87 As part of the analysis of Principle 1 of the MoJ Guidance.

> 5.7 It may be appropriate to require associated persons to undergo training. This will be particularly relevant for high risk associated persons. In any event, organisations may wish to encourage associated persons to adopt bribery prevention training.'

8.117

Given this guidance, which appears to create the expectation of training, the practical question for training in anything other than a small company dealing in low risk areas is not 'if' training will occur but rather 'who' will be trained, 'when' will they be trained, 'how' will they be trained and 'what' will training include. These are considered below.

Who will be trained

8.118

The emphasis both in the MoJ Guidance and in other industry guidance appears to be on risk based approach. Larger companies may seek to include essential bribery and corruption training as part of any induction process for all staff, and otherwise require basic revision (or new training for older staff) using e-learning over a period of time. For employees in higher risk areas, usually as identified by the risk assessment or experience, additional more focused training may also be prudent.

When will they be trained

8.119

The MoJ Guidance provides little assistance on timing for training, other than that it *could* be made mandatory at the start of employment. With a paucity of Guidance, it is suggested that although training is an important tool, it is one of many, and providing the training given is robust and part of broader ethical based training, re-training every two or more years may well be sufficient for employees not particularly exposed to risk, even in companies that otherwise have medium or even higher risk business areas. In practice, much will depend on the risk/ethos of the company and the totality of its other controls, and for some companies or groups of employees, one year intervals between some form of training with a periodic face-to-face component (see 8.120 below) for higher risk individuals may be more appropriate.[88]

88 A company could also, it is suggested, take into account how proportionate it would be in its wider programme to train on all risk areas (eg trade sanction, international trade rules, health and safety, competition laws, FSA regulation, money laundering) on a yearly basis.

How will they be trained

8.120

As the MoJ Guidance indicates, there are a number of means of delivering training. Many vendor companies now supply e-learning products that can either be bought off the shelf or tailored at a relatively low cost to an organisation's risk and activities. Better training materials tend to provide relevant case studies, and face-to-face training is the 'gold standard' for higher risk employees such as senior management located in high risk countries (or in procurement or commission based sales), government affairs groups and employees who regularly deal with public officials.

Face-to-face training allows small groups to explore issues in a supported forum with a compliance practitioner and/or lawyer with relevant training and expertise.

What will training include

8.121

The content of training will of course depend on the audience and, as mentioned above, relevant case studies and practical examples are helpful, some of which can be found in documents such as Transparency International's 'How to Bribe' published in January 2014[89] or indeed their free and comprehensive Global Anti-Bribery Guidance Portal[90] or RESIST's publicly available documents and case studies[91] or the UN's e-learning tools.[92] However, common denominators in tailored training appear to be an explanation of the 'zero-tolerance approach', perhaps an outline of relevant bribery offences in the US and UK, examples of enforcement and penalties, practical case studies, and information on where further guidance can be obtained (including a whistleblowing or 'speak up' service).

8.122

In relation to particularly high risk employees, such as decision makers in the procurement function, there may be more focused materials that build on the standard training to incorporate a broader range of ethical and/or practical issues such as further knowledge of red flags, more detailed consideration of internal processes and controls and additional or different points for escalating concerns and questions.

---

89 www.transparency.org.uk/sites/default/files/pdf/publications/How_to_Bribe_A_Typology_of_Bribe_Paying_and_How_to_Stop_It_0.pdf.

90 www.antibriberyguidance.org/.

91 https://images.transparencycdn.org/images/2001_RESIST_EN.pdf.

92 http://thefightagainstcorruption.org/certificate/.

8.123

Whatever the training, it can be helpful to convey the following message in a form suitable for the business and culture: 'We mean it. Bribes are not payable even if this means a loss for the company. You can always speak up about bribery concerns and are encouraged to do so.'

Documentation/training records

8.124

Documenting and recording training is as important as documenting any other part of adequate procedures, given that the burden of proof is on the organisation to show that the training took place.

Principle 6: monitoring and review

8.125

As regards Principle 6, monitoring and review, the MoJ Guidance emphasises the need to continually monitor the progress of the compliance programme in an effort to help senior management correct any errors and consider making improvements; Specifically, Principle 6 states as follows:

> 'Monitoring and review
>
> The commercial organisation monitors and reviews procedures designed to prevent bribery by persons associated with it and makes improvements where necessary.'
>
> 'Procedures
>
> 6.2 There is a wide range of internal and external review mechanisms which commercial organisations could consider using. Systems set up to deter, detect and investigate bribery, and monitor the ethical quality of transactions, such as internal financial control mechanisms, will help provide insight into the effectiveness of procedures designed to prevent bribery. Staff surveys, questionnaires and feedback from training can also provide an important source of information on effectiveness and a means by which employees and other associated persons can inform continuing improvement of anti-bribery policies.
>
> 6.3 Organisations could also consider formal periodic reviews and reports for top-level management. Organisations could also draw on information on other organizations' practices, for example relevant trade bodies or regulators might highlight examples of good or bad practice in their publications.'

8.126

In purely practical terms, monitoring begins with collating information from different parts of the company (eg audit, investigations, legal, procurement, finance and speak up line). Some of this information may be pre-packaged and available for commercial reasons to management in any event, eg financial data about spending in different countries or in relation to particular types of counter-parties such as joint venturers. Other information may benefit from being collated separately so that the overall data available includes sufficient detail to adequately monitor the corruption risk, eg the number of employees passing training, the number of corruption investigations and speak up reports, staff feedback and data regarding the retention of high risk counter-parties.

8.127

Larger companies and banks are likely to have systems and controls to assist in monitoring risk, but for many smaller companies a senior committee or individual tasked with helping the monitoring process may be a useful focus point. In any event it appears to be the MoJ Guidance's intention that internal management information is collected on an on-going basis, to which there is added external information identified by the programme manager(s) or by others stakeholders (eg news reports, information provided by NGOs or government, and industry body updates on new or emerging risks).

8.128

Finally, in relation to monitoring generally, 'no news is not necessarily good news'. A working adequate procedure will usually generate information (and trends that can be identified). That information, even if at first difficult to digest, should always be welcomed; it may lead to better management and commercial savings as well as a reduction in bribery risk.

8.129

As regards actions from monitoring, it is suggested that the thrust of the MoJ Guidance is that it is for senior management to ask itself common sense questions such as 'why has there been a significant drop in corruption reports this quarter?', 'why is there so much more audit activity in one part of the business?', or 'what has caused an increase in the pass rate for training high-risk employees?'. The key issues for management in this regard are therefore likely to be as simple or difficult as asking the questions:

- What does the information really mean?
- What is the data's strengths and weaknesses?
- What more ought we try and find out before making a decision?

- How should policies and procedures (including monitoring itself) be refined?
- Where should the company's compliance resources be applied or supplemented?

Trends

8.130

Trends and predictions should always be treated with caution but below are some thoughts on the development of adequate procedures and the guidance surrounding them.

8.131

First, there is a still small but growing availability of resources and professional advisors in relation to adequate procedures. Ultimately this ought to reduce costs for corporate compliance and help in tasks such as benchmarking and the common understanding of industry norms during contract negotiations.[93] This is assisted by a further positive trend, the increasing collaboration between anti-corruption practitioners globally and a greater sharing of compliance and financial crime related data.

8.132

Secondly, as the world adapts to life with COVID-19, and the greater attention to financial crime that it has brought, we can expect a more international and connected approach to compliance and at national level a more joined up approach to corporate criminal liability, including in the UK through additional financial crime offences aimed at corporates, including for fraud and money-laundering, similar in nature to the UKBA and the anti-tax evasion offences brought in by section 45 and 46 of the Criminal Finances Act 2017.

8.133

Finally, in the medium term, as adequate procedures under the UKBA are 'effectively required' for most companies with part of their business in the UK, and given the concerns expressed by small and medium businesses referred to in paragraph 8.132 above, there is likely to be continued discussion of the provision of further statutory or even non-binding guidance from a relevant body. Much could be written on this topic – and there are valid differing views – but the current situation appears to lack some of the benefits of 'opinions' given in US matters by the SEC and the authoritative guidance that can be provided by, for instance, the Financial Conduct Authority in the UK.

93 As regards contracts a good example of contract updating are the new standard Oil and Gas UK and AIPN joint venture agreements.

9 Internal company investigations

Introduction

9.1

This chapter contains an overview of key principles and practical issues relating to internal corporate investigations that arise in the UK from Bribery Act 2010 ('UKBA') corruption concerns or allegations. The content of the chapter is divided by sub-sections, which provide a summary of 'why' investigations are a useful tool in a well-designed compliance programme, 'what' issues or allegations might trigger an investigation and of course 'how' investigations are effectively and ethically conducted.

9.2

Given the complex, sensitive and unique nature of most investigations and the challenging legal, compliance and ethical issues they give rise to, this chapter is intended only as an overview of those matters most likely to be pertinent to small to medium sized enterprises ('SME') where: (a) the enterprise is subject to the UKBA, and (b) a director, senior manager or partner has been asked to be a 'sponsor' for a 'formal' investigation.

9.3

Although the chapter is primarily intended for directors and executive management, it includes sample checklists, examples and information relevant to investigators, legal practitioners and/or compliance professionals.

Key points

9.4

- Internal investigations and confidential reporting mechanisms are a useful and often essential hallmark of a commercial organisation's efforts to prevent, detect and respond to corruption.
- To maintain trust in the reporting and investigations processes it is important to embed a culture and procedures that respect and protect the rights and privileges of all those involved including the fundamental principle of non-retaliation.

- Internal investigations can be disruptive, frustrating, costly and discover unpleasant facts that are difficult to deal with, including the impact on investigation participants and work environments. They are unlikely to be implemented well or carried out effectively without the explicit support of senior leadership, which allows investigations to be properly scoped and assists in ensuring reasonable access to company records and witnesses.

- To be credible, internal investigations must be as independent as reasonably possible, carefully managed, properly resourced and recorded, as well as objective and fair. Investigators should of course be competent and well trained. The level of investigation does not always need to be 'gold plated' but should be appropriate (eg timely and proportionate to the risk and nature of the complaint).

- Any sizeable investigation is likely to need expert advice, professional case handling and digital forensic or eDiscovery resources, which will often mean at least considering external assistance. However, this will not always necessitate retaining a respected but costly external law firm (or other consultancy practice[1]) to conduct the investigation in its entirety.

- Allowing for investigative independence, the relationship between the investigation team and its business sponsor will usually run more smoothly where the investigation team provides interim reports, risk insights, and, as required, interim advice from legal to the sponsor. This can assist the sponsor in making pressing business decisions which are likely to be required during the course of the investigation (eg employee related matters including team and welfare management, suspending contracts, making contingency plans for replacement providers, reporting to listing authorities or other corporate disclosures[2] or delaying investment decisions).

- An investigation will often conclude with recommendations (including disciplinary actions and control and process improvements upon review by and guidance from human resources and compliance teams, respectively) and legal advice arising from the factual findings. Any such recommendations should be informed by a root cause analysis, monitored and recorded. Sharing lessons learned to employees and third parties (as appropriate) may also help to raise awareness and prevent reoccurrence.

---

1 A useful resource here may be the ACi (https://my-aci.com/).

2 Including Annual reports, sustainability reports, investor relations/reports etc.

Why carry out investigations

9.4

There is little practical guidance contained in the DoJ Resource Guide or MoJ Guidance[3] in relation to the key practical issues of 'why', 'when' or 'how' to carry out an internal investigation into alleged corruption.

The MoJ Guidance is almost silent as regards investigations. However, the US guidance does helpfully indicate that a thorough and immediate investigation may be a mitigating factor in relation to either the decision to prosecute or in relation to the level of fine imposed.[4]

9.5

In any event, internal investigations are, as explained below, a practical and significant tool in both helping to mitigate corruption risk and maintaining the trust and faith of employees, regulators, prosecutors, shareholders, partners, communities and customers in the organisation's 'zero-tolerance' to bribery..

9.6

By way of explanation, as regards corruption risk, it is often only by properly investigating allegations of breach of trust or corruption that a commercial organisation can achieve the following:

- identify and stop secret and improper practices;
- gain the support of whistleblowers (nowadays often referred to as the 'reporting party') (and therefore encourage a 'speak and listen-up' culture);
- discipline/remove or where appropriate re-train relevant personnel or associated parties;
- strengthen governance, administration procedures and controls to prevent re-occurrence and improve transparency;
- inform corporate strategy; and
- assess liability and determine next steps

---

3 The most relevant section of the MoJ Guidance states as follows at page 31:
'Procedures
6.2. There is a wide range of internal and external review mechanisms which commercial organisations could consider using. Systems set up to deter, detect and *investigate* bribery, and monitor the ethical quality of transactions, such as internal financial control mechanisms, will help provide insight into the effectiveness of procedures designed to prevent bribery.' (emphasis added)

4 'Factors taken into account when deciding whether or not to proceed in the US', Resources Guide page 78. Also required by the Sarbanes-Oxley Act and the 2010 SEC Enforcement Cooperation Initiative, which sets out where credit might be awarded for co-operation with the SEC.

9.7

As regards the Serious Fraud Office ('SFO'), it would also seem that internal investigations are in practice considered as a usual part of the process a company would go through prior to self-reporting an alleged corruption offence. This is evident from the guidance for corporate self-reporting (last updated in October 2012)[5] which states as follows:

> 'Should I self-report directly to the SFO?
>
> The decision to approach us may not be easy for a corporation or business when it discovers a problem relating to fraud or corruption within the organisation. *We understand that you may not want to approach us unless you have decided, following advice and some investigation by your professional advisers, that there is a real issue that should be reported.*' (emphasis added)

9.8

The practice of at least *some* investigating prior to self-reporting is further supported by the process the SFO requests during self-reporting (ie that internal investigation reports and related documents (excluding privileged documents) will be shared with the SFO, if a company is to fully benefit from its co-operation).[6]

What to investigate

9.9

What to investigate will depend partly on the company's policy requirements, resources available internally and externally to the commercial organisation, the seriousness of the allegations and issues and their credibility. The following table contains a non-exhaustive list of issues that may be relevant to the decision to launch an 'internal investigation'.

5 SFO's Guidance – Corporate self-reporting, available at www.sfo.gov.uk/publications/guidance-policy-and-protocols/corporate-self-reporting/.

6 The following is an outline of the process to be adopted by corporate bodies and/or their advisers when self-reporting to the Serious Fraud Office: (i) Initial contact, and all subsequent communication, must be made through the SFO's Intelligence Unit, through the secure reporting form. The Intelligence Unit is the only business area within the SFO authorised to handle self-reports; (ii) Hard copy reports setting out the nature and scope of any internal investigation must be provided to the SFO's Intelligence Unit as part of the self-reporting process; (iii) All supporting evidence including, but not limited to, emails, banking evidence and witness accounts, must be provided to the SFO's Intelligence Unit as part of the self-reporting process.

Table of factors relevant to decision to investigate

- whether the allegation, if true, would present a material risk (including on reputation, social or legal licence to operate) or liability to the company or a serious crime by an individual that may result in dismissal
- the harm, damage or other consequential impact (including ongoing cooperation with regulators or enforcement agencies) that would be occurring if the allegations are true
- whether senior leaders are involved in the allegation or concerns are in relation to retaliation of a whistleblower/reporting party
- the breadth/size/complexity of the issues
- whether the issue if true could be the 'tip of the iceberg' including the possibility for systemic control issues or violations
- the value of the alleged wrongdoing or the value of the benefit (or loss or damage) of the wrongdoing
- whether the issue already has the attention of the press or other interested third parties (such as minority shareholders and suppliers)
- whether other avenues of review are available or more appropriate (eg audit or other assurance functions)
- as regards third parties, the contractual right to conduct or participate in an investigation
- the likely sale of the entity or transfer of an asset to which the allegation relates and so discovery by a third party of misconduct
- whether other available information exists relating to the relevant business (or named individuals) which suggests it is high risk, including previous investigations or reports that raise 'red flags' but which may not themselves have led to an investigation or resulted in a substantiated outcome
- whether there are similarities between the allegations and previous observed and concerning behaviour or anomalies in the business or similar businesses either inside or outside of the company

When to investigate

9.10

Assuming a decision is taken that an investigation is required, it is usually appropriate to begin an investigation as soon as it is at all practicable. There is 'no time like the present', and regulators are unlikely to understand inexplicable delays or inadequately scoped preliminary actions to preserve material evidence and data. However, despite the need to proceed quickly, for obvious reasons, this should not be done at the cost of the integrity of the process. In other words, investigations can themselves be complex and cross-disciplinary projects involving highly trained investigators, forensic accountants, digital forensic and eDiscovery specialists and lawyers.

9.11

The start of an investigation may not always immediately involve arranging numerous interviews and compiling case theories. It is more likely to consist of efforts by the investigation team to quickly preserve and collate available information, as well as agreeing accountabilities and a communications protocol (confidential 'need-to-know' list). Identifying initial resources and creating a written plan (including, if possible, an initial timeline). During this stage there is also likely to be at least some work relating to identifying and considering key legal issues such as data protection and any immediate money laundering reporting requirements. Where relevant, this might also include considering local law issues, such as mandatory requirements to notify law enforcement agencies, certain restrictions on transfer or review of documents or data processed or stored in-country or rights of employees involved in an investigation.[7]

How to investigate

Internal or external resources

9.12

A significant early issue to consider in any investigation is whether to conduct an investigation using internal resources or whether to out-source the investigation to a trusted third party law firm (or consultancy practice).

9.13

Five factors usually relevant to this decision are set out below:

(1) in-house resources and capacity – are there sufficiently expert internal available resources, with skills aligned to the scope and access to tools

7 See Global Investigations Review (GIR) Practitioner's Guide to Global Investigations – Fourth edition (2020); see also *Lissack and Horlick on Bribery and Corruption* (3rd edn, LexisNexis, 2020).

including data management systems, digital forensics software and eDiscovery platforms to conduct the investigation required;

(2) perception of conflict – is independence likely to be a particularly important factor, for instance where a previous in-house review has been shown to have failed;

(3) seriousness of the matter – the more serious the matter, the more likely that at least some independent oversight, assurance or professional credibility will be deemed appropriate by stakeholders;

(4) available funds of the organisation and the likely cost of retaining external resources; and

(5) complicating practical, data, compliance or legal issues that make the use of external resources appropriate and sometimes more efficient. For example, investigations that cross a number of jurisdictions and time-zones may be more suited to an international law firm or other consultancy, or may require specialist IT support, forensic equipment and in-country presence.[8]

Independence

9.14

Whatever the investigation is and however it is conducted, if it does not have a professional, competent and ethical investigation team and a responsible sponsor that meets the two criteria below, it is likely to fail in its aims.

9.15

Requirements for the business sponsor of an investigation

First, the internal sponsor who initially instructs the investigation team to conduct an independent investigation should, for their own benefit and the benefit of the investigation, not be conflicted in anyway and should not have any vested interest in the investigation's outcome (including in relation to those potentially involved). They cannot, for instance, be conflicted or the subject of the investigation. In an SME, the audit committee or the chair of that committee may therefore be an appropriate sponsor, although a senior business leader or non-executive director can also be appropriate in the right circumstances.

8 Issues of legal privilege will also be relevant to investigations in countries where in-house legal advice does not attract privilege from disclosure in court proceedings but external legal advice carries that protection.

> Secondly, the sponsor should be of *sufficient seniority* in the organisation to ensure sufficient access is provided to documents, data and employees, direct funds and resources to the investigation, as the investigation reasonably requires them, and to compel the implementation of decisions made following recommendations during the investigation or in the investigation report. This authority is important whether the investigation is outsourced to an external law firm or other consultancy, conducted internally or conducted internally with external assurance.

Resources overview

9.16

Depending on what is being investigated, a larger investigation will often include legal advice or legal oversight and / or the use of specialist investigators trained in serious and complex investigations, cognitive interview techniques, case management and data governance. Other external resources with relevant expertise for larger investigations might include:

- forensic accountants who may be engaged to review invoices and accounting information and documentation;
- digital forensic and eDiscovery experts to retrieve and process emails and other electronic sources of information;
- specialist first level document reviewers to assess, categorise and refer documents for second level review.

9.17

Often at an early stage it will be difficult to determine the amount of work and time an investigation will take, and therefore to predict costs. However, generally speaking, as with any corporate project, the more serious the issues, the wider the geographical area, the longer the relevant time periods and the greater the amount of documentation, the more resources and costs are likely to be involved. It is therefore advisable to carefully scope, prioritise and phase investigations appropriately.

Scope

9.18

As indicated above, the scope of an investigation can vary considerably. Therefore, one issue to consider at the outset is a record of the intended aims and scope of the investigation. This task must be done on a case by case basis, and of course should not create a scope that is so narrow as to render the investigation ineffective or so wide that the investigation covers areas that are irrelevant.

9.19

Whatever the scope, it will only rarely be the case that a UKBA investigation will seek only to understand whether an allegation of corruption is 'true'. In order to assess the liability and improve compliance structures and internal controls, it may well also be important to understand if the required parts of the relevant offence have occurred and to understand the strength of any 'adequate procedures' defence. As part of this, it will often be necessary to understand individual actions and accountability, particularly that of any relevant senior leaders.

9.20

The scope of an investigation can (and should) be monitored and may be amended as new matters or information comes to light. By way of example, new allegations or concerns (eg other types of bribery) could arise that may be best considered within the investigation, and other issues may arise which may not require investigation or which may be best suitable to be referred to another assurance process, for audit or for review by a prosecutor or a third party.

Managing employees

9.21

Inevitably the time, cost and particularly the need for the investigation team to withhold confidential/sensitive information during an investigation can cause employees to become stressed, whether they were responsible for misconduct or not. Although this stress cannot realistically be completely avoided, it can often be reduced using the following techniques:

- strong tone from the top – ie support from senior management;
- interim updates on the investigations to relevant employee teams, that for instance thank employees for their co-operation, ask for their continued support, empathise with problems that may arise given the disruption occurring and re-affirm the corporate commitment to ethical business practice;
- professional, polite and responsive investigation teams who adopt an empathetic approach;
- taking heed of the requirement not to retaliate against whistleblowers and, in support of this, maintaining the anonymity of any whistleblower

and keeping the whistleblower (or 'concerned individual') informed of the company's commitment to the investigation and, if possible, the likely timeline for closure of the matter.

Finally, where possible, it is usually helpful to at least consider informing whistleblowers of the outcome of the investigation This is for instance standard practice under the EU Whistleblower Protection Directive.

9.22

Critically, investigation teams operating in the regulated sector must be cognisant of several offences for tipping-off and prejudicing an investigation that apply under the Proceeds of Crime Act 2002 ('POCA'). Under POCA 'tipping off' means alerting a relevant individual, for example, the person suspected of laundering money or a close associate of his, that an investigation into the suspected money laundering is either in progress or pending. Two separate tipping off offences are covered under POCA, that relate to situations before and after a Suspicious Activity Report ('SAR') has been made.

9.23

Elements of a tipping off offence under POCA:

i. A person discloses to a third party that he has made a relevant disclosure to the National Crime Agency (NCA), or any other relevant individual OR discloses that an investigation into allegations that an offence under POCA has been committed is being contemplated or is being carried out;

ii. That disclosure is likely to prejudice any investigation that might be conducted following the disclosure; and

iii. The information on which the disclosure is based came to the person in the course of a business in the regulated sector.

Walmart case study[9]

9.24

Considering some of the above themes, below is a case study concerning *allegations* relating to Walmart, published in the *New York Times* by the Pulitzer prize winners David Barstow and Alejandra Xanic von Bertrab in April 2012.

9 See http://searchcompliance.techtarget.com/guides/FAQ-Wal-Mart-de-Mexico-scandal-and-how-it-triggered-FCPA-violations and www.fcpablog.com/blog/2012/11/16/wal-marts-latest-fcpa-disclosure-november-2012.html.

Walmart Case Study

In April 2012, the New York Times reported on alleged corruption within Walmart in a detailed article, which included the following statement:

> 'Wal-Mart dispatched investigators to Mexico City, and within days they unearthed evidence of widespread bribery. They found a paper trail of hundreds *of suspect payments totaling more than $24 million.* They also found documents showing that Wal-Mart de Mexico's top executives not only knew about the payments, but had taken steps to conceal them from Wal-Mart's headquarters in Bentonville, Ark.
>
> In a confidential report to his superiors, Wal-Mart's lead investigator, a former F.B.I. special agent, summed up their initial findings this way: "There is reasonable suspicion to believe that Mexican and USA laws have been violated."
>
> *The lead investigator recommended that Wal-Mart expand the investigation. Instead, an examination by the New York Times found, Wal-Mart's leaders shut it down.*' (emphasis added)

It was further reported that WalMart management sent the above matter to be investigated by a legal officer alleged to have been involved with wrongdoing, essentially thwarting a proper review.

Predictably perhaps, these allegations have been very negative for Walmart, showing just how damaging even allegation of a cover-up/ failure to investigate properly can be. In particular:

- An investigation led by the US DoJ and Securities and Exchange Commission ('SEC') was started and continues as at October 2013 in relation to Walmart's actions.
- Senior management figures resigned or left office and may face prosecution in due course.
- In March 2013, Walmart disclosed that legal costs alone relating to the matter were running at US$604,000 per day.
- The share price of Walmart was materially impacted following the disclosure of the allegation in the New York Times.
- In November 2012, Walmart notified the listing authorities that its investigations had spread to include India, China and Brazil.

In June 2019, Walmart announced that it would pay US$282 million to settle what was by that time a seven-year long global probe into potential FCPA violations by its entities in Mexico, Brazil, China and India.

Information gathering

9.25

Investigations inevitably focus on three types of fact gathering: (i) documentary fact gathering (including electronic sources of information: emails, telecommunication records, computer and mobile devices and other electronic records and recordings (potentially also using on-line resources and due diligence tools)); (ii) interviews; and (iii) financial records, including internal account records and bank statements.

9.26

There is no established best practice as to whether to proceed first with document review or with interviews or to proceed with both in parallel. This will depend on the matter under review.

9.27

In interviews, investigators/investigative lawyers in the UK will often provide what is sometimes called in America an Upjohn warning or a corporate Miranda warning. In this statement, the investigator might explain to the interviewee the company policy as regards conducting fair investigations (and often the principle of non-retaliation), that the investigation process is confidential, and therefore that the interviewee should not discuss it with any person (other than their lawyer[10] if appointed, a member of the internal review team or other approved person such as a labour council representative or nominated support person), that the notes of the interview will be taken by the review team, that the company may assert 'privilege' (see paras 9.45–46 below) over those notes in the event of related or associated proceedings or provide them to a third party, such as a regulator. The investigator may also say that any lawyer present represents the company rather than the interviewee.[11]

9.28

An example of an Upjohn warning for US matters, issued by the American Bar Association's White Collar Crime Committee Working Group, follows below:

> 'I am a lawyer for Corporation A. I represent only Corporation A, and I do not represent you personally or any other employees of Corporation A.
>
> I am conducting this interview with you and other Corporation A employees to gather facts in order to provide legal advice for

10 In some cases it may be appropriate for an employee to have separate legal representation, possibly at the company's cost. This is relatively unusual and is considered on a case by case basis.

11 See *Upjohn Co v United States* 449 US 383 (1981).

Corporation A. This interview is part of an investigation to determine the facts and circumstances of X in order to advise Corporation A how best to proceed.

Your communications with me are protected by /the attorney-client privilege. But the attorney-client privilege belongs solely to Corporation A, not you. That means Corporation A alone may elect to waive the attorney-client privilege and reveal our discussion to third parties. Corporation A alone may decide to waive the privilege and disclose this discussion to such third parties as federal or state agencies, at its sole discretion, and without notifying you.

In order for this discussion to be subject to the privilege, it must be kept in confidence. In other words, with the exception of your own attorney, you may not disclose the substance of this interview to any third party, including other employees or anyone outside of the company. You may discuss the facts of what happened but you may not discuss this discussion.

Do you understand what I have explained to you?

Do you have any questions?

Are you willing to proceed?'

9.29

In relation to document review, documents (including electronic sources of information, data from computer and mobile devices and informed stored in web-based repositories) are usually identified and moved or copied for removal to a suitable site for processing, recording and review. Where there are considerable numbers of electronic or documentary sources of information, it is common practice in the UK and in the US to apply a proportionate approach to review what may be hundreds of thousands, or in some cases millions of emails and documents, eg 30.5 million documents were collected by Airbus from relevant custodians in the course of the SFO's investigation). This is a science in its own right but it is frequently the case that investigators will undertake (or instruct a specialist to undertake) the following steps:

(a) collate and forensically process the documents/electronic data into a single and easy to use data review platform (eg Reveal; Brainspace; Relativity; Nuix; Ringtail; Everlaw; Logikcull; ZyLAB; Sightline; Intella; Celebrite; OSForensics; and Encase);

(b) remove 'duplicate' documents eg email reviews will often collect emails sent by one person and received by another, making one of these sets of emails a duplicate (or near duplicate) of the original;

(c) apply 'search terms' across the emails/data to identify potentially responsive emails (eg searching for emails referring to, for instance, 'special commissions', 'bonuses' or 'fees);[12]

(d) use threading to review a series or string of emails or communications which derive from the same thread.

(e) use of artificial intelligence such as machine learning or predictive coding to email review. Typically, these tools are applied to help identify the most useful documents as quickly as possible and often involve natural language processing to work across different languages and exclude irrelevant data.

  – An effective method is the use of Continuous Active Learning which works by separating items into two sets: (1) those typically associated with a 'positive' result; and (2) those typically associated with a 'negative' result. Positive labels are often items coded as 'relevant' or 'key' whilst negative labels have been coded as 'not relevant'. Common patterns in a representative sample set allow for a calculated weighting/value to be assigned to each item enabling the sorting of documents more likely to be relevant or key which can be prioritised for review. The system continues to intelligently learn each time a label is assigned (positive or negative), building a more accurate pattern to apply across the data set.

(f) identifying events and connections through use of interactive timelines, concept search, metadata analysis and visualised social mapping tools;

(g) adoption of machine translation to assist with the prioritisation and review of documents. It is advisable for potentially hot or key items to be reviewed in their native language and where there is doubt as to the accuracy of translation.

Document preservation

9.30

Few matters in an investigation cause as many problems or garner as much attention from prosecutors as document preservation. Specific advice will usually be sought in relation to document preservation during an investigation. However, it is common practice for an investigation team or legal advisors to circulate what are known variously as 'document holds', 'litigation document hold notices' or 'document preservation notices' to potentially relevant employees and third parties at a very early stage in an investigation to prevent the intentional or unintentional deletion of relevant data. In some cases, this is

12 Other documents that may be reviewed include any other form of recording, such as tape/audio recordings, written notes, draft documents, diary entries etc.

further strengthened by early copying or removal of documents – in whatever form – that may be relevant to the concerns raised.

9.31

In the US, failures in the above regard have been connected to criminal charges and in the UK deletion of data can also potentially lead to civil and criminal liabilities as well as to obvious reputational damage.[13]

9.32

Where investigations include numerous parties, an electronic document retention system may be advantageous in tracking document holds and any exceptions.

Data protection

9.33

Data protection will always be a consideration for investigators and is particularly key when information gathered is personal or sensitive in nature or needs to be processed in or transferred between countries. However, as regards investigations conducted in the UK regarding UK employees, applicable laws under the Data Protection Act 2018 (the DPA 2018) that reasonably aim to protect employees' sensitive and personal data are unlikely to prevent a legitimate corruption investigation, where appropriate mitigating steps such as obtaining informed consent and redacting irrelevant information are taken.

9.34

In some circumstances, exemptions under Schedules 2 and 4 of the DPA 2018 may apply to relieve a corporate from certain data protection obligations, such as the right to be informed, reporting personal data breaches and other individual rights. One such exemption includes circumstances where a company is required by law to disclose certain formation in response to a warrant or mandatory regulatory notice.

This is not always the case in countries such as Spain, Germany and France, where data protection and employee rights issues generally are likely to require more thought and action.[14]

13 See Lomas and Kramer (eds), *Corporate Internal Investigations: An International Guide* (2nd edn, Oxford University Press, 2013), paras 4.136–4.140.

14 See Data Protection Act 1998 and *Corporate Internal Investigations*, paras 4.150–4.187.

Interim decision making during the investigation

9.35

Business goes on during investigations as of course does business decision-making. A really effective investigation team must therefore 'issue spot' and provide interim briefings and legal advice sufficient for the sponsor to make key decisions and interventions that simply cannot reasonably wait until the close of the investigation but may also have an impact on investigations.

9.36

Relevant interim decisions will of course depend on the nature of the business and investigation but common issues are as follows: whether to suspend, terminate or renew (if they are coming to an end) employee[15] or supplier contracts; whether to continue to sell goods or services that may in some way be 'tainted'; whether to file SARs pursuant to Part 7 of POCA or the Terrorism Act 2000; whether and how to respond to requests from the press or other third parties;[16] whether to make contingency plans for replacement providers; when and how to report to listing authorities; and whether to 'press ahead with' or delay investment and divestment decisions.

9.37

All of the above decisions of course benefit from a sponsor who has not only the authority to take decisions but who has sufficient experience of the organisation to be capable of decisive action, even in difficult situations where not all of the salient facts are available.

Report writing

9.38

Investigation report writing is a complicated skill, and it can be difficult to try and capture the important information and themes for a major project in one document, which is often prepared by a lawyer in relation to more significant matters for privilege reasons (see paras 9.45–46 below).

9.39

Although investigation reports are prepared on a case by case basis, they will usually include key sections, which are as follows:

---

15 It is helpful to consider the termination arrangements of any employee who is leaving, both in relation to cooperation obligations and severance packages, which may seem excessive if corruption is proved. As regards suspension, it can be helpful to set out the terms of the suspension, particularly as regards access to people, IT and offices.

16 It will often be helpful to prepare, in advance, a short press statement and to consider a press strategy. A PR consultant may also be helpful.

Methodology

9.40

A methodology section is an essential part of the report and explains the steps that have been taken, the resources applied and importantly an explanation of why some steps or avenues of investigation were not pursued (eg for reasons of proportionality).

Findings

9.41

No report is complete without clearly setting out the findings and making conclusions clear and evidence based. However, care must be taken not to over or under state what can be deduced from the facts.

Legal analysis

9.42

Arguably the most important section of the report, this section explains the legal issues (often interspersed in the findings) and how the law applies to the company. In relation to corruption issues, lawyers explain potential liabilities, continuing legal risks and self-reporting obligations, laws and requirements as well as analysis of breaches of adequate procedures. Reports will also often include advice on any relevant money laundering issues.

Recommendations

9.43

Last but by no means least, investigation reports will often provide the sponsor with recommendations. Inevitably these will be case specific. However, common recommendations may relate to discipline regarding employees, actions to be brought against third parties, the strengthening of controls and procedures (including training and communications), monitoring, relationships with third parties and self-reporting to enforcement authorities such as the Serious Fraud Office of City of London Police / Action Fraud.[17]

9.44

Whatever the recommendations are, it is important for both commercial and ethical reasons that lessons are learnt. It is therefore helpful for companies to

17 See the SFO's guidance on Corporate Self-Reporting at www.sfo.gov.uk/publications/guidance-policy-and-protocols/corporate-self-reporting/.

monitor and where possible record the implementation of recommendations that are accepted by the sponsor.

Privilege and investigation

9.45

Privilege is an over-arching issue relating to not only investigations but to all documentation created relating to corruption issues. The short point of principle, protected by English law, is that any person, either a company or individual, ought to be able to seek advice from their lawyer honestly and frankly, without fearing that those documents containing advice will be disclosed in court proceedings or be produced to prosecutors.[18]

9.46

The general rule therefore in English common law is that investigation documents can be subject to privilege if they remain confidential and either contain legal advice for the sponsor or are produced for the dominant purpose of contemplated litigation, which includes a prosecution.

9.47

In 2018, the UK Court of Appeal's ('COA') decision in *The Director of the Serious Fraud Office v Eurasian Natural Resources Corporation Limited* [2018] EWCA Civ 2006 (the *SFO v ENRC*) unanimously overturned a controversial High Court ruling regarding the scope of privilege covering investigation material, including notes taken by lawyers during investigation interviews and materials generated by forensic accountants. At first instance, the High Court denied a claim of litigation privilege in relation to said documents.

9.48

The COA diverged from the view taken by the High Court on a number of important points of general principle, finding that:

- whilst a party anticipating possible prosecution will often need to make further investigations before it can say with certainty that proceedings are likely, that uncertainty does not of itself prevent proceedings being in reasonable contemplation;
- the High Court was wrong that litigation privilege cannot attach until either: (a) the defendant knows the full details of what is likely to be unearthed; or (b) a decision to prosecute has been taken; and

18 In many countries 'privilege' is very limited or does not exist as a concept, and in such countries it may be possible for the Court to require a copy of relevant investigation documents.

- the fact that a formal criminal investigation has not yet been commenced will be a part of the factual matrix when determining whether litigation is reasonably in contemplation, but it will not necessarily be determinative.

9.49

Despite the COA's decision in the *SFO v ENRC*, privilege in England remains narrower than many think (and differs from the broader position in the US). With this in mind, advice should usually be sought from legal representatives in relation to the creation and control of privileged documents at the outset of a major issue. However, as regards investigations, 'golden rules' include the following:

- Use internal or external lawyers.
- Restrict production of unnecessary investigation documents.
- Label relevant new investigation documents 'privileged and confidential'.
- Restrict the number of recipients of investigation documents to those people who are essential to decision making or undertaking the investigation.
- Set out in the investigation report (and potentially any other key documents) the primary reasons for conducting the investigation.
- Carefully consider statements of opinion in documents created during an investigation, including emails, and particularly whether such statements are accurate and necessary.
- Give thought to whether it is appropriate to entirely 'outsource' investigations to accountancy practices, where privilege will not normally apply to correspondence between accountants and their clients.[19]

Further resources

9.50

For those interested in this area or in benchmarking their own processes, there is a lack of UK material that is inexpensively available. However, available material does helpfully include the following:

- Lomas and Kramer (eds), *Corporate Internal Investigations: An International Guide* (2nd edn, OUP, January 2013);[20]

19 *R (on the application of Prudential plc and another) (Appellants) v Special Commissioner of Income Tax and another (Respondents)* [2013] UKSC 1. On appeal from [2010] EWCA Civ 1094.

20 www.freshfields.com/en/news/Second_edition_of_Corporate_Internal_Investigations_gives_unique_guide_to_quickening_pace_and_widening_scope_of_international_regulation/?LanguageId=2057.

- Linklaters LLP, '*Internal Investigations – a Practical Guide*', published online in May 2013;[21]
- Global Investigations Review (GIR) *'Practitioner's Guide to Global Investigations'* – Fourth edition (2020); and
- *Lissack and Horlick on Bribery and Corruption* (3rd edn, LexisNexis, 2020);
- *The Association for Corporate Investigations* (ACi). The ACi is a not-for-profit association established to meet the needs of corporate investigation professionals who require training, networking opportunities and a centralised resource for members (www.my-aci.com).

21 www.linklaters.com/Publications/Investigations_Regulatory_Enforcement/Conduct_Investigations/Pages/Guidance_Conduct_of_Investigations.aspx.

10 Self-reporting

Introduction

10.01

A decision to co-operate includes:

> 'identifying suspected wrong-doing and criminal conduct together with the people responsible, regardless of their seniority or position in the organisation; reporting this to the SFO within a reasonable time of the suspicions coming to light; and preserving available evidence and providing it promptly in an evidentially sound format'.[1]

The discovery by an organisation of potential wrongdoing within its business requires prompt action to investigate, identify and, if necessary, stop and eradicate any problem, but perhaps the most difficult question that must be tackled is whether or not to report what has happened to a regulator or prosecuting agency. This is a commercial decision for the company, rather than a legal requirement. This is a separate question from whether a company should or ought to make a SAR (but if it does, then the SFO may come to hear of the matter in any event).

10.02

As noted above, self-reporting in the UK is already a regular feature of money laundering regimes, and in recent years the practice has been actively encouraged by prosecuting agencies investigating corporate offending (principally the Serious Fraud Office ('SFO')). No guarantees can be given; however self-reporting will generally have a positive impact on any action that may be taken in relation to the company, and regularly this will take the form of a more lenient outcome than might otherwise be the case. This has been clarified by the SFO in recent years. In April 2019 Lisa Osofsky, the Director of the SFO, announced that the SFO would issue new guidance to companies to give them added transparency about what they might expect if they decide to self-report fraud or corruption to the SFO.

10.03

The SFO has, to date, published:

1 SFO Corporate Co-operation Guidance August 2019.

- Deferred Prosecution Agreement Guidance (SFO Operational Handbook), on 23 October 2020.
- Corporate Co-operation Guidance (SFO Operational Handbook), on 6 August 2019.
- The SFO Deferred Prosecution Agreements Code of Practice ('DPA Code'), on 14 February 2014.
- Guidance on Corporate Self-Reporting (last revised in October 2012 and prior to the introduction of DPAs. It is still available on the SFO's website and remains useful so far as it refers to the self-reporting process).

10.04

The above guidance has clarified the general approach that the SFO will take to self-reporting and cooperation by companies. The SFO has made clear that 'co-operation by organisations benefits the public and advances the interests of justice by enabling the Serious Fraud Office more quickly and reliably to understand the facts, obtain admissible evidence, and progress an investigation to the stage where the prosecutor can apply the law to the facts.'[2] As set out in the DPA Code, self-reporting and cooperation is a public interest factor tending against prosecution when management has adopted a 'genuinely proactive approach' upon learning of the offending (§32 (a) DPA Code 2.8.2 (i)).

10.05

However, despite the increased clarity as to the weight that will be given to self-reporting by the SFO, self-reporting is not an action that can be taken or viewed in isolation. The act of reporting potential or actual misconduct is likely to impact upon a company's business and will frequently result in action by more than one regulator in several countries (in cases where the SFO does not prosecute a self-reporting corporate body, the SFO reserves the right to provide information on the reported violation to other interested bodies such as foreign investigating authorities), as well as having implications for the business once the issue becomes public (or in the event that the report is leaked). As a result, self-reporting must be a well-considered and carefully planned step which forms part of a company's overall strategy to address any potential unethical behaviour by individuals within the business.

10.06

Ideally, the object of self-reporting is either to start a company down the path to a DPA, or to persuade the regulator or prosecutor that the company's own internal investigation has dealt with the problem adequately and that there is no need for intervention. However, whether that aim is achieved depends on numerous and variable factors including the nature and seriousness of any

2 SFO Corporate Co-operation Guidance.

allegations, the timing of the self-report and the accuracy or completeness of the information received. In particular, the timing of the report, the quality of the information disclosed and the cooperation provided to the prosecuting body (or regulator) will influence how much trust is placed in the company concerned and therefore how intrusive any investigation by the regulator or prosecutor might be.

10.07

Although self-reporting is encouraged it remains a relatively recent concept in the UK. Traditionally, companies in the UK have been less enthusiastic about laying themselves open to prosecutors than, say, in the US where the culture of self-reporting is more established. However, the principal, and largely effective, carrot is the potential avoidance of a criminal conviction via Deferred Prosecution Agreements ('DPAs'), as to which see Chapter 11. As a result, something of a sea change in attitude towards self-reporting has commenced over the past seven years. The introduction of DPAs on 24 February 2014 is part of a specific policy to encourage self-reporting; as was observed in *SFO v XYZ Ltd*, incentivising self-reporting is a core purpose of DPAs and the weight the self-report attracts depends on the totality of the information provided [§45]:

> '… it is important to send a clear message, reflecting a policy choice in bringing DPAs into the law of England and Wales, that a company's shareholders, customers and employees (as well as all those with whom it deals) are far better served by self-reporting and putting in place effective compliance structures. When it does so, that openness must be rewarded and be seen to be worthwhile.'

10.08

It is a very tempting carrot, given that no prosecution following a DPA has resulted in the conviction of the individuals involved, suggesting that perhaps companies may have entered into DPAs in circumstances where the evidence was insufficient to convict the individual actors, although there are other commercial reasons why a company would nevertheless find a DPA attractive. There have been 12 deferred prosecution agreements to date, and in all of them the cooperation of the company involved has been cited as a factor tending against prosecution and in favour of a DPA.

Key points

10.09

There can be no question but that self-reporting is laden with risk and lacking in certainty as to how 'bitter the pill' might be at the end of it all. However, the pitfalls can be mitigated if self-reporting forms part of a highly planned strategy.

This chapter aims to address the principal issues that those responsible for the internal investigation will wish to consider which are as follows:

(1) What is self-reporting and what are the advantages?

(2) When to self-report.

(3) To whom to self-report.

(4) How much information should be provided?

(5) How to self-report.

(6) What are the risks of self-reporting and how to counter them?

What is self-reporting and what are the advantages?

- Advantages
  - The potential for more lenient treatment by a regulator or prosecution agency
  - Likelihood of non-criminal disposal increased by introduction of DPAs
  - Helps to preserve a company's reputation and moral imperative
  - Sustains shareholder confidence
  - Increases a company's ability to continue to trade
- Disadvantages
  - The company will lose at least some control over the problem and over any internal investigation
  - There are no guarantees of lenient treatment in the UK
  - To be most effective, self-reports should be made at an early stage, which may be before the full facts can be assessed by the company
  - Business disruption
  - Information may be disseminated to agencies in other countries with little flexibility for non-criminal sanctions

What is self-reporting?

10.10

Whereas self-reporting in anti-money laundering terms can be a mechanism used to distance a business from misconduct by third parties, in this context it is the opposite. Self-reporting involves revealing to a prosecutor or regulator misconduct that is known or suspected to have taken place and the measures taken or proposed to deal with it. There is no doubt but that regulators, particularly in the US and more recently in the UK, look favourably upon self-reporting and a business culture where self-reporting is not only acceptable but considered proper ethical conduct is being actively encouraged. This can be seen as part of the wider drive to promote ethical business spearheaded by the Bribery Act 2010. This is resulting in, or perhaps coinciding with, a growing expectation on the part of shareholders and the market place in the UK and elsewhere that business will be conducted properly, responsibly and ethically.

10.11

In times of reduced resources and high expectations, it is in the interests of the authorities to give companies a reason to self-report, and to foster a culture of self-policing and self-discipline. For a start, it brings concealed or secretive misbehaviour, such as corruption, to their attention where otherwise it may have remained invisible. It permits involvement by a prosecutor or regulator with an internal investigation without bearing the cost, and enables the direction of resources and manpower elsewhere. Furthermore, self-reporting which leads to an agreed outcome and remedy or sanction is a very cost-effective means of investigation and disposal of alleged or potential criminal conduct.

What are the advantages of self-reporting?

10.12

So far as companies themselves are concerned there are several advantages that come from self-reporting. First and foremost, the prosecutor or regulator should be predisposed to act more leniently and less intrusively towards the company and, in the best case scenario, may be persuaded not to take any action at all. However, quite what form the more lenient treatment will take is difficult to predict and there is no guarantee that a prosecution will not result where the SFO takes the view that the facts require one. The SFO Guidance on Corporate Self-Reporting, issued on 9 October 2012, provides that a decision whether or not to instigate a prosecution will be determined by what is known as the 'Full Code Test'. In other words, the SFO will consider first whether the evidence gives rise to a realistic prospect of conviction (the sufficient evidence test), and secondly whether a prosecution would be in the public interest.

10.13

The guidance goes on to state that a self-report can be taken into consideration as a public interest factor tending against prosecution. The internal SFO guidance on DPAs also states that 'Co-operation is a key factor to consider when deciding whether to enter into a DPA.' However, co-operation must be part of a 'genuinely proactive approach adopted by the corporate management team'. This is an important caveat. Furthermore, this phrase has been adopted by the 'Deferred Prosecution Agreements Code of Practice 2014' issued by the Serious Fraud Office and Crown Prosecution Service on 14 February 2014 and reproduced in Appendix 7, which states that considerable weight may be given to such an approach when considering whether or not to prosecute an offence. In other words, the mere fact of a self-report is insufficient; the SFO will expect to receive full cooperation from the company concerned. The guidance also warns that self-reporting brings no guarantee that a prosecution will not follow. That being said, the possibility of a non-criminal disposal has not been ruled out entirely. The SFO retains a discretion whether or not to offer a company a DPA, or negotiations with a view to a DPA. In addition, although it has not done so for several years, the SFO still has powers of civil recovery under proceeds of crime legislation as an alternative to prosecution.

10.14

The internal SFO Corporate Cooperation Guidance makes the above explicit, stating that:

- Co-operation means providing assistance to the SFO that goes above and beyond what the law requires. It includes: identifying suspected wrong-doing and criminal conduct together with the people responsible, regardless of their seniority or position in the organisation; reporting this to the SFO within a reasonable time of the suspicions coming to light; and preserving available evidence and providing it promptly in an evidentially sound format.
- Genuine co-operation is inconsistent with: protecting specific individuals or unjustifiably blaming others; putting subjects on notice and creating a danger of tampering with evidence or testimony; silence about selected issues; and tactical delay or information overloads.
- It is important that organisations seeking to co-operate understand that co-operation – even full, robust co-operation – does not guarantee any particular outcome. The very nature of co-operation means that no checklist exists that can cover every case. Each case will turn on its own facts.

10.15

Secondly, while self-reporting often results in a loss of control over an investigation, self-reporting can, in some circumstances, allow the company to retain more control over the investigation and its affairs that it would otherwise have were it to be investigated covertly by a regulator or prosecutor and then the subject of a dawn raid. The company can provide industry background, context and detail of common practices and potential defences that are particular to the market or industry which can help shape the investigative approach. Self-reporting provides a company with knowledge of the information passed to the regulator. In short, there are fewer surprises. In some circumstances, where the relationship with the regulator is a reasonable one, self-reporting can provide the company with the opportunity to discuss publication of information with the prosecutor or regulator in advance, permitting steps to be taken to ameliorate any potential negative consequences. A company that self-reports to a regulator is much more likely to gain the regulator's trust and thus permit the establishment of a relationship where cooperation and openness is provided by each party. The more confidence a prosecutor has in the internal investigation and the information provided by the company, the less likely it is to launch its own investigation or to take over any existing investigation from the management. If, as a result, a company is permitted to keep control over the internal investigation, then any investigation by the regulator is likely to be significantly less invasive and business disruption should be minimised.

10.16

Thirdly, a company will also wish to be seen to be acting ethically and removing corruption where it may exist within the company. Self-reporting as part of an effective internal investigation will reassure clients and investors that any further wrongdoing is being prevented, thus assisting in the preservation of the company's reputation and market confidence in its business. This impact has been highlighted in the judgment of Sir Brian Leveson PQBD in approving the DPA in *SFO v Tesco Ltd* (in which Tesco accepted responsibility for false accounting practices between February and September 2014). In his concluding remarks Sir Brian noted that cooperation with the prosecuting authorities was a way in which a company could demonstrate 'integrity':

> '115 … As I have said, any corporate entity is only a structure that operates through its directors and employees. If they commit crime in apparent interests of the company, that criminal offence is personal to them unless they are a controlling mind in which case the crime can be brought home against the company itself. Although there is reputational damage however junior the employee, the higher up the chain of management, the more serious the damage. That damage can only be limited by the demonstration of integrity, by the company operating through its most senior management.
>
> 116. There are, of course, different ways in which discovered criminality can be managed. I sought to address these possibilities in *SFO v Rolls-Royce plc* (U20170036), when I put the matter in this way (at [143]):

> "A cynic (or irresponsible company) might look at the costs which Rolls-Royce have incurred in their own investigation and wonder whether it be more sensible to keep quiet and hope that its conduct does not fall under the eye of the authorities. Quite apart from the total failure to acknowledge the difference between right and wrong, that is to fail to understand that such an approach carries with it cataclysmic risks. Whatever the costs Rolls-Royce have incurred, they are modest compared to the cost of seeking to brazen out an investigation which commences; absent self-disclosure and full co-operation, prosecution would require the attention of the company to be entirely focused on litigation at the expense of whatever business it is trying to conduct and conviction would almost inevitably spell a far greater disaster than has befallen Rolls-Royce."

117. Another way of making the same point is to identify what demonstration of integrity means. It generally requires self-reporting to the authorities, co-operation with an investigation, a willingness to learn the lessons and recognition that where corporate liability could be established, a penalty must be imposed for punishment and deterrence. In that way, the company concerned can demonstrate to its Board, its employees, its agents, its customers and its shareholders that it has learnt and will adhere to the highest standards required of those engaged in corporate activity in this country. In that regard, from 19 September 2014, after learning of the misstatement, Tesco Plc and Tesco Stores have done as much as possible to learn from what has happened and to start to rebuild the trust necessary to operate in a society where that trust is so important. Both deserve great credit for doing so.'

What are the disadvantages of self-reporting?

10.17

Of course, self-reporting is not entirely risk free. There is no guarantee that embarking upon such a process will not result in a criminal conviction for either the corporate or its employees, with attendant consequences for the company and the stability of its business that may not otherwise have taken place. Conversely, there is always the possibility that, despite initial suspicions, no criminal behaviour has in fact taken place, or facts may be viewed differently after a full investigation or further information comes to light. As a result of an early self-report the company may receive negative publicity, investors or clients may be discouraged and business activity disrupted. For this reason, the timing of any self- report would have to be very carefully considered. Furthermore, the company's view of the facts may differ from that taken by the regulator or prosecutor who may decide to take matters into its own hands, leading to inevitable business disruption with the consequence of placing the company on the back foot.

10.18

In summary, while no outcome is ruled out, frank and cooperative self-reporting will normally result in at least some benefit to the reporting corporation compared to the likely consequences of a prosecutor-instigated criminal investigation. It also opens the door to the possibility of a non-criminal sanction, and where this is achieved it may also result in the avoidance of the mandatory debarment provisions under section 57 of the Public Contracts Regulations 2015, thus allowing a company to continue to tender for public sector contracts. Even where a prosecution occurs, a company may earn a reduction in sentence as a result of having fully co-operated with the investigation, as occurred with the sentencing of GPT Special Project Management for corruption in April 2021.

Case Study: Effects of Co-operation on DPAs

The SFO's first DPA was with Standard Bank in 2015. Subsequent DPAs were agreed with Sarclad Ltd in 2016 and with Rolls-Royce and Tesco in 2017. In 2019, DPAs were agreed with Serco Geografix Ltd and Güralp Systems Ltd. In 2020, DPAs were agreed with Airbus SE, G4S Care & Justice Services (UK) Ltd and Airline Services Ltd.

Each DPA contained a discussion of the impact of cooperation by the relevant companies upon the decision to approve the DPA. All companies involved in the DPAs cooperated with the SFO (although as noted in the judgment in G4S and Airbus, cooperation with the SFO investigations was a little slow to start although generally the companies made up for initial deficiencies with extensive cooperation thereafter) and in three cases where the investigation was triggered solely by a self-report, this was specifically recognised in the judgment and, in two cases, it also had an effect on financial penalties.

Sarclad Ltd (also known as XYZ Ltd)

The DPA between Sarclad and the SFO was approved by the High Court in July 2016. Under the DPA Sarclad agreed to pay financial orders of £6,553,085, comprised of a £6,201,085 disgorgement of gross profits and a £352,000 financial penalty.

Sarclad designed and manufactured technology-based products for the steel manufacturing industry globally, generating the majority of its revenue from exports to Asian markets. In February 2000, it was acquired by Heico Companies LLC ('Heico') which was a US registered corporation.

During the period June 2004 to June 2012, Sarclad was involved in the systematic offer and/or payment of bribes to secure contracts in foreign jurisdictions. In the period 2004–2013, a total of £17.24 million was paid to Sarclad on the 28 implicated contracts on which bribes were offered. This sum represented 15.81% of the total turnover of Sarclad in the period (being £109 million).

The conspiracy involved a course of systematic conduct over eight years. It implicated seven agents in as many jurisdictions, generated £6.5 million of gross profit (£2.5 million net) and caused detriment to other potential competitors. It was, in the view of Sir Brian Leveson PQBD (who approved the DPA) part of Sarclad's 'established business conduct' and as such had to be considered conduct of the utmost gravity.

By its own admission, prior to 2012, Sarclad did not have adequate compliance provisions in place. In order to address this problem, in late 2011, Heico sought to improve matters in its subsidiary by implementing its global compliance programme within Sarclad. It was within the context of this compliance programme that, at the end of August 2012, concerns came to light about the way in which a number of contracts had been secured. Sarclad took immediate action and on 4 September 2012 it retained a law firm McGuireWoods LLP, to undertake an independent internal investigation.

On 13 November 2012, the lawyers met with the SFO and confirmed that Sarclad would be making a written self-report following the conclusion of the internal investigation. It was agreed that the written self-report would be submitted to the SFO by 31 January 2013. McGuireWoods delivered the self-report to the SFO on the agreed date. It was 39 pages in length and set out details of the evidence identified in relation to 16 implicated contracts and 20 suspicious contracts. Between 26 April 2013 and 14 January 2016, with the full co-operation of Sarclad, the SFO conducted its own investigation. Further, through McGuireWoods, Sarclad made continuing efforts to investigate and supplement the self-report.

In conducting the exercise in weighing up whether approval of the DPA was in the interests of justice in the preliminary judgment, the President noted the systematic nature of the conduct concerned and the period for which it continued but also noted that:

> "36. ...very considerable weight must be attached, reflecting a core purpose of the creation of DPAs being to incentivise the exposure (and self- reporting) of corporate wrongdoing, is the timeframe and sequence of events leading up to Sarclad's self-report to the SFO and the manner in which it adopted a genuinely proactive approach to the wrongdoing it uncovered: see para. 2.8.2(i) of the DPA Code of

Practice and Joint Prosecution Guidance to the Bribery Act 2010 (page 7). In that regard, the promptness of the self-report and the extent to which the prosecutor has been involved are to be taken into account: see para. 2.9.2 of the DPA Code of Practice.

37. In that context it is also important to underline that, had it not been for the self-report, the offending might otherwise have remained unknown to the prosecutor: see para. 2.8.2(i) of the DPA Code of Practice. In that regard, the conduct had lasted eight years without being detected. There is no suggestion of a whistle-blower or any other mechanism whereby the matter might have come to the attention of the authorities."

The President approved the DPA, and also took into account the impact of the self-report in deciding the financial penalty. He applied a discount of a third given the self-report and admission of the conduct, and then further discounted the penalty to 50% overall, taking into account how far in advance of the first reasonable opportunity to be charged the admissions had been given. Sir Brian also noted that one purpose of the 50% discount was 'not least to encourage others how to conduct themselves when confronting criminality as Sarclad has'. The eventual financial penalty was reduced even further upon reflection of what Sarclad would be able to pay without becoming insolvent, but which would be proportionate to the gravity of the conduct.

Sarclad was relatively small company, which committed offences of bribery and corruption on a 'prolific scale'. That a DPA was achieved, that the financial penalty reflected Sarclad's ability to pay and that the SFO did not seek costs (payment of which would also have been likely to make the company insolvent) can be attributed in part to the manner in which Sarclad conducted itself and the extent of its co-operation with the SFO once the wrongdoing was discovered by those within the company.

Guralp Systems

On 22 October 2019, the SFO and Güralp Systems Ltd finalised a Deferred Prosecution Agreement, under which Güralp Systems Ltd ('GSL') accepted the charges of conspiracy to make corrupt payments and failure to prevent bribery and agreed to pay a total of £2,069,861. Guralp was a UK registered company specialising in seismic measurement equipment. The misconduct related to payments made over a period of 12 years to an individual named Dr Chi who had held various positions with a government funded research institute in the Republic of South Korea.

The conduct had come to light after the appointment of Dr Christopher Potts as executive chairman of GSL in December 2014. In September 2015 he formed suspicions around the relationship between GSL and Dr Chi. Having spoken to individuals with knowledge of GSL's dealings with Dr Chi, Dr Potts terminated all contractual and other relationships existing between GSL and Dr Chi. Dr Potts then instructed a firm of solicitors, Addleshaw Goddard, to undertake an internal review.

As a result of that review, on 23 October 2015, GSL reported its concerns to the SFO and to the United States Department of Justice. A report by way of a presentation from Addleshaw Goddard was provided on 19 November 2015 to the SFO.

In conducting the balance as to whether the DPA was in the interests of justice, Davis J noted that:

> '27. The first matter to be set in the balance in favour of a DPA is the fact that GSL reported the making of the corrupt payments to the authorities both in this country and in the United States. This reporting did not consist simply of an indication to the authorities of a suspicion of corrupt payments with an offer to assist in any investigation. Rather, GSL engaged an outside law firm to assess the position. Upon that law firm reaching its conclusions, GSL required the law firm to make a detailed presentation of its findings. Much of the core material relied on for the purpose of the application for a DPA and in the extant criminal proceedings is drawn from the findings of the outside law firm instructed by GSL albeit that the SFO conducted its own thorough investigation to establish the nature and extent of the criminality involved.
>
> …
>
> 50. …the relevant conduct did not come to light in the context of another enquiry (as was the case with Serco) or via an internal whistle-blower (Tesco) or through internet postings (Rolls-Royce) or due to the intervention of an associated enterprise (Standard Bank and Sarclad). In this instance those who had taken over the running of the company in 2015 identified the conduct, instructed outside solicitors to investigate and self-reported to the SFO. Had they wished to do so, they presumably could have covered up what had gone on and/or allowed the corrupt practices to continue.'

Davis J went on to consider that GSL had not previously engaged in criminal conduct and substantial steps had been taken once Dr Potts had discovered what was going on vis-à-vis Dr Chi. Taking these factors into account Davis J found that it was in the interests of justice for the conduct of GSL to be resolved through the mechanism of a DPA.

Airline Services Ltd

On 30 October 2020, the SFO entered into a DPA with Airline Services Limited ('ASL'), with the approval of Mrs Justice May. Under the terms of the DPA, ASL accepted responsibility for three counts of failing to prevent bribery arising from the company's use of an agent to win three contracts between 2011–13, together worth over £7.3 million, to refit commercial airliners for Lufthansa.

In 2014 concerns within ASL led it to instruct external solicitors to examine a series of unrelated contracts involving a different agent and a different airline ('Agent X/Airline Y'). Although these solicitors reported allaying ASL's original concerns in relation to Agent X, the process incidentally threw light upon the activities of an agent in Germany. At this point ASL once more instructed external solicitors to investigate. The results of that investigation prompted ASL to make self-disclosure to the SFO, which ASL did initially on 30 July 2015. The SFO thereafter conducted its own investigation, using material provided by ASL both voluntarily and through use by the SFO of its compulsory powers.

May J was satisfied that the public interest lay against prosecution. She noted that ASL's offending behaviour was 'egregious' and took place over a sustained period of time. However, ASL mounted its own investigation, made a timely self-report and provided full cooperation to the SFO. May J noted that 'This is an important consideration given that the core purpose of the creation of DPAs was to "incentivise" the exposure and self-report of corporate wrong-doing'. May J then went on to consider the financial penalty, and took the self-report into account in doing so:

> '71. Ordinarily, a guilty plea would engage a maximum one third discount, or 33%. However it has been recognised in DPA cases that a further discount may be appropriate, for the reasons given by Leveson LJ in *Sarclad*, at [69]:
>
> > "In addition, given that the admissions are far in advance of the first reasonable opportunity having been charged and brought before the court, that discount can be increased as representing additional mitigation. In the circumstances, a discount of 50% could be appropriate not least to encourage others how to conduct themselves when confronting criminality..."
>
> 72. ...in addition to early reporting and acceptance of wrongdoing, ASL has demonstrated a very high degree of cooperation, including a (limited) waiver of legal

professional privilege in respect of ASL's own investigation into the Lufthansa agreements and the previous one into the activities of Agent X/Airline Y. He also drew my attention to the requirement, identified at Step 9 of the Guideline, to consider the totality of offending where, as here, there is more than one offence.'

Mrs Justice May therefore applied a discount of 50% to the financial penalty. She finished by noting that:

> '79. DPAs are still relatively rare, this being the ninth to be approved since the enactment of the 2013 Act. The present DPA requires ASL to disgorge all profit made from the business obtained through bribery and also to pay a significant financial penalty. The penalty, and the discount, serve to convey two important messages: the first is that corporate offending will be visited by the imposition of a very heavy financial penalty over and above the disgorging of profits wrongly made; the second, via the discount of 50% on that penalty, conveying a positive and substantial incentive toward self- reporting and cooperation where offending is detected.'

When to self-report?

- Before, during or after an internal investigation?
- What are the views of the relevant agencies on the timing of self-reports?
- Is the company subject to any regulatory rules on self-reporting?
- What is the impact on personnel?
- How will the timing affect the business of the company?

10.19

Certainly, so far as UK and US regulators and prosecuting agencies are concerned, the emphasis is on early disclosure; the earlier the better. It has been argued that making an initial report as soon as suspected criminality has been discovered protects the company against the SFO finding out through other channels whilst the company investigates further. However, from the company's perspective, the optimal or most prudent time to self-report is not easy to identify, particularly since a report once made cannot be withdrawn. Should it be as soon as a suggestion of improper conduct is made? This would provide the best opportunity to persuade a regulator that the company is trustworthy and can be relied upon to deal with the problem by way of internal investigation, however this cedes control before the company will have had the time to fully establish the facts and which personnel is involved. Alternatively, should it be during the internal investigation once sufficient facts are known to allow the company to be aware of the issues and the nature of the alleged corrupt conduct, with the concordant risk that the whistle may be blown in the interim?

10.20

Alternatively, should a report take place after the internal investigation has concluded and once the company is in possession of the results of that investigation, when the facts are known and no further facts are likely to come to light to alter the position, thus allowing the company to settle its strategy before the matter is reported?

10.21

Identifying when to report is a difficult decision, fraught with tension both in terms of the company's best interests and internal divisions – especially for those whose conduct is the subject of investigation and who may, along with the company, face prosecution.

10.22

However, it is not solely the company and the views of its personnel that should be considered. Regulators around the world have varying views about whether and when companies should self-report. Therefore, when to self-report may be informed by the identity and jurisdiction of the particular regulator(s) under whose remit the matter falls.

10.23

In the UK, the principal prosecution agency with responsibility for corruption offences is the SFO. While it does not have a formal procedure that will apply to all companies that choose to self-report, the likelihood of a non-criminal disposal has been improved with the introduction of DPAs in February 2014. DPAs are considered in more detail in Chapter 11 but a decision to offer a DPA will be influenced by whether or not the company self-reported the matter to the SFO. The DPA Code of Practice appears to infer that a self-report will be a starting point for the consideration of a DPA. According to the Code, the factors that will be taken into account when considering such a course include:

(1) the totality of the information provided by the company to the prosecutor – the withholding of relevant information will be considered a strong factor in favour of prosecution (paragraph 2.9.1);

(2) how early the company self-reports; this includes the extent to which the company involves the prosecutor in the early stages of an investigation, allowing a degree of direction to be provided (paragraph 2.9.2); and

(3) whether not reporting at an earlier stage has prejudiced the investigation, and in particular whether the manner of the internal investigation could have led to the destruction of material or the gathering of first accounts being delayed, increasing the risk of fabrication (paragraph 2.9.3).

This is supported by the internal SFO DPA guidance, which states that 'Co-operation is a key factor to consider when deciding whether to enter into a DPA.'

10.24

The DPA Code also lists certain indicators of co-operation which includes 'Within a reasonable time of offending coming to light reporting the Company's offending otherwise unknown to the prosecutor.' The DPA Guidance states that 'Voluntary self-reporting suspected wrongdoing within a reasonable time of these suspicions coming to light is an important aspect of co-operation.' While failure to self-report is not a bar to negotiations per se, it must be considered as a factor when assessing whether a DPA is in the public interest.

10.25

In addition to the SFO, the Rules of the Financial Conduct Authority ('FCA') and the Prudential Regulatory Authority ('PRA') require prompt (and in some cases, immediate) self-reporting. Corporations will wish to consider and where necessary take advice concerning their own regulatory obligations. Those companies which provide financial services or which are listed on an exchange will also wish to consider whether any other relevant regulator or listing authority requires self-reporting or market reporting at an early stage.

10.26

Relationships with regulators and prosecutors are becoming more sophisticated than in the past, not least through the involvement of law firms which frequently run internal investigations and which act as intermediaries between the company and prosecutors. This is particularly so in the area of anti-corruption legislation. Several individuals have left the SFO in order to work in the private sector and secondments to, or from, the SFO are becoming increasingly common. As knowledge and understanding of the SFO's expectations, processes and relationships with its personnel grows, this has led to a greater degree of confidence between all parties involved in the process.

10.27

Nevertheless, self-reporting too early can in fact cause more problems than it was intended to resolve. Premature reporting, before the facts have been clarified, can lead to needless expense and unnecessary intrusive investigation by regulators, not to mention unnecessary damage to reputation. A high degree of caution should therefore be exercised before informing a regulator, particularly where that information is likely to seep into the market place. At the beginning of an investigation, the facts are likely to lack clarity or be incomplete. Therefore, if a company is going to report at an early stage, it is important that it provides the regulator with an accurate portrayal of what the company knows or has unearthed thus far so as to avoid presenting a misleading picture or one which has to be corrected at a later date. This will involve the admission of uncertainties and providing a balanced summary of the investigation.

10.28

Further, a number of the DPAs have made clear that it is overall cooperation that is important, rather than simply looking at the matter of the date of the first self-report. In *SFO v Airbus Ltd,* Sharp PQBD noted that concerns had arisen in Airbus in October 2014 at which point it started internal investigations, however matters did not come to the attention of the SFO until April 2016 and the true catalyst was Sharp PQBD noted that Airbus could have moved more quickly after a 'slow start', however Airbus had cooperated with prosecuting authorities to the fullest extent possible, [§68]:

> 'A core purpose of the creation of DPAs was to "incentivise"' the exposure and self-report of corporate wrongdoing: see Sarclad at para 16 of the final judgment. Self-reporting, as it is called, and the subsequent level and quality of co-operation can therefore be critical factors when considering the interests of justice. It would be wrong to look at the issue of self-reporting purely from the perspective of the first report of wrongdoing, however. Even if the prosecuting authorities became aware of the relevant conduct by the actions of a third party, if subsequent self-reporting or co-operation overall, is of a high quality and brings significant wrongdoing to light that would not otherwise have come to the attention of the authorities, this will be a significant factor in favour of a DPA: see Rolls Royce para 22 of the final judgment and Sarclad at paras 37 to 38 of the preliminary judgment. To that extent, there is no necessary bright line between self-reporting and co-operation.'

Rolls Royce Ltd's DPA demonstrates that in some circumstances, a self-report does not always have to be made before the SFO is aware of the existence of allegations in order for a company to be given a DPA. In that case, the investigation was not triggered by a self-report but by publication of concerns on a public internet posting. However, the SFO described the cooperation provided subsequently by Rolls Royce as 'extraordinary' which persuaded Leveson PQBD to draw no distinction between the company and those who had self-reported from outset.

10.29

In conclusion, there is no one answer as to the best time to self-report. It is a fact-sensitive decision, which should take into account the specific circumstances of each company, its industry, the nature of the potentially corrupt conduct, the quality of the evidence of misconduct, how matters have come to light, the risk of pre-emptive whistleblowing to the authorities and the identities of the individuals whose conduct has led to the concern. The decision will both inform and be informed by the company's overall strategy with respect to all relevant regulators, the procedure for internal investigations, and the need for sensitive handling of employees who are at risk of prosecution as well as shareholders, investors and clients all balanced against the risk of the regulatory/ prosecution action.

Case Study: Rolls Royce

This case study demonstrates that a company can still benefit from cooperation even if an investigation has not been triggered by a self-report, however the cooperation of the company during the investigation will have to be of the highest order.

On 17 January 2017, Sir Brian Leveson approved a DPA between the SFO and Rolls Royce. It was then the largest DPA approved by the High Court and Rolls Royce were required to pay £497.25 million plus interest and the SFO's costs of £13 million.

The indictment, which was suspended for the term of the DPA, covered 12 counts of conspiracy to corrupt, false accounting and failure to prevent bribery. The conduct spanned three decades and involved Rolls-Royce's Civil Aerospace and Defence Aerospace businesses and its former Energy business and related to the sale of aero engines, energy systems and related services. The conduct covered by the UK DPA took place across seven jurisdictions: Indonesia, Thailand, India, Russia, Nigeria, China and Malaysia.

The conduct was described in the judgment approving the DPA as 'the most serious breaches of the criminal law in the areas of bribery and corruption' some of which implicated senior management and, on the face of it, controlling minds of the company.

The conduct had come to light in early 2012, when internet postings which raised concerns about the operation of Rolls Royce's civil business in China and Indonesia came to the attention of the SFO which subsequently sought information from Rolls-Royce. An investigation was immediately commenced by Rolls-Royce itself which led to a report on the findings into these and other issues in its civil and defence work.

Starting in 2013, Rolls-Royce voluntarily supplied to the SFO reports in respect of its internal investigations into its energy, defence, civil, and marine businesses. The investigation included collection of data and review of email containers from relevant employees together with a review of relevant archive material and 229 internal investigation interviews. The SFO examined the internal investigations (including interviews, over which Rolls-Royce waived any claim for legal professional privilege on a limited basis). The investigation by the SFO was conducted with what was described as the 'extraordinary cooperation' of Rolls Royce.

The cooperation of Rolls Royce entailed the following:

i) genuine cooperation with the SFO in the conduct of Rolls-Royce's own internal investigation, including deferring interviews until the SFO had first completed its interview, and the audio recording of interviews where requested;

ii) disclosure of all interview memoranda was made (on a limited waiver basis), despite Rolls-Royce's belief that the material was capable of resisting an order for disclosure, on the basis that it was privileged;

iii) providing all material requested by the SFO voluntarily, that is to say without requiring recourse to compulsory powers (in one case at least, effectively relinquishing control to the SFO); and

iv) consulting the SFO in respect of developments in media coverage, and seeking the SFO's permission before winding up companies that may have been implicated in the SFO's investigation.

The investigation was not triggered by a self-report, and normally this would have been counted against Rolls-Royce in assessing the interests of justice and the balance between prosecution and DPA. However, Sir Brian noted in the judgment at §22 that:

> 'the nature and extent of the co-operation provided by Rolls-Royce in this case has persuaded the SFO not only to use the word "extraordinary" to describe it but also to advance the argument that, in the particular circumstances of this case, I should not distinguish between its assistance and that of those who have self-reported from the outset. Given that what has been reported has clearly been far more extensive (and of a

> different order) than what may have been exposed without the co-operation provided, I am prepared to accede to that submission.'
>
> In assessing 'cooperation' as a public interest factor tending against prosecution, Leveson PQBD stated that although the SFO had been prompted to ask questions of Rolls-Royce by reason of public postings on the internet, 'I am entirely satisfied that from that moment, the company could not have done more to expose its own misconduct, limited neither by time, jurisdiction or area of business.' [§38]

To whom to self-report?

- Prosecution agencies and/or regulators?
- Agencies in other jurisdictions?
- To whom is information likely to be disclosed?

10.30

As noted above, the lead prosecutor in the UK for most offences of corruption occurring in the business sphere is the SFO. As a result, it is the natural first port of call for a company or individual wishing to report corrupt behaviour. However, regulated companies may also be under an expectation, if not a duty, to inform their regulator, whether it be the FCA, PRA, Ofgem or another similar regulator.

10.31

Companies whose shares are listed on an exchange may also be under a duty to inform the listing authority, depending on the rules of that exchange. For example, companies listed in the UK Stock Exchange may be required to inform the UK Listing Authority. Rules may vary across different markets and investor bases, so separate advice may be necessary.

10.32

Identifying the appropriate authority or authorities frequently requires an international perspective. Companies that operate in several jurisdictions may be regulated by multiple regulators and will frequently, where corruption is concerned, come under the jurisdiction of more than one prosecuting agency in more than one state. For this reason, it is important that the company obtains legal advice with respect to corporate criminal liability and the regulatory framework relevant to each country. It should be borne in mind that prosecuting and regulatory agencies regularly speak to each other and their counterparts abroad. Therefore, to whom to report will rarely be a decision that can be taken in isolation of other potentially relevant jurisdictions.

10.33

Tensions can arise within a company as a result of a decision to report in one jurisdiction where that may create a perceived obligation to report in another jurisdiction which does not have a strong expectation of self-reporting, which may not typically reward voluntary disclosure, or where penalties for corrupt conduct might be significant.

10.34

Equally, such tensions may arise between different departments or different arms of the same firm who may have opposing views on the best course of action for the company. Any such tensions will need sensitive handling.

10.35

A company may wish to receive and consider legal advice on whether or not it should inform all regulators who may have an interest in the matter being investigated. One issue for consideration may be publicity. A company may lose credibility if it is seen to be cooperating with one regulator but not with others, or not with different but involved jurisdictions.

10.36

The more cautious course is to proceed on the basis that the information contained in any report is likely to be disclosed to all relevant regulators or prosecutors. Within the European Union and many other states besides, there exist varying degrees of cooperation. The Brexit deal made provision for judicial co-operation and law enforcement between the UK and the EU. While there were some losses for the UK, most specifically access to the Second Schengen Information System, much has been retained and it would be risky to assume that a prosecution agency in the UK would not inform its counterparts of relevant intelligence – particularly as all states stand to gain from co-operation on intelligence and potential criminal activity. Importantly, there is nothing to prohibit disclosure by a UK agency to other agencies where that is for the purpose of providing intelligence for the proper conduct of that agency's duties. Indeed, the SFO guidance on self-reporting makes plain that in cases where the SFO does not prosecute a self-reporting corporate body, the SFO reserves the right: (i) to prosecute it for any unreported violations of the law; and (ii) lawfully to provide information on reported violations to other bodies, for example foreign investigative bodies.

10.37

Inter-agency cooperation is only likely to increase in the future. A self-reporting strategy which concentrates on one regulator (where more than one may have an interest) is likely to be short sighted. A company is likely to be best served by a comprehensive strategy which addresses the interests of all regulators concerned, and which considers the management of any competing interests and how they may impact on the company.

10.38

Specific, but not sole, account will frequently need to be taken of the likely role of US prosecutors and regulators, largely as a result of their extra-jurisdictional reach.

10.39

In summary, companies will want to consider who to approach, whether to cascade multiple approaches or make them simultaneously, and whether or not individual reports need to be tailored in any way.

10.40

All of these considerations will be driven by the individual facts and circumstances relating to the company and its business, relevant regulators and countries, the quality of the evidence available and the stage of the investigation. Factors to bear in mind include the overall interests of the company, its shareholders, its employees, publicity and overall likely outcome. If the company, or specific employees, are at serious fault, then controlled self-reporting, either simultaneous or reports made in close proximity, leading to a single, global resolution, is likely to be a better outcome for the company and its shareholders than multiple disclosures to different regulators, potentially in different jurisdictions at different times, leading to numerous resolutions and additional media exposure.

Case study: SFO v Airbus SE

In January 2020, the record breaking DPA entered into between the SFO and the global aerospace company Airbus SE saw Airbus SE agree to pay €991 million in the UK and in total €3.6 billion as part of the world's largest global resolution for bribery. In addition to the DPA, Airbus SE also reached a Convention Judicaire d'Intérêt Public with the Parquet National Financier ('PNF') to pay €2,083,137,455 and a Deferred Prosecution Agreement with the US Department of Justice and US Department of State requiring it to pay €525,655,000 to the US authorities.

How much information to disclose?

- The SFO will seek full information about the potential misconduct and nature of the investigation
- The quality and quantity of disclosure is likely to impact on action taken by prosecutor
- Material subject to legal professional privilege is not required to be disclosed
- A company may wish to consider jurisdiction-specific reports
- Companies should consider the risk of, and prepare for, the potential consequences of disclosure to third parties

The contents of a self-report

10.41

When considering the contents of a report, companies should have at the centre of their thinking the ultimate goal of avoiding a criminal prosecution. There are two requirements which need to be fulfilled in order to commence a criminal prosecution. The first is the identification of sufficient evidence to create a realistic prospect of conviction. The second is to determine that it is in the public interest to prosecute. Corruption is a serious offence. Where there is sufficient evidence to prosecute, it will frequently be in the public interest to prosecute corporate corruption. In order to avoid prosecution, the company must be able to set out the full facts and to demonstrate to the prosecutor that it has taken all possible measures to prevent a recurrence of the criminal conduct. These include:

- conducting an independent and thorough investigation;
- making detailed admissions without exceeding the true extent of its responsibility;
- taking action as required against relevant individuals;
- enhancing its procedures to ensure that such conduct does not happen again;
- cooperating fully with any regulators and prosecution bodies;
- being prepared to pay back in full the proceeds of any criminal conduct.

If the company is able to demonstrate the above in its report, then it should stand the best possible chance of persuading a prosecutor that the company has done all it can, and that far from being in the public interest, further investigation and prosecution would damage the company and put the employment of innocent employees at risk.

10.42

The SFO Guidance on Corporate Co-operation, published in August 2019, has also provided some indicators of good practice in self-reporting although it emphasises that some items will be inapplicable in certain cases and do not create legally enforceable rights, expectations or liabilities. It defines co-operation as including 'identifying suspected wrong-doing and criminal conduct together with the people responsible, regardless of their seniority or position in the organisation; reporting this to the SFO within a reasonable times of the suspicions coming to light and preserving available evidence and providing it promptly in an evidentially sound format' and, importantly, notes that 'it is a public interest factor tending against prosecution when management has adopted a "genuinely proactive approach" upon learning of the offending'.

10.43

The guidance sets out examples of good practice, in particular the preservation and provision of evidence:

- Good general practice: including the preservation of digital and hard copy material; ensuring that the integrity of digital material is preserved, prompt provision of material; clear lists of document custodians and locations including third parties and material held abroad; provision of material in a useful structured way; informing the SFO of any delays or reasons for data loss; providing schedules of documents withheld on the basis of privilege; identifying material capable of assisting the defence and undermining the prosecution.

- Digital evidence: providing digital material in a format that the SFO requests; creating an audit trail of acquisition and handling of digital material and identifying a person who can provide a witness statement re continuity; be alert to ageing technology and information systems; alert the SFO to digital material that the organisation cannot access; preserve passwords and access keys.

- Hard copy evidence: create and maintain an audit trail of the acquisition and handling of hard copy material.

- Financial records and analysis: Provide records that show relevant money flows; provide relevant organisational financial documents in a structured way. Alert the SFO to relevant financial material that the organisation cannot access; create and maintain an audit trail or acquisition and handling of financial material; provided financial calculations and information relevant to profit and disgorgement of profits, financial penalty calculations and ability to pay.

- Industry background: provide industry knowledge, context and common practices; identify potential defences that are particular to the market or industry; notify the SFO of other government agencies by whom the organisation has been contacted or to whom it has reported.
- Individuals: consult in a timely way before interviewing potential witnesses or suspects; identify personal witnesses including third parties; refrain from tainting a potential witness' recollection; make individuals available for SFO interviews; provide last known contact details of ex-employees, agents and consultants.

10.44

It follows from the above that a limited report to the prosecutor which seeks to avoid responsibility, fails to provide the full facts, or which fails to indicate the sufficient measures have been taken is unlikely to result in the outcome that the corporate body seeks. Furthermore, it is likely that prosecutors will require a report to be relatively detailed. If a prosecutor finds that the information provided is not complete, that there are unanswered questions or that a misleading picture has been presented, then they may well not accept the report at face value. That said, if a company decides that it wishes to report at an early stage in the investigation, before all facts are known, in order to put down a marker for 'co-operation credit' purposes, it is not uncommon for a high level summary to be provided to the SFO's investigation unit with a fuller report of the investigation findings to follow.

10.45

It is worth remembering that the DPA Code of Practice provides that a failure to report properly and fully the extent of the criminal conduct is a factor in favour of prosecution. Paragraph 2.8.1(vi) provides that 'reporting the wrongdoing but failing to verify it, or reporting it, knowing or believing it to be inaccurate, misleading or incomplete' are factors that will weigh in favour of a prosecution. Furthermore, in order to assess whether a company has adopted a 'genuinely proactively approach', the SFO will need to establish whether sufficient information about the operation of the company in its entirety has been supplied (paragraph 2.8.2(i)). Cooperation will include identifying relevant witnesses, disclosing their accounts and the documents shown to them; where practicable, this will involve making witnesses available for interview. It will also include providing a report in respect of any internal investigation, including source documents (paragraph 2.8.2(i)). It follows that a company making a self-report must ensure that it does not withhold material that may jeopardise an effective investigation or prosecution. To do so would, according to the Code, be a very strong factor in favour of prosecution (paragraph 2.9(i)). The Code of Practice also warns that the provision of inaccurate, misleading or incomplete information, where the company knew or ought to have known that the information was inaccurate, misleading or incomplete, may lead to prosecution of the company, either for the offences which were envisaged to be the subject of the DPA or separately for the fact of providing such information (paragraph 3.8).

10.46

Self-evidently, when considering how much information to include in a self-report, the corporate body should consider the nature of the disclosures and any risks that may flow from disclosing particular information, such as the likelihood of prosecution or a wider investigation than the company believes to be necessary. This is not with a view to reducing the content of a report but rather preparing for consequences that may flow from it. This judgment call is not made easier by the fact that different jurisdictions and regulators around the world have different views about how transparent companies should be.

10.47

Tactically, the company will of course wish to consider how the disclosure of facts will impact on any defence that might be available, in the event that settlement negotiations fail, or in the event that the company faces civil proceedings from third parties. Again, this should be with a view to preparing the company's defence rather than editing the report in any way.

10.48

What happens to the information once it is disclosed to the regulator will be a key concern. It seems reasonable to suppose that at least part of the information may be released into the public domain, whether as a result of a leak or because the regulator/prosecutor wishes to make a press release. The better the relationship with the authority, the greater the likelihood that the company may be able to influence the content and timing of any press release. One solution may be for the company to 'bite the bullet' and to make its own, simultaneous, announcement to the press and the markets in conjunction with the relevant authorities – but not before having first discussed the wording with them. This is dealt with at paragraphs 10.60–65 below.

10.49

In the context of UK investigations, it is very rarely advisable to disclose communications to and from lawyers, as this material is privileged and prosecution agencies in the UK do not, generally, require companies to provide privileged material. The Court of Appeal judgment in *SFO v ENRC* [2018] EWCA Civ 2006 confirmed that documents, including interview notes, generated by mining company ENRC during an internal corruption investigation were protected by privilege and therefore did not have to be disclosed to the Serious Fraud Office, as a criminal prosecution was in the reasonable contemplation of ENRC at the time the notes were made.

10.50

That being said, disclosure of privileged material is not without precedent and may be disclosed as part of a specific strategy to demonstrate complete cooperation and openness with a prosecutor or regulator. The SFO Corporate Co-operation Guidance refers to witness accounts and the waiving or privilege as follows:

- Organisations seeking credit for co-operation by providing witness accounts should additionally provide any recording, notes and/or transcripts of the interview and identify a witness competent to speak to the contents of each interview.
- When an organisation elects not to waive privilege, the SFO nonetheless has obligations to prospective individual defendants with respect to disclosable materials.
- The existence of a valid privilege claim must be properly established.
- During the investigation, if the organisation claims privilege, it will be expected to provide certification by independent counsel that the material in question is privileged.
- If privilege is not waived and a trial proceeds, where appropriate, the SFO will apply for a witness summons under section 2 Criminal Procedure (Attendance of Witnesses) Act 1965.[3]
- An organisation that does not waive privilege and provide witness accounts does not attain the corresponding factor against prosecution that is found in the DPA Code [...] but will not be penalised by the SFO.[4]

10.51

Disclosure of privileged material should not be undertaken without independent legal advice on the matter. Such disclosure, even if deemed to be limited or inadvertent, can result in all documents having a bearing on that material being disclosed either to a UK prosecutor or to a prosecutor abroad. Specific advice should be taken on the nature of the documents that may attract legal privilege, bearing in mind that the rules applying to privileged material and waiver of privilege can differ, sometimes significantly, across jurisdictions. The

3 See www.sfo.gov.uk/publications/guidance-policy-and-protocols/guidance-for-corporates/corporate-co-operation-guidance/#_ftn4.

4 See www.sfo.gov.uk/publications/guidance-policy-and-protocols/guidance-for-corporates/corporate-co-operation-guidance/#_ftn5.

DPA Code of Practice specifically protects privilege by providing that it does not, nor cannot alter the law on privilege. Nonetheless, the Code also states that the prosecutor will expect to be provided with a report dealing with any internal investigation. As such reports are typically prepared by lawyers who have carried out the investigation they will normally contain legal advice, and therefore be subject to privilege. A solution would therefore appear to be to provide the prosecutor with a version of the report that includes all of the facts but not any legal advice.

10.52

It should also be borne in mind that the SFO has onerous disclosure obligations. It must provide to any person or entity whom it prosecutes all information in its possession which might reasonably be considered capable of undermining the SFO's case or assisting the case of the accused. Such material must not be withheld by reporting companies (it, or individual employees, may be committing the separate offence of perverting the course of justice), but it is prudent to identify what material is likely to be provided to third parties and what the consequences might be for the company's business or any future or concurrent litigation.

10.53

In some circumstances, the difficulty with providing material that might trigger waiver of privilege in another jurisdiction may be mitigated by the provision of an oral or partly oral report.

10.54

In order to be satisfied that the internal investigation is sufficient for the regulator's purposes, the regulator will wish to be assured about the adequacy and focus of the investigation. With that in mind, the regulator is therefore likely to require the following information about any internal investigation:

(1) its scope;

(2) who has conducted it;

(3) who within the firm is responsible and accountable for it;

(4) the methodology employed;

(5) the timing of its conduct; and

(6) the independence or otherwise of the investigation from the company and individuals within its scope;

(7) Any action taken or proposed in relation to any employees.

Finally, it should be noted that self-reporting is rarely the end of the matter. Once an issue has been reported the regulator is likely to require further documentation.

Case study: ENRC

This example highlights the SFO's expectation of self-reporting as 'part of a genuinely proactive approach' adopted by the corporate management team and demonstrates the action it will take when not satisfied with the information provided.

Eurasian Natural Resources Corporation ('ENRC'), a FTSE 100 mining company, self-reported accusations of corruption to the SFO in 2011. Instead of opening a formal investigation into the company, the SFO decided to permit ENRC to report the findings of the internal investigation itself.

However, in April 2013, the company parted with the US law firm that had been instructed to run the investigation and retained new counsel in its stead. ENRC had provided a report to the SFO concerning the company's operations in Kazakhstan prior to changing its legal representation. However, it had not supplied a second report concerning its investigation into its subsidiary in Africa.

Seven months later, in November 2013, the SFO announced that it had launched its own criminal investigation into allegations of corruption regarding the activities of the company or its subsidiaries in Kazakhstan and Africa. Although the SFO did not say so, the implication of this move was that the SFO was no longer content to rely upon the company's own investigation or its reports on the conduct that is alleged to have taken place.

How to self-report?

- Simultaneous or staged reporting
- Responsibility for the reporting process
- Oral or written report?
- How and when will further supporting evidence be supplied?
- Consistency of information supplied to multiple agencies

10.55

Once a corporate body has identified which regulators or prosecuting agencies it wishes to report to, then it is advisable to consider whether broadly simultaneous or staged reporting is the best option, bearing in mind that significant lapses of time between contacting regulators reduces the opportunity to get to a particular regulator or prosecutor first. There is always the risk of the authorities' trust in the corporate organisation being eroded if information is provided to it by a third party rather than by the company itself. The corporate may also wish to bear in mind which jurisdictions have the greatest expectation of self-reporting.

10.56

The nature of internal investigations, in particular their human and IT demands, mean that third parties are frequently involved, normally a law firm and/or accountants (internal investigations are dealt with in Chapter 9). It is often preferable for the personnel from the law firm overseeing the investigation to contact the regulator or prosecutor. This provides helpful neutrality from the conduct under investigation, underscores the independence of the investigation, and frequently those involved will know the relevant counterparty at the regulator or prosecuting agency as a result of regular dealing. All of this can help to ensure that the creation of the contact and the relationship with the regulator throughout the investigation process is frank, as informal as it can be and that there are good lines of communication between the parties.

10.57

An open dialogue with the prosecutor or regulator is likely to lead to a better relationship which reduces the potential for surprises, may help to limit the scope of activity that is under investigation and may increase the likelihood of the regulator or prosecutor deciding that the internal investigation has been conducted fully and satisfactorily.

So far as the SFO is concerned, its guidance on corporate prosecutions outlines the following regarding the way in which self-reports should be made:

(1) Initial contact and all subsequent communication must be made through the SFO's Intelligence Unit.

(2) Hard copy reports setting out the nature and scope of any internal investigation must be provided to the Intelligence Unit as part of the self-reporting process.

(3) All supporting evidence including, but not limited to emails, banking evidence and witness accounts must be provided as part of the self-reporting process.

(4) Further supporting evidence may be provided during the course of any on-going internal investigation.

10.58

Where multiple self-reports are concerned, it is essential that the information provided to the authorities is consistent. One way to ensure that, and to reduce the potential for inadvertent disclosure, is to designate a very small pool of people who have direct contact with any relevant agencies or indeed with third parties in general. It is also advisable to maintain an audit trail and to log the disclosure of material to one or more regulators.

Risks of reporting and how to counter them

- Prosecution of the company and/or individuals
- Negative publicity
- Possibility of arrest of individuals
- Staff uncertainty
- Impact on markets
- Risk of prosecution as a result of not reporting

Prosecution

10.59

Although the aim of self-reporting is to avoid the need for prosecution of the company, or obtain a DPA, (DPAs are dealt with in more detail in the Chapter 11), there is always a risk that a prosecutor may decide that it is in the public interest to prosecute because of the nature of the misconduct, or that individuals within the company, perhaps with senior positions, should be prosecuted in any event. In such circumstances it will be necessary to prepare for negative publicity, loss of key personnel and a period of turbulence in the functioning of the company and the health of its business. In the event that a company is prosecuted it will still have available to it the lesser-used option of a plea agreement in order to avoid a trial.

Negative publicity

10.60

The risks of premature reporting have been dealt with above. Releasing information about an internal investigation to a third party carries an inherent risk that some material may be released into the public domain, which could give rise to speculation and cause significant damage to the company's trading activity. Depending on the nature of the risk, in order to limit damage and to avoid appearing reactive, companies should consider various actions to counter it. These may include taking the initiative and making a brief and carefully worded press release before the self-report becomes public.

10.61

The strategy for dealing with publicity must recognise the importance of issuing a consistent message, and one that is designed to preserve the company's reputation, for example by restating a commitment to ethical business.

Any announcement should:

- be measured and accurate;
- be consistent with all other messages or press releases issued by the company and indeed by a regulator or prosecutor;
- avoid making assertions, especially as to vindication or innocence at an early stage, since the discovery of new facts might make the company appear over confident or suspect;
- avoid the need to make amendments, corrections or to provide updates at a later stage;
- confirm that the company is taking appropriate, responsible and independent action to reassure interested parties, stakeholders and clients;
- re-state the company's commitment to ethical business;
- re-state the company's commitment to a zero tolerance approach to corruption;
- ensure compliance with the rules of the relevant regulatory body (eg the FCA) governing the content of such announcements.

Before the self-report is made, a media strategy should be put in place and a central body, comprising a small pool of designated personnel, should be appointed with responsibility for issuing statements to the media and for dealing with queries. All company personnel with public facing roles should be appraised of the communications procedure and know to whom to refer any inquiries.

10.62

It might, in some circumstances, be appropriate to engage a public relations firm who can advise on how to best deal with the media as well as protecting a company's global reputation. Good communication is not just vital between the company and the outside world but also between all elements of the investigation, including management, legal advisors, forensic accountants and staff.

10.63

If a regulator or prosecutor has already received a self-report then the company will wish to notify it of the wording of any announcement in advance, in order to avoid the potential for conflict with any announcement that the regulator or prosecutor intends to make and, if matters are not yet public, avoid tipping off potential suspects within the organisation. Taking action to avoid tipping off any suspects is an important part of co-operation.

10.64

Companies should be aware that the regulator or prosecutor is likely to have its own media strategy. While it is unlikely that a joint strategy can be pursued, it should be possible to ask what information they intend to release into the public sphere, and more importantly whether there is any information which ought not to be released. Channels of communication on this issue should be kept open so that neither party is taken by surprise.

10.65

Once the information has become public, it is likely to impact on a number of groups or stakeholders, including but not limited to the markets, shareholders, investors or clients. A strategy should therefore be devised in order to mitigate the impact such an announcement might have on the company's business. This is particularly important if the company is on the verge of concluding a deal or contract, or is about to publish a financial statement. It would also be wise to plan for a period of economic uncertainty for both the business and staff during the period of the internal investigation.

Possible arrests

10.66

There is little certainty as to what action a regulator or prosecutor might take once a disclosure has been made, and therefore action should be taken to prepare for all outcomes. Depending on the information provided to the agency, the arrest of any suspects may occur immediately. Arrests of senior management will be particularly disruptive to business as they may need to be placed on immediate leave. If the individuals at risk are not already on leave from the company then a strategy should be in place to allocate their work elsewhere and to inform clients of the changes in the event it is necessary. Depending on the level of knowledge those members of staff have of the investigation, consideration may need to be given to the level of advance warning, if any, which they should be given about a self-report to a regulator or prosecutor. A company needs to tread extremely carefully not to tip off individuals within the company, those whose involvement has not yet been identified. This is particularly if consideration is to be given to entering into a DPA, as one factor in favour of prosecution is whether the conduct of any internal investigation could have led to material being destroyed or created the opportunity for fabrication of a suspect's account (DPA Code of Practice paragraph 2.9.3). It will not be uncommon for the company to give no advance warning to its employees, save for the board of directors and the tightly identified privilege group.

Staff uncertainty

10.67

Confirmation of a self-report, particularly if accompanied by arrests, is likely to cause unease and concern among staff and affect morale. Companies may therefore wish to consider what information is divulged to staff, whether or not regular updates might provide reassurance and what instructions to give them about communicating externally about the matter. For example, a simple instruction to make no comment or assign a person to whom to refer queries might provide clarity for the staff and reduce the risk of unauthorised disclosure.

Impact on stock market

10.68

The disclosure obligations on a listed corporate body are likely to depend on the applicable listing rules. For example, in the UK those rules include the Listing Rules, the Listing Principles, the Disclosure Rules and Transparency Rules. There may well be a requirement to provide specific information to the market to ensure the company is transparent about its risk profile. Whether or not to make an announcement, and whether or not an announcement is required can be a complex issue and specific legal advice should be obtained. Any market announcement would post-date the making of a self-report.

What are the risks of not reporting?

10.69

The risk of not reporting lies in the possibility that allegations of criminal conduct may come to the attention of the regulator or prosecutor via another source depriving the company of the opportunity to get its foot in the door with cooperation credit. Such a risk is unquantifiable since information can be provided to the SFO by various means, including via a foreign authority, other

UK criminal justice agencies, disgruntled competitors or, increasingly likely, a whistleblower.

10.70

Reporting by whistleblowers is something the government in the UK seeks to encourage. When the National Crime Agency was created, the Home Office published its 'Serious and Organised Crime Strategy' (October 2013) in which it announced its intention to make it easier to report corruption, and that in order to incentivise whistleblowing it would be examining 'the successful Qui Tam provisions' deployed in the US. However, to date there are no financial incentives for whistleblowers, and a 2014 Report by the Bank of England and Financial Conduct Authority concluded that 'introducing financial incentives for whistleblowers would be unlikely to increase the number or quality of the disclosures we receive from them'. Their protection lies in the Public Interest Disclosure Act 1998 which provides for the right not to suffer detriment or unfair dismissal.

10.71

Failure to self-report in a timely manner, or a decision not to do so, could have far reaching consequences for a company. The SFO has made plain that if and when it uncovers corruption it will assume that the company has deliberately chosen not to self-report the conduct in question. In such circumstances, the SFO is likely to conduct its own investigation, potentially by way of a dawn raid. Any resulting investigation is likely to involve significant intrusion into the company's business, as well as publicity which is almost bound to be damaging. The uncovering of criminal activity, particularly if it was known about at a high level, will result in both shareholder and public outrage as well as difficulties for the conduct of the company's business as mentioned elsewhere in this chapter. However, most significantly, a company should be aware that where it chooses not to make a self-report, it runs the risk of committing one or more criminal offences related to money laundering under sections 327–9 of the Proceeds of Crime Act 2002.

Conclusion and checklist

10.72

Following the introduction of the Bribery Act 2010, the interest of the authorities in identifying, investigating and prosecuting corporate offences, particularly corruption, is unlikely to diminish in the future and it seems reasonable to suppose that both prosecutors and companies at risk of investigation will see advantages in negotiating settlements in order to avoid the full cost and significant disruption caused by a high profile prosecution. As the SFO has pointed out, a self-report at the very least mitigates the chances of a corporate being prosecuted and also opens up the possibility of a DPA.

10.73

The introduction of DPAs in particular has caused law firms and their clients to rethink the advantages of self-reporting, and as a result this is an area that compliance officers and directors alike can ill afford to disregard. The judicial statements within the DPAs approved to date have emphasised the key role of DPAs in incentivising self-reporting and the weight that will be given to self-reporting in determining whether a DPA will be approved as being within the interests of justice, but also in determining, in certain cases, the financial penalty.

Checklist

10.74

The following is a non-exhaustive checklist of matters that a company considering whether to self-report may wish to consider:

First steps

(1) What information is known about the conduct in question and what further information is required?

(2) Should an internal investigation be conducted and, if so, should an external law firm have oversight?

(3) What legal advice is likely to be required (corporate criminal liability, white collar criminal advice in relation to different jurisdictions, regulatory, money laundering)?

(4) What is the evidence of misconduct, has a potential offence been committed and should the company be considering self-reporting?

(5) Given what is known about the conduct, what are the potential implications of self-reporting at this stage?

(6) Given what is known about the conduct, what are the potential disadvantages of not self-reporting at this stage?

(7) What other parties, or who else within the organisation, knows about the conduct?

(8) What is the likelihood of a whistleblower approaching a regulator or prosecutor?

(9) What, realistically, might be achieved from self-reporting?

(10) What is the likelihood of prosecution, or a DPA?

Timing

(11) Would the company be justified in seeking further information before informing any relevant regulators or prosecutors?

(12) Is the company more likely to gain the confidence of the regulator/prosecutor and avoid an external investigation by self-reporting at an early stage?

(13) What are the risks of self-reporting now, given the information known about the conduct, and given any significant business-related steps or transactions that may be being conducted at this time?

(14) What is the risk of not reporting at this stage? Is it possible that the authorities may discover the conduct through different channels?

(15) Who are the agencies who stand to be informed and what are their expectations in relation to self-reporting?

To whom to self report

(16) Which is the most appropriate prosecution agency and/or regulator?

(17) Are agencies in other jurisdictions likely to be involved as well?

(18) What are the attitudes of those agencies to self-reporting and what action are they likely to take?

(19) Should all relevant agencies be informed more or less simultaneously?

(20) If not, what is the likelihood that any agency that is informed will pass on intelligence to other agencies?

How much information to disclose

(21) How much information does the company wish to disclose and how much information is the investigating agency likely to acquire in any event?

(22) What are the potential implications of providing less information than the company currently holds?

(23) Is staged disclosure appropriate? For example, an overview of the investigation to date followed by an agreement to provide such information as is required by the regulator or prosecutor?

(24) Does the regulator or relevant body have any rules about the nature of the information to be provided?

(25) What information is considered privileged (a) by the UK, (b) by any other relevant jurisdiction, and does not have to be disclosed?

(26) Might the disclosure of any information in one jurisdiction be considered as a loss of confidentiality or waiver of privilege in another?

(27) What information about the nature of the investigation should be provided?

How to self-report

(28) Who should deal with communications between the company and the regulator or prosecutor?

(29) Are there designated channels for a self-report?

(30) Will all relevant agencies be informed simultaneously or will reporting be a staged process?

(31) Should the report be in writing or will an oral report together with the key documentation be acceptable?

(32) Who should be responsible for dealing with external agencies and providing information to them?

(33) How should the company ensure that the information provided to third parties is, and remains, consistent?

(34) What are the risks and how can they be countered?

(35) Who within the company is at risk of arrest and or prosecution?

(36) How should the company best prepare for their (potential) absence?

(37) What is the likely result on business in the event that the market becomes aware of the self-report?

(38) What is the risk of information leaking into the public sphere?

(40) What is the best way to mitigate that risk?

(41) What information should be provided to staff and how should their concerns be allayed?

Publicity (both internal and external)

(42) Is the very fact of the investigation to be kept confidential?

(43) How much information should employees be provided with?

(44) What information is likely to be provided to the press by any regulator or prosecutor involved in the matter?

(45) Is a press release to be issued and if so, in which country/countries?

(46) Should any agency be informed of the press released in advance?

(47) How should any press release be worded?

11 Deferred prosecution agreements

Introduction and background

11.1

Deferred prosecution agreements ('DPAs') were introduced by Schedule 17 of the Crime and Courts Act 2013 ('Schedule 17'of 'the 2013 Act'). Available since February 2014, they have now become a well-established way of responding to alleged acts of fraud, bribery and other economic crime committed by commercial organisations. They are intended as 'a discretionary tool' which will enable the Serious Fraud Office ('SFO') and the Crown Prosecution Service ('CPS') to conclude criminal investigations into corporate organisations as an alternative to prosecution,[1] by imposing requirements such as financial penalties, compensation and compliance programmes. They are subject to judicial approval, and involve the suspension of a criminal indictment for an agreed period. After a hesitant start, there has been a steady growth in the use of DPAs: between 2015 and 2021, the SFO entered into some twelve DPAs with major corporations. These are summarised at 11.149 below. A further two or three DPAs are anticipated in 2021.

11.2

A Code of Practice for DPAs, intended for prosecutors, ('the Code') was published jointly by the SFO and the CPs on 14 February 2014 after public consultation. It remains in place. It was designed to give, and continues to offer, guidance to prosecutors when negotiating DPAs with the organisations concerned; when applying to the court for its approval of the agreements; and when overseeing DPAs once the court's approval has been obtained, particularly where the terms of the agreement require variation, or where a breach of the agreement has occurred. The Code also provides guidance as to what to do when the agreement is completed or terminated for some other reason.

11.3

The SFO have also published an Operational Handbook, ('Operational Handbook') which sets out standard processes, instructions and guidance on

1 SFO/CPS Code of Practice 11 February 2014, and SFO Operational Handbook (revised 23 October 2020).

the conduct of SFO casework. This was updated in October 2020 to include a chapter on DPAs.[2]

11.4

Further instructions on DPAs can be found in the Criminal Procedure Rules 2020, Part 11 ('Part 11 CPR') which are designed to correspond with the Code.

11.5

The motivation behind the legislation which introduced DPAs had its roots in the US where prosecuting authorities have been using DPAs and related non-prosecution agreements ('NPAs) since the 1990s, largely but not exclusively to resolve enforcement actions under the Foreign Corrupt Practices Act 1977. These are often related to criminal activities with little connection to the US. Many, if not the majority of such cases in the US are settled in this way.

11.6

While US judges have the ultimate power to refuse to sanction such deals, and occasionally do,[3] final judicial approval is largely seen as a rubber stamp exercise. This has led to considerable criticism in the US about the growing tendency to circumvent the criminal trial process, and attempts at greater judicial intervention. Past observations from one senior US judge suggested that the US Department of Justice's use of regulatory settlements to resolve criminal investigations without holding individuals to account was 'morally and legally suspect'.[4] Nonetheless, DPAs and NPAs appear to operate comfortably within the US criminal justice system where plea agreements in return for reduced criminal penalties have climbed in value between 2000 and 2020, and are now the norm. The DoJ and the US Securities and Exchange Commission can enter into negotiations and deals with corporations and their directors and even seek civil sanctions, unfettered by the need for court supervision or prior approval.

2 www.gov.uk/publications/guidance-policy-and-protocols/sfo-operational-handbook/.

3 Examples include Judge Jed Rakoff's rejection of a US$285 million settlement between the SEC and Citycorp Bank; Judge Richard Leon's refusal to approve a settlement between the SEC and IBM over bribery allegations; the blocking by New York District Judge Richard Sullivan of a deal of a US$600 million deal between the SEC and SAC Capital Management – a hedge fund accused of insider trading. The judge commented that there was something 'counter-intuitive and incongruous' about settling for such a large amount if the company 'truly did nothing wrong.'

4 Judge Jed Rakoff's comments were made in a speech to the New York City Bar Association on 12 November 2013. He was appointed by President Clinton to sit on the US District Court for the Southern District of New York where he has assumed senior status, and is a leading authority on securities law and white collar crime.

11.7

The SFO under the tenure of a former Director[5] – no doubt with an eye to the substantial sums of money earned and saved by its US counterparts – made clear its wish to encourage a climate of corporate engagement by entering into negotiated settlements with co-operating defendants. Since then, as already noted above, the SFO's use of DPAs has expanded considerably. Furthermore, the benefits of effective corporate compliance structures have been acknowledged, and the courts have adopted a flexible approach so as to provide companies with sufficient incentive to self-report.[6]

11.8

Despite this, a more circumspect approach to the use of DPAs is incorporated in the Code. This states that these organisations 'are first and foremost prosecutors, and it will only be in specific circumstances deemed by their directors to be appropriate that they will decide to offer a DPA instead of pursuing the full prosecution of the alleged conduct'. Additionally, the SFO's Operational Handbook comments on the need to pursue a DPA only if prosecution of the company is not in the public interest, The test requires 'a balancing act of the factors that tend to support the Prosecution and those that do not'. These factors will be determined by the individual prosecutor on a case-by-case basis.

It should be noted however, that, 'a decision as to whether to enter DPA discussions is not a guarantee that a DPA will be offered at the conclusion of the discussions.'[7] Whether to offer a DPA is a matter for the prosecutor's discretion; corporate organisations have no right to be invited to negotiate a DPA.

11.9

Concerned by 'forbiddingly long, expensive and complicated investigations and trials', the Ministry of Justice launched a consultation between May and August 2012, seeking the views of lawyers, judges, commercial organisations and others on the desirability of entering into DPAs in 'less serious cases'. It was always intended that these agreements would be sanctioned by judges and blocked if not in the public interest. The objective was to arrive at a solution which commanded public confidence and ensured:

- Transparency.
- Consistency of approach.
- Judicial oversight.

---

5 Richard Alderman.
6 Per Leveson LJ in *SFO v Standard Bank PLC* (2015 No: U20150854).
7 Code of Practice 2.1.

- The protection of free and without prejudice discussions between the parties, whilst avoiding the perception of a cosy deal being struck.
- The imposition of financial penalties.
- The disgorgement of illicit profits.
- Reparation to victims balanced with the desire to save the company and the jobs of its employees.

11.10

The response to the consultation was largely supportive, and resulted in Schedule 17 of the 2013 Act which received Royal Assent on 25 April 2013. The relevant provisions became operative in February 2014. The scheme envisaged by Schedule 17 relies on transparency and proper supervision, and gives the UK courts a very important role to play. From the earliest stage, a judge will be asked to determine in principle whether the circumstances of the case are appropriate for the use of a DPA, before deciding whether to sanction the terms and conditions agreed. The process, which has been adapted to fit within the UK legal system and in which the judge's power to supervise, control or even veto has been enshrined, has been described by a former Solicitor General[8] as 'particularly British'.

11.11

After a period of consultation, the joint SFO/CPS Code, (see 11.2 above) was issued on 11 February 2014, and remains in place. It was designed to give, and continues to offer guidance to prosecutors when negotiating DPAs with the organisations concerned; when applying to the court for its approval of the agreements; and when overseeing DPAs once the court's approval has been obtained, particularly where the terms of the agreement require variation, or where a breach of the agreement has occurred. The Code also provides guidance as to what to do when the agreement is completed or terminated for some other reason.

11.12

The Code must be taken into account by prosecutors when exercising their functions under the 2013 Act. It sets out the criteria governing which cases will be deemed suitable for DPAs, and provides guidance when negotiating and applying for DPAs. It also outlines what happens once agreement is reached, and spells out the consequences should negotiations fall through, or if the court declines to give its approval.

8 Oliver Heald QC.

Order of topics in this chapter

11.13

The topics covered in this chapter are not dealt with in precisely the same order as they appear in Schedule 17, paragraphs 1–39. Instead they have been rearranged sequentially – and hopefully in a more practical way – to help the reader better understand the nature of the process, and the rules which govern it. To that end, additional explanatory and corresponding references relating to procedural requirements and practical guidance contained in the DPA Code and Part 11 of the CPR have been interpolated wherever it has been thought helpful to do so.

11.14

For ease of reference, Schedule 17 of the 2013 Act is reproduced in this book and can be found at Appendix 5, the Code is included at Appendix 7, and Part 11 of the Rules ('CPR Part 11') at Appendix 6. Where the topic of financial penalties arises in this chapter, reference is made to the Sentencing Guidelines for Economic Crimes, including Bribery, which were published in their approved form by the Sentencing Council in February 2014. The relevant section of the Guidelines is reproduced with the kind permission of the Sentencing Council, and can be found at Appendix 4.

11.15

The key issues in this chapter are set out as follows:

- Characteristics of a deferred prosecution agreement.
- Offences in relation to which a DPA may be entered into.
- Designated prosecutors.
- Persons who may enter into a DPA with a prosecutor.
- The two stage test.
- Factors in the public interest which may be taken into account when deciding whether to enter into a DPA or not.
- The Full Code Test.
- Additional factors in the public interest for and against prosecution.
- Letter of invitation to enter into DPA negotiations.
- The substance and character of negotiations.
- Unused material and disclosure.
- The end of the negotiation period.

- Confidentiality.
- Use of civil recovery orders.
- Content of a DPA:
  - Statement of facts
  - Expiry date
  - Terms of DPA
  - Guiding principles.
- Monitors.
- Preliminary court hearing:
  - Application to approve a proposal
  - Preferring a Bill of indictment.
- Final hearings and approval of the terms of a DPA.
- Financial penalties and new sentencing guidelines.
- Breach of DPA.
- Late payments.
- Variation of DPA.
- Subsequent use of information obtained by the prosecutor during the negotiation period.
- Discontinuance of proceedings on expiry of DPA.
- Money received by the prosecutor.
- Re-instituting proceedings.
- Publication.
- Postponement of publication.

Characteristics of a deferred prosecution agreement

11.16

Paragraph 1 of Schedule 17 defines a DPA as 'an agreement between a designated prosecutor and a person ('P') whom the prosecutor is considering prosecuting for an offence or ancillary offence specified in Part 2 (the "alleged offence").'

11.17

As we will see, (at 11.23 below) in contrast to the position in the US, P cannot be an individual but must be a corporate entity, a partnership or unincorporated association.[9]

11.18

In essence, where such an organisation is suspected of committing a criminal offence, the prosecutor may invite the organisation to enter into negotiations to agree a DPA as an alternative to prosecution. If no agreement is reached, or an agreement is breached, the prosecution may proceed as usual.

Offences in relation to which a DPA may be entered into

11.19

Paragraphs 15–27 of Schedule 17 set out a list of common law and statutory offences which can be the subject of a DPA, and which may have occurred before the Schedule came into force. Included amongst the list of offences of financial and economic crimes, in respect of which a DPA may be entered into, are specific offences under the Bribery Act 2010 ('UKBA'): section 1 (bribing another person), section 2 (being bribed), section 6 (bribery of foreign public officials) and section 7 (failure of a commercial organisation to prevent bribery).

11.20

DPAs can also relate to ancillary offences such as aiding, abetting, counselling or procuring, attempting or conspiring to commit bribery.[10]

Designated prosecutors

11.21

Paragraph 3 of Schedule 17 identifies designated prosecutors as:

(a) the Director of Public Prosecutions;

(b) the Director of the Serious Fraud Office;

(c) any prosecutor designated under this paragraph by an order made by the Secretary of State.

---

9 On 13 November 2013 the US SEC announced the first DPA ever agreed with an individual –Scott Herckis of the Hepplewhite Fund LP. Herckis was granted immunity from prosecution in exchange for his co-operation in providing information about the company's misappropriation of fund money and misinformation to investors.

10 Schedule 17, para 29.

11.22

This paragraph further stipulates that the designated prosecutor must personally exercise the power to enter into a DPA, or if unavailable, by a person authorised in writing by the designated prosecutor.

Persons who may enter into a DPA with a prosecutor

11.23

Paragraph 4 of Schedule 17 makes clear that a body corporate, a partnership or an unincorporated association may enter into a DPA, but not an individual, partner, or member of an association.

11.24

Any money payable under a DPA must be paid from the funds of the partnership or association.[11]

The two stage test

11.25

The Code[11] suggests that the starting point for determining whether a DPA will be appropriate in any given circumstance is to apply a two stage test about which prosecutors must be satisfied and record.

1. **The evidential stage:**

   (i) Either:

   (a) the evidential stage of the Full Code Test in the Code for Crown Prosecutors[12] [must be] satisfied (paragraph 11.26 below) or, if this is not met,

   (b) there is at least a reasonable suspicion that the commercial organisation has committed the offence, and that there are reasonable grounds for believing that a continued investigation would provide further evidence within a reasonable period of time, so that all the evidence together would be capable of establishing a realistic prospect of conviction in accordance with the Full Code Test.

2. **The public interest stage:**

   (ii) And the public interest would be properly served by the prosecutor not prosecuting but instead entering into a DPA with P in accordance with [certain] criteria.

11 Schedule 17, para 4(2-3).
12 Code section 1.2.

The Full Code Test

11.26

The Full Code Test for Crown prosecutors, which must be applied at the evidential stage of the process, requires prosecutors to be satisfied on *objective grounds* that there is sufficient evidence to provide a realistic prospect of conviction against each suspect on each charge. They must also consider what the defence case may be, and how it is likely to affect the prospects of conviction. A case which does not pass the evidential stage must not proceed, no matter how serious or sensitive it may be.

11.27

If the evidence gathered is insufficient to meet the Full Code Test, the prosecutor must next ask whether there are reasonable grounds to believe that by continuing the investigation for a reasonable period of time, further evidence could be uncovered which would make a conviction more likely.

11.28

What can be said to constitute 'reasonable' grounds to believe, or what can be considered a 'reasonable' period of time, is likely to be case specific, and will obviously depend on the individual views of the prosecutor, the complexity of the investigation, and the resources available. The absence of a more precise definition might be thought to introduce an element of uncertainty in the way in which the test might be applied. However, the legal test for establishing what is or is not reasonable is not wholly subjective. A decision is considered unreasonable if it can be said that no reasonable person acting reasonably could have made it.[13]

11.29

In cases where neither limb of the evidential test can be met at the conclusion of the DPA negotiations, and/or it is not considered to be in the public interest to prosecute or enter into DPA negotiations, the prosecutor should consider whether the case is appropriate for a Civil Recovery Order. In these circumstances, reference should be made to the Attorney General's guidance on asset recovery powers under the Proceeds of Crime Act 2002.

Public interest factors

11.30

As set out above, deciding whether a DPA is appropriate involves an assessment of whether or not it would be in the public interest to enter into such an agreement

13 *Associated Provincial Picture Houses Ltd v Wednesbury Corporation* [1948] 1 KB 223.

rather than to prosecute. Public interest considerations will take account of both the overall seriousness of the offence and the issue of deterrence. They will include not just the value of any gain or loss, but also the risk of harm to the victim, to the public, to shareholders, and to creditors, as well as the stability and integrity of financial markets and international trade. In particular, prosecutors must have regard to the UK's commitment to the OECD[14] Convention on Combating Bribery of Foreign Officials in International Business Transactions 2011, particularly in respect of key industry sectors and large corporations. The Code emphasises Article 5 of the OECD Convention which states that investigation and prosecution of bribery of a foreign public official should not be influenced by considerations of national economic interest, the potential effect upon relations with another state or the identity of the natural or legal persons involved.[15]

Additional public interest factors in favour of prosecution

11.31

The Code lists a number of further factors to be weighed in the balance *in favour* of prosecution when considering the public interest aspect of the test:[16]

- Where there is a history of similar conduct by the company (including prior criminal, civil, and regulatory enforcement actions against it).
- Where the conduct alleged is part of the established business practices of the company.
- Where the offence was committed at a time when the company had an ineffective compliance programme.
- Where the company had been previously subject to warnings, sanctions or criminal charges, and has nonetheless failed to take adequate action to prevent future unlawful conduct, or has continued to engage in the conduct.
- Where there has been failure to report wrongdoing within a reasonable time of the offending conduct coming to light, or reporting it knowing it to be inaccurate, misleading or incomplete.
- Where a significant level of harm has been caused to the victims of the wrongdoing, or where a substantial adverse impact to the integrity or confidence of markets, local or national governments has occurred.

14 Organization for Economic Co-operation and Development.
15 Code section 2.7.
16 Code section 2.8.1(i)–(vii).

Additional public interest factors against prosecution

11.32

Further public interest criteria *against* prosecution listed[17] include:

- A genuinely proactive approach adopted by the corporate management team when the offending is brought to their notice. This will involve self-reporting (the advantages of which are spelt out in Chapter 10 paragraphs 10.12–16), the timeliness of the self-reporting, and remedial actions such as compensating the victims.
- Proactive compliance, including making witnesses available and disclosure of the details of any internal investigation. Holding back important information which jeopardises an effective investigation or the destruction of material would be a strong factor in favour of prosecution.
- A lack of history of similar conduct.
- The existence of a proactive corporate compliance programme at the time of offending and at the time or reporting, although it failed to be effective in this instance.
- The offending represents isolated actions by individuals, for example a rogue director.
- The offending is not recent in nature, and the company in its current form is effectively a different body to that which committed the offences.
- A conviction is likely to have disproportionate consequences for the company under the law of another jurisdiction including European Law. In this respect, the Code recognises the draconian effect caused by the EU Directive which excludes companies convicted of fraud, corruption and other such offences from participating in public contracts within the European Community.[18]

Letter of invitation

11.33

An invitation to negotiate a DPA is a matter for the discretion of the prosecutor and not P.[19] Since DPAs are entirely voluntary, the prosecutor is no obligation to invite P to negotiate, and P is under no obligation to accept. Neither side is obliged to agree any particular term.[20]

17 Code section 2.8.2(i)–(vi).

18 See Article 45 of Directive 2004/18//EC of the European Parliament and of the Council on the coordination of procedures for the award of public work contracts, public supply contracts and public service contracts.

19 Code section 2.1.

20 Code section 2.2.

11.34

The Code dictates how an invitation to enter into DPA negotiations should be made, and the way in which discussions should be conducted.[21] If the prosecutor decides to offer P the opportunity to enter into DPA negotiations, a formal letter of invitation marking the beginning of the negotiation period will be sent outlining the way in which negotiations will proceed.[22] The letter will:

- confirm the prosecutor's decision to offer P the opportunity to enter into DPA negotiations;
- ask P to confirm whether or not it wishes to enter into negotiations in accordance with the 2013 Act and the Code;
- set out a timeframe within which P must notify the prosecutor whether it accepts the invitation to enter into DPA negotiations.

11.35

If P agrees to engage in such negotiations, then a further letter from the prosecutor to P should contain the following undertakings:[23]

- To keep confidential the fact that DPA negotiations are taking place.
- That information which is provided in the course of the negotiations will remain confidential, and its disclosure will be restricted,[24] except as permitted by Schedule 17, paragraph 13 of the 2013 Act, or where permitted by law. (As to the nature of such material and the circumstances in which it can be used in subsequent criminal proceedings, see paras 11.98–103 below.)
- In exceptional circumstances, the prosecutor may agree in writing to different terms regarding the confidentiality of information.[25] However, until the issues of confidentiality, use and retention of information have been agreed to the satisfaction of both parties, and the agreement is reflected in signed undertakings, the prosecutor must not continue with the substantive negotiations.[26]

11.36

The letter should also include the following matters:

(a) A statement of the prosecutor's responsibility for disclosure of material pursuant to the Code.[27]

21 Code section 3.
22 Code section 3.5.
23 Code section 3.6.
24 Code section 3.9(i).
25 Code section 3.10.
26 Code section 3.11.
27 Code section 3.8(i).

(b) The statement will make it clear that the law in relation to the disclosure of *unused* material may require the prosecutor to provide information received in the course of the negotiations to a defendant in criminal proceedings.[28]

(c) A warning that the provision of inaccurate, misleading or incomplete information where P ought to have known that this was the case may lead to a prosecution of P:

  (i) for providing such information;

  (ii) for the offence or offences which are the subject of an agreed DPA.[29]

(d) The practical means by which the discussions will be conducted, including appropriate time limits.[30]

(e) A requirement that P will provide an undertaking:

  (i) that the information provided by the prosecutor in the course of the negotiations will be treated as confidential, and not be disclosed to any other party, other than for the purpose of the negotiations or as required by law;

  (ii) that all documentation or other material relevant to the matters the prosecutor is considering prosecuting is retained by P, until the prosecutor releases P from the obligation.[31]

The substance and character of negotiations

11.37

The negotiations must be transparent, and the prosecutor must:

- Ensure that a full and accurate record of negotiations is prepared and retained. It is essential that a full written record is kept of every key action and event in the discussion process, including details of every offer or concession made by each party, and the reasons for every decision taken by the prosecutor. All meetings should be minuted, signed and agreed.[32]
- Ensure that the prosecution and P have obtained sufficient information from each other so each can play an informed part in the negotiations.[33]
- Ensure that the DPA ultimately placed before the court fully and fairly reflects P's alleged offending.[34]

28 Code section 3.7(ii).
29 Code section 3.8(ii)2B22.
30 Code section 3.8(iii).
31 Code section 3.9(ii).
32 Code section 3.4(i).
33 Code section 3.4(ii).
34 Code section 3.4(iv).

- Not agree additional matters with P which are not recorded in the DPA and not made known to the court.[35]

There is a balance to be struck between encouraging all parties to be able to negotiate freely, and the risk that P may seek (knowingly or when P should have known) to induce the prosecutor to enter into a DPA on an inaccurate, misleading or incomplete basis.[36] It is clear, however, that incorrect information provided by P intentionally or recklessly in order to avoid prosecution will inevitably attract it.

Unused material and disclosure

11.38

Since a DPA is an agreement, it is essential that negotiations between the parties are fair, and that P should in principle have sufficient information to play an informed part in the negotiations. For instance, P must not be misled as to the strength of the prosecution case.[37]

11.39

Since DPA negotiations will precede the formal instigation of proceedings, the prosecutor will not at that stage be under any statutory legal obligation under the Criminal Procedure and Investigations Act 1996 ('CPIA 1996') to disclose all the evidence that it intends to rely on at trial, or other material pertaining to the case, or 'unused material' which it does not intend to use, but which undermines the prosecution case or lends support to the defence case.[38] Nonetheless the prosecutor must always be alive to the potential need to disclose such evidence or unused material in the interests of justice and fairness in the particular circumstances of the case.[39]

11.40

Consideration should therefore be given to reasonable and specific requests for disclosure by P. Where the need for such disclosure is not apparent to the prosecutor, any disclosure will depend on what P chooses to reveal to the prosecutor about its case in order to justify the request.[40]

11.42

Where a DPA is approved by the court at a final hearing and a bill of indictment is preferred upon entering into a DPA, the provisions of the CPIA 1996 will apply,

35 Code section 3.4(v).
36 Code section 4.2.
37 These requirements are echoed in the Operational Handbook under the subheading 'Disclosure'.
38 Code section 5.1.
39 Code section 5.2.
40 Code section 5.3. and updated Handbook subheading: 'DPA Disclosure'.

and disclosure obligations will be triggered. Such obligations are immediately at an end if and when the indictment is suspended. The statutory disclosure obligations and standard directions providing time limits for compliance will only apply if the suspension is lifted in the event of termination of the DPA, and the prosecution of P.[41]

11.43

Just as with disclosure under the CPIA, the prosecutor and the Principal Investigator/Disclosure Officer should work together to conduct DPA disclosure in a 'thinking manner'. The Prosecutor's duty to disclose material is a continuing one, and even extends to material that comes to light after the DPA has been agreed, provided it satisfies the test for disclosure as outlined in the Code.[42]

11.44

The investigator's duty to pursue reasonable lines of inquiry in accordance with the CPIA 1996 Code of Practice is not affected by the introduction of DPAs or the application of the Code. What is reasonable in each case will depend on the particular circumstances.[43]

The end of the negotiation period

11.45

The negotiating period will end when one or both parties withdraw from the process, or when the court approves or refuses a DPA at a final hearing.[44]

Civil Recovery Orders

11.46

If, by the end of negotiations, the two stage test has not been met, and it is not thought appropriate to continue the criminal investigation, the prosecutor should consider whether a Civil Recovery Order is appropriate. In this respect, the Code draws the prosecutor's attention to *The Attorney General's Guidance to Prosecuting Bodies on their Asset Recovery Powers under the Proceeds of Crime Act 2002*, issued on 5 November 2009.[45] In January 2018, new guidance was issued to authorities involved in asset recovery and financial investigation under POCA, including the SFO and CPS. The guidance reminds prosecutors that, in accordance with public interest factors including

41 Code section 5.7.
42 Code section 5.8. and updated Handbook subheading: 'DPA Disclosure'.
43 Code section 5.4.
44 Code section 3.2. and updated Handbook subheading: 'Formal letter of invitation'.
45 Code section 1.6.

the reduction of crime, care must be taken not to allow an individual or body corporate to avoid a criminal investigation and prosecution by consenting to the making of a civil recovery order in circumstances where a criminal disposal would be justified.[46]

11.47

The Proceeds of Crime Act 2002 ('POCA') provides the courts with a variety of additional civil powers in relation to the confiscation of property and assets related to criminal activity. These powers allow investigating agencies and prosecuting authorities, including the Crown Prosecution Service (CPS) and SFO, to seek court orders that specified properties are recoverable on the basis that they are, or represent, the proceeds of criminal conduct. This can be done can without criminal convictions against the party accused of the offence. Which path is chosen will depend on a combination of factors, not least the strength of the evidence and the weighing of the various factors in deciding whether to prosecute. Civil recovery orders, made in civil proceedings by the High Court against property located in England and Wales[47] and shown to be the proceeds of crime, have become an important part of the SFO's enforcement armoury, even in a world where there are DPAs. These powers have been considerably extended by the Criminal Finances Act 2017 ('CFA'), which has introduced new asset recovery and investigation powers under POCA, and made amendments to existing powers.

11.48

One innovation created by the CFA is Unexplained Wealth Orders ('UWOs'). UWOs may be granted by the High Court if satisfied that:

- There is reasonable cause to believe that the respondent holds the property (whether in its entirety or in part with others), and the value of the property is greater than £50,000.
- There are reasonable grounds for suspecting that the known sources of the respondent's lawfully obtained income would have been insufficient for the purposes of enabling the respondent to obtain the property.
- The respondent is either a politically exposed person ('PEP') or there are reasonable grounds for suspecting that the respondent (or a person connected to the respondent) is, or has been, entrusted with prominent state functions by an international organisation or by a state (other than the UK) or an individual who is a family member or known to be a close associate of a PEP.[48]

---

46 The Handbook provides additional new areas of guidance, eg the 2017 Memorandum of Understanding on Tackling Foreign Bribery.

47 *Perry & Others v Serious Organised Crime Agency (No 2)* [2012] UKSC 35.

48 CFA (2017), s 362B(7).

11.49

A UWO requires the respondent to provide a statement setting out the nature and extent of their interest in the property; how they obtained it; details of any settlement that holds the property; and any other information requested in connection with the property. Once the respondent has complied with the UWO, the enforcement authority must decide within 60 days what, if any, enforcement or regulatory proceedings (eg civil recovery proceedings) ought to be taken. Guidance on the scope of statutory powers underlying UFOs was provided by the Court of Appeal in *NCA v Hajiyeva*.[49]

Content of a DPA

1. Statement of facts

11.50

The content of a DPA is governed by the provisions of Schedule 17, paragraph 5. It includes a statement of facts.

11.51

Paragraph 5(1) provides:

> '(1) A DPA must contain a statement of facts relating to the alleged offence, which may include admissions made by P.'

11.52

The contents of a statement of facts must:

- Give particulars relating to each alleged offence.
- Include details of any financial gain or loss, with reference to key documents that must be attached.[50]

11.53

Since the court does not have the power to adjudicate upon factual differences in DPA proceedings, the parties should resolve any factual issue necessary to allow the court to agree the terms of the DPA on a clear, fair and accurate basis.[51]

49 2020] EWCA Civ 108; [2020] All ER 34.
50 Code section 6.1(i)–(ii), and updated Handbook subheading: 'Statement of Facts'.
51 Code section 6.2.

11.54

There is no requirement for formal admissions of guilt in respect of offences charged by the indictment, though it will be necessary to admit the contents and meaning of key documents referred to in the statement of facts.[52]

11.55

However, it is important to remember that if P is prosecuted for the alleged offence addressed by a court approved DPA, Schedule 17, paragraph 13 (2) makes the statement of facts admissible against P in any subsequent criminal proceedings as an admission by P under section 10 of the Criminal Justice Act 1967.[53] Where linked individuals are prosecuted following a DPA, the statement of facts and DPA itself may be admissible, though this will depend on a number of case specific factors.

11.56

The final statement of facts will ultimately be a public document and should be drafted accurately, concisely and in a way that is accessible to all. When detailing the gains and losses made, it can be helpful to distil complex transactions down to key transactions, and summarise complex payment trails. In respect of bribery cases, it may be sufficient to simply list the dates and amounts of the corrupt payments.

2. Expiry Date

11.57

A DPA must specify an expiry date, which is the date on which the DPA ceases to have effect if it has not already been terminated as a result of a breach.[54] In determining the expiry date, the time period must be sufficient to ensure that the company is capable of complying with the obligations in the DPA. Consideration should also be given to the time required for the Company to complete the following obligations:

- co-operation with ongoing investigations and prosecutions, in particular, those of linked individuals;
- fulfilment of the financial obligations, including payment of compensation, disgorgement, financial penalty and costs, which may be in instalments if strong evidence is provided for doing so;
- implementation/improvements to the Company's compliance programme; and

52 Code section 6.3.
53 Code section 6.4.
54 Schedule 17 para 5(2).

- (if applicable) a monitor's assessment or external review of the organisation's implementation/improvement of a compliance programme.[55]

3. Terms of a DPA

11.58

Schedule 17, paragraphs 5(3) (a)–(g) of the 2103 Act set out terms which, if agreement is reached, may be imposed on P. The list provided is not intended to be exhaustive. It can require P:

(a) to pay the prosecutor a financial penalty;

(b) to compensate victims of the alleged offence;

(c) to donate money to a charity or other third party;

(d) to disgorge any profits made by P from the alleged offence;

(e) to implement a compliance programme or make changes to an existing compliance programme relating to P's policies, or to the training of P's employees or both;

(f) to co-operate in any investigation of the alleged offence;

(g) to pay any reasonable costs of the prosecutor in relation to the alleged offence or the DPA.

11.59

Schedule 17 paragraph 5(5) states that a DPA may include a term setting out the consequences of a failure by P to comply with any of its terms.

The guiding principles

11.60

The prosecutor and P will be required to agree terms which are fair, and reasonable. What terms are fair and reasonable can only be determined on a case-by-case basis. The Operational Handbook and Code provide general guidance.[56] They state, amongst other things, that the terms:

(i) must set out clearly the measures with which P must comply. Clarity is important so P understands what is required, and ambiguity is avoided if a breach occurs;

(ii) must be proportionate to the offence and tailored to the specific facts of the case;

---

55 Code section 7.2.

56 Handbook subsection: Term of the Agreement.

(iii) must specify the start and end date of the DPA which is the date on which the DPA ceases to have effect if it has not already been terminated by virtue of a breach (see paragraph 11.57 above).

(iv) must record that the DPA relates only to the offences particularised in the draft indictment. It follows that prosecutors should not agree to a term that would prevent P from being prosecuted for conduct not included in the indictment, even where the conduct has been disclosed during the course of the DPA negotiations but not charged.

(v) must include a warranty from P that the information provided to the prosecutor throughout the DPA negotiation and upon which the DPA is based contains no inaccurate, misleading or incomplete information relevant to the matters covered by the DPA.

(vi) should require P to notify the prosecutor and provide where requested, any documentation or other material that it becomes aware of when the DPA is in force;

(vii) may include but are not confined to the financial terms listed in paragraph 5(3) of the Act (see paragraph 11.59 above). There is no compulsion on P to submit to any of these terms, all of which are a matter of negotiation with P and subject to judicial oversight.

Monitors

11.61

A further term of a DPA may involve the appointment of monitors. The use of monitors must be fair, reasonable, and proportionate. It should be approached with care, and the individual facts of the case will determine whether or not such a step is appropriate. A monitor is a person capable of overseeing and supervising the terms of the agreement. In the context of a DPA, a monitor's 'primary responsibility is to assess and monitor P's internal controls, and advise of necessary compliance improvements that will reduce the risk of future recurrence of the conduct subject to the DPA, and report misconduct to the prosecutor.'[57]

11.62

The Code suggests the following terms which might be incorporated into a monitor's agreement.[58] They include:

- A code of conduct.
- An appropriate education programme.

57 Code section 7.12. and updated Handbook, subsection: 'Monitors'.
58 Code section 7.21.

- Internal procedures which enable officers and employees to report issues in a safe and confidential manner.
- Processes for identifying key strategic risk areas.
- A gift and hospitality policy
- Procurement procedures which minimise the opportunity for misconduct.
- Internal management and audit processes which include reasonable controls against misconduct.

11.63

It is P's duty at the preliminary hearing to provide the prosecutor and the court with details of three potential monitors, including their relevant qualifications, specialist knowledge and experience, and the reasons why they have been selected. In order to avoid any actual or potential conflicts of interest, where a monitor has or has had any associations with P or companies or persons either associated with P, or with companies or person featured in the DPA, this should be made known. Although the prosecutor should ordinarily accept P's proposed monitors, the prosecutor or the court may veto the proposed appointment if it is considered that that there is a conflict of interest or that the monitor lacks the necessary experience and authority, or that the appointment is inappropriate for some other reason.

11.64

P should also supply an estimate of the costs for the monitoring process.[59] Where the terms require a monitor to be appointed, P will bear the cost of the selection, appointment, and remuneration, as well as the reasonable costs incurred by the prosecutor during the monitoring period.

11.65

The Code also addresses other issues such as the length of time the monitors should be appointed; an extension of time if the organisation has not satisfied its obligations during the term of the initial period;[60] and confidentiality of monitors' reports and associated correspondence, with disclosure restricted to the prosecutor, organisation and the court, save as otherwise permitted by law.[61]

59 Code section 7.15.
60 Code section 7.19.
61 Code section 7.19.

Preliminary court hearings

1. Application to approve a proposal to enter an agreement

11.66

Applications to the court to approve a proposal to enter an agreement take place before the proposed terms have been finally agreed between the parties. The process is governed by Schedule 17, paragraph 7 of the 2013 Act, which provides that:

> '(1) After the commencement of negotiations between a prosecutor and P in respect of a DPA, but before the terms of the DPA are agreed, the prosecutor must apply to the Crown Court for a declaration that –
>
> (a) entering into a DPA is likely to be in the interests of justice, and
>
> (b) the proposed terms of the DPA are fair, reasonable and proportionate.[62]
>
> (2) The court must give reasons for its decision on whether or not to make a declaration under sub-paragraph (1).
>
> (3) The prosecutor may make a further application to the court for a declaration under sub-paragraph (1) if, following the previous application, the court declined to make a declaration.
>
> (4) A hearing at which an application under this paragraph is determined must be held in private, and reasons under sub-paragraph (2) must be given in private.'

11.67

The Criminal Procedure Rules set out in detail what must be included in the application.[63] It must be served on the court and P in writing as soon as practicable after the parties have begun to negotiate the proposal, and should, amongst other things:

- Identify the parties to the proposed agreement;
- Attach a copy of the proposed indictment;

62 7.20.

63 Paragraph 11.3(1) of the Criminal Procedure Rules provides that where the prosecutor seeks approval, s/he must apply in writing as soon as practicable after the parties have begun to negotiate the proposal, and serve the application on the court officer and the defendant. Paragraph 11.3(3)-(4) of the Rules also sets out detailed requirements for the content of the application. See also updated Handbook, subsection: 'Court application'.

- Include or attach a statement of facts proposed for inclusion in the agreement, providing full particulars of each offence, and details of any financial gain or loss.
- Explain why the proposed agreement is likely to be in the interests of justice and is 'fair, reasonable and proportionate'. In doing so, the prosecutor may be called on to address such issues such as on-going and/or subsequent ancillary proceedings if relevant, and/or any conduct within the scope of the DPA which P has disclosed to the prosecutor but which does not form part of the draft indictment.[64]
- Include any information about P that would be relevant to sentence, in the event of conviction for the offence(s) (see paragraphs 11.80 onwards).
- Specify the proposed expiry date of the agreement.
- Describe the proposed terms of the agreement, including such matters as compensation, reparation, or donations agreed to be paid.
- Set out the details of any profits or other financial benefits to be surrendered.
- Include any details of any arrangements being made to the management or conduct of the defendant's business.
- Detail any arrangement to monitor P's compliance with any term.
- Contain or attach P's written consent.
- The prosecutor should contact a court designated to approve DPAs to request a listing, and provide a realistic time estimate for a preliminary hearing.[65]

2. Preferring and suspending a Bill of Indictment

11.68

If a DPA is considered appropriate by the prosecutor, and approved by the court, proceedings will be formally instituted by the prosecutor by the preferment of a draft Bill of Indictment, which will immediately be suspended pending the satisfactory performance, or otherwise, of the DPA.[66] The procedure will be as follows:

- The Crown Court judge will be asked to approve the DPA;
- Once approval has been obtained, consent must be sought from the judge for the indictment to be preferred;

64 See also Code section 9.4.

65 Code section 9.2.

66 Section 1(2)(g) of the Criminal Procedure and Investigations Act 1996 has been amended by Schedule 17 para 37 of the Crime and Courts Act 2013.

- As soon as proceedings are instituted in this way, they are automatically suspended;
- The suspension can only be lifted on an application to the Crown Court by the prosecutor, and no such application may be made at any time when the DPA is in force;
- At a time when the proceedings are suspended, no other person may prosecute P for the alleged offence.

The final hearing – court approval of terms of a DPA

11.69

Before the final hearing, further negotiations will take place having given further thought to the terms which were proposed at the preliminary hearing. By the time of the final hearing, the prosecutor and P will have concluded these discussions and reached final agreement on the statement of facts and component parts of the DPA. The court will continue to maintain tight control over the proceedings. The mere fact that agreement has been reached between the prosecutor and P does not mean that the DPA will follow. The court's approval is required.

11.70

Paragraph 8 of Schedule 17 states:

> '(1) When a prosecutor and P have agreed the terms of a DPA, the prosecutor must apply to the Crown Court for a declaration that –
>
> (a) the DPA is in the interests of justice, and
>
> (b) the terms of the DPA are fair, reasonable and proportionate.
>
> (2) But the prosecutor may not make an application under sub-paragraph (1) unless the court has made a declaration under paragraph 7(1) (declaration on preliminary hearing).
>
> (3) A DPA only comes into force when it is approved by the Crown Court making a declaration under sub-paragraph (1)
>
> (4) The court must give reasons for its decision on whether or not to make a declaration under sub-paragraph (1).'

11.71

The application for a declaration at the final hearing must be served by the prosecution on the court and P in writing.[67] It must also:

---

67 CPR section 11.4(f); Code section 10.4.

- attach the agreement, signed by the Director of the SFO and the Company;
- indicate in what respect, if any, the terms of the agreement differ from those proposed in the original application at the preliminary hearing;
- contain or attach the defendant's written consent to the agreement;
- explain why the agreement is in the interests of justice, and why the terms of the agreement are fair, reasonable and proportionate;
- attach a draft indictment relating to the offences which are subject to the agreement; and
- include in the application for the hearing to be held in private.[68]

11.72

The court will once again need to satisfy itself that the agreement is in the interests of justice and that the terms are fair, reasonable, and proportionate. Where relevant, issues such as on-going and/or subsequent ancillary proceedings must also be addressed by the prosecutor at the final hearing. Agreements reached between P and regulatory bodies or prosecuting authorities in other jurisdictions must also be raised with the court, if relevant.

11.73

Relevant considerations for cases where a DPA is under consideration and where there is a parallel investigation by an overseas and/or other UK agency will include:

- Early communication and de-confliction in respect of investigative activity, including interviews and use of statutory powers, which may affect admissibility of evidence (eg section 2 powers, interviews under caution, co-operating suspects).
- Early communication and de-confliction in respect of interaction with the Company and the Company's position with respect to the SFO and other agencies on matters such as LPP.
- Laws regarding disclosure of material in respective jurisdictions (both between agencies and those relating to defendants) and potential impact.
- Ensuring the terms of negotiations allow for communication and sharing of information provided by the Company with the relevant agencies.
- Whether the Company has taken a consistent position on the admission of facts and liability in its respective jurisdictions.

68 Handbook, subheading: Final Application.

- Co-ordination of court listing dates to ensure that resolutions can be approved simultaneously where possible. This may be critical to the confidentiality terms and is likely to be a key concern for the company to achieve full national and/or global coverage in respect of the conduct.
- Ensuring liaison between the Company's respective press offices.
- Awareness of different market announcement requirements for public companies in different jurisdictions. For example, when the obligation to make a market announcement is triggered.

11.74

The application seeking approval of the DPA may be made in open court, but is more likely to be made in private, since the prosecutor and P will be uncertain as to whether the court will grant a declaration under paragraph 8(1). The reason for this is easily understood. If the parties were to make an application in open court which was refused, it might lead to uncertainties and destabilisation that private preliminary proceedings are designed to avoid.[69]

11.75

The court may adjourn a final hearing as many times as it wishes, if it requires more information about the facts or terms of a proposed DPA before it can make the full declaration under paragraph 8(1) of Schedule 17.[70]

11.76

If a DPA is approved, the court must give its declaration to that effect in open court.[71]

Financial penalties

11.77

Paragraph 5(4) of Schedule 17 states that the amount of any financial penalty agreed between the prosecutor and P must be 'broadly comparable to the fine that a court would have imposed on P on conviction for the alleged offence following a guilty plea'. This is intended to enable the parties and the courts to have regard to relevant pre-existing sentencing principles and guidelines in order to determine the appropriate level for a financial penalty in an individual case.

69 Code section 10.4, and updated Handbook, subsection: 'Naming of Relevant Parties'.
70 Operational Handbook, subsection: 'Introduction'.
71 Schedule 17 para 5(6); Code section 11.1.

11.78

By creating a transparent and consistent approach to the setting of a financial penalty analogous to the sentencing framework, the parties and the court will know what the appropriate starting point is before they enter into the process.[72] To this end, the prosecutor should assist the court, where possible and relevant, with the identification of the appropriate terms by drawing the judge's attention to the following information:[73]

- Any victim statement or other information available to the prosecutor as to the impact of the alleged offence on the victim.
- Any statutory provisions relevant to the offender and the offences under consideration.
- Any relevant Sentencing Council Guidelines (see below) and guideline cases.
- The aggravating and mitigating factors of the alleged offence under consideration.

11.79

If such information is relevant and available, it should form part of the agreed written application to be provided to the court at the final hearing.[74]

New sentencing guidelines

11.80

The Sentencing Council for England and Wales have published new sentencing guidelines for a range of economic crimes, which for the first time include sentences for bribery as well as specific and separate guidelines for corporate offenders, and individual offenders.[75] The purpose of the guidelines is threefold:

- to help the courts achieve consistency of approach;
- to ensure that any fine imposed on a corporate entity convicted of offences under the UKBA is be substantial enough to have a real economic impact on it; and
- to send a strong deterrent message to the business community.

72 Code section 8.3.
73 Code section 8.1. and updated Handbook, subsection: 'Financial terms'.
74 Code section 8.2.
75 See –Appendix 4.

11.81

In formulating its sentencing guidelines for corporations convicted of section 7 bribery offences, the Sentencing Council has taken into account existing practices here and abroad, in particular:

- regulatory and civil penalty regimes used by such bodies as the Financial Services Authority (now the Financial Conduct Authority (FCA)), the Office of Fair Trading, HM Revenue and Customs and the SFO;
- relevant domestic criminal case law;
- civil and criminal penalties imposed in other jurisdictions (notably the US);
- fine regimes for corporations in the definitive guideline for corporate manslaughter and the draft environmental guideline;
- sentencing guideline for corporations produced by the United States Sentencing Commission.

11.82

Noting that offences of this kind encompass a wide range of behaviour and that the circumstances of the offender could vary considerably, from a small organisation with very limited resources to a huge multi-national with vast resources, the Council has urged the need for flexibility.

11.83

The fine for a corporate offence under the 2013 Act is unlimited. The Guidelines set out a ten step exercise to be conducted by the sentencing court when determining the nature of the financial penalty and fixing the size of any fine. Although not every aspect of the exercise will apply in securing agreement and court approval of a DPA, it is submitted that in order to achieve a 'broadly comparable' financial penalty under a DPA, the parties and ultimately the court should comply with the following relevant steps before a declaration is made at the final hearing:

- The court should first consider whether it wishes to make a compensation order, requiring the offender to pay compensation for any personal injury, loss or damage which should be prioritised over the payment of a fine. Compensation is usually paid to the victim directly by the compensating party or through an intermediary agreed by the parties and approved by the court. Where it is not possible to agree compensation, reasons for this must be given in the DPA application.
- Relevant considerations in deciding whether compensation should be a term of the DPA may include:[76]

---

76 Updated Handbook, subsection: 'Compensation'.

- whether a victim can be identified;
- whether the relevant wrongdoing has caused loss;
- whether any loss is quantifiable so that it can be used as a basis for compensation, such as the cost by which a contract has been inflated to take account of the bribe payment;
- if not easily quantifiable, whether the civil courts would be a better forum to resolve the issue;
- what steps the victim has already taken to recover their loss, and if they have, how much has been recovered or is likely to be recovered;
- the risk that the payment of compensation to any overseas victims might lead to the funds being vulnerable to corruption once again, and the extent to which such risks can be mitigated;
- whether a financial payment is the best means of achieving compensation or other measures are possible;
- whether it is practicable to obtain the views of the victim and, if so, what those views are;
- where there are victims in other jurisdictions, consideration will be given to the General Principles to compensate overseas victims (including affected states) in bribery, corruption, and economic crime cases agreed between the SFO, CPS and NCA.[77] The need to obtain victim impact statements by individuals or companies and/or relevant country expert statements will also be considered;
- Early engagement with the relevant government department, if itself the victim.

• The court must next determine the category of the offence by reference to culpability and harm. Consideration will be given to the main factual elements of the offence in order to determine whether levels of culpability and harm are high, medium or low.

Key factors in determining a high level of culpability include the following non-exhaustive characteristics:

• where the role played by the corporation in the planned, unlawful activity was central;
• wilful obstruction of detection (eg destruction of evidence, misleading investigators, suborning employees);
• where the corruption targeted local or national government ministers or officials, including those performing a law enforcement role;

77 Published on 1 June 2018.

- where there was abuse of the corporation's dominant market position;
- where the offending conduct was committed over a sustained period of time (relevant to UKBA section 7 offences only); or
- where a culture of wilful disregard prevailed in relation to the commission of offences by employees or agents with no effort to put effective systems in place(relevant to UKBA section 7 offences only).

11.84

Factors in concluding medium culpability include:

- where the corporation played a significant role in unlawful activity organised by others;
- where the activity was not unlawful from the outset.

11.85

Factors in concluding lesser culpability include:

- where the corporation played a minor, peripheral role in unlawful activity organised by others;
- where, in respect of a section 7 offence some effort has been made to put bribery prevention measures in place, but it was insufficient to amount to a defence.

11.86

The level of *harm* must be also assessed. This is represented by a financial figure which, for offences under the UKBA, will normally be the gross profit from the contract obtained, retained, sought or avoided, as a result of the offending. An alternative measure for offences under section 7 may be the likely cost avoided by failing to put in place appropriate measures to prevent bribery.

11.87

Where the actual or intended gain cannot be established, the appropriate measure will be the amount that the court considers was likely to be achieved in all the circumstances. In the absence of sufficient evidence of the amount that was likely to be obtained, 10–20% of the relevant revenue (ie between 10 and 20% of the worldwide revenue derived from the product or business area to which the offence relates for the period of the offending) *may* be the appropriate measure. In cases of bribery in which the true harm is to commerce or markets generally, a greater harm figure may be justified.

Fixing the starting point and sentencing range

11.88

Once the court has determined the culpability level, it should use the table reproduced below to determine the starting point within the category range. The starting point applies to all offenders irrespective of plea or previous convictions.

11.89

The harm figure at step three is multiplied by the relevant percentage figure representing culpability.

Culpability Level

	A	B	C
Harm figure multiplier	**Starting point** 300%	**Starting point** 200%	**Starting point** 100%
	Category range 250%–400%	**Category range** 100%–300%	**Category range** 20%–150%

11.90

So where culpability is found to have been high, the range is 250%–400% with a suggested multiplier starting at 300%; where culpability is fixed as medium, the range is 100%–300% with a suggested multiplier starting at 200%; and where culpability is assessed as low, the range is 20%–150%, with the suggested starting point at 100%. Thus, for example, where a corporation's culpability level is assessed as medium and the harm figure assessed as £1 million, the starting point would be £2 million (with a range of £1 million–£3 million).[78]

11.91

Having determined the appropriate starting point, the court should then consider adjustment within the category range for aggravating and mitigating features. In some cases, having considered these factors, it may be appropriate to move outside the identified category range.

11.92

Factors *increasing* seriousness may include:

---

78 The use of a multiplier applied to a harm figure is broadly bases on the US system of determining fines for corporations where the range of multipliers is .05 to 4 (www.ussc.gov/Guidelines/Organizational_Guidelines/guidelines_chapter_8.htm).

- Previous relevant convictions or subject to previous relevant civil or regulatory enforcement action.
- Endemic fraudulent activity within the corporation.
- Attempts made to conceal misconduct.
- Substantial harm to the confidence of the markets, or to the integrity of local or national governments (This form of harm is an aggravating factor and will not be taken into account in the initial assessment of harm.)
- Offence committed across borders or jurisdictions.

11.93

Factors *reducing* seriousness or reflecting personal mitigation will include:

- No previous relevant convictions or previous relevant civil or regulatory enforcement action.
- Victims voluntarily reimbursed or compensated.
- No actual loss to victims.
- Where the offending was committed under previous directors or management.
- Little or no actual gain to the corporation from offending.

11.94

The Court will also follow 'general principles' when setting a fine in accordance with sections 118–132 of the Sentencing Act 2020, which requires that the fine must reflect the seriousness of the offence, and will require the court to take account of the financial circumstances of the offending corporation.[79]

11.95

As to the kind of financial information required, specific guidance is provided to companies, and partnerships delivering public or charitable services. In the context of DPA negotiations, the absence of disclosure of documents such as relevant audited accounts is likely to jeopardise the agreement.

Adjustment of fine

11.96

Having arrived at a fine level, the court should consider whether there are any further factors which indicate an adjustment in the level of the fine,

79 Section 164 of the Criminal Justice Act 2003 has been repealed by the Sentencing Act 2020, Sch 28, para 1.

having regard to the overall effect of the various orders made.[80] Consideration should be given to any further factors relevant to the setting of the level of the fine, 'to ensure that the fine is proportionate having regard to the size and financial position of the offending organisation and the seriousness of the offence.' The fine must be big enough 'to have a real economic impact which will bring home to both management and shareholders the need to operate within the law. Whether the fine will have the effect of putting the offender out of business will be relevant; in some bad cases this may be an acceptable consequence,' but this will be balanced against the risk of unacceptable harm to third parties.

11.97

The Guidelines set out a list of non-exhaustive factors in making any adjustment to the fine, whether a reduction or increase, to ensure that the fine is proportionate to the size and financial position of the organisation. These include:

- Whether the fine fulfils the objectives of punishment, deterrence and the removal of gain.
- The value, worth and available means of the corporation.
- Whether the fine impacts on the company's ability to implement effective compliance programmes.
- The impact of a fine on the employment of staff, service users, customers and local economy (but not shareholders).
- The impact of a fine on performance of a public or charitable function.
- Whether the fine impairs the offender's ability to make restitution to victims.

Consideration of factors which would indicate a reduction in sentence, such as assistance to the prosecution

11.98

One important consideration is whether the company has demonstrated co-operation with the investigation over and above mere compliance with coercive measures,[81] including where early admissions have been made, and/or the offending has been voluntarily reported. The court will take particular account of sections 73 and 74 of the Serious Organised Crime and Police Act 2005 ('SOCPA') so further reductions will be given for any special and additional

80 Updated Handbook, subsection: 'Adjustment of financial penalty'.
81 Code section 8.5.

assistance shown by the corporation to the prosecutor or investigator (such as helping to expose the criminal activity of others).[82]

Reduction for guilty pleas

11.99

The court should take into account any potential reduction in the level of fines for guilty pleas, in accordance with section 73 of the Sentencing Act 2020[83] and the *Guilty Plea* guideline. Since discounts of one third are given for pleas of guilty entered at the first available opportunity, it is submitted that in terms of financial penalties, a DPA (particularly one where prompt self reporting is a feature) will normally equate to a guilty plea at the earliest opportunity, and an organisation who enters into such an arrangement will legitimately expect a full discount of at least one third.

Breach of DPA

11.100

If, before the DPA has expired, the prosecutor believes that P is in breach, they should where possible ask P directly to rectify the alleged breach immediately.[84] In cases of minor breaches, it may be possible for a solution to be reached efficiently in this way, without the need for an application to the court.

11.101

The prosecutor will be required to publish details of the breach pursuant to paragraph 9(8) of Schedule 17.[85]

11.102

If a satisfactory outcome cannot be achieved in this way, the prosecutor may apply to the court under Schedule 17, paragraph 9, seeking a finding that P is in breach of the term as alleged, and explaining the reasons for the remedy sought.

11.103

Paragraph 9 of Schedule 17 states:

82 *R v Blackburn* [2007] EWCA Crim 2290 and *R v Dougall* [2010] EWCA Crim 1048 for reduction in sentences for providing evidence in criminal proceedings under the SOCPA.
83 Section 144 of the Criminal Justice Act 2003 has been repealed by the Sentencing Act 2020, Sch 28, para 1.
84 Updated Handbook, subheading 'Rectifying the breach'.
85 Code section 11.2.

'(1) At any time when a DPA is in force, if the prosecutor believes that P has failed to comply with the terms of the DPA, the prosecutor may make an application to the Crown Court under this paragraph.

(2) On an application under sub-paragraph (1) the court must decide whether, on the balance of probabilities, P has failed to comply with the terms of the DPA.

(3) If the court finds that P has failed to comply with the terms of the DPA, it may –

(a) invite the prosecutor and P to agree proposals to remedy P's failure to comply, or

(b) terminate the DPA.

(4) The Court must give its reasons for its decisions under sub-paragraphs (2) and (3)'

11.104

The Criminal Procedure Rules[86] provide, amongst other things, that the application:

- must be made in writing, as soon as practicable after becoming aware of the grounds for doing so; and
- must specify each respect in which the prosecutor believes that P has failed to comply with the terms of the agreement, and explain the reasons for the prosecutor's belief, attaching the necessary evidence.

If P wishes to make representations, they must be served on the court and the prosecutor in writing, within 20 business days of service of the application.[87]

11.105

The court must then decide on a balance of probabilities, whether there has been such a failure. If the court finds there has been a failure, it may either *invite* but not order the prosecutor and P to agree suitable proposals to remedy P's failure to comply, or terminate the DPA. It is likely that this mechanism will be reserved for comparatively minor breaches of the DPA.[88]

11.106

If suitable proposals are made and accepted, the court must then declare that the remedy is 'in the interests of justice', and 'fair, reasonable and proportionate.'[89]

86 CrimPR 11.5.
87 CPR section 11.5.(4).
88 Schedule 17 para 9; Code section 12.5.
89 Code section 11.5 and updated Handbook, subheading 'Rectifying the Breach'.

11.107

If the breach is more substantial, or where no suitable remedy can be found, or if the court refuses to approve the proposal, the court may order that the DPA is terminated. If that occurs, the DPA will cease to take effect immediately, and the prosecutor may apply to have the suspension of the indictment covered by the DPA lifted, in accordance with Schedule 17, paragraph 2.[90]

11.108

Where a DPA has been terminated in this way, P is not entitled to the return of any monies already paid under the DPA, nor to any other form of relief for detriment arising from its compliance with the DPA up until that point. The Code cites as an example, the costs of a monitoring programme.[91] P will also liable for the costs of the application. The court may not determine an application for breach of the DPA in the prosecutor's absence; or in the absence of the defendant, unless the defendant has had at least 20 days in which to make representations.

Late payments

11.109

A late payment, which may include financial obligations such as payment of compensation, disgorgement, financial penalties and costs, may constitute a breach of the DPA leading to breach and termination. Time in which to pay and payment in instalments can be incorporated into the terms of the DPA. It is pointed out in the Code that it may be appropriate to make provision for short delays requiring the payment of interest on any payment(s) not paid by the agreed date. It is also suggested that the rate of interest should ordinarily be not less than the rate of interest payable on post judgment debts at the date when the DPA is approved.

Variation of DPA

11.110

Variations of DPAs are governed by paragraph 10 of Schedule 17, which provides:

> '(1) At any time when a DPA is in force, the prosecutor and P may agree to vary its terms if –
>
> (a) the court has invited the parties to vary the terms of the DPA under paragraph 9(3)(a), or

90 Code section 11.5 and updated Handbook, subheading 'Termination'.
91 Code section 11.6 and updated Handbook, subheading 'Termination'.

(b) variation is necessary to avoid a failure by P to comply with its terms in circumstances that were not, and could not have been, foreseen by the prosecutor or P at the time that the DPA was agreed.

(2) When the prosecutor and P have agreed to vary the terms of the DPA, the prosecutor must apply to the Crown Court for a declaration that –

(a) the variation is in the interests of justice, and

(b) the terms of the DPA as varied are fair, reasonable and proportionate.

(3) A variation of a DPA only takes effect when it is approved by the Crown Court making a declaration under sub-paragraph (2).

(4) The court must give reasons for its decision on whether or not to make a declaration under sub-paragraph (2).'

11.111

It will be noted that variation can take place during the currency of the DPA, where the court has invited the parties to do so, or where a variation is necessary 'to avoid failure by P to comply with its terms in circumstances that were not, and could not have been foreseen by P or the Prosecutor at the time that the DPA was agreed'.

11.112

An application for a declaration seeking to vary the terms of a DPA must be justified on the ground that it is the interests of justice to do so, and the variations sought must be 'fair, reasonable and proportionate'.[92]

11.113

The Code anticipates two possible situations in which variation may be necessary.[93] The first is where a breach *has* occurred in respect of which an application has been made under paragraph 9 of Schedule 17, and the court has invited the parties to agree a solution, which it may or may not approve. The second is where the breach *has not yet* occurred, but save for the variation, is likely to occur.[94] A variation in this category will only be approved by the court if, in the words of section 10(1)(b) of Schedule 17, it arises from 'circumstances that were not, and could not have been foreseen by the prosecutor or P at the time that the DPA was agreed.'

92 Schedule17 para10(1)(b) and 10(2).
93 See also updated Handbook, subheading: 'Variation of a DPA'.
94 Code section 13.2(i)–(ii).

11.114

The Code points out that the process whereby parties can seek a variation of the DPA is not intended as a mechanism that exists for mere convenience or efficiency. Rather 'the DPA is a serious sanction for criminal conduct and will have been approved by the court on that basis'. It is therefore suggested that in the vast majority of cases, the terms of the DPA that are approved at a final hearing will be expected to be strictly complied with in their entirety, failing which P risks losing the benefit of the DPA.

11.115

In both situations, whilst P may approach the prosecutor to request a variation, it is the prosecutor and not P who may apply to the court to seek a declaration that a variation is acceptable,[95] and that varied terms are fair, reasonable and proportionate.[96]

11.116

The hearing can take place in private, but the decision refusing or granting the application and the reasons for it must be given in open court unless Schedule 17 paragraph 12 applies.[97]

11.117

Where the court decides not to approve the variation, the prosecutor must publish the court's decision and the reasons for it, unless prevented from doing so by any enactment or by an order of the court under Schedule 17 paragraph 12.[98] Where approval is given, the prosecutor must publish (a) the DPA, as varied, and (b) the court's declaration and the reasons for it, unless prevented from doing so under any enactment or by an order of the court under paragraph 12.[99]

Subsequent use of material in criminal proceedings

11.118

Paragraph 13 of Schedule 17 deals with the use of material in criminal proceedings where either (i) a DPA has been approved by the Crown Court in a final hearing under Schedule 17 paragraph 8 and has been subsequently terminated, or (ii) where a prosecutor and P have entered into negotiations for a DPA, but the DPA has not been approved by the Crown Court under paragraph 8.

95 Code section 13.3.
96 Updated Handbook, subheading: 'Variation of a DPA'.
97 Schedule 17 para 10(5)–(6).
98 Schedule 17 para 10(7).
99 Schedule 17 para 10(8).

Where a DPA has been approved by the Crown Court under Schedule 17 paragraph 8(1)

11.119

Where a DPA has been approved by the Crown Court under Schedule 17 paragraph 8(1), Schedule 17 paragraph 13(2) provides:

> '(2) The statement of facts contained in the DPA in any criminal proceedings brought against P for the alleged offence, [is] to be treated as an admission by P under section 10 of the Criminal Justice Act 1967 (proof by formal admission)'.

11.120

An admission under section 10 of the 1967 Act applies to the admission of any fact of which oral evidence may be given in any criminal proceedings by or on behalf of the prosecutor or defendant, and the admission of such a fact by any party shall be conclusive evidence in those proceedings *against* that party of the fact admitted.

11.121

Although an admission under this section can be withdrawn with the leave of the court, leave is unlikely to be given if the admission is in writing, prepared as an agreed document, and has been drafted with the benefit of legal advice.[100] Since a statement of facts is likely to contain an account by P, tantamount in law to an admission of culpability, the introduction of this material in a criminal trial could be determinative of guilt.

Where a prosecutor and P have entered into negotiations for a DPA, but the DPA has not been approved by the Crown Court under Schedule 17 paragraph 8(3)

11.122

Paragraph 13(3) of Schedule 17 governs the admission of material arising from negotiations between the prosecutor and P for a DPA, but where the DPA has not been approved by the Crown Court under paragraph 8.

11.123

Paragraph 13(6) of Schedule 17 defines the material as:

> '(a) material that shows that P entered into negotiations for a DPA, including in particular –

100 *R v Kolton* [2000] Crim LR 761, CA.

(i) any draft of the DPA;

(ii) any draft of a statement of facts intended to be included within the DPA;

(iii) any statement indicating that P entered into such negotiations;

(b) material that was created solely for the purpose of preparing the DPA or statement of facts.'

11.124

Pursuant to the provisions of paragraph 13(4), however, such material may only be used in evidence against P:

'(a) on prosecution for an offence consisting of the provision of inaccurate, misleading or incomplete information, or

(b) on a prosecution for some other offence where in giving evidence P makes a statement inconsistent with the material.'

11.125

The admission of material under paragraph 13(4)(b) is qualified by paragraph 13(5) which states:

> '…Material may not be used against P by virtue of paragraph 4(b) unless evidence relating to it is adduced, or a question relating to it is asked, by or on behalf of P in the proceedings arising out of the prosecution.'[101]

11.126

Apart from the material described at paragraph 13(6) of Schedule 17, there is no limitation on the use to which other information obtained by the prosecutor during the DPA negotiation period may subsequently be put during in criminal proceedings brought against P, or anyone else (so far as the rules of evidence permit.)[102]

11.127

The Code provides, by way of 'non-exhaustive' example, the following types of document which, if provided to a prosecutor during DPA negotiations, would be available to be used by the prosecutor in a subsequent prosecution of P if the negotiations had failed:[103]

101 This provision corresponds with section 119 of the Criminal Justice Act 2003, which governs the admissibility of previous inconsistent statements in criminal proceedings.

102 Code section 4.5.

103 Code section 4.6(i)–(v).

(i) pre-existing contemporary key documentation such as contracts, accountancy records including payments of any kind, any records evidencing the transfer of money, email or other communications etc;

(ii) any internal or independent investigation report carried out by P prior to the DPA negotiation period commencing;

(iii) any interview note or witness statement obtained from an employee of P prior to the DPA negotiation period commencing;

(iv) any document obtained by the prosecutor at any time obtained from any source other than P; and

(v) any information obtained by the prosecutor as a result of enquiries made as a result of information provided by P at any time.

Discontinuance of proceedings on expiry of the DPA

11.128

Paragraph 11 of Schedule 17 states that:

> '(1) If a DPA remains in force until its expiry date, then after the expiry of the DPA the proceedings instituted under paragraph 2(1) are to be discontinued by the prosecutor giving notice to the Crown Court that the prosecutor does not wish the proceedings to continue.'

11.129

The wording of paragraph 11(1) suggests both a mandatory requirement on the prosecutor to discontinue proceedings once the DPA has come to an end, and a discretionary element, namely a requirement that the prosecutor notifies the court that the decision to discontinue the proceedings has been made because he 'does not want the proceedings to continue'. In this respect, the section is somewhat confusing. It may be an attempt to ensure that decisions to prosecute or not are for the prosecuting body and not for the court, but it begs the question: what if the prosecutor wishes the proceedings to continue despite full compliance by P with the terms of the order? It is submitted that in this unlikely event, the prosecutor would be bound by the mandatory requirement which is the clear intention of the 2013 Act. Any decision to the contrary would arguably be unfair, unreasonable, disproportionate and contrary to the interests of justice, and would be subject to judicial review.

11.130

Once the DPA has expired and proceedings are discontinued,[104] fresh criminal proceedings may not be instituted against P for the same offence[105] unless

104 Updated Handbook, subheading: 'Discontinuance'.

105 Schedule 17 para 11(2).

the prosecutor finds that during the negotiations for the DPA P knowingly provided inaccurate, misleading or incomplete information, or ought to have known that it was.[106]

11.131

A DPA will normally expire on the date specified in the agreement. However, this will not always be the case. Schedule 17 paragraph 11(5) sets out the circumstances when a DPA will be deemed to have expired on an earlier date.[107]

11.132

Paragraph 11(4) of Schedule 17 states that a DPA is not to be treated as having expired, if, on the expiry date specified in the DPA:

(a) an application made by the prosecutor under paragraph 9 (breach) has not yet been decided by the court;

(b) following an application under paragraph 9, the court has invited the parties to agree proposals to remedy P's failure to comply, but the parties have not yet reached an agreement; or

(c) the parties have agreed proposals to remedy P's failure to comply following an invitation of the court under paragraph 9(3)(a) but P has not yet complied with the agreement.

11.133

A DPA is not deemed to have 'expired' for the purposes of Schedule 17 paragraph 11 if an allegation of breach has yet to be determined by the court, or the parties have not agreed to accept the court's proposals to address the breach, or having agreed the proposals P has failed to act on them; nor has a DPA expired if the court has terminated it for non-compliance.[108]

11.134

As with breaches and variations in the terms of DPAs, where a decision has been made to discontinue proceedings, the fact that proceedings have been discontinued and all details of P's compliance with it must be published, subject to paragraph 12.[109]

---

106 Schedule 17 para 11(3)(a) and (3)(b). The position contrasts with discontinuance of proceedings under section 23A (5) of the Prosecution of Offences Act 1985, which do not prevent the institution of fresh proceedings in respect of the same offence.

107 Schedule 17 para 11(5)–(11)(7).

108 Schedule 17 paras 11(4)(a), (b) and (c) and 11(5)(a),(b) and (c), (6) and (7).

109 Schedule 17 para 11(8)(a) and (b).

11.135

Prior to discontinuance, and where considered necessary, consultation should take place with the investigator and any monitor appointed by the court. (See paragraphs 11.62–11.66 above regarding monitors.)

11.136

Discontinuance notices[110] should be sent to the court as soon as practicable after the decision to discontinue, and copies should be sent to P and the investigator.[111] The notices should state:

- The effective date of the discontinuance;
- The offences to be discontinued;
- Confirmation that the DPA has expired.[112]

11.137

No discontinuance notice is needed where the court terminates the DPA.[113]

Money received by the prosecutor under a DPA

11.138

Paragraph 14 of Schedule 17 provides that any money received by a prosecutor under the term of a DPA that provides for P to pay a financial penalty to the prosecutor or to disgorge profits from the alleged offence is to be paid into the Consolidated Fund. In practical terms this will be done via the prosecutor. Charitable donations and compensation will be paid by P directly or through an intermediary agreed by the parties and approved by the court as part of the DPA. P will be required to provide to the prosecutor confirmation and supporting evidence that this has occurred.[114]

11.139

The Code suggests that as a starting point, moneys should be ordered to be paid within seven days of the final hearing unless it would be unfair, unreasonable or disproportionate to do so.[115]

110 Updated Handbook, subheading: 'Discontinuance'.
111 Code section 14.3.
112 Code section14.4.
113 Schedule 17 para 11(5)(b).
114 Code section 7.9(v).
115 Updated Handbook, subheading: 'Applying for a suspension of the indictment to be lifted'.

Re-instituting criminal proceedings

11.140

The lifting of the suspension of the indictment would reinstitute criminal proceedings,[116] although the prosecutor might not be in a position to commence without time for further investigation and preparation.[117] In this event, the prosecutor should inform the court what needs to be done and how long it is likely to take.[118]

11.141

Before re-commencing proceedings, the prosecutor must be satisfied that the Full Code Test under the Code for Crown Prosecutors is met in relation to each charge. The court will have been informed at the final hearing if the original charge was pursuant to the second limb of the evidential stage above,[119] in which case the prosecutor will need to be satisfied that the more stringent evidential stage of the Full Code Test is met. Furthermore, the public interest position will need to be reassessed in light of the breach.[120]

Publication

11.142

Paragraph 8(7) of Schedule 17 provides that once the court has approved the DPA, the prosecutor is under a duty to publish:

(a) the DPA;

(b) the declaration of the court under paragraph 7 and its reasons for making that declaration.

(c) in a case where the court initially declined to make a declaration under paragraph 7, the court's reason for that decision, and

(d) the court's declaration under this paragraph and its decision to make the declaration unless the prosecutor is prevented from doing so by an enactment or by an order of the court under paragraph 12 (postponement of publication to avoid prejudicing proceedings).

11.143

Paragraph 9(5), 9(6) and 9(7) of Schedule 17 deal with the prosecutor's obligations to publish the court's decisions in various circumstances, unless he

116 Code section 7.9(ii).
117 Code section 12.8.
118 Code section 12.10.
119 Ie on the basis that further evidence could be gathered if the charge was pursued; see 11.27 above.
120 Code section 12.9.

or she is prevented from doing so by an enactment or by an order of the court under paragraph 12 (see paragraph 11.145 below).

11.144

Where the prosecutor believes that P has failed to comply with the terms of the DPA but decides not to make an application to the Crown Court, he or she will nevertheless be required to publish details of it pursuant to paragraph 9(8) of Schedule 17.[121] Where a conclusion has been reached by a prosecutor alone that no breach has in fact occurred, then there is no requirement to publish it.[122]

Postponement of publication of information by prosecutor – Schedule 17 paragraph 12

11.145

Section 16.1 of the Code reminds the parties that 'transparency remains a key aspect of the success and proper operation of DPAs, and accordingly Schedule 17 of the 2013 Act requires in prescribed circumstances the prosecutor to publish on its website orders made by the court or decisions made by the prosecutor.' However, paragraph 12 of the Schedule permits the court to order that the publication of information under paragraph 8(7) (Final Hearings) be postponed 'for such period as it considers necessary if it appears that postponement is necessary for avoiding a substantial risk of prejudice to the administration of justice in any legal proceedings.'

11.146

This provision also applies to the postponement of publication of information in relation to Schedule 17 paragraphs 9(5), (6), (7) or (8) (Breach of DPA); paragraph 10(7) (Variation of DPA); or paragraph 11(8) (Discontinuance of Proceedings).

11.147

One example where postponement of the publication of information might well be ordered is where the prosecution is proceeding against an individual, such as a director, or other companies or partnerships caught in the chain of liability. In these circumstances, publication could be highly prejudicial to a fair trial.

11.148

Any postponement of publication will be temporary, so P's offence and the sanctions provided for in the DPA will be made public at some point.

---

121 Code section 12.2.
122 Code section 16.3.

11.149

Between 2015 and 2020, the SFO has entered into twelve DPAs with major corporations summarised below.

SFO v Standard Bank PLC (2015)[123]

In November 2015, the SFO secured the UK's first DPA with ICBC Standard Bank plc (Standard Bank) which admitted liability for failing to prevent bribery in its Tanzanian subsidiary, Stanbic Bank, Tanzania. Under the terms of the DPA, Standard Bank agreed to pay US$32.5 million, including costs and compensation to the Government of Tanzania. It was also agreed that the indictment against Standard bank would be suspended for three years dependent on the company meeting certain conditions. These included cooperating in the investigation of culpable individuals, and conducting an independent review of the bank's internal anti-corruption compliance controls.

SFO v Sarclad Ltd (2016)

Sarclad Ltd, which supplies advanced technologies to the metals industry, had been charged with conspiracy to corrupt and failure to prevent bribery. Under the terms of the agreement, the company was ordered to pay £6,553,085 consisting of a financial penalty and disgorgement of gross profits. The company also undertook to co-operate fully with the SFO, and to prepare a report on the effectiveness of its existing anti-bribery and corruption controls and procedures within 12 months of the DPA and every 12 months thereafter. It also agreed to provide details of all third party transactions. Three connected individuals were prosecuted for agreeing bribes in relation to overseas contracts, but acquitted. The DPA expired with their acquittals.

SFO v Rolls-Royce PLC (2017)

In January 2017, the SFO entered into a DPA with Rolls-Royce Plc ('Rolls Royce') arising from allegations of worldwide misconduct in relation to its Civil Aerosplace and Defence Aerospace businesses, and its former Energy business. The suspended indictment consisted of 12 counts of conspiracy to corrupt, false accounting, and failure to prevent bribery. Despite the company's considerable co-operation with the authorities, and a 50% discount on the penalty, a total fine of £671 million was imposed, coupled with an undertaking requiring the company to continue to co-operate with the SFO, and to complete an anti-bribery and corruption compliance programme.

123 [2015] 11 WLUK 804.

***SFO v Tesco Stores Ltd* (2017)**

In April 2017, a DPA was reached between the SFO and Tesco relating to the company's illegal practices in 2014, including improperly 'putting forward' income from subsequent reporting periods in order to meet accounting targets, and dishonestly creating a false account of its financial position by overstating profits. Under the DPA, Tesco agreed to pay a £129 million fine and investigation costs of £3 million, and to undertake and implement a compliance programme over a three year period.

***SFO v Serco Geografix Ltd* (2019)**

In July 2017, Serco Geografix Ltd ('SGL') took responsibility for three offences of fraud and two offences of false accounting. It arose from a scheme to dishonestly mislead the Ministry of Justice ('MoJ') as to the true extent of the profits being made, between 2010 and 2013, by SLG's parent company, Serco Ltd ('SL'), for the provision of electronic monitoring services. SLG agreed to pay a financial penalty of £19.2 million, and the SFO's costs, in addition to £12.8 million compensation already paid by SL to the MoJ in an earlier civil settlement. SGL and Serco also agreed to additional conditions which included full cooperation and annual reporting to the authorities on the effectiveness of the companies' ethics and compliance programmes.

***SFO v Güralp Systems Ltd* (2019)**

In October 2019, the SFO entered into a DPA with Güralp Systems ('Güralp') following the company's admitted failure to prevent bribery and conspiracy to make corrupt payments to a South Korean public official between 2002 and 2015. Three individuals were acquitted in related prosecutions. Included in the conditions of the agreement with Güralp were the disgorgement of gross profits in the sum of £2,069,861, full and truthful cooperation with the SFO, and undertakings to review and maintain existing internal controls, policies and procedures for compliance with the Bribery Act 2010.

***SFO v Airbus SE* (2020)**

In January 2020, the SFO reached a wide-ranging global DPA with Airbus SE ('Airbus'), a Dutch and French domiciled company, following allegations that the company had used external consultants to bribe customers to purchase aircrafts. Airbus accepted that it had failed to have adequate procedures in place designed to prevent those associated with it from carrying out bribery offences. The company agreed to pay an amount in excess of £840 million including a penalty of £350 million.

***SFO v G4S Care and Justice Services UK Ltd* (2020)**

G4S Care and Justice Services Ltd ('G4SC') provided electronic monitoring services for the Ministry of Justice ('MoJ'). The company engaged in fraudulent conduct whereby invoices were paid to G4SC by MoJ for monitoring people, when in fact no monitoring had taken place. The company accepted that it had falsely represented that costs had been genuinely incurred, and cooperated fully with the SFO investigation. The SFO and G4SC entered into a DPA in July 2020 in which a financial penalty of £38.952 million will be paid.

***SFO v Airline Services Ltd* (2020)]**

In October 2020, the SFO entered into a DPA with Airline Service Ltd ('ASL') which had provided services and products to commercial airlines for the refurbishment of airline interiors since 1982. ASL ceased trading in 2018, but self-reported and continued to exist as a non-trading company so as to allow the SFO to carry out its investigations. Accepting responsibility for three counts of failing to prevent bribery in relation to contracts worth £7.3 million, the company paid £2,979,685, consisting of a financial penalty of £1,238,714, disgorgement of profits representing the profit made by the criminal conduct, and costs of £750,000.

***SFO v Amec Foster Wheeler Energy Ltd* (2021)**

In July 2021, the SFO entered into a DPA with Amec Foster Wheeler Ltd ('AFWEL') relating to the use of corrupt agents in the oil and gas sector across the world from 1996–2014. Under the terms of the DPA, AFWEL will pay a financial penalty and costs amounting to £103 million in the UK, which forms part of the US$177 million global settlement with UK, US and Brazilian authorities. The amounts to be paid by AFWEL in the UK include costs of £3.4 million and payment of compensation to the people of Nigeria of £210,610.

On 19 July 2021 the SFO received approval for separate DPAs with two companies registered and operated in the UK in relation to bribes paid for multi-million UK contracts. The charges related to offences contrary to sections 1 and 7 of the Bribery Act 2007, and the companies, who cannot be named for legal reasons, will pay a total of £2,510,065, comprising disgorgement of profits and a financial penalty.

Summary – stages of a deferred prosecution agreement

Prosecution applies Two Stage Test and Full Code Test, to consider whether to offer organisation 'P' the opportunity to enter into negotiations to agree a DPA.

If yes:

Prosecution issues a letter to P, setting out offer.

P will accept or decline the offer in writing.

If yes:

Negotiations will take place. Full records should be kept.
Any agreement must include:

- written statement of facts relating to alleged offence;
- proposed expiry date;
- preliminary terms, including if appropriate the appointment of monitors.

Preliminary court hearing:

- Parties apply for declaration that DPA is in interests of justice, and terms are reasonable and proportionate If DPA is approved...
- Bill of Indictment will be preferred and suspended.

Period of further negotiation between the parties, and final terms agreed.

Final court hearing:

- Court will be asked to approve terms of DPA, including nature and scale of any financial penalty.
- Agreement to be submitted in writing, indicating if and how terms differ from those agreed at preliminary hearing.
- Written consent signed by all parties, explaining why agreement is in interests of justice.
- Copy of indictment to be attached to application.
- If approval given, court will make a declaration that DPA is in interests of justice, and that terms are fair, reasonable and proportionate.

Applications, if required, for variation of term(s) in DPA.

Proceedings discontinued on expiry of DTA or in event of breach of terms.

12 What to do if you are being investigated as an individual

12.1

The interests of the individual and the company are not always necessarily the same. Some of the general matters that are referred to in Chapter 9 on investigations (eg preservation of evidence) also apply to individuals. However, this chapter considers where the interests may diverge and common issues for individuals are their lawyers.

Internal investigations or disciplinary proceedings

12.2

Conflict between employer and employee is at its most acute when there is an internal investigation or disciplinary proceedings are contemplated against the employee. The company may consider that there is evidence of wrongdoing, that such wrongdoing will require disciplinary proceedings, and perhaps that it may suit the company to pursue a defence strategy of a 'rogue' employee to any corporate prosecution. This may include reporting an employee to the police or other investigator or prosecutor such as the National Crime Agency of Serious Fraud Office.

12.3

The key difficulty for employees is the conflict between their desire to retain their jobs and protecting themselves in future criminal proceedings. At interviews or hearings, there will be great pressure for the employee to provide a full account of his actions. Some companies even have a 'duty to cooperate with internal investigations' written into codes of conduct or terms of employment. Even if such a clause is absent, the employee who refuses to cooperate is unlikely to have improved their chances of keeping their job.

12.4

However, speaking 'on the record' at such an early stage is treated with suspicion by criminal lawyers (who may have to defend the employee in a criminal trial at some later date).

12.5

Again, if there is a genuine concern that internal investigations or disciplinary hearings may lead to criminal prosecutions, then a criminal defence lawyer's expertise should be sought. In some circumstances, corporates may cover the costs of an employee's legal fees in connection with an internal investigation or disciplinary hearing, which is often covered by the company's directors' and officers' liability ('D&O') insurance policy. This process enables employees to instruct an independent legal advisor of their choice, provided their chosen adviser is suitably skilled and experienced.

12.6

The starting point is whether there is a risk that the employee's statements during investigation/disciplinary proceedings can be admitted in criminal court proceedings later.

12.7

The short answer is that there is always such a risk. This may not present a huge problem, however it should be remembered that statements made in the relatively informal circumstances of an investigation/hearing may be perceived very differently in a court room in front of a jury some years later. Also, at the time of the internal investigation, there may only be limited information available to the employee about the evidence against him.

12.8

Whether or not these statements can be admitted in court later depends upon the circumstances in which the statement was taken.

12.9

If a statement during an internal investigation is made under certain formalities, the likelihood that it would be admissible in future criminal proceedings is increased. For this purpose the employee would be informed:

(a) that the interview could be used in future criminal proceedings;

(b) that he is allowed or offered the assistance of legal advice;[1] and

(c) that he is 'cautioned'.[2]

If the formalities above are carried out by the investigator, it is likely that the interview can be used in future criminal proceedings.

1 If Codes apply, then it is a requirement that the individual under investigation should have allowed legal representatives under s 58 of the Police and Criminal Evidence Act 1984 ('PACE') – Code C, paras 3.1, 3.2 and 6.

2 If Codes apply, a caution must be given under Code C, para 10.1.

12.10

If the formalities are NOT carried out, then the interview's admissibility depends on what the purpose and context of the internal investigation is and what happens during the trial. There are two issues to consider:

(i) If at the time of the internal investigation it is clear that criminal proceedings may result in future, then the formalities in paragraph 10.29 should be complied with. If they are not complied with, then there will be a good argument that they cannot be relied on in criminal proceedings.[3]

(ii) If at the time of the internal investigation it has the appearance of a line manager conducting interviews as part of a disciplinary panel concerning whether or not the employee should be dismissed, then the formalities DO NOT have to be complied with.[4]

12.11

Much of this would be subject to argument in a criminal trial and also depends upon what happens during the course of the trial (if for example the employee gives evidence in trial which is inconsistent with their earlier statements during the internal investigation). So although the above factors have been set out, the best advice remains that there is a *risk* that internal investigatory interviews could be later be used in a criminal trial.

What happens if the police/SFO wish to interview you

12.12

It should be confirmed whether you are being interviewed as a witness or a suspect and under what legislative power the authorities wish to speak to you.

Witness

12.13

If you are asked to give a witness statement, it should be remembered that you are under no duty to sign any such statement. Whilst, there can be circumstances in which you are required to attend an interview, answer questions and/or hand over documents (see paragraph 12.21), the authorities cannot *compel* you to sign a statement. Once you sign a statement, it becomes easier to compel you to attend court in the future.

---

3 Investigators will be caught by s 67(9) of PACE; Failure to observe the codes may result in an application under s 78 of PACE for the interviews to be excluded from the criminal case.

4 Following *R v Welcher* [2007] EWCA Crim 480, such an investigator is NOT caught by s 67(9), and so the formalities in para 12.31 need not necessarily be complied with.

Suspect

12.14

If you are approached as a suspect, then you may be asked to attend an interview as a 'volunteer' or you may be arrested.

12.15

The police have the power to arrest a person who they have reasonable suspicion is about to commit, is in the act of committing, or has committed an offence.[5]

12.16

The powers of arrest can only be exercised if the arresting officer has reasonable grounds for believing that arrest is necessary. In the context of corruption enquiries, the most likely justification is that the arrest is necessary to allow the prompt and effective investigation of the offence.[6]

12.17

Often, there will be no choice in the matter – the authorities can attend without notice and arrest. However, there are occasions in which the authorities will have been in contact and arranged a time for the individual to attend for an interview. In those circumstances, it can be argued that an arrest is not 'necessary' and that the individual can choose to remain a 'volunteer' at the police station.[7] This will mean that the individual can leave at any point.

12.18

In such a case, it is often an advantage for an executive to maintain that there has been no arrest (either for professional or public relations term). This should be balanced against the fact that the authorities may still arrest in future (although the same arguments about necessity will apply). Furthermore, the authorities will be limited in the length of time that they can keep anyone detained following arrest.[8]

12.19

If you are arrested, you should remember that you have some rights including those listed below.

---

5 PACE s 24.

6 PACE s 24(5)(e). Code G states that this condition may be satisfied if there are grounds to believe that evidence may be destroyed or where it is necessary to obtain evidence by questioning.

7 *Richardson v Chief Constable of West Midlands Police* [2011] EWHC 773 (QB).

8 The normal time limit for detention is 24 hours but it can be extended in certain circumstances up to 36 hours by a senior officer, or a further 72 hours after that by a magistrates' court.

You must be 'cautioned' before an interview
You have the right to consult a lawyer of your choice
You have the right to let someone know of your arrest
You have the right to make a telephone call

12.20

The decision whether or not to answer questions, or whether to exercise your 'right to silence' in an interview is a can be complicated, as there are legal consequences to both answering questions and remaining silent. Specialist advice should be sought prior to agreeing to be interviewed under caution.

Compulsory Powers by the SFO

12.21

The SFO have specific powers to compel individuals to attend interviews, answer questions and produce documentation. This will occur if the SFO have issue a notice under section 2 of the Criminal Justice Act 1987 ('CJA', section 2A relates specifically to bribery and corruption offences).

12.22

S2 powers are known as 'compulsory' powers and are draconian in nature because:

- a failure to comply with a section 2 notice, without a reasonable excuse, is an offence (CJA, section 2(13));
- giving false or misleading information in response to a notice is an offence (CJA, section 2(14));
- the 'right to silence' does not apply to information obtained under section 2(2) of the CJA because it cannot be used in evidence unless a formal witness statement is obtained.

12.23

Section 2 notices are designed to obtain information during an investigation and can either require documents to be delivered up or information provided verbally. The fact that a notice is sent to an individual or company does not mean that person is suspected of an offence. Indeed, recipients will often be professional persons who owe a duty of confidence which would otherwise preclude them from cooperating without a court order and who will request a section 2 notice from the SFO to prevent claims for breaches of contract or fiduciary duties.

12.24

The issue of a section 2 notice overrides any obligations of confidentiality or secrecy attaching to the information or to the holder other than Legal Professional Privilege. As regards privilege, privilege protects legal advice and documents created for litigation, but specific legal advice will often be required, not only because this is a complex area of law but because the privilege will often belong not to the individual who is subject to the section 2 notice but to the company for which they work.

Section 2 Interview Process

12.25

Section 2 interviews are almost always conducted by the SFO in person, usually at the SFO's offices. The audio of the interview is always recorded, and on some occasions a video is also taken. At the start of the process the interviewee will be reminded that it is a criminal offence to provide false or misleading information during the interview.

12.26

On 6 June 2016, the SFO published new guidance in relation to the attendance of lawyers at section 2 interviews. Pursuant to this guidance, the relevant SFO case controller will allow a practising solicitor, barrister or chartered legal executive to accompany the interviewee to the interview if the case controller 'believes it likely they will assist the purpose of the interview and/or investigation, or that they will provide essential assistance to the interviewee by way of legal advice or pastoral support'.[9]

12.27

Lawyers attending section 2 interviews will be asked to provide a number of undertakings in the name of their firm as a condition for their attendance, including that they do not represent any individual or legal person who is a suspect in the investigation and that they will treat any documents provided ahead of the interview confidentially and hold them securely. They must also agree that they 'must not do anything to undermine the free flow of full and truthful information which the interviewee, by law, is required to give'.[10] If

9 Serious Fraud Office guidance on 'Presence of interviewee's legal adviser at a section 2 interview', online at: www.sfo.gov.uk/download/sfo-operational-guidance-presence-interviewees-legal-adviser-section-2-interview-internal-guidance/.

10 ibid.

the lawyer fails to adhere to these requirements or is otherwise inappropriately disruptive, they may be excluded by the SFO from the interview.

12.28

The SFO guidance was amended on 28 February 2019 to allow an additional legal representative to attend the interview for the sole purpose of taking a note. That legal representative must also be covered by the relevant undertakings. As the SFO does not allow interviewees or their legal representatives to use digital devices in the interview room, any note taken will be by hand.[11]

12.29

The answers given in the course of section 2 interview cannot be used directly in a criminal trial, but the information can be used to assist in the investigation so that evidence can be admitted in the correct form later. The SFO may also draft the responses provided during the interview into a witness statement, to be agreed with the interviewee, which may then be used in court proceedings.

Conclusion

12.30

It can be seen that individuals will need to take a number of steps in reaction to any material investigation and will have to obtain legal advice where criminal allegations are made.

11 ibid.

13 Managing bribery risk: a financial services perspective

Introduction

13.1

This chapter provides a perspective on managing bribery risk in a financial institution through the lens of foundational requirements for an effective risk management programme. This chapter will also provide some food for thought about where bribery risk programmes need to be enhanced to meet the changing needs of the world post pandemic.

The financial Services Context

13.2

The role of Financial Institutions is pivotal in every economy, providing liquidity, supporting economic growth, providing access to investments and capital markets, brokerage, financing, lending, and banking services. Customers of financial institutions include personal customers, commercial enterprises, corporates, government bodies and non-profit organisations among others, each with their own unique financial requirements. Access to a reliable and trustworthy financial system is important at all levels of society, financial institutions are the connection point for anyone that uses financial services, impacting all aspects of our lives.

13.3

The World Bank in its call for papers on anti-corruption analytics said, 'Corruption erodes trust in government and undermines the social contract[1] and this also resonates for the financial services industry. The role of banks and the influence the industry has on our lives in terms of providing the means to maintain financial security requires that it be operated with integrity and continuously earn the trust of society. Public trust was lost during the 2008 financial crisis and a number of high-profile money laundering prosecutions

1 Combating Corruption, available at www.worldbank.org/en/topic/governance/brief/anti-corruption.

and fines as well as regulatory scandals since then have continued to undermine efforts by the industry to rebuild trust. Financial institutions must operate to the highest standards of integrity and transparency and establish a policy and culture of zero tolerance for bribery as part of efforts to rebuild public confidence in the industry.

13.4

Part of the challenge the industry faces is the size and complexity of the problem, the estimated US$1.75 trillion in bribery annually[2] will undoubtably touch the financial services industry somewhere. However as bribes can be any benefit or advantage, and not necessarily cash or a financial transaction, spotting bribery and managing this risk requires a more nuanced approach than following the proceeds of crime.

13.5

The global reach of anti-bribery laws, the increase in legislation, increase in prosecutions and international enforcement and fines means that managing bribery risk effectively is critical for the financial services industry. Guidance from the UK Ministry of Justice ('MOJ'), the Foreign Corrupt Practices Act of 1977 ('FCPA') guidance and the Financial Conduct Authority ('FCA') make it clear that a bribery programmes cannot be a paper or box-ticking exercise.

Managing Bribery Risk in Financial Institutions

13.6

The management and oversight of bribery risk in financial institutions is similar to other types of industries because the legislation applies in the same way. However, the nature of financial services means that there is a significant focus on the financial crime risk associated with customers' activity when managing financial crime risk and, in particular, on the proceeds of crime. This stands to reason when we consider that the bulk of financial activity is with or for customers and can give rise to both a direct criminal liability under bribery legislation for the financial institution as well as exposing it to different types of financial crime risks such as money laundering, fraud, and tax evasion.

13.7

The focus on customers and the associated transactional activities in managing financial crime such as fraud, anti-money laundering ('AML') and sanctions can pose challenges in ensuring that the anti-bribery programme has the right scope and is adequately resourced with the right skillsets. The programme must include the risks posed by employees and third parties across the organisation

2 Transparency International corruption statistics.

and not just the customer related risks. That said, the reality is that bribery risk must be managed alongside the demands of many other regulatory and legal requirements.

13.8

The bribery risk in a financial organisation, in particular, can sometimes be obscured by the significant money laundering risks where customers utilise products or services in the giving or receiving of bribes in the course of their own activities. To be effective, the anti-bribery programme must be able to have a life of its own while still working in parallel with anti-money laundering and fraud controls and finding ways to manage risk across not only customers but employees and third parties such as introducers and intermediaries.

13.9

Increasingly, since bribery can be a lagging indicator for broader corruption, the focus is shifting to connect with the underlying criminal activity as part of the wider anti-corruption agenda. This includes understanding how managing bribery and corruption risk is connected and integrated with other aspects of the Environmental, Social and Governance ('ESG') agenda such as human trafficking, modern slavery, wildlife trafficking and environmental issues.

Bribery Risk Regulatory framework

13.10

Similar to other commercial organisations, financial institutions are expected to comply with all applicable laws and regulations designed to combat bribery and corruption. This includes legislation with extraterritorial jurisdictional reach such as the FCPA and the UK Bribery Act 2010 ('UKBA').

13.11

In the UK, financial institutions are regulated by both the Prudential Regulatory Authority ('PRA') on behalf of the Bank of England and the FCA whose role is to look after the interests of consumers and improve market integrity and promote competition.

13.12

Unlike the Securities and Exchange Commission ('SEC') in the US, the FCA does not enforce the UK Bribery Act but sets out guidance for impacted organisations to establish and maintain effective systems and controls necessary to mitigate financial crime risk. The FCA provides guidance on good practice in the Regulatory Guide section under Financial Crime: A Guide for Firms ('FCG').[3] [4]

13.13

The FCA includes corruption risk within the guidance and therefor the scope of the guidance is wider than the UKBA, specifying that the FCA may take action if the organisation has deficient systems and controls relating to anti bribery and corruption regardless of whether bribery or corruption has actually occurred.[5]

13.14

Other useful guidance focused on financial services can also be found on the The Wolfsberg Group website, Wolfsberg Anti-Bribery and Corruption Compliance Programme Guidance.[6]

13.15

In contrast, the SEC works alongside the US Department of Justice and will pursue civil enforcement of the FCPA. In 2020 the SEC brought civil enforcement against eight companies with fines over US$1.5 billion in total. The settlement agreed by Goldman Sachs accounted for US$1 billion of this total for violations of books and records, and internal accounting controls provisions in connection with the 1Malaysia Development Berhad ('1MDB') bribery scheme.[7] However, the total fine imposed on Goldman Sachs was US$2.9 billion which also included £96.6 million imposed by the PRA and FCA for failures relating to systems and controls.[8]

13.16

As regards enforcement in the UK alone, between 2015 and 2020 the Serious Fraud Office ('SFO'), the UK authority responsible for prosecutions under the UKBA has imposed one Deferred Prosecution arrangement on a financial institution, for the section 7 offence of failure to prevent bribery, namely Standard Bank in 2015. In that case, Standard Bank was ordered to pay US$25.2 million in fines and a further US$7 million compensation the Government of

3 Regulatory Guides – FCA Handbook, available at www.handbook.fca.org.uk/regulatory-guides.
4 FCA Handbook, FCG6.1.3 and FCG6.1.4, available at www.handbook.fca.org.uk/regulatory-guides.
5 FCG Section 6.2.
6 Wolfsberg-Group-ABC-Guidance-June-2017.pdf (wolfsberg-principles.com).
7 See www.sec.gov/enforce/sec-enforcement-actions-fcpa-cases.
8 See www.bankofengland.co.uk/-/media/boe/files/prudential-regulation/regulatory-action/final-notice-to-goldman-sachs-international.pdf?la=en&hash=0905E04952BFE7C4B05B7AFBB11467F21A069E3F.

Tanzania. The suspended charges related to alleged payments made by Stanbic Bank to members of the Government of Tanzania to gain favoured treatment in relation to a private placement.[9]

Key Components of a good AB&C Programme

13.17

The AB&C programme should be designed to mitigate bribery risk in the organisation by tailoring controls to relevant business areas and functions and the activities they undertake.

13.18

The principles for an anti-bribery programme are covered in Chapter 8, therefore this section focuses on the specific FCA expectations to provide an interpretation of a programme as it applies in a financial institution, actual design and implementation will vary from one organisation to another.

13.19

The FCA Financial Crime Guide[10] broadly aligns with the six principles set out in the Ministry of Justice guidance, however, provides practical examples drawn from thematic reviews. The areas specific to managing bribery and corruption risk covered in the guidance include:

- Governance.
- Staff Vetting, Training and Remuneration.
- Policies and Procedures.
- Training and Awareness.
- Risk Assessment.
- Third parties.

The processes and controls relating to employees, third parties, organisational risks and transactional activities will all be managed through the effective implementation of the core elements of the above components in conjunction with the six principles covered in the MOJ Guidance.

9 SFO agrees first UK DPA with Standard Bank – Serious Fraud Office, available at www.sfo.gov.uk/2015/11/30/sfo-agrees-first-uk-dpa-with-standard-bank/.

10 FCA Handbook – FCA Handbook, Regulatory Guides, FCG Financial Crime Guide: A firm's guide to countering financial crime risks (FCG), available at www.handbook.fca.org.uk/handbook/FCG/.

Governance

13.20

The FCG sets out a general expectation that 'senior management take clear responsibility for managing financial crime risk [and] be actively engaged in the organisation's approach to addressing the risks.'[11] This includes setting the right tone from the top, taking action to prevent financial crime and clear escalation processes.

13.21

In practice this means that financial crime topics including bribery and corruption are included in the senior level risk committees and that there are standing agenda items for reporting on bribery and corruption risk as part of the financial crime management information.

13.22

The FCG sets out the expectation that senior management maintain awareness of current bribery and corruption issues, periodically review the Anti-Bribery and Corruption programme, be able to demonstrate understanding and use this knowledge in assessing risks in relation to the organisation's business activities.[12]

13.23

It should be clear from the above that the FCA expectation is that leaders in financial institutions model behaviours that align to the values and culture of the organisation and breathe life into the application of the policies. Policies are not enough on their own as a defence against failure to prevent bribery, they must be communicated, supported by a robust anti bribery programme, and apply equally to all employees from the top down.

13.24

The 'tone from the top' commitment from senior management will be included in the code of conduct which is an internal policy and will also be referenced in the organisation's public statements. The Anti-Bribery public statement highlights to external stakeholders the approach taken by the financial institution in managing bribery risk and increasingly is linked to other ESG related statements such as climate change, modern slavery and human trafficking and wildlife trafficking.

---

11 FCG Box 2.1 Governance.

12 FCG Box 6.1 – Governance.

13.25

In practical terms anti-bribery topics will be included within the governance of financial crime risk management. As a result, the challenge for leaders in financial institutions is in ensuring that where the focus on financial crime tends to be on customer risk, that third party and employee related bribery and corruption risks are given equal significance and are properly understood and mitigated where possible. For instance bribery specific typologies ought to be taken into account when implementing software related to managing payments to third parties.

Policies and Procedures

13.26

The FCG sets out the topics that should be included under the Anti-Bribery and Corruption Policy including staff recruitment, vetting, training, remuneration, conflicts of interest, expenses, gifts, and hospitality, third parties, whistleblowing, monitoring, and breach handling. The policy should establish in clear and unambiguous language a zero tolerance to bribery, and provide guidance on limited exceptions, such as the payment of a bribe in situations where employee safety or liberty is at risk.

13.27

The examples of good and poor practice indicate that the FCA is interested in how financial institutions have 'embedded' the policies into practice by focusing not just on 'what' must be in the policies and procedures but also 'how' the organisation demonstrates that the policies and procedures are actually helping employees to identify bribery and corruption issues.

13.28

The FCA expects policies to be kept up to date, taking into account internal and external bribery and corruption issues with senior management accountability to review and approve the content. In recent years in the development of AB&C policies greater focus has been on ensuring a clear link between the requirements set out in the policy and the actual controls that sit within the risk and control framework to evidence the effectiveness of the policies.

13.29

There is an expectation that the organisation uses a risk-based approach and conducts additional monitoring and due diligence for 'jurisdictions, sectors and business relationships identified as higher risk. The risk-based approach will need to be explained within the policies and integrated into end-to-end processes through more detailed business procedures.[13]

13 FCG – Box 6.3 Policies and Procedures.

13.30

There will be multiple policies covering the regulatory requirements impacting the activities of the organisation. A key consideration for the anti-bribery and corruption policy is how this document will sit within the overall policy framework and governance of the organisation in order to give effect to the requirement that the procedures are clear and accessible to all employees and applies across the whole organisation.

13.31

The Bribery policy should also link to Environmental, Social and Governance ('ESG') public statements on anti-bribery and corruption, human trafficking, modern slavery, wildlife trafficking and environmental and sustainability policies. These statements set out the Financial Institutions own principles in these areas and will set an expectation in how the organisation interacts with customers and third parties which in turn links back to the relevant policies and procedures impacting these relationships.

Procedures

13.32

Procedures underpin the policy, providing more detailed requirements for implementation of effective controls. For example where the policy will set out a requirement to establish controls for bribery risk in employee hiring, the procedures will provide the detail of the standards expected and which function is responsible for the controls, in order to assess and mitigate the risk effectively. Given the complexity of a financial institution and the number of different processes that must take into consideration bribery risks, each function and business area will need to integrate the anti-bribery elements into their procedures to enable the policy to be embedded.

Training and Awareness

13.33

Principle 5 of the MOJ Guidance covering communication (including training), emphasises the need for effective internal and external communications and training to ensure the policies and procedures are embedded.

13.34

The FCG requirements apply across all financial crime and focuses on the need to ensure that employees are given training that is appropriate to their roles. The guidance specifies that training should be tailored, using practical case studies, some level of testing of understanding, be updated regularly and supported by appropriate records of training completion data.

13.35

As a practical matter, financial institutions may provide training to all employees on basic awareness of anti-bribery and corruption and provide employees engaged in higher risk activities tailored training specific to their role or function.

13.36

Anti-bribery training is essential to develop a broader awareness of the risks across the organisation. It should include updating employees on new developments in anti-bribery legislation and regulations; 'lessons learnt' from key prosecutions or internal monitoring. Generic organisation wide anti-bribery training will include the key principles regarding record-keeping, transparency, approvals, escalation paths, zero tolerance for bribery. The training will also explain core definitions such as the meaning of active and passive bribery, and public officials (and how this definition differs from the definition of Politically Exposed Persons used in AML training).

13.37

In terms of the specific training for higher risk roles, this training would include employees managing higher risk customers such as state owned entities and government bodies, business areas focused on higher risk transactions such as infrastructure financing and other complex transactions where there may be intermediaries or public officials involved in licensing or approvals. However it should also be tailored for functions that have oversight of employee and third-party risk or who deal with public officials or government organisations. This would include functions such as procurement who deal with supplier or third-party relationships and human resources who will deal with recruitment as well as areas dealing with the corporate real estate for the organisation. The more targeted and tailored the training is, the easier it is for employees to embed 'doing the right thing' into their day-to-day activities.

13.38

Training tends to be an annual event and may be delivered with other financial crime topics therefore regular communications to raise awareness across the organisation helps to support a 'tone from the top' anti-bribery culture. An education programme that includes clear and regular messaging from senior leadership can be an important element in a defence against failure to prevent bribery. A good example of this is the charges against a former Morgan Stanley executive in 2012.[14] In their investigation the DOJ decided not to pursue FCPA violations against Morgan Stanley because the organisation was able to demonstrate that the employee had received numerous reminders about the anti-bribery policy over and above the regular training.

13.39

There is also an expectation in the FCG that financial institutions provide anti-bribery training to their third parties where appropriate.[15] Typically the focus will be on third parties that act on behalf of the organisation or third parties that may represent higher risk to the organisation, for example interacting with public officials. Similar to employee training it can cover the overarching principles but may also be tailored to the specific service provided by the third party. This training ensures third parties understand the expectations of the financial institution but also has the benefit of sharing best practice in aspects of financial crime risk management and assisting third parties in navigating the challenges of managing bribery and corruption risk.

Risk Assessment

13.40

The FCG sets out principles for risk assessment within financial institutions for all financial crime[16] as well as specific requirements for Anti-Bribery and Corruption.[17] The emphasis in the guidance is on understanding the financial crime risks in order to apply proportionate systems and controls. This means taking into consideration the main financial crime risks, having the ability to identify new and emerging risks and that the risk assessment is subject to appropriate check and challenge and sign off at a senior level. The FCA would also expect to see how the output from the risk assessment links to the regular updating of policies and procedures.

13.41

In terms of the specific anti-bribery and corruption expectations, the FCG guidance includes anyone 'acting on the organisation's behalf' and therefore includes assessment of employee and third-party related controls as a key element of the anti-bribery risk assessment. The guidance also focuses on risks associated with products and services, customer risk, exposure to public officials, as well as specific anti-bribery controls such as gifts and entertainment, charitable and political donations.

---

14 SEC Press Release 2012-78: SEC Charges Former Morgan Stanley Executive with FCPA Violations and Investment Adviser Fraud.

15 FCG Box 6.4 – Dealing with Third Parties.

16 FCG Box 2.3 – Risk Assessment.

17 FCB Box 6.2 – Risk Assessment.

13.42

In the thematic examples, the FSG emphasis is on employee understanding of the bribery and corruption risk exposure, challenging 'downplaying' of bribery risk, and using appropriate sources both internal and external to inform the risk assessment.

13.43

Financial institutions may include the anti-bribery and corruption risk assessment in the overall financial crime risk assessment. This provides the benefit of enabling senior management to 'look across' multiple financial crime risks and will also leverage of other financial crime controls to resolve anti-bribery and corruption risks where possible.

13.44

A key challenge is that the anti-bribery focus on third parties and employee risk may mean it does not get the same level of attention as other financial crime risks such as AML, sanctions and fraud given the predominance of customer risk in terms of materiality of risk for the organisation. Aligning the anti-bribery and corruption risk assessment impact with the organisation's ESG commitments can support providing the right context and materiality of the risk exposure to the organisation.

Processes and Controls to manage Bribery Risk

13.45

Every industry has its own particular bribery and corruption challenges, in this section, we will look at some specific challenges through the lens of three areas where financial institutions have faced prosecution and fines, namely recruitment, transactional risk and third-party risk.

13.46

The control framework will predominantly be focused on the most material processes within the financial institution. Anti-bribery controls are generally part of the overall process and are more easily adhered to when they are integrated into an end-to-end process rather than stand-alone. Each function or business area must assess their own processes for bribery risk. An example of an exception to this is gifts and entertainment and charitable donation controls, where a single process and recording tool across the organisation is more efficient for managing approvals and gathering data for reporting purposes.

Recruitment

13.47

The FSG focuses on ensuring that employees have appropriate skills, knowledge, and expertise to perform their role, that the remuneration policy does not reward taking on unacceptable financial crime risk and the individual is subject to appropriate vetting. In financial services however a particular risk is where potential recruits are connected to customers, third parties, public officials or politically exposed persons and the hiring is linked to an improper business advantage for the organisation.

13.48

Careers in financial services are highly sought after, the industry offers higher remuneration than most other industries and candidates or family members may be incentivised by the potential status and recognition. It is unsurprising therefore that the hiring process itself can be subject to bribery risks by way of offering of mandates or deals in return for hiring the individual. Once onboard there may also be an ongoing risk that such employees may use their status or connection improperly.

13.49

In terms of hiring, Human Resources is usually the function responsible for establishing appropriate controls. Hiring processes should include vetting of potential candidates and processes designed to identify if the candidate is connected to government officials or other connected parties such as customers or third parties. Whilst the hiring decision rests with the hiring manager, it is important that there are independent checks during the process to ensure that the hiring is based on merit and is not influenced by an improper advantage to the business.

13.50

Similar to third party and customer due diligence the information collected about a potential employee at onboarding will be risk based and dependent on the role they are applying for in the organisation. A connected hire question should be asked of all potential recruits as this will trigger additional bribery risk assessments if required.

13.51

Notable examples of bribery cases related to hiring is JP Morgan Chase ordered to pay US$264 million to settle FCPA charges for giving jobs and internships to relatives and friends of government officials in China in order to win business. Over a seven-year period the bank hired approximately 100 individuals at the request of foreign government officials resulting in over US$100 million in revenues for the bank.[18]

13.52

In a similar case in 2018 the SEC fined Credit Suisse US$30 million for a similar scheme.[19] In the press release commentary the Chief of the SEC Enforcement FCPA division noted that 'bribery can take many forms, including granting of employment to friends and relatives of government officials.'

Transactional Risk

13.53

In financial institutions, due diligence is most often considered in the context of onboarding customers and is also referred to as 'know your customer'. Transaction due diligence refers to the risk assessment that applies to complex transactions and will consider, among other risks the potential for bribery and corruption risk within the transaction structure. Examples include infrastructure finance, mergers, acquisitions, public offerings, corporate lending, supply chain finance and debt capital markets.

13.54

For anti-bribery purposes the risk assessment is focused on the potential for bribes to be paid up front, during the transaction or as part of any ongoing process in order to secure an improper advantage or benefit. This means that additional scrutiny is required to explain the role of any third parties involved in the transaction, for example intermediaries or public officials, the rationale and transparency of any incentives offered as part of the transaction, whether fees and commissions are in line with the services provided (ie not excessively high or suspiciously low), the amount and purpose of payments to third parties, the requirement for licences or regulatory approvals and whether the transaction is subject to a public tender process.

13.55

Anti-bribery assessments should be integrated into the existing transaction or mandate approvals and due diligence processes to ensure senior management involved in approving the deals has a holistic overview of the risks.

13.56

The information gathered to manage other risks such as money laundering and fraud will be leveraged to assess the bribery risk. For example, information

18 SEC Release 2016-241.
19 SEC Release 2018-128.

such as the financial crime risk of the jurisdiction, the know your customer due diligence information, information on the target in the case of a merger or acquisition, and the purpose of the transaction will support a risk-based approach for the bribery risk assessment.

13.57

Payment of bribes can, and often do occur outside the transaction itself. For example, the offering of lavish gifts to an intermediary or public official outside the transaction itself to gain an advantage in a tender process. Transparency over any individuals involved in approvals in a mandate or tender process and monitoring of deal team gifts and entertainment records and expense claims is key.

13.58

As bribes are often paid from low-risk countries to higher-risk countries, it is important not to just focus on the transaction elements or parties in the higher risk country. The assessment must also include any parties, including third parties, customers or the organisation's own employees who may be influencing the transaction from a low-risk country.

13.59

As discussed earlier in this chapter, Goldman Sachs agreed to pay a total of US$2.9 billion in penalties, £96.6 million of which went to UK regulatory authorities for its involvement in the Malaysian state-owned development company 1MDB, the FCA and Prudential Regulatory Authority found that the organisation had failed to holistically assess risk factors. These included that a third party raised red flags, the appropriateness of very high fees, the size of the bond offering and failure to record how the transaction review committee assessed and managed the risk of the transaction.[20]

Third parties

13.60

The FCG sets out the expectation that financial institutions undertake appropriate risk-based measures to assess the risk that third parties acting on behalf of the organisation may engage in bribery or corruption.

13.61

Similar to customers, third party due diligence will be risk based depending on the type of service provided and the type of third party. At a high level, for third

20 Final notice – Goldman Sachs International, available at www.bankofengland.co.uk/-/media/boe/files/prudential-regulation/regulatory-action/final-notice-to-goldman-sachs-international.pdf?la=en&hash=0905E04952BFE7C4B05B7AFBB11467F21A069E3F.

parties the due diligence information will consider two elements: identification of the third party and assessing the bribery risks associated with the service to be provided.

13.62

In terms of bribery risk the starting point will be to understand if the third party is acting on behalf of the financial institution as this creates a direct liability if the third party were to bribe others.

13.63

Typical considerations for the risk assessment include:

- the third party's approach to managing bribery risk, ie is there an anti-bribery programme in place;
- ensuring that the choice of third party went through an appropriate selection process;
- assessment of the services that the third party is offering is commensurate with their experience, ie, does the third party have the necessary expertise and are they the best choice for providing the service against the selection process utilised in the financial institution; and
- anti-bribery clauses to be included in contracts.

An additional consideration for the Financial Institution will be the possibility that the third party is also a customer. This element brings in the additional bribery risk consideration of whether the existence of a customer relationship is improperly influencing the selection of the third party over others.

13.64

The number of types of third parties and the different services they provide make it much more difficult to centralise the onboarding process for all third parties in the way that customers are managed. This means there is much more reliance on business areas or the third-party relationship manager in understanding what the inherent bribery risks are and assessing the risk in a consistent way.

13.65

Intermediaries or consultants can present higher bribery risk by the nature of the services they provide and may be onboarded for a specific project or transaction. For example, intermediaries or consultants who act on the financial institution's behalf with Public Officials in an infrastructure financing transaction to obtain licenses or approvals. These relationships can arise in different areas of the organisation and may be challenging to subject to standardised procurement controls. The relationships may be small in financial terms or undertake limited numbers of transactions or be established for a particular transaction. Intermediaries represent a higher risk and the controls to manage these risks may need to be manual and tailored to the relationship.

13.66

In the case of the SEC and FCPA, enforcement of Deutsche Bank in relation to violations involving third party intermediaries, 'Business Development Consultants', acted as conduits for bribes to Public Officials and their families in order to gain or retain business. Weaknesses in payment controls were exploited by employees and records falsified to make the payments look legitimate.[21]

13.67

Standard controls designed for supply chain activities may not be adequate to capture this type of bespoke activity. What is more useful in these situations is for Compliance to work with the business areas to identify where the services of these types of third party are likely to be used and to support the business or function in developing appropriate bespoke controls. These controls can then be included within periodic monitoring activities and payments to third parties.

Bribery Risk – looking ahead

13.68

Despite the increase in legislation, the prosecutions and the fines, corruption and bribery are on the increase. Do we need to think again about how we are managing bribery and corruption risk and is the financial services sector doing enough?

Data Challenges

13.69

There have been significant advances in the use of data to manage financial crime risk in financial institutions, however this has historically been focused on anti-money laundering, sanctions, and fraud. Use of third party and employee data in the management of bribery risk remains a challenge in financial institutions in linking up different data systems and where the data is unstructured (eg descriptive text).

21 SEC.gov | SEC Charges Deutsche Bank with FCPA Violations Related to Third-Party Intermediaries, available at www.sec.gov/news/press-release/2021-3.

13.70

Technology solutions rely on good quality structured data to provide meaningful information about patterns and indicators of bribery risk. Whilst there have been significant advances in financial institutions in machine learning and ability to aggregate data, more development is needed to enable the look across the customer, employee, and third-party data. The data for these three risk areas may be held in separate systems and pooling the data may be subject to data privacy challenges, particularly in relation to employees and retail customers.

13.71

The criminals involved in bribery cover their tracks by using more than one financial institution and the transactions are often cross border adding to the legal complexity of prosecution. Perhaps the answer is to focus on technology solutions that offer the possibility of data pooling without infringing on individual privacy for the purposes of looking for activity patterns and connections related to criminal activity. Development of shared technology solutions could also support a more consistent and collaborative effort in combatting bribery and corruption.

Culture and Looking Beyond Proceeds of Crime

13.72

The behavioural aspect of bribery and corruption does not lend itself to a purely data driven, transactional solution. Therefore, the focus on culture change and a 'hearts and minds' approach is also required. All staff must be engaged or motivated to actively 'do the right thing' when dealing with customers and third parties. This requires financial institutions to look harder at the effectiveness of culture change and alignment to the organisation's purpose, balancing profit with the needs of society to combat bribery and corruption.

13.73

The transactional nature of financial institutions, the amount of money that flows through system on any given day and the plethora of rules to be followed can serve to de-sensitise employees to the impact of bribery and it may be viewed as a victimless crime. To ensure that staff are fully committed to managing bribery risk it is essential to link up bribery in financial services with communities and environment that are impacted by bribery and corruption. Training that incorporates the impact of bribery using case studies and victim testimonies can be a powerful way to connect employees to the need for change.

The ESG Agenda

13.74

Financial Institutions are pivotal in enabling businesses to operate. In committing to tackling climate change, financial services organisations are potentially in a position to work with these businesses as well as civil society, communities and governments in driving the ESG agenda. This in turn may further the fight against bribery and corruption by influencing third parties and customers to support change. The focus of the compliance function is in protecting the organisation, employee, customer, and investor interests. Becoming more externally focused on supporting customers and third parties in implementing their own effective anti-bribery and corruption programmes as part of the social aspects of the ESG agenda could create more of a movement for change.

13.75

Financial institutions are central to country economies and are the connectors of communities, governments and business both inside and outside the country in which they are established. There may be reluctance to stand out in what might be a political issue, however financial services have access to knowledge and the technical skills that can help communities deal with corruption. Assisting with training programmes, knowledge, and processes to both raise awareness and help businesses and communities take action themselves should be possible in this globalised world more than ever before.

Collective action

13.76

There can be multiple touchpoints that give rise to bribery risk in a Financial Institution. At the same time, the connectivity in linking customers and third parties across business activities and geographies can help to promote good standards in anti-bribery practices. Particularly where processes such as due diligence standards are encouraged or where training on anti-bribery and corruption is shared to improve understanding of the nature of bribery, the benefits of good governance practices and its impact of bribery and corruption on communities.

13.77

The focus in managing bribery risk in financial institutions to date has potentially been rooted in the concepts of anti-money laundering and fraud controls in that it is focused on finding the proceeds of the crime of bribery. To manage bribery risk effectively financial institutions need to be able to join up the dots between the corrupt behaviours that that leads to bribery as well as the underlying activity that is being influenced. In practice this means better collaboration across the financial services industry, with customers, third parties, governments, civil society, and the communities in which the activity takes place and finding ways to undertake more outcomes focused collective action.

14 Corporate hospitality

Introduction

14.1

Corporate hospitality – the entertaining carried out by businesses for the benefit of their actual or potential clients (or, sometimes, their staff) – is a common and accepted feature of business life. The fear that corporate hospitality could fall foul of the Bribery Act dogged the legislation's progress with repeated warnings that curtailment of such accepted norms would damage British business.[1] Indeed the delay in the publication of the Ministry of Justice Guidance was attributed to concerns about how to deal with issue of corporate hospitality.

In the event, the Secretary of State's statement on the publication of the Guidance sought to allay the concerns that the business community had about corporate hospitality:

> 'Bribery is one of those things we know when we see – it is a cynical attempt to manipulate someone's judgement by financial or similar means. The guidance makes clear that no one is going to try to stop businesses getting to know their clients by taking them to events like Wimbledon, Twickenham or the Grand Prix. Reasonable hospitality to meet, network and improve relationships with customers is a normal part of business'.[2]

Although the vague 'you will know it when you see it' attitude of distinguishing corporate hospitality from bribery is perhaps at the core of how the British government sought to deal with the matter. Action would be taken where corporate hospitality was a cover or ruse for what were 'plainly corrupt payments'.

However, there is a wide range of such activities from the clearly innocuous to the clearly corrupt, and businesses need better guidance as to where to draw the line and how to best protect themselves.

1 Law Commission Report, 'Reforming Bribery', Appendix D.
2 Ministry of Justice Statement dated 31 March 2011.

What is corporate hospitality?

14.2

Hospitality (also commonly referred to as 'entertainment') differs from gift giving in that the person providing the hospitality, or their representative, is generally in attendance throughout the relevant activity. As such, tickets to a sporting event for the recipient to attend on their own (or with their friends / family) would be a gift, whereas tickets to attend in the company of the giver would be hospitality. While the principles governing provision of gifts and hospitality are generally the same, there is often less of a prima facie business justification for providing a gift than for providing hospitality. As a result, some companies have stricter requirements and value thresholds for gift giving than for hospitality.

14.3

This chapter deals primarily with hospitality rather than more general gift giving because gift giving of any real value is unusual in most UK businesses, whereas provision of some level of hospitality is commonplace. Nevertheless, some points relating to gift giving are included throughout the chapter and specifically discussed in paragraph 14.10 below.

14.4

According to the Institute of Business Ethics, the giving and accepting of gifts and hospitality has an important role facilitating business relationships and practice 'a meal out with a supplier can help build a relationship; a pen with your firm's name on it can remind a customer of you when they need a quote'.[3]

14.5

These minor examples of low value gifts / hospitality will still constitute a 'financial advantage' but on their own are unlikely to amount to a bribe. In order to provide a framework to understand how to distinguish between corporate hospitality and a bribe, it is important to return to the distinguishing features of a 'bribe'.

What is the distinguishing feature of a 'bribe'

14.6

The essence of what a bribe is hoping to achieve is improper performance of a function or activity (or influencing a foreign public official and thus obtaining a business advantage). There is without doubt an element of reciprocity – ie a

3 *The IBE Business Ethics Toolkit*, Gifts and Hospitality, November 2020.

direct connection between the giving/receiving of an advantage and activity which is improperly performed.

14.7

Therefore, genuine corporate hospitality, which seeks to cultivate better relations with customers or other business partners rather than inducing or rewarding improper performance, is not caught within the Act.

14.8

Business transactions are complicated, however, and corporate hospitality will often go well beyond the examples given in paragraph 14.4 above. To help distinguish, there is some guidance available.

Guidance from the SFO, CPS and MoJ

14.9

On 9 October 2012, the Serious Fraud Office confirmed the following:

> 'Bona fide hospitality or promotional or other legitimate business expenditure is recognised as an established and important part of doing business. It is also the case, however, that bribes are sometimes disguised as legitimate business expenditure.'[4]

This again reiterated the element of disguised expenditure. The short statement from the SFO also referred to the Joint Guidance from the Director of Public Prosecutions and Director of the SFO first issued in March 2011 and updated in September 2019.

14.10

It is worth quoting in full from the updated 2019 Joint Guidance from the Director of Public Prosecutions and Director of the SFO:

> 'Hospitality or promotional expenditure which is reasonable, proportionate and made in good faith is an established and important part of doing business. The Act does not seek to penalise such activity.
>
> Hospitality and promotional expenditure could, however, form the basis of offences under s1 (bribing another person) or s6 (bribing a foreign public official) and constitute a bribe for the purpose of s7 (failure to prevent bribery). Under section 1 there must be an element of "improper performance". Under section 6, it will be necessary to show that the provision of hospitality or promotional expenditure was

4 UK Serious Fraud Office 'Bribery Act Guidance', online at: www.sfo.gov.uk/publications/guidance-policy-and-protocols/bribery-act-guidance/.

intended to influence the foreign public official so as to obtain or retain business, or an advantage in the conduct of business.

The more lavish the hospitality or expenditure (beyond what may be reasonable standards in the particular circumstances) the greater the inference that it is intended to encourage or reward improper performance or influence an official. Lavishness is just one factor that may be taken into account in determining whether an offence has been committed. The full circumstances of each case would need to be considered. Other factors might include that the hospitality or expenditure was not clearly connected with legitimate business activity or was concealed.'[5]

14.11

This mirrors the 2011 MoJ Guidance on Adequate Procedures, which usefully also gives examples:

'The provision by a UK mining company of reasonable travel and expenditure to allow foreign public officials to visit their distant mining operations so that those officials may be satisfied of the high standard and safety of the company's installations and operating systems are circumstances that fall outside the intended scope of the offence. Flights and accommodation to allow foreign public officials to meet with senior executives of a UK commercial organisation in New York as a matter of genuine mutual convenience, and some reasonable hospitality for the individual and his or her partner, such as fine dining and attendance at a baseball match are facts that are, in themselves, unlikely to raise the necessary inferences.

However, if the choice of New York as the most convenient venue was in doubt because the organisation's senior executives could easily have seen the official with all the relevant documentation when they had visited the relevant country the previous week then the necessary inference might be raised.

Similarly supplementing information provided to a foreign public official on a commercial organisation's background track record and expertise in providing private health care with an offer of ordinary travel and lodgings to enable a visit to a hospital run by the commercial organisation is unlikely to engage section 6. On the other hand, the provision by that same commercial organisation of a five-star holiday for the foreign public official which is unrelated to a demonstration of

5 Bribery Act 2010: 'Joint Prosecution Guidance of The Director of the Serious Fraud Office and The Director of Public Prosecutions', reviewed September 2019, online at: www.cps.gov.uk/legal-guidance/bribery-act-2010-joint-prosecution-guidance-director-serious-fraud-office-and.

the organisation's services is, all things being equal, far more likely to raise the necessary inference.'[6]

These two examples can be seen as implementing the principles which are outlined below, namely that consideration needs to be given to the context within which the corporate hospitality is given, the proportionality of that gift/hospitality and the relevance to the business itself.

14.12

The concept of a gift or hospitality being 'lavish' is also reflected in the US Department of Justice Guide to the FCPA (updated in November 2020). The guide states that the 'larger or more extravagant the gift … the more likely it was given with an improper purpose.'[7] The DoJ uses example cases that have involved single instances of large, extravagant gift-giving (such as sports cars, fur coats, and other luxury items). It also refers to widespread gifts of smaller items as part of a pattern of bribes. The reasoning behind this Guidance is similar to that in the guidance in the UK, and the examples used are instructive.

Principles of corporate hospitality

14.13

Using both sets of Guidance and using some of the cases decided in the US under the FCPA, a number of principles that businesses should consider when dealing with corporate hospitality/gifts can be suggested.

1. **Whether the corporate hospitality placed the receiver under any obligation**

   As referred to in paragraph 14.4, the element of 'reciprocity' is key and perhaps the most fundamental principle when considering the hospitality on offer. There should be no sense of obligation created whatsoever from the receiver's point of view.

2. **Proportionality**

   Proportionality is another fundamental principle. The trip to Silverstone referred to at the start of the chapter might be acceptable – but an all expenses paid trip to the World Cup finals for a foreign official from a developing country and all of his family, with a total cost running to tens of thousands of pounds, would be more likely to be challenged under the legislation. This means that the context in which the corporate hospitality is offered, and the industry norms, are important.

6 UK Ministry of Justice, 'Guidance about procedures which relevant commercial organisations can put into place to prevent persons associated with them from bribing', page 14, para 31.

7 US Department of Justice, 'A Resource Guide to the U.S. Foreign Corrupt Practices Act: Second Edition', page 15.

As noted previously, what might be acceptable in the world of English Premiership football is unlikely to be acceptable in many other industries. Thus the proportionality that is being considered is the effect on (or inference that the effect might have on) the recipient.

Indeed, during the Joint Committee hearings on the draft Bribery Bill, the DPP indicated that:

> 'to an extent, it might be possible resolve some of the issues as to what is acceptable through adoption and implementation of codes of practices in industries and professions'.

The importance of proportionality is reflected in the fact that both the MoJ Guidance and the SFO/DPP Guidance refer to 'lavish expenditure' being more likely to be unacceptable. This again suggests something out of the ordinary and beyond what would be expected.

3. **Business content**

While the whole of the event need not be devoted to discussing business matters, it is best practice for corporate hospitality to contain a business element that is proportionate to, and balances out, the entertainment aspect. By way of example, it is now common practice for hospitality provided at longer and higher profile sports events (such as the Olympics) to include significant business elements such as technical show cases and / or meetings between senior executives on specific business topics. By contrast, an invitation to a multi-day conference held at a luxury resort that involved only a minimal amount of business content (eg 1–2 hours of presentations on the first morning) would have little genuine business purpose and is therefore more likely to be perceived as being intended to influence inappropriately and so attract scrutiny.

4. **Transparency / Documentation**

When prosecutors consider hospitality, their focus is often on disguised payments. The more open and the clearer the record of what was given, the less likely that it was meant for an illicit purpose. However, any documentation should completely and accurately describe what the hospitality was. There are a number of US cases where the description involved 'training days / inspections' regarding an all expenses paid trip to examine, for example, a factory – but in reality there was a minimal work-related element and extensive and lavish sightseeing.[8]

5. **Working in another country**

Local cultural norms can be taken into consideration when providing gifts and hospitality in other jurisdictions

The Law Commission indicated that:

8 *SEC v Avery Dennison Corporation* and *SEC v Lucent Technologies Inc.*

> 'if one country traditionally entertains all visiting business executives far more lavishly than is customary in other countries, that fact will still have a relevance under our scheme. It would evidence, tending to show that in spite of the fact that hospitality was accepted, it did not mean that the executives departed from standards of good faith or of impartiality that would be observed by a person of moral integrity.'

However, there is no suggestion that there is a defence against bribery based on cultural norms in a different country – it is but one factor that needs to be taken into account.

One point worth noting is the MoJ focus on the section 6 offence (ie the influencing of a foreign public official) in relation to corporate hospitality. The MoJ Guidance maintains that for a section 6 offence there must be an intention for a financial or other advantage to influence the official in his or her official role and thereby secure business or a business advantage. According to the Guidance (paragraph 27), in this regard it may be in some circumstances that hospitality or promotional expenditure in the form of travel and accommodation costs does not even amount to a 'financial or other advantage' to the relevant official because it is a cost that would otherwise be borne by the relevant foreign government rather than the official him or herself.

However, companies should be wary of relying on this guidance alone. What a foreign public official may be able to claim by way of expenses covered by his or her relevant own government may be very different from the five star accommodation that may be available by way of corporate hospitality. Anything above and beyond what the official would ordinarily be able to claim from his or her government would thus still constitute a financial or other advantage.

6. **Identity of recipient**

The giver of a gift or hospitality should always be mindful of who the recipient is. The more targeted the corporate hospitality, then the more the inference is that its intent is to improperly influence them / induce them into improper performance, rather than to cement links with the supplier or keep the existence of the supplier at the forefront of someone's mind when it comes to placing orders.

If, for example, the only recipient of the hospitality is the sole decision maker related to a tender or other key aspect of a business relationship, then suspicion may arise.

Furthermore, it can rarely be right that family members of decision makers are included in corporate hospitality (although the MoJ Guidance does suggest that meals for family members are in some cases permissible).

7. **Timing of hospitality**

   Care should also be taken when giving or accepting corporate hospitality shortly before a large contract or piece of work is due to be offered. It is best practice not to provide *any* hospitality when engaged in a tender process being run by the recipient, and the rules of the tender will often require this.

8. **Seeking assurances from recipients**

   If you are inviting your business partner to an event, it is worth including in the invitation wording to the effect that they should check that accepting such an invitation would not breach any internal or external rules before RSVPing. Having such wording makes it difficult for investigators to allege that you knew or believed that the acceptance of the offer would be improper performance on the part of the recipient. It also reduces the risk of committing an offence under Case 2 of Section 1 of the UK Bribery Act, whereby it is prohibited to offer a financial or other advantage to another person while knowing or believing that their accepting it would in itself constitute the improper performance of their duties (e.g. by being in violation of their company's internal policies).

Principles of Gift Giving

14.14

As discussed at the beginning of this chapter, gift giving of any real value is relatively uncommon in most UK businesses, and is often limited to major public holidays or religious festivals such as Christmas or Eid. In general, gifts pose greater risks of being perceived as intending to influence the recipient than hospitality, as gifts are enjoyed in the absence of the giver and therefore have a less immediately apparent business purpose. There is also a risk with a gift that it could be taken and sold by the recipient, therefore realising an immediate cash value.

14.15

The principles in relation to provision of hospitality set out above also generally apply to gift giving, particularly with respect to not creating any obligation, proportionality, transparency / documentation and timing. Some companies also choose to only provide gifts that are emblazoned with their official branding, which can make the gift's business connection more apparent. However, you should be mindful that, while company branding may reduce the value of a gift in some jurisdictions, in other locations it may provide a certain additional status to the recipient, particularly if it demonstrates the recipient's connection to a large and high-profile multi-national.

14.16

While it may technically count as a gift, providing a free sample of a low-value product to demonstrate its purpose and / or quality is also generally regarded as acceptable. However, this would not apply to free samples of high-value or luxury items such as cars, watches or consumer electronics.

14.17

A simple, practical test to apply when considering whether a gift is appropriate is to think about how the giver (and their company) would feel if the gift were publicly known (eg through being reported in a newspaper). If this would cause embarrassment or potentially raise awkward questions, it is likely that the gift is not appropriate and should not be given.

Private/public sector

14.18

From the Law Commission document, it is clear that there was a distinction between ordinary hospitality in the private sector and corporate hospitality in the public sector.

According to the Law Commission's footnote (Law Com number 313/2008), acceptance of hospitality of a 'special kind' would be a breach of the expectation of the position of trust held by a recipient working in the public sector. It is not clear what 'special kind' refers to, but most public sector organisations such as local authorities or civil services will have strict rules already in place about the acceptance of corporate hospitality.

14.19

With this in mind, many companies choose to apply additional controls with respect to any gifts and hospitality provided to public officials. This may include lower thresholds for requiring approval, more direct review by compliance, and specific recording procedures.

Different types of corporate hospitality

14.20

Corporate hospitality can take a wide range of different forms, from dinner and drinks at a local restaurant to front row tickets at an Opera premiere. Some general categories of hospitality that can create particular risks are as follows:

1. Sporting and cultural events.
2. Sightseeing.

3. Provision of travel / hotels.

4. Sexual entertainment.

Sporting and cultural events

14.21

In many ways this is the cliché or stereotypical image when one thinks of corporate hospitality. There is a whole industry that is devoted to providing seats at high profile football matches, Wimbledon, Grand Prix or other iconic sporting events. The MoJ Guidance (and indeed the Secretary of State when introducing the guidance) is at pains to confirm that such corporate hospitality is still deemed to be permissible.

14.22

Nevertheless, some care must be taken. Many of these items are in themselves quite expensive. If for example the recipient is known to have been seeking tickets to such events for some time and the corporate hospitality has been defined as a way of targeting him, then care must be taken.

14.23

The following checklist might be useful in relation to dealing with this type of corporate hospitality:

1. How generous is the entertainment, ie the cost?
2. Has it been targeted or solicited by the recipient?
3. How much time would it require out of the office?
4. Are other associated expenses such as travel paid for?
5. Would these expenses include flights (if abroad)?
6. Can it be indicated that there is a potential for the recipient to be under any sort of obligation?
7. How frequently has the entertainment been offered to the recipient?

14.24

Determining the value of tickets to a cultural or sporting event may not always be straightforward. While a ticket may have a reasonable retail face value, if the event is particularly exclusive or availability of tickets is limited (eg for certain concerts, music festivals or high profile sporting events) then it may have a far higher re-sale / grey market value which the recipient would in reality have to pay themselves if they wanted to attend. As noted above, value can also be highly subjective, and a recipient may value a ticket to see his or her favourite performer much more than that ticket's face price. While companies will obviously want to invite business partners to events that those partners would actually want to attend, care should be taken not to be seen as targeting specific individuals with tickets to their favourite events or performances which the company would not otherwise have provided to anyone else.

Sightseeing

14.25

An analysis of US bribery cases involving corporate hospitality shows that whilst paying for sightseeing is permitted, it should be incidental to the purpose of the hospitality rather than the main focus. Where for example business partners are invited to a meeting in New York from a different jurisdiction, there can be no objection to including a one-day sightseeing trip around the attractions of Manhattan. However, if on the same trip the donor company also paid for two weeks sightseeing ranging from the Grand Canyon to Las Vegas and Disney World, then it could be argued that the business meeting itself was a ruse, and that the real objective was to reward members of the donor company / a foreign public official with an all-expenses paid holiday.

14.26

For example, in *SEC v Siemens Aktiengesellschaft*, 4,000 payments to government officials totalling £1.4 billion were made. Some of the payments included trips to holiday destinations such as Las Vegas, which the SEC found to have no legitimate business purpose.

Travel and hotels

14.27

The purpose of any travel and the level of expenditure involved (eg whether or not the recipient is travelling first class) must be made clear. What is appropriate may well depend on industry norms and also on the position and expectations of the recipient. For example, board members of a large, multinational partner company may be accustomed to travelling in business or first class and staying in 5 star hotels, and are therefore unlikely to be improperly influenced if such travel and accommodation is provided to them (indeed, they may potentially be offended if it is not). However, such travel might be more novel for a mid-level public official or procurement manager, who are therefore likely to value it much more highly. In reality, it is unlikely that many SMEs will be able to justify providing first class travel to their business partners.

In all cases, payment should be made directly to the hotel / airline / travel company rather than to the individual.

Sexual entertainment

14.28

Sexual entertainment, even if lawful, is unlikely to be tolerated by the recipient company and hence it can be inferred that an executive/company officer is being induced to improper performance by the provision of such hospitality. Most companies will explicitly prohibit any such expenditure in their codes of conduct.

Checklist of high risk/low risk factors

14.29

From the principles and different types of corporate hospitality, a checklist of low and high risk examples can be drawn up, as shown below.

Low risk	**High risk**
Taking your contacts out for a meal	Paying cash for your business contact and their family to dine without you there
Paying for you and your contact to attend a sporting event in the UK	An all expenses paid, weekend trip to see a high profile sporting event abroad, with five star hotel accommodation and spending money
Paying for your business contact to attend a series of meetings in the UK where the business relationship can be discussed, and paying for a sightseeing event during the course of that trip	Paying for your business contact to attend the UK for three weeks for one meeting, and funding a number of sightseeing trips in the meantime
Paying for low level promotional items such as corporate pens	Paying for high level items such as expensive watches
Attending a concert with a business contact	Arranging for a business contact's favourite artist to provide them with a private performance

This does not mean that 'high risk' examples cannot be undertaken as corporate hospitality, BUT additional care must be taken, with particular consideration to industry norms, codes of practice etc.

14.30

When making decisions on whether to give or accept corporate hospitality, the principle and factors outlined in this chapter need to be observed. A corporation should ensure that it has adequate procedures in place to prevent corporate hospitality from turning into bribery. Further guidance is given on this in Chapter 8, and particularly paragraph 8.74 in relation to corporate hospitality or gifts and entertainment.

14.31

There should always be a policy specifically dealing with corporate hospitality. A model of such a policy is set out in the Annex below. This is a 'core' policy but it should be amended to take into account the individual circumstances of your corporation.

14.32

As with all policies, it is only as good as the people who observe it and the people who enforce it. There should be regular reminders of the policy, with a register of gifts and a potential audit. In these ways, the risks to individuals and corporations can be minimised.

14.33

It is also important for employees to understand that they cannot circumvent the policy by paying for corporate hospitality themselves and not claiming the cost back as an expense. If an employee is meeting with a business partner or potential customer there is a general presumption that they are acting on behalf of the company and therefore must follow the relevant principles and requirements at all times.

Annex – Example corporate hospitality/gift policy wording

14.34

The following is an example of the sort of content that a company may consider including in its corporate gifts and hospitality policy, and is not intended to be copied word-for-word. All companies should carefully consider their own business and risk profiles and create bespoke policies to fit these, taking appropriate legal advice where needed.

> [Our company] values require a commitment to being open and honest, and treating everyone with fairness, consideration and respect. These values underpin our ethical standards, and provide us with guidance as

to acceptable behaviours. This policy sets out specific expectations with regard to gifts, tips and hospitality.

Scope

The policy applies to all employees of [company].

Purpose

This policy sets out the responsibilities of all staff throughout [company] to ensure appropriate and consistent handling of any gifts or hospitality which may be offered to them or which they wish to provide to others. Adhering to the requirements of this policy will protect staff against potential bribery allegations.

Company policy

[Company name] recognises that giving and receiving gifts/hospitality is often an established and important part of doing business. This policy does not prohibit the giving or accepting of reasonable and proportionate gifts and hospitality for legitimate purposes such as building relationships, maintaining our image or reputation, or marketing our products and services. However, giving and receiving gifts/hospitality can create a bribery risk if not done appropriately and transparently.

In particular, extra care must be taken when spending on Public Officials, as laws and regulations for dealing with them can vary from place to place and are often stricter than the rules that apply to commercial Third Parties. While in some countries reasonable and proportionate spending on Public Officials is permitted, in other jurisdictions *all* gifts and hospitality provided to Public Officials are treated as bribery and are illegal.

Under no circumstances should you actively solicit a gift or corporate hospitality. Doing so will result in an investigation being undertaken, which may lead to disciplinary action. Gifts, tips and offers of corporate hospitality must be dealt with in a manner consistent with the details set out below.

A gift or hospitality will not be appropriate if it is unduly lavish or extravagant, or could be seen as a request or reward for any preferential treatment (for example, during contractual negotiations or a tender process). Gifts must be of an appropriate type and value depending on the circumstances and taking account of the reason for the gift. Gifts must not include cash or cash equivalent (such as vouchers), or be given in secret. Gifts must be given in our name, not your name.

Business gifts

You may give or receive gifts to / from suppliers, customers or other business contacts up to a value of £[50] without prior approval. Examples of appropriate gifts may include diaries, pens, other branded stationary, or modest food / drink items or hampers.

If you wish to give a gift to a third party of a value greater than set out above, you must obtain pre-approval from the [Chief Compliance Officer]. You must inform the [Chief Compliance Officer] by email of the exact or estimated value of the gift, its business purpose, the details of the recipient, and why a gift of a value below the approval threshold is not appropriate in this case.

In circumstances where you have received a gift with an estimated value above the approval threshold, the [Chief Compliance Officer] will decide what to do with it. This may involve you keeping the gift, returning the gift to the giver, donating the gift to charity, or sharing the gift for the collective benefit of your team.

Corporate hospitality

You may give or receive corporate hospitality to / from suppliers, customers or other business contacts up to a value of £[100] without prior approval. Examples of appropriate hospitality may include meals at restaurants, tickets to concerts or sporting events, or drinks in bars.

As with gifts, if you wish to provide corporate hospitality to a third party of a value greater than set out above, you must obtain pre-approval from the [Chief Compliance Officer]. You must inform the [Chief Compliance Officer] by email of the exact or estimated value of the hospitality, its business purpose, the details of the recipient, and why hospitality of a value below the approval threshold is not appropriate in this case.

If you are invited to a corporate day or other event, you must seek approval from your Line Manager. This will only be given where the hospitality is reasonable and justifiable. It is not generally permissible to accept more than one such invitation from any company within a 12 month period.

When attending free business events, such as seminars or conferences, the travel and other agreed costs must be met by [company]. There is an exception in circumstances where you are speaking at the event on behalf of the company – in such cases travel and accommodation costs may be settled by the event organiser, but should be of a level consistent with our own travel and expenses policy. Approval to attend any such events must be sought from your Line Manager.

Attendance at professional institute events undertaken voluntarily during your own time does not require approval, and is encouraged.

Important considerations

You should as much as possible consider the total spend on single individuals by others within [company]. If a number of other people have recently given gifts / hospitality to a Third Party or Public Official, it may not be appropriate for you to do so, even when the gift / hospitality is of modest value and is within the approval threshold. You should consult with the [Chief Compliance Officer] if in any doubt on this point.

On some occasions you may be offered a gift / hospitality of a value greater than the approval threshold in circumstances where it would be rude or culturally inappropriate to refuse. Alternately, you may be put in a position where you feel obliged to pay a bill for a value greater than that amount without having obtained pre-approval. In such circumstances, you may accept the gift or pay the bill, but must immediately report it to the [Chief Compliance Officer] for guidance and recording.

You should be mindful of the fact that it is a potential criminal offence to offer a gift or hospitality to someone when you know that they are not allowed to receive it, for example due to their own corporate policies. In this regard, it is best practice to always confirm with the recipient what they are permitted or prohibited from receiving before making any offer.

Attempting to circumvent this policy by providing multiple gifts or frequent hospitality to a single recipient at just below the approval threshold is a serious disciplinary matter that may have consequences up to and including dismissal.

Recording gifts and hospitality

Any gifts or hospitality that you give or receive which exceed the approval thresholds set out in this Policy must be properly recorded in company's] Gifts and Hospitality Register (the '**Register**'). When the giver or recipient is a Public Official, this must be clearly noted in the Register.

The Register will be maintained by [the Chief Compliance Officer], who is responsible for recording the details of applicable gifts / hospitality once they have been approved.

You must also submit all expenses claims relating to hospitality, gifts or payments made to Third Parties in accordance with our expenses policy and record the reason for expenditure.

All accounts, invoices, and other records relating to dealings with Third Parties should be prepared with strict accuracy and completeness. Accounts must not be kept 'off-book' to facilitate or conceal improper payments.

Roles and responsibilities

Every member of staff at [company] has a personal responsibility to behave in line with our values.

If you become aware of behaviour by one of your colleagues which you believe breaches this policy, you should report your concerns using the company's whistleblowing policy.

Suspected breaches of this policy may be investigated. Any member of staff found to have acted outside the policy will face disciplinary action, and this may result in dismissal.

Further guidance

If you are unsure whether or not your actions are appropriate with regard to gifts or hospitality, you can seek clarification from any of the following:

[The Chief Compliance Officer]

[A Manager from the People team];

[A member of the Operating Board];

[The Group Internal Audit Manager].

Some examples are provided on the following page which may assist you.

Examples of the policy in practice

1. A potential supplier offers to pay for travel and accommodation to allow you to visit their factory & ensure that they are able to meet our requirements.

   - Provided the travel and accommodation is within the scope of our expenses policy, this is acceptable. An offer which exceeds our standards should be referred to the Chief Compliance Officer.

2. You wish to provide a long-standing supplier with a number of tickets to a ballet performance, valued at £300.

- You must seek approval from the [Chief Compliance Officer] before providing the tickets, and ensure that these are properly recorded in the gifts and hospitality register.

3. A Public Official conducts a day-long inspection of one of our [facilities / buildings]. At the end of the inspection you wish to take the inspector to a local pub for dinner.

   - As the recipient of the hospitality in this case is a Public Official, care should be taken in relation to any hospitality provided, even if it is within the approval threshold. You should discuss this with the [Chief Compliance Officer] before proceeding.

4. A service provider who you have worked with regularly in the past sends you a crate of wine from a boutique vineyard as a Christmas gift. You estimate the total value of the crate as approximately £160.

   - As the estimated value of the gift exceeds the approval limit of £50, you should consult the [Chief Compliance Officer] on how to proceed. It may be most appropriate for the wine to be shared among your team at an office social event rather than retained for your personal consumption. Whatever decision is arrived at, the gift should be recorded in the gifts and hospitality register.

5. A representative from a potential new customer travels from overseas for a business meeting. After the meeting is complete, you suggest that you take the representative out to dinner. The representative readily agrees and suggests that you go to a restaurant known for its luxury cuisine and expensive menu.

   - In this circumstance, you should be aware of the likelihood that the dinner will cost more than the allowable threshold of [£100] set out in this policy for hospitality that can be given to a third party without prior approval. You should therefore contact the [Chief Compliance Officer] and seek pre-approval for the dinner before agreeing the choice of restaurant. Alternately, you could suggest another restaurant to the customer's representative that is known to be within the price range that does not require pre-approval.

Appendix 1: Small bribes management discussion

In relation to small bribes, senior executives, perhaps using the Panalpina case study in Chapter 2 and to Chapter 5 generally, could take time to consider a selection of the following questions – ideally with real examples selected from the business.

Generating top-level discussion

1. Is it appropriate to make a small payment, where is it culturally acceptable or simply the business norm? Does the desire to be culturally sensitive (and thereby increase potential business opportunities) override the legal requirement not to pay bribes?
2. Is it appropriate to make a small payment to protect oneself from reasonable fear of injury or false imprisonment? Does the protection of an employee override the legal requirement not to pay bribes?
3. Is it appropriate to make a small payment to prevent a long delay to a critical business meeting? Does the business's need override the legal requirement not to pay bribes?
4. Is it appropriate to make a small payment to prevent loss of property or sometimes significant business damage (loss of a new contract, loss of perishable goods). Does the business need override the legal requirement not to pay bribes?
5. Is it appropriate to make a payment where not to make a payment would delay a shipment of medicine or food that is perishable and without which others will suffer? Does the short-term protection of non-employees override the legal requirement not to pay bribes?
6. Is it appropriate to make a small payment where the person requesting it is underpaid and needs the additional income small bribes provide to provide for his or her family? Does the medium to long-term welfare of a non- employee become an over-riding issue?

Further sub-issues for thought or discussion are as follows:

- For the topics above, remove the word 'small' and insert the word 'large' before 'bribe'; reconsider the questions. Does it alter the outcome and does it alter the efforts that should be taken not to pay the money requested?
- In relation to the topics above, consider whether an employee in the company being discussed could reasonably believe that they ought to be praised or at least not disciplined for breaching company policy in relation to any of the above, or finding ambiguity in which to try and justify a decision to make a small payment? Might such employees be tempted to falsify accounts so as not to cause embarrassment for management or to allow what they consider a good act to take place that the rules (by oversight and omission) do not allow?

The issues raised in relation to the topics do not necessarily have particularly easy or comfortable answers but they can generate helpful debate. Legal and ethical analysis is suggested below for the leader/facilitator of the discussion.

1. Paying bribes to meet cultural norms is not a defence under the Bribery Act 2010 (or under the US FCPA) and this would not be a legal reason to allow a bribe.
2. A payment could well be appropriate in these circumstances and a defence is available under the law of duress.
3. English law does not allow mere inconvenience as a reason for paying a small bribe.
4. Arguably the law of extortion may provide a defence here but it is very limited, if available at all, and would not be likely to be available on an on-going basis.
5. Such a payment may fall into the law of necessity or duress but the law is quite untested in this area. This commentator's view is that the law would be extended to cover this issue if the payment was unexpected and that in such circumstances a prosecutor would not consider it in the public interest to prosecute. However, if the payment was made regularly by, for instance, an employee of a pharmaceutical company, it is suggested that the better opinion is that duress/necessity will not apply.
6. These reasons are not sufficient to pay a bribe under English law but a company might ask what it is doing to deal with such ethical issues – in terms of (1) reducing the issues but also (2) in terms of informing employees that the company recognises this as a cause of bribes and is taking steps to trade ethically and fairly in a manner that does support local business and communities.

Appendix 2: Red flags

The following is a non-exhaustive list of generic 'red flags' that could arise in relation to third party transactions.

- The country in which the third party is incorporated or in which the activities are to occur is 'high risk'.
- The third party has a reputation for unethical or illegal acts.
- The third party has been investigated for or been prosecuted for corruption, money laundering, fraud or similar crimes of dishonesty.
- The owners of the third party have been investigated for or been prosecuted for corruption, money-laundering, fraud or similar crimes of dishonesty.
- The third party has no or little trading record/has only very recently been incorporated.
- A government official connected with the transaction recommends or requires the use or one or a small number of counterparties.
- Part ownership of the third party by government officials.
- The third party wishes to keep normally available commercial information secret or undisclosed, eg names of directors, addresses, accounts.
- The transaction relies disproportionately on the payment of 'commissions'.
- The third party does not appear to have the skills, resources or personnel to conduct the required business.
- The third party can only provide non-descript services or the contract amounts to services that rely primarily on 'contacts' or influencing.
- The third party is to be paid in cash or in a country which either has no obvious connection to the contract or third party and/or is a country known for poor money laundering controls.
- There have been accounts in the press/wider media of improper conduct.
- The local law relevant to the business activities requires the use of a small group of agents or there is otherwise a monopoly.
- The third party ownership structure is unclear or convoluted/the beneficial owners are unknown.

- The transaction is structured in way that appears unnecessarily complex.
- The third party refuses to provide detailed invoices or to agree reasonable anti-corruption contract terms.
- The third party requests for any cash sums to 'get the deal through' or similar.
- Training provided to the third party reveals a lack of understanding of bribery risk and of the zero-tolerance to bribery approach to business.
- The third party, its shareholders or directors are known to be closely connected with decision making public officials relevant to the business activity or to other relevant decision makers (eg managers in a procurement department).
- The third party has no or only a weak compliance culture but is operating in a medium or high-risk area.
- The counterpart has unusual wealth or influence as against its size and industry norms.
- There are departures from the usual tendering process or the deal struck appears uncommercial.
- The amount paid appears to materially exceed the value being provided.
- A request is made to create misleading or false documents.
- The third party will be moving goods or people across borders or engaging with public officials in relation to low level payments.
- There are any peculiar acts which seem to indicate the third party does not wish to be transparent in its dealings.

Appendix 3: Ministry of Justice Guidance on the Bribery Act 2010

Guidance about procedures which relevant commercial organisations can put into place to prevent persons associated with them from bribing (section 9 of the Bribery Act 2010).

Foreword

Bribery blights lives. Its immediate victims include firms that lose out unfairly. The wider victims are government and society, undermined by a weakened rule of law and damaged social and economic development. At stake is the principle of free and fair competition, which stands diminished by each bribe offered or accepted.

Tackling this scourge is a priority for anyone who cares about the future of business, the developing world or international trade. That is why the entry into force of the Bribery Act on 1 July 2011 is an important step forward for both the UK and UK plc. In line with the Act's statutory requirements, I am publishing this guidance to help organisations understand the legislation and deal with the risks of bribery. My aim is that it offers clarity on how the law will operate.

Readers of this document will be aware that the Act creates offences of offering or receiving bribes, bribery of foreign public officials and of failure to prevent a bribe being paid on an organisation's behalf. These are certainly tough rules. But readers should understand too that they are directed at making life difficult for the mavericks responsible for corruption, not unduly burdening the vast majority of decent, law-abiding firms.

I have listened carefully to business representatives to ensure the Act is implemented in a workable way – especially for small firms that have limited resources. And, as I hope this guidance shows, combating the risks of bribery is largely about common sense, not burdensome procedures. The core principle it sets out is proportionality. It also offers case study examples that help illuminate the application of the Act. Rest assured – no one wants to stop firms getting to know their clients by taking them to events like Wimbledon or the Grand Prix. Separately, we are publishing non-statutory 'quick start' guidance. I encourage small businesses to turn to this for a concise introduction to how they can meet the requirements of the law.

Ultimately, the Bribery Act matters for Britain because our existing legislation is out of date. In updating our rules, I say to our international partners that the UK wants to play a leading role in stamping out corruption and supporting trade-led international development. But I would argue too that the Act is directly beneficial for business. That's because it creates clarity and a level playing field, helping to align trading nations around decent standards. It also establishes a statutory defence: organisations which have adequate procedures in place to prevent bribery are in a stronger position if isolated incidents have occurred in spite of their efforts.

Some have asked whether business can afford this legislation – especially at a time of economic recovery. But the choice is a false one. We don't have to decide between tackling corruption and supporting growth. Addressing bribery is good for business because it creates the conditions for free markets to flourish.

Everyone agrees bribery is wrong and that rules need reform. In implementing this Act, we are striking a blow for the rule of law and growth of trade. I commend this guidance to you as a helping hand in doing business competitively and fairly.

Kenneth Clarke
Secretary of State for Justice
March 2011

Introduction

1 The Bribery Act 2010 received Royal Assent on 8 April 2010. A full copy of the Act and its Explanatory Notes can be accessed at: www.opsi.gov.uk/acts/acts2010/ukpga_20100023_en_1 The Act creates a new offence under section 7 which can be committed by commercial organisations[1] which fail to prevent persons associated with them from committing bribery on their behalf. It is a full defence for an organisation to prove that despite a particular case of bribery it nevertheless had adequate procedures in place to prevent persons associated with it from bribing. Section 9 of the Act requires the Secretary of State to publish guidance about procedures which commercial organisations can put in place to prevent persons associated with them from bribing. This document sets out that guidance.

2 The Act extends to England & Wales, Scotland and Northern Ireland. This guidance is for use in all parts of the United Kingdom. In accordance with section 9(3) of the Act, the Scottish Ministers have been consulted

1 See paragraph 35 below on the definition of the phrase 'commercial organisation'.

regarding the content of this guidance. The Northern Ireland Assembly has also been consulted.

3 This guidance explains the policy behind section 7 and is intended to help commercial organisations of all sizes and sectors understand what sorts of procedures they can put in place to prevent bribery as mentioned in section 7(1).

4 The guidance is designed to be of general application and is formulated around six guiding principles, each followed by commentary and examples. The guidance is not prescriptive and is not a one-size-fits-all document. The question of whether an organisation had adequate procedures in place to prevent bribery in the context of a particular prosecution is a matter that can only be resolved by the courts taking into account the particular facts and circumstances of the case. The onus will remain on the organisation, in any case where it seeks to rely on the defence, to prove that it had adequate procedures in place to prevent bribery. However, departures from the suggested procedures contained within the guidance will not of itself give rise to a presumption that an organisation does not have adequate procedures.

5 If your organisation is small or medium sized the application of the principles is likely to suggest procedures that are different from those that may be right for a large multinational organisation. The guidance suggests certain procedures, but they may not all be applicable to your circumstances. Sometimes, you may have alternatives in place that are also adequate.

6 As the principles make clear commercial organisations should adopt a risk-based approach to managing bribery risks. Procedures should be proportionate to the risks faced by an organisation. No policies or procedures are capable of detecting and preventing all bribery. A risk-based approach will, however, serve to focus the effort where it is needed and will have most impact. A risk-based approach recognises that the bribery threat to organisations varies across jurisdictions, business sectors, business partners and transactions.

7 The language used in this guidance reflects its non-prescriptive nature. The six principles are intended to be of general application and are therefore expressed in neutral but affirmative language. The commentary following each of the principles is expressed more broadly.

8 All terms used in this guidance have the same meaning as in the Bribery Act 2010. Any examples of particular types of conduct are provided for illustrative purposes only and do not constitute exhaustive lists of relevant conduct.

Government policy and section 7 of the Bribery Act

9 Bribery undermines democracy and the rule of law and poses very serious threats to sustained economic progress in developing and emerging economies and to the proper operation of free markets more generally. The Bribery Act 2010 is intended to respond to these threats and to the extremely broad range of ways that bribery can be committed. It does this by providing robust offences, enhanced sentencing powers for the courts (raising the maximum sentence for bribery committed by an individual from 7 to 10 years imprisonment) and wide jurisdictional powers (see paragraphs 15 and 16 on page 9).

10 The Act contains two general offences covering the offering, promising or giving of a bribe (active bribery) and the requesting, agreeing to receive or accepting of a bribe (passive bribery) at sections 1 and 2 respectively. It also sets out two further offences which specifically address commercial bribery. Section 6 of the Act creates an offence relating to bribery of a foreign public official in order to obtain or retain business or an advantage in the conduct of business[2], and section 7 creates a new form of corporate liability for failing to prevent bribery on behalf of a commercial organisation. More detail about the sections 1, 6 and 7 offences is provided under the separate headings below.

11 The objective of the Act is not to bring the full force of the criminal law to bear upon well run commercial organisations that experience an isolated incident of bribery on their behalf. So in order to achieve an appropriate balance, section 7 provides a full defence. This is in recognition of the fact that no bribery prevention regime will be capable of preventing bribery at all times. However, the defence is also included in order to encourage commercial organisations to put procedures in place to prevent bribery by persons associated with them.

12 The application of bribery prevention procedures by commercial organisations is of significant interest to those investigating bribery and is relevant if an organisation wishes to report an incident of bribery to the prosecution authorities – for example to the Serious Fraud Office (SFO) which operates a policy in England and Wales and Northern Ireland of co-operation with commercial organisations that self-refer incidents of bribery (see 'Approach of the SFO to dealing with overseas corruption' on the SFO website). The commercial organisation's willingness to co-operate with an investigation under the Bribery Act and to make a full disclosure will also be taken into account in any decision as to whether it is appropriate to commence criminal proceedings.

---

2 Conduct amounting to bribery of a foreign public official could also be charged under section 1 of the Act. It will be for prosecutors to select the most appropriate charge.

13 In order to be liable under section 7 a commercial organisation must have failed to prevent conduct that would amount to the commission of an offence under sections 1 or 6, but it is irrelevant whether a person has been convicted of such an offence. Where the prosecution cannot prove beyond reasonable doubt that a sections 1 or 6 offence has been committed the section 7 offence will not be triggered.

14 The section 7 offence is in addition to, and does not displace, liability which might arise under sections 1 or 6 of the Act where the commercial organisation itself commits an offence by virtue of the common law 'identification' principle.[3]

Jurisdiction

15 Section 12 of the Act provides that the courts will have jurisdiction over the sections 1, 2[4] or 6 offences committed in the UK, but they will also have jurisdiction over offences committed outside the UK where the person committing them has a close connection with the UK by virtue of being a British national or ordinarily resident in the UK, a body incorporated in the UK or a Scottish partnership.

16 However, as regards section 7, the requirement of a close connection with the UK does not apply. Section 7(3) makes clear that a commercial organisation can be liable for conduct amounting to a section 1 or 6 offence on the part of a person who is neither a UK national or resident in the UK, nor a body incorporated or formed in the UK. In addition, section 12(5) provides that it does not matter whether the acts or omissions which form part of the section 7 offence take part in the UK or elsewhere. So, provided the organisation is incorporated or formed in the UK, or that the organisation carries on a business or part of a business in the UK (wherever in the world it may be incorporated or formed) then UK courts will have jurisdiction (see more on this at paragraphs 34 to 36).

Section 1: Offences of bribing another person

17 Section 1 makes it an offence for a person ('P') to offer, promise or give a financial or other advantage to another person in one of two cases:

- **Case 1** applies where P intends the advantage to bring about the improper performance by another person of a relevant function or activity or to reward such improper performance.

---

3 See section 5 and Schedule 1 to the Interpretation Act 1978 which provides that the word 'person' where used in an Act includes bodies corporate and unincorporate. Note also the common law 'identification principle' as defined by cases such as Tesco Supermarkets v Nattrass [1972] AC 153 which provides that corporate liability arises only where the offence is committed by a natural person who is the directing mind or will of the organisation.

4 Although this particular offence is not relevant for the purposes of section 7.

- **Case 2** applies where P knows or believes that the acceptance of the advantage offered, promised or given in itself constitutes the improper performance of a relevant function or activity.

18 'Improper performance' is defined at sections 3, 4 and 5. In summary, this means performance which amounts to a breach of an expectation that a person will act in good faith, impartially, or in accordance with a position of trust. The offence applies to bribery relating to any function of a public nature, connected with a business, performed in the course of a person's employment or performed on behalf of a company or another body of persons. Therefore, bribery in both the public and private sectors is covered.

19 For the purposes of deciding whether a function or activity has been performed improperly the test of what is expected is a test of what a reasonable person in the UK would expect in relation to the performance of that function or activity. Where the performance of the function or activity is not subject to UK law (for example, it takes place in a country outside UK jurisdiction) then any local custom or practice must be disregarded – unless permitted or required by the written law applicable to that particular country. Written law means any written constitution, provision made by or under legislation applicable to the country concerned or any judicial decision evidenced in published written sources.

20 By way of illustration, in order to proceed with a case under section 1 based on an allegation that hospitality was intended as a bribe, the prosecution would need to show that the hospitality was intended to induce conduct that amounts to a breach of an expectation that a person will act in good faith, impartially, or in accordance with a position of trust. This would be judged by what a reasonable person in the UK thought. So, for example, an invitation to foreign clients to attend a Six Nations match at Twickenham as part of a public relations exercise designed to cement good relations or enhance knowledge in the organisation's field is extremely unlikely to engage section 1 as there is unlikely to be evidence of an intention to induce improper performance of a relevant function.

Section 6: Bribery of a foreign public official

21 Section 6 creates a standalone offence of bribery of a foreign public official. The offence is committed where a person offers, promises or gives a financial or other advantage to a foreign public official with the intention of influencing the official in the performance of his or her official functions. The person offering, promising or giving the advantage must also intend to obtain or retain business or an advantage in the conduct of business by doing so. However, the offence is not committed where the official is permitted or required by the applicable written law to be influenced by the advantage.

22 A 'foreign public official' includes officials, whether elected or appointed, who hold a legislative, administrative or judicial position of any kind of a country or territory outside the UK. It also includes any person who performs public functions in any branch of the national, local or municipal government of such a country or territory or who exercises a public function for any public agency or public enterprise of such a country or territory, such as professionals working for public health agencies and officers exercising public functions in state-owned enterprises. Foreign public officials can also be an official or agent of a public international organisation, such as the UN or the World Bank.

23 Sections 1 and 6 may capture the same conduct but will do so in different ways. The policy that founds the offence at section 6 is the need to prohibit the influencing of decision making in the context of publicly funded business opportunities by the inducement of personal enrichment of foreign public officials or to others at the official's request, assent or acquiescence. Such activity is very likely to involve conduct which amounts to 'improper performance' of a relevant function or activity to which section 1 applies, but, unlike section 1, section 6 does not require proof of it or an intention to induce it. This is because the exact nature of the functions of persons regarded as foreign public officials is often very difficult to ascertain with any accuracy, and the securing of evidence will often be reliant on the co-operation of the state any such officials serve. To require the prosecution to rely entirely on section 1 would amount to a very significant deficiency in the ability of the legislation to address this particular mischief. That said, it is not the Government's intention to criminalise behaviour where no such mischief occurs, but merely to formulate the offence to take account of the evidential difficulties referred to above. In view of its wide scope, and its role in the new form of corporate liability at section 7, the Government offers the following further explanation of issues arising from the formulation of section 6.

Local law

24 For the purposes of section 6 prosecutors will be required to show not only that an 'advantage' was offered, promised or given to the official or to another person at the official's request, assent or acquiescence, but that the advantage was one that the official was not permitted or required to be influenced by as determined by the written law applicable to the foreign official.

25 In seeking tenders for publicly funded contracts Governments often permit or require those tendering for the contract to offer, in addition to the principal tender, some kind of additional investment in the local economy or benefit to the local community. Such arrangements could in certain circumstances amount to a financial or other 'advantage' to

a public official or to another person at the official's request, assent or acquiescence. Where, however, relevant 'written law' permits or requires the official to be influenced by such arrangements they will fall outside the scope of the offence. So, for example, where local planning law permits community investment or requires a foreign public official to minimise the cost of public procurement administration through cost sharing with contractors, a prospective contractor's offer of free training is very unlikely to engage section 6. In circumstances where the additional investment would amount to an advantage to a foreign public official and the local law is silent as to whether the official is permitted or required to be influenced by it, prosecutors will consider the public interest in prosecuting. This will provide an appropriate backstop in circumstances where the evidence suggests that the offer of additional investment is a legitimate part of a tender exercise.

Hospitality, promotional, and other business expenditure

26 Bona fide hospitality and promotional, or other business expenditure which seeks to improve the image of a commercial organisation, better to present products and services, or establish cordial relations, is recognised as an established and important part of doing business and it is not the intention of the Act to criminalise such behaviour. The Government does not intend for the Act to prohibit reasonable and proportionate hospitality and promotional or other similar business expenditure intended for these purposes. It is, however, clear that hospitality and promotional or other similar business expenditure can be employed as bribes.

27 In order to amount to a bribe under section 6 there must be an intention for a financial or other advantage to influence the official in his or her official role and thereby secure business or a business advantage. In this regard, it may be in some circumstances that hospitality or promotional expenditure in the form of travel and accommodation costs does not even amount to 'a financial or other advantage' to the relevant official because it is a cost that would otherwise be borne by the relevant foreign Government rather than the official him or herself.

28 Where the prosecution is able to establish a financial or other advantage has been offered, promised or given, it must then show that there is a sufficient connection between the advantage and the intention to influence and secure business or a business advantage. Where the prosecution cannot prove this to the requisite standard then no offence under section 6 will be committed. There may be direct evidence to support the existence of this connection and such evidence may indeed relate to relatively modest expenditure. In many cases, however, the question as to whether such a connection can be established will depend on the totality of the evidence which takes into account all of the surrounding circumstances.

It would include matters such as the type and level of advantage offered, the manner and form in which the advantage is provided, and the level of influence the particular foreign public official has over awarding the business. In this circumstantial context, the more lavish the hospitality or the higher the expenditure in relation to travel, accommodation or other similar business expenditure provided to a foreign public official, then, generally, the greater the inference that it is intended to influence the official to grant business or a business advantage in return.

29 The standards or norms applying in a particular sector may also be relevant here. However, simply providing hospitality or promotional, or other similar business expenditure which is commensurate with such norms is not, of itself, evidence that no bribe was paid if there is other evidence to the contrary; particularly if the norms in question are extravagant.

30 Levels of expenditure will not, therefore, be the only consideration in determining whether a section 6 offence has been committed. But in the absence of any further evidence demonstrating the required connection, it is unlikely, for example, that incidental provision of a routine business courtesy will raise the inference that it was intended to have a direct impact on decision making, particularly where such hospitality is commensurate with the reasonable and proportionate norms for the particular industry; e.g. the provision of airport to hotel transfer services to facilitate an on-site visit, or dining and tickets to an event.

31 Some further examples might be helpful. The provision by a UK mining company of reasonable travel and accommodation to allow foreign public officials to visit their distant mining operations so that those officials may be satisfied of the high standard and safety of the company's installations and operating systems are circumstances that fall outside the intended scope of the offence. Flights and accommodation to allow foreign public officials to meet with senior executives of a UK commercial organisation in New York as a matter of genuine mutual convenience, and some reasonable hospitality for the individual and his or her partner, such as fine dining and attendance at a baseball match are facts that are, in themselves, unlikely to raise the necessary inferences. However, if the choice of New York as the most convenient venue was in doubt because the organisation's senior executives could easily have seen the official with all the relevant documentation when they had visited the relevant country the previous week then the necessary inference might be raised. Similarly, supplementing information provided to a foreign public official on a commercial organisation's background, track record and expertise in providing private health care with an offer of ordinary travel and lodgings to enable a visit to a hospital run by the commercial organisation is unlikely to engage section 6. On the other hand, the provision by that same commercial organisation of a five-star holiday for the foreign public official which is unrelated to a demonstration of the organisation's

services is, all things being equal, far more likely to raise the necessary inference.

32 It may be that, as a result of the introduction of the section 7 offence, commercial organisations will review their policies on hospitality and promotional or other similar business expenditure as part of the selection and implementation of bribery prevention procedures, so as to ensure that they are seen to be acting both competitively and fairly. It is, however, for individual organisations, or business representative bodies, to establish and disseminate appropriate standards for hospitality and promotional or other similar expenditure.

Section 7: Failure of commercial organisations to prevent bribery

33 A commercial organisation will be liable to prosecution if a person associated with it bribes another person intending to obtain or retain business or an advantage in the conduct of business for that organisation. As set out above, the commercial organisation will have a full defence if it can show that despite a particular case of bribery it nevertheless had adequate procedures in place to prevent persons associated with it from bribing. In accordance with established case law, the standard of proof which the commercial organisation would need to discharge in order to prove the defence, in the event it was prosecuted, is the balance of probabilities.

Commercial organisation

34 Only a 'relevant commercial organisation' can commit an offence under section 7 of the Bribery Act. A 'relevant commercial organisation' is defined at section 7(5) as a body or partnership incorporated or formed in the UK irrespective of where it carries on a business, or an incorporated body or partnership which carries on a business or part of a business in the UK irrespective of the place of incorporation or formation. The key concept here is that of an organisation which 'carries on a business'. The courts will be the final arbiter as to whether an organisation 'carries on a business' in the UK taking into account the particular facts in individual cases. However, the following paragraphs set out the Government's intention as regards the application of the phrase.

35 As regards bodies incorporated, or partnerships formed, in the UK, despite the fact that there are many ways in which a body corporate or a partnership can pursue business objectives, the Government expects that whether such a body or partnership can be said to be carrying on a business will be answered by applying a common sense approach. So long as the organisation in question is incorporated (by whatever means), or is a partnership, it does not matter if it pursues primarily charitable or

educational aims or purely public functions. It will be caught if it engages in commercial activities, irrespective of the purpose for which profits are made.

36 As regards bodies incorporated, or partnerships formed, outside the United Kingdom, whether such bodies can properly be regarded as carrying on a business or part of a business 'in any part of the United Kingdom' will again be answered by applying a common sense approach. Where there is a particular dispute as to whether a business presence in the United Kingdom satisfies the test in the Act, the final arbiter, in any particular case, will be the courts as set out above. However, the Government anticipates that applying a common sense approach would mean that organisations that do not have a demonstrable business presence in the United Kingdom would not be caught. The Government would not expect, for example, the mere fact that a company's securities have been admitted to the UK Listing Authority's Official List and therefore admitted to trading on the London Stock Exchange, in itself, to qualify that company as carrying on a business or part of a business in the UK and therefore falling within the definition of a 'relevant commercial organisation' for the purposes of section 7. Likewise, having a UK subsidiary will not, in itself, mean that a parent company is carrying on a business in the UK, since a subsidiary may act independently of its parent or other group companies.

Associated person

37 A commercial organisation is liable under section 7 if a person 'associated' with it bribes another person intending to obtain or retain business or a business advantage for the organisation. A person associated with a commercial organisation is defined at section 8 as a person who 'performs services' for or on behalf of the organisation. This person can be an individual or an incorporated or unincorporated body. Section 8 provides that the capacity in which a person performs services for or on behalf of the organisation does not matter, so employees (who are presumed to be performing services for their employer), agents and subsidiaries are included. Section 8(4), however, makes it clear that the question as to whether a person is performing services for an organisation is to be determined by reference to all the relevant circumstances and not merely by reference to the nature of the relationship between that person and the organisation. The concept of a person who 'performs services for or on behalf of' the organisation is intended to give section 7 broad scope so as to embrace the whole range of persons connected to an organisation who might be capable of committing bribery on the organisation's behalf.

38 This broad scope means that contractors could be 'associated' persons to the extent that they are performing services for or on behalf of a commercial organisation. Also, where a supplier can properly be said to

be performing services for a commercial organisation rather than simply acting as the seller of goods, it may also be an 'associated' person.

39 Where a supply chain involves several entities or a project is to be performed by a prime contractor with a series of sub-contractors, an organisation is likely only to exercise control over its relationship with its contractual counterparty. Indeed, the organisation may only know the identity of its contractual counterparty. It is likely that persons who contract with that counterparty will be performing services for the counterparty and not for other persons in the contractual chain. The principal way in which commercial organisations may decide to approach bribery risks which arise as a result of a supply chain is by employing the types of anti-bribery procedures referred to elsewhere in this guidance (e.g. risk-based due diligence and the use of anti-bribery terms and conditions) in the relationship with their contractual counterparty, and by requesting that counterparty to adopt a similar approach with the next party in the chain.

40 As for joint ventures, these come in many different forms, sometimes operating through a separate legal entity, but at other times through contractual arrangements. In the case of a joint venture operating through a separate legal entity, a bribe paid by the joint venture entity may lead to liability for a member of the joint venture if the joint venture is performing services for the member and the bribe is paid with the intention of benefiting that member. However, the existence of a joint venture entity will not of itself mean that it is 'associated' with any of its members. A bribe paid on behalf of the joint venture entity by one of its employees or agents will therefore not trigger liability for members of the joint venture simply by virtue of them benefiting indirectly from the bribe through their investment in or ownership of the joint venture.

41 The situation will be different where the joint venture is conducted through a contractual arrangement. The degree of control that a participant has over that arrangement is likely to be one of the 'relevant circumstances' that would be taken into account in deciding whether a person who paid a bribe in the conduct of the joint venture business was 'performing services for or on behalf of' a participant in that arrangement. It may be, for example, that an employee of such a participant who has paid a bribe in order to benefit his employer is not to be regarded as a person 'associated' with all the other participants in the joint venture. Ordinarily, the employee of a participant will be presumed to be a person performing services for and on behalf of his employer. Likewise, an agent engaged by a participant in a contractual joint venture is likely to be regarded as a person associated with that participant in the absence of evidence that the agent is acting on behalf of the contractual joint venture as a whole.

42 Even if it can properly be said that an agent, a subsidiary, or another person acting for a member of a joint venture, was performing services for the

organisation, an offence will be committed only if that agent, subsidiary or person intended to obtain or retain business or an advantage in the conduct of business for the organisation. The fact that an organisation benefits indirectly from a bribe is very unlikely, in itself, to amount to proof of the specific intention required by the offence. Without proof of the required intention, liability will not accrue through simple corporate ownership or investment, or through the payment of dividends or provision of loans by a subsidiary to its parent. So, for example, a bribe on behalf of a subsidiary by one of its employees or agents will not automatically involve liability on the part of its parent company, or any other subsidiaries of the parent company, if it cannot be shown the employee or agent intended to obtain or retain business or a business advantage for the parent company or other subsidiaries. This is so even though the parent company or subsidiaries may benefit indirectly from the bribe. By the same token, liability for a parent company could arise where a subsidiary is the 'person' which pays a bribe which it intends will result in the parent company obtaining or retaining business or vice versa.

43 The question of adequacy of bribery prevention procedures will depend in the final analysis on the facts of each case, including matters such as the level of control over the activities of the associated person and the degree of risk that requires mitigation. The scope of the definition at section 8 needs to be appreciated within this context. This point is developed in more detail under the six principles set out on pages 20 to 31.

Facilitation payments

44 Small bribes paid to facilitate routine Government action – otherwise called 'facilitation payments' – could trigger either the section 6 offence or, where there is an intention to induce improper conduct, including where the acceptance of such payments is itself improper, the section 1 offence and therefore potential liability under section 7.

45 As was the case under the old law, the Bribery Act does not (unlike US foreign bribery law) provide any exemption for such payments. The 2009 Recommendation of the Organisation for Economic Co-operation and Development[5] recognises the corrosive effect of facilitation payments and asks adhering countries to discourage companies from making such payments. Exemptions in this context create artificial distinctions that are difficult to enforce, undermine corporate anti-bribery procedures, confuse anti-bribery communication with employees and other associated persons, perpetuate an existing 'culture' of bribery and have the potential to be abused.

5 Recommendation of the Council for Further Combating Bribery of Foreign Public Officials in International Business Transactions.

46 The Government does, however, recognise the problems that commercial organisations face in some parts of the world and in certain sectors. The eradication of facilitation payments is recognised at the national and international level as a long term objective that will require economic and social progress and sustained commitment to the rule of law in those parts of the world where the problem is most prevalent. It will also require collaboration between international bodies, governments, the anti-bribery lobby, business representative bodies and sectoral organisations. Businesses themselves also have a role to play and the guidance below offers an indication of how the problem may be addressed through the selection of bribery prevention procedures by commercial organisations.

47 Issues relating to the prosecution of facilitation payments in England and Wales are referred to in the guidance of the Director of the Serious Fraud Office and the Director of Public Prosecutions.[6]

Duress

48 It is recognised that there are circumstances in which individuals are left with no alternative but to make payments in order to protect against loss of life, limb or liberty. The common law defence of duress is very likely to be available in such circumstances.

Prosecutorial discretion

49 Whether to prosecute an offence under the Act is a matter for the prosecuting authorities. In deciding whether to proceed, prosecutors must first decide if there is a sufficiency of evidence, and, if so, whether a prosecution is in the public interest. If the evidential test has been met, prosecutors will consider the general public interest in ensuring that bribery is effectively dealt with. The more serious the offence, the more likely it is that a prosecution will be required in the public interest.

50 In cases where hospitality, promotional expenditure or facilitation payments do, on their face, trigger the provisions of the Act prosecutors will consider very carefully what is in the public interest before deciding whether to prosecute. The operation of prosecutorial discretion provides a degree of flexibility which is helpful to ensure the just and fair operation of the Act.

51 Factors that weigh for and against the public interest in prosecuting in England and Wales are referred to in the joint guidance of the Director of the Serious Fraud Office and the Director of Public Prosecutions referred to at paragraph 47.

6 Bribery Act 2010: Joint Prosecution Guidance of the Director of the Serious Fraud Office and the Director of Public Prosecutions.

The six principles

The Government considers that procedures put in place by commercial organisations wishing to prevent bribery being committed on their behalf should be informed by six principles. These are set out below. Commentary and guidance on what procedures the application of the principles may produce accompanies each principle.

These principles are not prescriptive. They are intended to be flexible and outcome focussed, allowing for the huge variety of circumstances that commercial organisations find themselves in. Small organisations will, for example, face different challenges to those faced by large multi-national enterprises. Accordingly, the detail of how organisations might apply these principles, taken as a whole, will vary, but the outcome should always be robust and effective anti-bribery procedures.

As set out in more detail below, bribery prevention procedures should be proportionate to risk. Although commercial organisations with entirely domestic operations may require bribery prevention procedures, we believe that as a general proposition they will face lower risks of bribery on their behalf by associated persons than the risks that operate in foreign markets. In any event procedures put in place to mitigate domestic bribery risks are likely to be similar if not the same as those designed to mitigate those associated with foreign markets.

A series of case studies based on hypothetical scenarios is provided at Appendix A. These are designed to illustrate the application of the principles for small, medium and large organisations.

Principle 1

Proportionate procedures

A commercial organisation's procedures to prevent bribery by persons associated with it are proportionate to the bribery risks it faces and to the nature, scale and complexity of the commercial organisation's activities. They are also clear, practical, accessible, effectively implemented and enforced.

Commentary

1.1 The term 'procedures' is used in this guidance to embrace both bribery prevention policies and the procedures which implement them. Policies articulate a commercial organisation's anti-bribery stance, show how it will be maintained and help to create an anti-bribery culture. They are therefore a necessary measure in the prevention of bribery, but they will not achieve that objective unless they are properly implemented. Further guidance on implementation is provided through principles 2 to 6.

1.2 Adequate bribery prevention procedures ought to be proportionate to the bribery risks that the organisation faces. An initial assessment of risk across the organisation is therefore a necessary first step. To a certain extent the level of risk will be linked to the size of the organisation and the nature and complexity of its business, but size will not be the only determining factor. Some small organisations can face quite significant risks, and will need more extensive procedures than their counterparts facing limited risks. However, small organisations are unlikely to need procedures that are as extensive as those of a large multi-national organisation. For example, a very small business may be able to rely heavily on periodic oral briefings to communicate its policies while a large one may need to rely on extensive written communication.

1.3 The level of risk that organisations face will also vary with the type and nature of the persons associated with it. For example, a commercial organisation that properly assesses that there is no risk of bribery on the part of one of its associated persons will accordingly require nothing in the way of procedures to prevent bribery in the context of that relationship. By the same token the bribery risks associated with reliance on a third party agent representing a commercial organisation in negotiations with foreign public officials may be assessed as significant and accordingly require much more in the way of procedures to mitigate those risks. Organisations are likely to need to select procedures to cover a broad range of risks but any consideration by a court in an individual case of the adequacy of procedures is likely necessarily to focus on those procedures designed to prevent bribery on the part of the associated person committing the offence in question.

1.4 Bribery prevention procedures may be stand alone or form part of wider guidance, for example on recruitment or on managing a tender process in public procurement. Whatever the chosen model, the procedures should seek to ensure there is a practical and realistic means of achieving the organisation's stated anti-bribery policy objectives across all of the organisation's functions.

1.5 The Government recognises that applying these procedures retrospectively to existing associated persons is more difficult, but this should be done over time, adopting a risk-based approach and with due allowance for what is practicable and the level of control over existing arrangements.

Procedures

1.6 Commercial organisations' bribery prevention policies are likely to include certain common elements. As an indicative and not exhaustive list, an organisation may wish to cover in its policies:

- its commitment to bribery prevention (see Principle 2)

- its general approach to mitigation of specific bribery risks, such as those arising from the conduct of intermediaries and agents, or those associated with hospitality and promotional expenditure, facilitation payments or political and charitable donations or contributions; (see Principle 3 on risk assessment)
- an overview of its strategy to implement its bribery prevention policies.

1.7 The procedures put in place to implement an organisation's bribery prevention policies should be designed to mitigate identified risks as well as to prevent deliberate unethical conduct on the part of associated persons. The following is an indicative and not exhaustive list of the topics that bribery prevention procedures might embrace depending on the particular risks faced:

- The involvement of the organisation's top-level management (see Principle 2).
- Risk assessment procedures (see Principle 3).
- Due diligence of existing or prospective associated persons (see Principle 4).
- The provision of gifts, hospitality and promotional expenditure; charitable and political donations; or demands for facilitation payments.
- Direct and indirect employment, including recruitment, terms and conditions, disciplinary action and remuneration.
- Governance of business relationships with all other associated persons including pre and post contractual agreements.
- Financial and commercial controls such as adequate bookkeeping, auditing and approval of expenditure.
- Transparency of transactions and disclosure of information.
- Decision making, such as delegation of authority procedures, separation of functions and the avoidance of conflicts of interest.
- Enforcement, detailing discipline processes and sanctions for breaches of the organisation's anti-bribery rules.
- The reporting of bribery including 'speak up' or 'whistle blowing' procedures.
- The detail of the process by which the organisation plans to implement its bribery prevention procedures, for example, how its policy will be applied to individual projects and to different parts of the organisation.

- The communication of the organisation's policies and procedures, and training in their application (see Principle 5).
- The monitoring, review and evaluation of bribery prevention procedures (see Principle 6).

Principle 2

Top-level commitment

The top-level management of a commercial organisation (be it a board of directors, the owners or any other equivalent body or person) are committed to preventing bribery by persons associated with it. They foster a culture within the organisation in which bribery is never acceptable.

Commentary

2.1 Those at the top of an organisation are in the best position to foster a culture of integrity where bribery is unacceptable. The purpose of this principle is to encourage the involvement of top-level management in the determination of bribery prevention procedures. It is also to encourage top-level involvement in any key decision making relating to bribery risk where that is appropriate for the organisation's management structure.

Procedures

2.2 Whatever the size, structure or market of a commercial organisation, top-level management commitment to bribery prevention is likely to include (1) communication of the organisation's anti-bribery stance, and (2) an appropriate degree of involvement in developing bribery prevention procedures.

Internal and external communication of the commitment to zero tolerance to bribery

2.3 This could take a variety of forms. A formal statement appropriately communicated can be very effective in establishing an anti-bribery culture within an organisation. Communication might be tailored to different audiences. The statement would probably need to be drawn to people's attention on a periodic basis and could be generally available, for example on an organisation's intranet and/or internet site. Effective formal statements that demonstrate top level commitment are likely to include:

- a commitment to carry out business fairly, honestly and openly
- a commitment to zero tolerance towards bribery

- the consequences of breaching the policy for employees and managers
- for other associated persons the consequences of breaching contractual provisions relating to bribery prevention (this could include a reference to avoiding doing business with others who do not commit to doing business without bribery as a 'best practice' objective)
- articulation of the business benefits of rejecting bribery (reputational, customer and business partner confidence)
- reference to the range of bribery prevention procedures the commercial organisation has or is putting in place, including any protection and procedures for confidential reporting of bribery (whistle-blowing)
- key individuals and departments involved in the development and implementation of the organisation's bribery prevention procedures
- reference to the organisation's involvement in any collective action against bribery in, for example, the same business sector.

Top-level involvement in bribery prevention

2.4 Effective leadership in bribery prevention will take a variety of forms appropriate for and proportionate to the organisation's size, management structure and circumstances. In smaller organisations a proportionate response may require top-level managers to be personally involved in initiating, developing and implementing bribery prevention procedures and bribery critical decision making. In a large multi-national organisation the board should be responsible for setting bribery prevention policies, tasking management to design, operate and monitor bribery prevention procedures, and keeping these policies and procedures under regular review. But whatever the appropriate model, top-level engagement is likely to reflect the following elements:

- Engagement with relevant associated persons and external bodies, such as sectoral organisations and the media, to help articulate the organisation's policies.
- Specific involvement in high profile and critical decision making where appropriate.
- Assurance of risk assessment.
- General oversight of breaches of procedures and the provision of feedback to the board or equivalent, where appropriate, on levels of compliance.

- Selection and training of senior managers to lead anti-bribery work where appropriate.
- Leadership on key measures such as a code of conduct.
- Endorsement of all bribery prevention related publications.
- Leadership in awareness raising and encouraging transparent dialogue throughout the organisation so as to seek to ensure effective dissemination of anti-bribery policies and procedures to employees, subsidiaries, and associated persons, etc.

Principle 3

Risk Assessment

The commercial organisation assesses the nature and extent of its exposure to potential external and internal risks of bribery on its behalf by persons associated with it. The assessment is periodic, informed and documented.

Commentary

3.1 For many commercial organisations this principle will manifest itself as part of a more general risk assessment carried out in relation to business objectives. For others, its application may produce a more specific stand alone bribery risk assessment. The purpose of this principle is to promote the adoption of risk assessment procedures that are proportionate to the organisation's size and structure and to the nature, scale and location of its activities. But whatever approach is adopted the fuller the understanding of the bribery risks an organisation faces the more effective its efforts to prevent bribery are likely to be.

3.2 Some aspects of risk assessment involve procedures that fall within the generally accepted meaning of the term 'due diligence'. The role of due diligence as a risk mitigation tool is separately dealt with under Principle 4.

Procedures

3.3 Risk assessment procedures that enable the commercial organisation accurately to identify and prioritise the risks it faces will, whatever its size, activities, customers or markets, usually reflect a few basic characteristics. These are:

- Oversight of the risk assessment by top level management.
- Appropriate resourcing – this should reflect the scale of the organisation's business and the need to identify and prioritise all relevant risks.

- Identification of the internal and external information sources that will enable risk to be assessed and reviewed.
- Due diligence enquiries (see Principle 4).
- Accurate and appropriate documentation of the risk assessment and its conclusions.

3.4 As a commercial organisation's business evolves, so will the bribery risks it faces and hence so should its risk assessment. For example, the risk assessment that applies to a commercial organisation's domestic operations might not apply when it enters a new market in a part of the world in which it has not done business before (see Principle 6 for more on this).

Commonly encountered risks

3.5 Commonly encountered external risks can be categorised into five broad groups – country, sectoral, transaction, business opportunity and business partnership:

- *Country risk:* this is evidenced by perceived high levels of corruption, an absence of effectively implemented anti-bribery legislation and a failure of the foreign government, media, local business community and civil society effectively to promote transparent procurement and investment policies.
- *Sectoral risk:* some sectors are higher risk than others. Higher risk sectors include the extractive industries and the large scale infrastructure sector.
- *Transaction risk:* certain types of transaction give rise to higher risks, for example, charitable or political contributions, licences and permits, and transactions relating to public procurement.
- *Business opportunity risk:* such risks might arise in high value projects or with projects involving many contractors or intermediaries; or with projects which are not apparently undertaken at market prices, or which do not have a clear legitimate objective.
- *Business partnership risk:* certain relationships may involve higher risk, for example, the use of intermediaries in transactions with foreign public officials; consortia or joint venture partners; and relationships with politically exposed persons where the proposed business relationship involves, or is linked to, a prominent public official.

3.6 An assessment of external bribery risks is intended to help decide how those risks can be mitigated by procedures governing the relevant operations or business relationships; but a bribery risk assessment should also examine the extent to which internal structures or procedures may themselves add to the level of risk. Commonly encountered internal factors may include:

- deficiencies in employee training, skills and knowledge
- bonus culture that rewards excessive risk taking
- lack of clarity in the organisation's policies on, and procedures for, hospitality and promotional expenditure, and political or charitable contributions
- lack of clear financial controls
- lack of a clear anti-bribery message from the top-level management.

Principle 4

Due diligence

The commercial organisation applies due diligence procedures, taking a proportionate and risk based approach, in respect of persons who perform or will perform services for or on behalf of the organisation, in order to mitigate identified bribery risks.

Commentary

4.1 Due diligence is firmly established as an element of corporate good governance and it is envisaged that due diligence related to bribery prevention will often form part of a wider due diligence framework. Due diligence procedures are both a form of bribery risk assessment (see Principle 3) and a means of mitigating a risk. By way of illustration, a commercial organisation may identify risks that as a general proposition attach to doing business in reliance upon local third party intermediaries. Due diligence of specific prospective third party intermediaries could significantly mitigate these risks. The significance of the role of due diligence in bribery risk mitigation justifies its inclusion here as a Principle in its own right.

4.2 The purpose of this Principle is to encourage commercial organisations to put in place due diligence procedures that adequately inform the application of proportionate measures designed to prevent persons associated with them from bribing on their behalf.

Procedures

4.3 As this guidance emphasises throughout, due diligence procedures should be proportionate to the identified risk.

They can also be undertaken internally or by external consultants. A person 'associated' with a commercial organisation as set out at section 8 of the Bribery Act includes any person performing services for a commercial organisation. As explained at paragraphs 37 to 43 in the section 'Government Policy and section 7', the scope of this definition is broad and can embrace a wide range of business relationships. But the appropriate level of due diligence to prevent bribery will vary enormously depending on the risks arising from the particular relationship. So, for example, the appropriate level of due diligence required by a commercial organisation when contracting for the performance of information technology services may be low, to reflect low risks of bribery on its behalf. In contrast, an organisation that is selecting an intermediary to assist in establishing a business in foreign markets will typically require a much higher level of due diligence to mitigate the risks of bribery on its behalf.

4.4 Organisations will need to take considerable care in entering into certain business relationships, due to the particular circumstances in which the relationships come into existence. An example is where local law or convention dictates the use of local agents in circumstances where it may be difficult for a commercial organisation to extricate itself from a business relationship once established. The importance of thorough due diligence and risk mitigation prior to any commitment are paramount in such circumstances. Another relationship that carries particularly important due diligence implications is a merger of commercial organisations or an acquisition of one by another.

4.5 'Due diligence' for the purposes of Principle 4 should be conducted using a risk-based approach (as referred to on page 27). For example, in lower risk situations, commercial organisations may decide that there is no need to conduct much in the way of due diligence. In higher risk situations, due diligence may include conducting direct interrogative enquiries, indirect investigations, or general research on proposed associated persons. Appraisal and continued monitoring of recruited or engaged 'associated' persons may also be required, proportionate to the identified risks. Generally, more information is likely to be required from prospective and existing associated persons that are incorporated (e.g. companies) than from individuals. This is because on a basic level more individuals are likely to be involved in the performance of services by a company and the exact nature of the roles of such individuals or other connected bodies may not be immediately obvious. Accordingly, due diligence may involve direct requests for details on the background, expertise and business experience, of relevant individuals. This information can then be verified through research and the following up of references, etc.

4.6 A commercial organisation's employees are presumed to be persons 'associated' with the organisation for the purposes of the Bribery Act.

The organisation may wish, therefore, to incorporate in its recruitment and human resources procedures an appropriate level of due diligence to mitigate the risks of bribery being undertaken by employees which is proportionate to the risk associated with the post in question. Due diligence is unlikely to be needed in relation to lower risk posts.

Principle 5

Communication (including training)

The commercial organisation seeks to ensure that its bribery prevention policies and procedures are embedded and understood throughout the organisation through internal and external communication, including training, that is proportionate to the risks it faces.

Commentary

5.1 Communication and training deters bribery by associated persons by enhancing awareness and understanding of a commercial organisation's procedures and to the organisation's commitment to their proper application. Making information available assists in more effective monitoring, evaluation and review of bribery prevention procedures. Training provides the knowledge and skills needed to employ the organisation's procedures and deal with any bribery related problems or issues that may arise.

Procedures

Communication

5.2 The content, language and tone of communications for internal consumption may vary from that for external use in response to the different relationship the audience has with the commercial organisation. The nature of communication will vary enormously between commercial organisations in accordance with the different bribery risks faced, the size of the organisation and the scale and nature of its activities.

5.3 Internal communications should convey the 'tone from the top' but are also likely to focus on the implementation of the organisation's policies and procedures and the implications for employees.

Such communication includes policies on particular areas such as decision making, financial control, hospitality and promotional expenditure, facilitation payments, training, charitable and political donations and penalties for breach of rules and the articulation of management roles at different levels. Another important aspect of internal communications is the establishment of a secure, confidential and accessible means for internal or external parties to raise concerns about bribery on the part of associated persons, to provide suggestions for improvement of bribery prevention procedures and controls and for requesting advice. These so called 'speak up' procedures can amount to a very helpful management tool for commercial organisations with diverse operations that may be in many countries. If these procedures are to be effective there must be adequate protection for those reporting concerns.

5.4 External communication of bribery prevention policies through a statement or codes of conduct, for example, can reassure existing and prospective associated persons and can act as a deterrent to those intending to bribe on a commercial organisation's behalf. Such communications can include information on bribery prevention procedures and controls, sanctions, results of internal surveys, rules governing recruitment, procurement and tendering. A commercial organisation may consider it proportionate and appropriate to communicate its anti-bribery policies and commitment to them to a wider audience, such as other organisations in its sector and to sectoral organisations that would fall outside the scope of the range of its associated persons, or to the general public.

Training

5.5 Like all procedures training should be proportionate to risk but some training is likely to be effective in firmly establishing an anti-bribery culture whatever the level of risk. Training may take the form of education and awareness raising about the threats posed by bribery in general and in the sector or areas in which the organisation operates in particular, and the various ways it is being addressed.

5.6 General training could be mandatory for new employees or for agents (on a weighted risk basis) as part of an induction process, but it should also be tailored to the specific risks associated with specific posts. Consideration should also be given to tailoring training to the special needs of those involved in any 'speak up' procedures, and higher risk functions such as purchasing, contracting, distribution and marketing, and working in high risk countries. Effective training is continuous, and regularly monitored and evaluated.

5.7 It may be appropriate to require associated persons to undergo training. This will be particularly relevant for high risk associated persons. In any event, organisations may wish to encourage associated persons to adopt bribery prevention training.

5.8 Nowadays there are many different training formats available in addition to the traditional classroom or seminar formats, such as e-learning and other web-based tools. But whatever the format, the training ought to achieve its objective of ensuring that those participating in it develop a firm understanding of what the relevant policies and procedures mean in practice for them.

Principle 6

Monitoring and review

The commercial organisation monitors and reviews procedures designed to prevent bribery by persons associated with it and makes improvements where necessary.

Commentary

6.1 The bribery risks that a commercial organisation faces may change over time, as may the nature and scale of its activities, so the procedures required to mitigate those risks are also likely to change. Commercial organisations will therefore wish to consider how to monitor and evaluate the effectiveness of their bribery prevention procedures and adapt them where necessary. In addition to regular monitoring, an organisation might want to review its processes in response to other stimuli, for example governmental changes in countries in which they operate, an incident of bribery or negative press reports.

Procedures

6.2 There is a wide range of internal and external review mechanisms which commercial organisations could consider using. Systems set up to deter, detect and investigate bribery, and monitor the ethical quality of transactions, such as internal financial control mechanisms, will help provide insight into the effectiveness of procedures designed to prevent bribery. Staff surveys, questionnaires and feedback from training can also provide an important source of information on effectiveness and a means by which employees and other associated persons can inform continuing improvement of anti-bribery policies.

6.3 Organisations could also consider formal periodic reviews and reports for top-level management. Organisations could also draw on information on other organisations' practices, for example relevant trade bodies or regulators might highlight examples of good or bad practice in their publications.

6.4 In addition, organisations might wish to consider seeking some form of external verification or assurance of the effectiveness of anti-bribery procedures. Some organisations may be able to apply for certified compliance with one of the independently-verified anti-bribery standards maintained by industrial sector associations or multilateral bodies. However, such certification may not necessarily mean that a commercial organisation's bribery prevention procedures are 'adequate' for all purposes where an offence under section 7 of the Bribery Act could be charged.

Appendix A
Bribery Act 2010 case studies

Introduction

These case studies (which do not form part of the guidance issued under section 9 of the Act) look at how the application of the six principles might relate to a number of hypothetical scenarios commercial organisations may encounter. The Government believes that this illustrative context can assist commercial organisations in deciding what procedures to prevent persons associated with them from bribing on their behalf might be most suitable to their needs.

These case studies are illustrative. They are intended to complement the guidance. They do not replace or supersede any of the principles. The considerations set out below merely show in some circumstances how the principles can be applied, and should not be seen as standard setting, establishing any presumption, reflecting a minimum baseline of action or being appropriate for all organisations whatever their size. Accordingly, the considerations set out below are not:

- comprehensive of all considerations in all circumstances
- conclusive of adequate procedures
- conclusive of inadequate procedures if not all of the considerations are considered and/or applied.

All but one of these case studies focus on bribery risks associated with foreign markets. This is because bribery risks associated with foreign markets are generally higher than those associated with domestic markets. Accordingly case studies focussing on foreign markets are better suited as vehicles for the illustration of bribery prevention procedures.

Case study 1 – Principle 1

Facilitation payments

A medium sized company ('A') has acquired a new customer in a foreign country ('B') where it operates through its agent company ('C'). Its bribery risk assessment has identified facilitation payments as a significant problem in securing reliable importation into B and transport to its new customer's manufacturing locations. These sometimes take the form of 'inspection fees' required before B's import inspectors will issue a certificate of inspection and thereby facilitate the clearance of goods.

A could consider any or a combination of the following:

- Communication of its policy of non-payment of facilitation payments to C and its staff.

- Seeking advice on the law of B relating to certificates of inspection and fees for these to differentiate between properly payable fees and disguised requests for facilitation payments.
- Building realistic timescales into the planning of the project so that shipping, importation and delivery schedules allow where feasible for resisting and testing demands for facilitation payments.
- Requesting that C train its staff about resisting demands for facilitation payments and the relevant local law and provisions of the Bribery Act 2010.
- Proposing or including as part of any contractual arrangement certain procedures for C and its staff, which may include one or more of the following, if appropriate:
  - questioning of legitimacy of demands
  - requesting receipts and identification details of the official making the demand
  - requests to consult with superior officials
  - trying to avoid paying 'inspection fees' (if not properly due) in cash and directly to an official
  - informing those demanding payments that compliance with the demand may mean that A (and possibly C) will commit an offence under UK law
  - informing those demanding payments that it will be necessary for C to inform the UK embassy of the demand.
- Maintaining close liaison with C so as to keep abreast of any local developments that may provide solutions and encouraging C to develop its own strategies based on local knowledge.
- Use of any UK diplomatic channels or participation in locally active non-governmental organisations, so as to apply pressure on the authorities of B to take action to stop demands for facilitation payments.

Case study 2 – Principle 1

Proportionate Procedures

A small to medium sized installation company is operating entirely within the United Kingdom domestic market. It relies to varying degrees on independent consultants to facilitate business opportunities and to assist in the preparation of both pre-qualification submissions and formal tenders in seeking new business. Such consultants work on an arms-length-fee-plus-expenses basis. They are engaged by sales staff and selected because of their extensive network of business contacts and the specialist information they have. The reason for engaging them is to enhance the company's prospects of being included in tender and pre-qualification lists and of being selected as main or sub-contractors. The reliance on consultants and, in particular, difficulties in monitoring expenditure which sometimes involves cash transactions has been identified by the company as a source of medium to high risk of bribery being undertaken on the company's behalf.

In seeking to mitigate these risks the company could consider any or a combination of the following:

- Communication of a policy statement committing it to transparency and zero tolerance of bribery in pursuit of its business objectives. The statement could be communicated to the company's employees, known consultants and external contacts, such as sectoral bodies and local chambers of commerce.
- Firming up its due diligence before engaging consultants. This could include making enquiries through business contacts, local chambers of commerce, business associations, or internet searches and following up any business references and financial statements.
- Considering firming up the terms of the consultants' contracts so that they reflect a commitment to zero tolerance of bribery, set clear criteria for provision of bona fide hospitality on the company's behalf and define in detail the basis of remuneration, including expenses.
- Consider making consultants' contracts subject to periodic review and renewal.
- Drawing up key points guidance on preventing bribery for its sales staff and all other staff involved in bidding for business and when engaging consultants
- Periodically emphasising these policies and procedures at meetings – for example, this might form a standing item on meeting agendas every few months.
- Providing a confidential means for staff and external business contacts to air any suspicions of the use of bribery on the company's behalf.

Case study 3 – Principles 1 and 6

Joint venture

A medium sized company ('D') is interested in significant foreign mineral deposits. D proposes to enter into a joint venture with a local mining company ('E'). It is proposed that D and E would have an equal holding in the joint venture company ('DE'). D identifies the necessary interaction between DE and local public officials as a source of significant risks of bribery.

D could consider negotiating for the inclusion of any or a combination of the following bribery prevention procedures into the agreement setting up DE:

- Parity of representation on the board of DE.
- That DE put in place measures designed to ensure compliance with all applicable bribery and corruption laws. These measures might cover such issues as:
  - gifts and hospitality
  - agreed decision making rules
  - procurement
  - engagement of third parties, including due diligence requirements
  - conduct of relations with public officials
  - training for staff in high risk positions
  - record keeping and accounting.
- The establishment of an audit committee with at least one representative of each of D and E that has the power to view accounts and certain expenditure and prepare regular reports.
- Binding commitments by D and E to comply with all applicable bribery laws in relation to the operation of DE, with a breach by either D or E being a breach of the agreement between them. Where such a breach is a material breach this could lead to termination or other similarly significant consequences.

Case study 4 – Principles 1 and 5

Hospitality and Promotional expenditure

A firm of engineers ('F') maintains a programme of annual events providing entertainment, quality dining and attendance at various sporting occasions, as an expression of appreciation of its long association with its business partners. Private bodies and individuals are happy to meet their own travel and accommodation costs associated with attending these events. The costs of the travel and accommodation of any foreign public officials attending are, however, met by F.

F could consider any or a combination of the following:

- Conducting a bribery risk assessment relating to its dealings with business partners and foreign public officials and in particular the provision of hospitality and promotional expenditure.

- Publication of a policy statement committing it to transparent, proportionate, reasonable and bona fide hospitality and promotional expenditure.
- The issue of internal guidance on procedures that apply to the provision of hospitality and/or promotional expenditure providing:
  - that any procedures are designed to seek to ensure transparency and conformity with any relevant laws and codes applying to F
  - that any procedures are designed to seek to ensure transparency and conformity with the relevant laws and codes applying to foreign public officials
  - that any hospitality should reflect a desire to cement good relations and show appreciation, and that promotional expenditure should seek to improve the image of F as a commercial organisation, to better present its products or services, or establish cordial relations
  - that the recipient should not be given the impression that they are under an obligation to confer any business advantage or that the recipient's independence will be affected
  - criteria to be applied when deciding the appropriate levels of hospitality for both private and public business partners, clients, suppliers and foreign public officials and the type of hospitality that is appropriate in different sets of circumstances
  - that provision of hospitality for public officials be cleared with the relevant public body so that it is clear who and what the hospitality is for
  - for expenditure over certain limits, approval by an appropriately senior level of management may be a relevant consideration
  - accounting (book-keeping, orders, invoices, delivery notes, etc).
- Regular monitoring, review and evaluation of internal procedures and compliance with them.
- Appropriate training and supervision provided to staff.

Case study 5 – Principle 3

Assessing risks

A small specialist manufacturer is seeking to expand its business in one of several emerging markets, all of which offer comparable opportunities. It has no specialist risk assessment expertise and is unsure how to go about assessing the risks of entering a new market.

The small manufacturer could consider any or a combination of the following:

- Incorporating an assessment of bribery risk into research to identify the optimum market for expansion.
- Seeking advice from UK diplomatic services and government organisations such as UK Trade and Investment.
- Consulting general country assessments undertaken by local chambers of commerce, relevant non-governmental organisations and sectoral organisations.
- Seeking advice from industry representatives.
- Following up any general or specialist advice with further independent research.

Case study 6 – Principle 4

Due diligence of agents

A medium to large sized manufacturer of specialist equipment ('G') has an opportunity to enter an emerging market in a foreign country ('H') by way of a government contract to supply equipment to the state. Local convention requires any foreign commercial organisations to operate through a local agent. G is concerned to appoint a reputable agent and ensure that the risk of bribery being used to develop its business in the market is minimised.

G could consider any or a combination of the following:

- Compiling a suitable questionnaire for potential agents requiring for example, details of ownership if not an individual; CVs and references for those involved in performing the proposed service; details of any directorships held, existing partnerships and third party relationships and any relevant judicial or regulatory findings.
- Having a clear statement of the precise nature of the services offered, costs, commissions, fees and the preferred means of remuneration.
- Undertaking research, including internet searches, of the prospective agents and, if a corporate body, of every person identified as having a degree of control over its affairs.
- Making enquiries with the relevant authorities in H to verify the information received in response to the questionnaire.
- Following up references and clarifying any matters arising from the questionnaire or any other information received with the agents, arranging face to face meetings where appropriate.
- Requesting sight or evidence of any potential agent's own anti-bribery policies and, where a corporate body, reporting procedures and records.
- Being alert to key commercial questions such as:

  - Is the agent really required?
  - Does the agent have the required expertise?
  - Are they interacting with or closely connected to public officials?
  - Is what you are proposing to pay reasonable and commercial?
- Renewing due diligence enquiries on a periodic basis if an agent is appointed.

Case study 7 – Principle 5

Communicating and training

A small UK manufacturer of specialist equipment ('J') has engaged an individual as a local agent and adviser ('K') to assist with winning a contract and developing its business in a foreign country where the risk of bribery is assessed as high.

J could consider any or a combination of the following:

- Making employees of J engaged in bidding for business fully aware of J's anti-bribery statement, code of conduct and, where appropriate, that details of its anti-bribery policies are included in its tender.
- Including suitable contractual terms on bribery prevention measures in the agreement between J and K, for example: requiring K not to offer or pay bribes; giving J the ability to audit K's activities and expenditure; requiring K to report any requests for bribes by officials to J; and, in the event of suspicion arising as to K's activities, giving J the right to terminate the arrangement.
- Making employees of J fully aware of policies and procedures applying to relevant issues such as hospitality and facilitation payments, including all financial control mechanisms, sanctions for any breaches of the rules and instructions on how to report any suspicious conduct.
- Supplementing the information, where appropriate, with specially prepared training to J's staff involved with the foreign country.

Case study 8 – Principle 1, 4 and 6

Community benefits and charitable donations

A company ('L') exports a range of seed products to growers around the globe. Its representative travels to a foreign country ('M') to discuss with a local farming co-operative the possible supply of a new strain of wheat that is resistant to a disease which recently swept the region. In the meeting, the head of the co-operative tells L's representative about the problems which the relative unavailability of antiretroviral drugs cause locally in the face of a high HIV infection rate.

In a subsequent meeting with an official of M to discuss the approval of L's new wheat strain for import, the official suggests that L could pay for the necessary antiretroviral drugs and that this will be a very positive factor in the Government's consideration of the licence

to import the new seed strain. In a further meeting, the same official states that L should donate money to a certain charity suggested by the official which, the official assures, will then take the necessary steps to purchase and distribute the drugs. L identifies this as raising potential bribery risks.

L could consider any or a combination of the following:

- Making reasonable efforts to conduct due diligence, including consultation with staff members and any business partners it has in country M in order to satisfy itself that the suggested arrangement is legitimate and in conformity with any relevant laws and codes applying to the foreign public official responsible for approving the product. It could do this by obtaining information on:
  - M's local law on community benefits as part of Government procurement and, if no particular local law, the official status and legitimacy of the suggested arrangement
  - the particular charity in question including its legal status, its reputation in M, and whether it has conducted similar projects, and
  - any connections the charity might have with the foreign official in question, if possible.
- Adopting an internal communication plan designed to ensure that any relationships with charitable organisations are conducted in a transparent and open manner and do not raise any expectation of the award of a contract or licence.
- Adopting company-wide policies and procedures about the selection of charitable projects or initiatives which are informed by appropriate risk assessments.
- Training and support for staff in implementing the relevant policies and procedures of communication which allow issues to be reported and compliance to be monitored.
- If charitable donations made in country M are routinely channelled through government officials or to others at the official's request, a red flag should be raised and L may seek to monitor the way its contributions are ultimately applied, or investigate alternative methods of donation such as official 'off-set' or 'community gain' arrangements with the government of M.
- Evaluation of its policies relating to charitable donations as part of its next periodic review of its anti-bribery procedures.

Case study 9 – Principle 4

Due diligence of agents

A small UK company ('N') relies on agents in country ('P') from which it imports local high quality perishable produce and to which it exports finished goods. The bribery risks it faces arise entirely as a result of its reliance on agents and their relationship with local businessmen and officials. N is offered a new business opportunity in P through a new agent ('Q'). An agreement with Q needs to be concluded quickly.

N could consider any or a combination of the following:

- Conducting due diligence and background checks on Q that are proportionate to the risk before engaging Q; which could include:
  - making enquiries through N's business contacts, local chambers of commerce or business associations, or internet searches
  - seeking business references and a financial statement from Q and reviewing Q's CV to ensure Q has suitable experience.
- Considering how best to structure the relationship with Q, including how Q should be remunerated for its services and how to seek to ensure Q's compliance with relevant laws and codes applying to foreign public officials.
- Making the contract with Q renewable annually or periodically.
- Travelling to P periodically to review the agency situation.

Case study 10 – Principle 2

Top level commitment

A small to medium sized component manufacturer is seeking contracts in markets abroad where there is a risk of bribery. As part of its preparation, a senior manager has devoted some time to participation in the development of a sector wide anti-bribery initiative.

The top level management of the manufacturer could consider any or a combination of the following:

- The making of a clear statement disseminated to its staff and key business partners of its commitment to carry out business fairly, honestly and openly, referencing its key bribery prevention procedures and its involvement in the sectoral initiative.
- Establishing a code of conduct that includes suitable anti-bribery provisions and making it accessible to staff and third parties on its website.

- Considering an internal launch of a code of conduct, with a message of commitment to it from senior management.
- Senior management emphasising among the workforce and other associated persons the importance of understanding and applying the code of conduct and the consequences of breaching the policy or contractual provisions relating to bribery prevention for employees and managers and external associated persons.
- Identifying someone of a suitable level of seniority to be a point-person for queries and issues relating to bribery risks.

Case study 11

Proportionate procedures

A small export company operates through agents in a number of different foreign countries. Having identified bribery risks associated with its reliance on agents it is considering developing proportionate and risk based bribery prevention procedures.

The company could consider any or a combination of the following:

- Making use of any external sources of information (UKTI, sectoral organisations) on bribery risks in particular markets and using the data to inform relationships with particular agents.
- Making sure staff have a confidential means to raise any concerns about bribery.
- Using trade fairs and trade publications to communicate periodically its anti-bribery message and, where appropriate, some detail of its policies and procedures.
- Oral or written communication of its bribery prevention intentions to all of its agents.
- Adopting measures designed to address bribery on its behalf by associated persons, such as:
  - requesting relevant information and conducting background searches on the internet against information received
  - making sure references are in order and followed up
  - including anti-bribery commitments in any contract renewal
  - using existing internal arrangements such as periodic staff meetings to raise awareness of 'red flags' as regards agents' conduct, for example evasive answers to straightforward requests for information, overly elaborate payment arrangements involving further third parties, ad hoc or unusual requests for expense reimbursement not properly covered by accounting procedures.

Appendix 4: Sentencing Council Definitive Guideline on fraud, bribery and money laundering: corporate offenders

Applicability of guideline

In accordance with section 120 of the Coroners and Justice Act 2009, the Sentencing Council issues this definitive guideline. It applies to all organisations that are sentenced on or after 1 October 2014, regardless of the date of the offence.

Section 125(1) Coroners and Justice Act 2009 provides that when sentencing offences committed after 6 April 2010:

> 'Every court –
>
> (a) must, in sentencing an offender, follow any sentencing guideline which is relevant to the offender's case, and
>
> (b) must, in exercising any other function relating to the sentencing of offenders, follow any sentencing guidelines which are relevant to the exercise of the function,
>
> unless the court is satisfied that it would be contrary to the interests of justice to do so.'

Fraud, bribery and money laundering: corporate offenders

Fraud

Conspiracy to defraud (common law)
Cheat the public revenue (common law)
Triable only on indictment

Fraud Act 2006 (sections 1, 6 and 7)
Theft Act 1968 (section 17)

Value Added Tax Act 1994 (section 72)
Customs and Excise Management Act 1979 (section 170)
Triable either way

Bribery

Bribery Act 2010 (sections 1, 2, 6 and 7)
Triable either way

Money laundering

Proceeds of Crime Act 2002 (sections 327, 328 and 329)
Triable either way

Maximum: Unlimited fine

Most cases of corporate offending in this area are likely to merit allocation for trial to the Crown Court.

Committal for sentence is mandatory if confiscation (see step two) is to be considered. (Proceeds of Crime Act 2002 section 70).

Structure, ranges and starting points

For the purposes of section 60 of the Sentencing Code, the guideline specifies offence ranges – the range of sentences appropriate for each type of offence. Within each offence, the Council has specified a number of categories which reflect varying degrees of seriousness. The offence range is split into category ranges – sentences appropriate for each level of seriousness. The Council has also identified a starting point within each category.

Starting points define the position within a category range from which to start calculating the provisional sentence. The court should consider further features of the offence or the offender that warrant adjustment of the sentence within the range, including the aggravating and mitigating factors set out at step four and the further set of factors that may require a final adjustment to the sentence at step five. Starting points and ranges apply to all offenders, whether they have pleaded guilty or been convicted after trial. Credit for a guilty plea is taken into consideration only at step seven after the appropriate sentence has been identified.

Step One
Compensation

The court must consider making a compensation order requiring the offender to pay compensation for any personal injury, loss or damage resulting from the offence in such an amount as the court considers appropriate, having regard to the evidence and to the means of the offender.

Where the means of the offender are limited, priority should be given to the payment of compensation over payment of any other financial penalty.

Reasons should be given if a compensation order is not made. (See sections 55 and 133-135 of the Sentencing Code)

Step Two
Confiscation

Confiscation must be considered if either the Crown asks for it or the court thinks that it may be appropriate.

Confiscation must be dealt with before, and taken into account when assessing, any other fine or financial order (except compensation).

(See Proceeds of Crime Act 2002 sections 6 and 13)

Step Three
Determining the offence category

The court should determine the offence category with reference to **culpability** and **harm**.

Culpability

The sentencer should weigh up all the factors of the case to determine **culpability**. **Where there are characteristics present which fall under different categories, the court should balance these characteristics to reach a fair assessment of the offender's culpability.**

Culpability demonstrated by the offending corporation's role and motivation. May be demonstrated by one or more of the following **non-exhaustive** characteristics.

A – High culpability
Corporation plays a leading role in organised, planned unlawful activity (whether acting alone or with others)
Wilful obstruction of detection (for example destruction of evidence, misleading investigators, suborning employees)
Involving others through pressure or coercion (for example employees or suppliers)
Targeting of vulnerable victims or a large number of victims
Corruption of local or national government officials or ministers
Corruption of officials performing a law enforcement role
Abuse of dominant market position or position of trust or responsibility
Offending committed over a sustained period of time
Culture of wilful disregard of commission of offences by employees or agents with no effort to put effective systems in place (section 7 Bribery Act only)
B – Medium culpability
Corporation plays a significant role in unlawful activity organised by others
Activity not unlawful from the outset
Corporation reckless in making false statement (section 72 VAT Act 1994)
Other cases that fall between categories A or C because: (i) Factors are present in A and C which balance each other out and/or (ii) The offending corporation's culpability falls between the factors as described in A and C
C – Lesser culpability
Corporation plays a minor, peripheral role in unlawful activity organised by others
Some effort made to put bribery prevention measures in place but insufficient to amount to a defence (section 7 Bribery Act only)
Involvement through coercion, intimidation or exploitation

Harm

Harm is represented by a financial sum calculated by reference to the table below

Amount obtained or intended to be obtained (or loss avoided or intended to be avoided)

Fraud	For offences of fraud, conspiracy to defraud, cheating the Revenue and fraudulent evasion of duty or VAT, harm will normally be the actual or intended gross gain to the offender.

Bribery	For offences under the Bribery Act the appropriate figure will normally be the gross profit from the contract obtained, retained or sought as a result of the offending. An alternative measure for offences under section 7 may be the likely cost avoided by failing to put in place appropriate measures to prevent bribery.
Money laundering	For offences of money laundering the appropriate figure will normally be the amount laundered or, alternatively, the likely cost avoided by failing to put in place an effective anti-money laundering programme if this is higher.
General	Where the actual or intended gain cannot be established, the appropriate measure will be the amount that the court considers was likely to be achieved in all the circumstances In the absence of sufficient evidence of the amount that was likely to be obtained, 10–20 per cent of the relevant revenue (for instance between 10 and 20 per cent of the worldwide revenue derived from the product or business area to which the offence relates for the period of the offending) **may** be an appropriate measure. There may be large cases of fraud or bribery in which the true harm is to commerce or markets generally. That may justify adopting a harm figure beyond the normal measures here set out.

Step Four
Starting point and category range

Having determined the culpability level at step three, the court should use the table below to determine the starting point within the category range below. The starting point applies to all offenders irrespective of plea or previous convictions.

The harm figure at step three is multiplied by the relevant percentage figure representing culpability.

	Culpability Level		
	A	B	C
Harm figure multiplier	**Starting point** 300%	**Starting point** 200%	**Starting point** 100%
	Category range 250% to 400%	**Category range** 100% to 300%	**Category range** 20% to 150%

Having determined the appropriate starting point, the court should then consider adjustment within the category range for aggravating or mitigating features. In some cases, having considered these factors, it may be appropriate to move outside the identified category range. (See below for a **non-exhaustive** list of aggravating and mitigating factors.)

Factors increasing seriousness
Previous relevant convictions or subject to previous relevant civil or regulatory enforcement action
Corporation or subsidiary set up to commit fraudulent activity
Fraudulent activity endemic within corporation
Attempts made to conceal misconduct
Substantial harm (whether financial or otherwise) suffered by victims of offending or by third parties affected by offending
Risk of harm greater than actual or intended harm (for example in banking/credit fraud)
Substantial harm caused to integrity or confidence of markets
Substantial harm caused to integrity of local or national governments
Serious nature of underlying criminal activity (money laundering offences)
Offence committed across borders or jurisdictions

Factors reducing seriousness or reflecting mitigation
No previous relevant convictions or previous relevant civil or regulatory enforcement action
Victims voluntarily reimbursed/compensated
No actual loss to victims
Corporation co-operated with investigation, made early admissions and/or voluntarily reported offending
Offending committed under previous director(s)/managers
Little or no actual gain to corporation from offending

General principles to follow in setting a fine

The court should determine the appropriate level of fine in accordance with section 125 of the Sentencing Code, which requires that the fine must reflect the seriousness of the offence and requires the court to take into account the financial circumstances of the offender.

Obtaining financial information
Companies and bodies delivering public or charitable services

Where the offender is a company or a body which delivers a public or charitable service, it is expected to provide comprehensive accounts for the last three years, to enable the court to make an accurate assessment of its financial status. In the absence of such disclosure, or where the court is not satisfied that it has been given sufficient reliable information, the court will be entitled to draw reasonable inferences as to the offender's means from evidence it has heard and from all the circumstances of the case.

1. *For companies*: annual accounts. Particular attention should be paid to turnover; profit before tax; directors' remuneration, loan accounts and pension provision; and assets as disclosed by the balance sheet. Most companies are required to file audited accounts at Companies House. Failure to produce relevant recent accounts on request may properly lead to the conclusion that the company can pay any appropriate fine.

2. *For partnerships*: annual accounts. Particular attention should be paid to turnover; profit before tax; partners' drawings, loan accounts and pension provision; assets as above. Limited liability partnerships (LLPs) may be required to file audited accounts with Companies House. If adequate accounts are not produced on request, see paragraph 1.

3. *For local authorities, fire authorities and similar public bodies*: the Annual Revenue Budget ("ARB") is the equivalent of turnover and the best indication of the size of the defendant organisation. It is unlikely to be necessary to analyse specific expenditure or reserves unless inappropriate expenditure is suggested.

4. *For health trusts*: the independent regulator of NHS Foundation Trusts is Monitor. It publishes quarterly reports and annual figures for the financial strength and stability of trusts from which the annual income can be seen, available via www.monitor-nhsft.gov.uk. Detailed analysis of expenditure or reserves is unlikely to be called for.

5. *For charities*: it will be appropriate to inspect annual audited accounts. Detailed analysis of expenditure or reserves is unlikely to be called for unless there is a suggestion of unusual or unnecessary expenditure.

Step Five
Adjustment of fine

Having arrived at a fine level, the court should consider whether there are any further factors which indicate an adjustment in the level of the fine. The court should 'step back' and consider the overall effect of its orders. The combination of orders made, compensation, confiscation and fine ought to achieve:

- the removal of all gain
- appropriate additional punishment, and
- deterrence

The fine may be adjusted to ensure that these objectives are met in a fair way. The court should consider any further factors relevant to the setting of the level of the fine to ensure that the fine is proportionate, having regard to the size and financial position of the offending organisation and the seriousness of the offence.

The fine must be substantial enough to have a real economic impact which will bring home to both management and shareholders the need to operate within the law. Whether the fine will have the effect of putting the offender out of business will be relevant; in some bad cases this may be an acceptable consequence.

In considering the ability of the offending organisation to pay any financial penalty the court can take into account the power to allow time for payment or to order that the amount be paid in instalments.

The court should consider whether the level of fine would otherwise cause unacceptable harm to third parties. In doing so the court should bear in mind that the payment of any compensation determined at step one should take priority over the payment of any fine.

The table below contains a **non-exhaustive** list of additional factual elements for the court to consider. The Court should identify whether any combination of these, or other relevant factors, should result in a proportionate increase or reduction in the level of fine.

Factors to consider in adjusting the level of fine
Fine fulfils the objectives of punishment, deterrence and removal of gain
The value, worth or available means of the offender
Fine impairs offender's ability to make restitution to victims
Impact of fine on offender's ability to implement effective compliance programmes
Impact of fine on employment of staff, service users, customers and local economy (but not shareholders)
Impact of fine on performance of public or charitable function

Step Six
Consider any factors which would indicate a reduction, such as assistance to the prosecution

The court should take into account section 74 of the Sentencing Code (reduction in sentence for assistance to prosecution) and any other rule of law by virtue of which an offender may receive a discounted sentence in consequence of assistance given (or offered) to the prosecutor or investigator.

Step Seven
Reduction for guilty pleas

The court should take account of any potential reduction for a guilty plea in accordance with section 73 of the Sentencing Code and the Reduction in Sentence for a Guilty Plea guideline.

Step Eight
Ancillary Orders

In all cases the court must consider whether to make any ancillary orders.

Step Nine
Totality principle

If sentencing an offender for more than one offence, consider whether the total sentence is just and proportionate to the offending behaviour. See Totality guideline.

Step Ten
Reasons

Section 52 of the Sentencing Code imposes a duty to give reasons for, and explain the effect of, the sentence.

Appendix 5: Crime and Courts Act 2013 Schedule 17: Deferred prosecution agreements

Part 1 General

Characteristics of a deferred prosecution agreement

1

(1) A deferred prosecution agreement (a 'DPA') is an agreement between a designated prosecutor and a person ('P') whom the prosecutor is considering prosecuting for an offence specified in Part 2 (the 'alleged offence').

(2) Under a DPA—

(a) P agrees to comply with the requirements imposed on P by the agreement;

(b) the prosecutor agrees that, upon approval of the DPA by the court (see paragraph 8), paragraph 2 is to apply in relation to the prosecution of P for the alleged offence.

Effect of DPA on court proceedings

2

(1) Proceedings in respect of the alleged offence are to be instituted by the prosecutor in the Crown Court by preferring a bill of indictment charging P with the alleged offence (see section 2(2)(ba) of the Administration of Justice (Miscellaneous Provisions) Act 1933 (bill of indictment preferred with consent of Crown Court judge following DPA approval)).

(2) As soon as proceedings are instituted under sub-paragraph (1) they are automatically suspended.

(3) The suspension may only be lifted on an application to the Crown Court by the prosecutor; and no such application may be made at any time when the DPA is in force.

(4) At a time when proceedings are suspended under sub-paragraph (2), no other person may prosecute P for the alleged offence.

Designated prosecutors

3

(1) The following are designated prosecutors—

(a) the Director of Public Prosecutions;

(b) the Director of the Serious Fraud Office;

(c) any prosecutor designated under this paragraph by an order made by the Secretary of State.

(2) A designated prosecutor must exercise personally the power to enter into a DPA and, accordingly, any enactment that enables a function of a designated prosecutor to be exercised by a person other than the prosecutor concerned does not apply.

(3) But if the designated prosecutor is unavailable, the power to enter into a DPA may be exercised personally by a person authorised in writing by the designated prosecutor.

Persons who may enter into a DPA with a prosecutor

4

(1) P may be a body corporate, a partnership or an unincorporated association, but may not be an individual.

(2) In the case of a DPA between a prosecutor and a partnership—

(a) the DPA must be entered into in the name of the partnership (and not in that of any of the partners);

(b) any money payable under the DPA must be paid out of the funds of the partnership.

(3) In the case of a DPA between a prosecutor and an unincorporated association—

(a) the DPA must be entered into in the name of the association (and not in that of any of its members);

(b) any money payable under the DPA must be paid out of the funds of the association.

Content of a DPA

5

(1) A DPA must contain a statement of facts relating to the alleged offence, which may include admissions made by P.

(2) A DPA must specify an expiry date, which is the date on which the DPA ceases to have effect if it has not already been terminated under paragraph 9 (breach).

(3) The requirements that a DPA may impose on P include, but are not limited to, the following requirements—

(a) to pay to the prosecutor a financial penalty;

(b) to compensate victims of the alleged offence;

(c) to donate money to a charity or other third party;

(d) to disgorge any profits made by P from the alleged offence;

(e) to implement a compliance programme or make changes to an existing compliance programme relating to P's policies or to the training of P's employees or both;

(f) to co-operate in any investigation related to the alleged offence;

(g) to pay any reasonable costs of the prosecutor in relation to the alleged offence or the DPA.

The DPA may impose time limits within which P must comply with the requirements imposed on P.

(4) The amount of any financial penalty agreed between the prosecutor and P must be broadly comparable to the fine that a court would have imposed on P on conviction for the alleged offence following a guilty plea.

(5) A DPA may include a term setting out the consequences of a failure by P to comply with any of its terms.

Code on DPAs

6

(1) The Director of Public Prosecutions and the Director of the Serious Fraud Office must jointly issue a Code for prosecutors giving guidance on—

(a) the general principles to be applied in determining whether a DPA is likely to be appropriate in a given case, and

(b) the disclosure of information by a prosecutor to P in the course of negotiations for a DPA and after a DPA has been agreed.

(2) The Code may also give guidance on any other relevant matter, including—

(a) the use of information obtained by a prosecutor in the course of negotiations for a DPA;

(b) variation of a DPA;

(c) termination of a DPA and steps that may be taken by a prosecutor following termination;

(d) steps that may be taken by a prosecutor when the prosecutor suspects a breach of a DPA.

(3) The Code must be set out in the report made by the Director of Public Prosecutions to the Attorney General under section 9 of the Prosecution of Offences Act 1985 for the year in which the Code is issued.

(4) The Code may from time to time be altered or replaced by agreement between—

(a) the Director of Public Prosecutions,

(b) the Director of the Serious Fraud Office, and

(c) any prosecutor who is for the time being designated by an order made under paragraph 3.

(5) If the Code is altered or replaced, the new Code must be set out in the report made by the Director of Public Prosecutions to the Attorney General under section 9 of the Prosecution of Offences Act 1985 for the year in which the Code is altered or replaced.

(6) A prosecutor must take account of the Code in exercising functions under this Schedule.

Court approval of DPA: preliminary hearing

7

(1) After the commencement of negotiations between a prosecutor and P in respect of a DPA but before the terms of the DPA are agreed, the prosecutor must apply to the Crown Court for a declaration that—

(a) entering into a DPA with P is likely to be in the interests of justice, and

(b) the proposed terms of the DPA are fair, reasonable and proportionate.

(2) The court must give reasons for its decision on whether or not to make a declaration under sub-paragraph (1).

(3) The prosecutor may make a further application to the court for a declaration under sub-paragraph (1) if, following the previous application, the court declined to make a declaration.

(4) A hearing at which an application under this paragraph is determined must be held in private, any declaration under sub-paragraph (1) must be made in private, and reasons under sub-paragraph (2) must be given in private.

Court approval of DPA: final hearing

8

(1) When a prosecutor and P have agreed the terms of a DPA, the prosecutor must apply to the Crown Court for a declaration that—

(a) the DPA is in the interests of justice, and

(b) the terms of the DPA are fair, reasonable and proportionate.

(2) But the prosecutor may not make an application under sub-paragraph (1) unless the court has made a declaration under paragraph 7(1) (declaration on preliminary hearing).

(3) A DPA only comes into force when it is approved by the Crown Court making a declaration under sub-paragraph (1).

(4) The court must give reasons for its decision on whether or not to make a declaration under sub-paragraph (1).

(5) A hearing at which an application under this paragraph is determined may be held in private.

(6) But if the court decides to approve the DPA and make a declaration under sub-paragraph (1) it must do so, and give its reasons, in open court.

(7) Upon approval of the DPA by the court, the prosecutor must publish—

(a) the DPA,

(b) the declaration of the court under paragraph 7 and the reasons for its decision to make the declaration,

(c) in a case where the court initially declined to make a declaration under paragraph 7, the court's reason for that decision, and

(d) the court's declaration under this paragraph and the reasons for its decision to make the declaration, unless the prosecutor is prevented from doing so by an enactment or by an order of the court under paragraph 12 (postponement of publication to avoid prejudicing proceedings).

Breach of DPA

9

(1) At any time when a DPA is in force, if the prosecutor believes that P has failed to comply with the terms of the DPA, the prosecutor may make an application to the Crown Court under this paragraph.

(2) On an application under sub-paragraph (1) the court must decide whether, on the balance of probabilities, P has failed to comply with the terms of the DPA.

(3) If the court finds that P has failed to comply with the terms of the DPA, it may—

(a) invite the prosecutor and P to agree proposals to remedy P's failure to comply, or

(b) terminate the DPA.

(4) The court must give reasons for its decisions under sub-paragraphs (2) and (3).

(5) Where the court decides that P has not failed to comply with the terms of the DPA, the prosecutor must publish the court's decision and its reasons for that decision, unless the prosecutor is prevented from doing so by an enactment or by an order of the court under paragraph 12 (postponement of publication to avoid prejudicing proceedings).

(6) Where the court invites the prosecutor and P to agree proposals to remedy P's failure to comply, the prosecutor must publish the court's decisions under sub-paragraphs (2) and (3) and the reasons for those decisions, unless the prosecutor is prevented from doing so by an enactment or by an order of the court under paragraph 12 (postponement of publication to avoid prejudicing proceedings).

(7) Where the court terminates a DPA under sub-paragraph (3)(b), the prosecutor must publish—

(a) the fact that the DPA has been terminated by the court following a failure by P to comply with the terms of the DPA, and

(b) the court's reasons for its decisions under sub-paragraphs (2) and (3), unless the prosecutor is prevented from doing so by an enactment or by an order of the court under paragraph 12 (postponement of publication to avoid prejudicing proceedings).

(8) If the prosecutor believes that P has failed to comply with the terms of the DPA but decides not to make an application to the Crown Court under this paragraph, the prosecutor must publish details relating to that decision, including—

(a) the reasons for the prosecutor's belief that P has failed to comply, and

(b) the reasons for the prosecutor's decision not to make an application to the court,

unless the prosecutor is prevented from doing so by an enactment or by an order of the court under paragraph 12 (postponement of publication to avoid prejudicing proceedings).

Variation of DPA

10

(1) At any time when a DPA is in force, the prosecutor and P may agree to vary its terms if—

(a) the court has invited the parties to vary the DPA under paragraph 9(3)(a), or

(b) variation of the DPA is necessary to avoid a failure by P to comply with its terms in circumstances that were not, and could not have been, foreseen by the prosecutor or P at the time that the DPA was agreed.

(2) When the prosecutor and P have agreed to vary the terms of a DPA, the prosecutor must apply to the Crown Court for a declaration that—

(a) the variation is in the interests of justice, and

(b) the terms of the DPA as varied are fair, reasonable and proportionate.

(3) A variation of a DPA only takes effect when it is approved by the Crown Court making a declaration under sub-paragraph (2).

(4) The court must give reasons for its decision on whether or not to make a declaration under sub-paragraph (2).

(5) A hearing at which an application under this paragraph is determined may be held in private.

(6) But if the court decides to approve the variation and make a declaration under sub-paragraph (2) it must do so, and give its reasons, in open court.

(7) Where the court decides not to approve the variation, the prosecutor must publish the court's decision and the reasons for it, unless the prosecutor is prevented from doing so by an enactment or by an order of the court

under paragraph 12 (postponement of publication to avoid prejudicing proceedings).

(8) Where the court decides to approve the variation the prosecutor must publish—

(a) the DPA as varied, and

(b) the court's declaration under this paragraph and the reasons for its decision to make the declaration,

unless the prosecutor is prevented from doing so by an enactment or by an order of the court under paragraph 12 (postponement of publication to avoid prejudicing proceedings).

Discontinuance of proceedings on expiry of DPA

11

(1) If a DPA remains in force until its expiry date, then after the expiry of the DPA the proceedings instituted under paragraph 2(1) are to be discontinued by the prosecutor giving notice to the Crown Court that the prosecutor does not want the proceedings to continue.

(2) Where proceedings are discontinued under sub-paragraph (1), fresh criminal proceedings may not be instituted against P for the alleged offence.

(3) But sub-paragraph (2) does not prevent fresh proceedings from being instituted against P in a case where, after a DPA has expired, the prosecutor finds that, during the course of the negotiations for the DPA—

(a) P provided inaccurate, misleading or incomplete information to the prosecutor, and

(b) P knew or ought to have known that the information was inaccurate, misleading or incomplete.

(4) A DPA is not to be treated as having expired for the purposes of subparagraph (1) if, on the expiry date specified in the DPA—

(a) an application made by the prosecutor under paragraph 9 (breach) has not yet been decided by the court,

(b) following an application under paragraph 9 the court has invited the parties to agree proposals to remedy P's failure to comply, but the parties have not yet reached an agreement, or

(c) the parties have agreed proposals to remedy P's failure to comply following an invitation of the court under paragraph 9(3)(a) but P has not yet complied with the agreement.

(5) In the case mentioned in sub-paragraph (4)(a)—

(a) if the court decides that P has not failed to comply with the terms of the DPA, or that P has failed to comply but does not take action under paragraph 9(3), the DPA is to be treated as expiring when the application is decided;

(b) if the court terminates the DPA, the DPA is to be treated as not having remained in force until its expiry date (and sub-paragraph (1) therefore does not apply);

(c) if the court invites the parties to agree proposals to remedy P's failure to comply, the DPA is to be treated as expiring when the parties have reached such an agreement and P has complied with it.

(6) In the case mentioned in sub-paragraph (4)(b), the DPA is to be treated as expiring when the parties have reached an agreement and P has complied with it.

(7) In the case mentioned in sub-paragraph (4)(c), the DPA is to be treated as expiring when P complies with the agreement.

(8) Where proceedings are discontinued under sub-paragraph (1), the prosecutor must publish—

(a) the fact that the proceedings have been discontinued, and

(b) details of P's compliance with the DPA,

unless the prosecutor is prevented from doing so by an enactment or by an order of the court under paragraph 12 (postponement of publication to avoid prejudicing proceedings).

Court order postponing publication of information by prosecutor

12

The court may order that the publication of information by the prosecutor under paragraph 8(7), 9(5), (6), (7) or (8), 10(7) or (8) or 11(8) be postponed for such period as the court considers necessary if it appears to the court that postponement is necessary for avoiding a substantial risk of prejudice to the administration of justice in any legal proceedings.

Use of material in criminal proceedings

13

(1) Sub-paragraph (2) applies where a DPA between a prosecutor and P has been approved by the Crown Court under paragraph 8.

(2) The statement of facts contained in the DPA is, in any criminal proceedings brought against P for the alleged offence, to be treated as an admission

by P under section 10 of the Criminal Justice Act 1967 (proof by formal admission).

(3) Sub-paragraph (4) applies where a prosecutor and P have entered into negotiations for a DPA but the DPA has not been approved by the Crown Court under paragraph 8.

(4) Material described in sub-paragraph (6) may only be used in evidence against P—

(a) on a prosecution for an offence consisting of the provision of inaccurate, misleading or incomplete information, or

(b) on a prosecution for some other offence where in giving evidence P makes a statement inconsistent with the material.

(5) However, material may not be used against P by virtue of sub-paragraph (4)(b) unless evidence relating to it is adduced, or a question relating to it is asked, by or on behalf of P in the proceedings arising out of the prosecution.

(6) The material is—

(a) material that shows that P entered into negotiations for a DPA, including in particular—

(i) any draft of the DPA;

(ii) any draft of a statement of facts intended to be included within the DPA;

(iii) any statement indicating that P entered into such negotiations;

(b) material that was created solely for the purpose of preparing the DPA or statement of facts.

Money received by prosecutor under a DPA

14

Any money received by a prosecutor under a term of a DPA that provides for P to pay a financial penalty to the prosecutor or to disgorge profits made from the alleged offence is to be paid into the Consolidated Fund.

Part 2 Offences in relation to which a DPA may be entered into

Common law offences

15

Conspiracy to defraud.

16

Cheating the public revenue.

Statutory offences

17

An offence under any of the following sections of the Theft Act 1968—

(a) section 1 (theft);

(b) section 17 (false accounting);

(c) section 20 (suppression etc of documents);

(d) section 24A (dishonestly retaining a wrongful credit).

18

An offence under any of the following sections of the Customs and Excise Management Act 1979—

(a) section 68 (offences in relation to exportation of prohibited or restricted goods);

(b) section 167 (untrue declarations etc);

(c) section 170 (fraudulent evasion of duty etc).

19

An offence under any of the following sections of the Forgery and Counterfeiting Act 1981—

(a) section 1 (forgery);

(b) section 2 (copying a false instrument);

(c) section 3 (using a false instrument);

(d) section 4 (using a copy of a false instrument);

(e) section 5 (offences relating to money orders, share certificates, passports etc).

20

An offence under section 450 of the Companies Act 1985 (destroying, mutilating etc company documents).

21

An offence under section 72 of the Value Added Tax Act 1994 (fraudulent evasion of VAT).

22

An offence under any of the following sections of the Financial Services and Markets Act 2000—

(a) section 23 (contravention of prohibition of carrying on regulated activity unless authorised or exempt);

(b) section 25 (contravention of restrictions on financial promotion);

(c) section 85 (prohibition of dealing etc in transferable securities without approved prospectus);

(d) section 346 (provision of false or misleading statements to auditor or actuary);

(e) ....

(f) section 398 (misleading the FSA).

23

An offence under any of the following sections of the Proceeds of Crime Act 2002—

(a) section 327 (concealing etc criminal property);

(b) section 328 (arrangements facilitating acquisition etc of criminal property);

(c) section 329 (acquisition, use and possession of criminal property);

(d) section 330 (failing to disclose knowledge or suspicion of money laundering);

(e) section 333A (tipping off).

24

An offence under any of the following sections of the Companies Act 2006—

(a) section 658 (general rule against limited company acquiring its own shares);

(b) section 680 (prohibited financial assistance);

(c) section 993 (fraudulent trading).

25

An offence under any of the following sections of the Fraud Act 2006—

(a) section 1 (fraud);

(b) section 6 (possession etc of articles for use in frauds);

(c) section 7 (making or supplying articles for use in frauds);

(d) section 11 (obtaining services dishonestly).

26

An offence under any of the following sections of the Bribery Act 2010—

(a) section 1 (bribing another person);

(b) section 2 (being bribed);

(c) section 6 (bribery of foreign public officials);

(d) section 7 (failure of commercial organisations to prevent bribery).

26ZA

An offence under any of the following sections of the Financial Services Act 2012—

(a) section 89 (misleading statements);

(b) section 90 (misleading impressions);

(c) section 91 (misleading statements etc. in relation to benchmarks).

26A

(1) An offence under an instrument made under section 2(2) of the European Communities Act 1972 for the purpose of implementing, or otherwise in relation to, EU obligations created or arising by or under an EU financial sanctions Regulation.

(2) An offence under an Act or under subordinate legislation where the offence was created for the purpose of implementing a UN financial sanctions Resolution.

(3) An offence under paragraph 7 of Schedule 3 to the Anti-terrorism, Crime and Security Act 2001 (freezing orders).

(4) An offence under paragraph 30 or 30A of Schedule 7 to the Counter-Terrorism Act 2008 where the offence relates to a requirement of the kind mentioned in paragraph 13 of that Schedule.

(5) An offence under paragraph 31 of Schedule 7 to the Counter-Terrorism Act 2008.

(5A) An offence under regulations made under section 1 of the Sanctions and Anti-Money Laundering Act 2018 (sanctions regulations).

(6) In this paragraph—

"EU financial sanctions Regulation" and "UN financial sanctions Resolution" have the same meanings as in Part 8 of the Policing and Crime Act 2017 (see section 143 of that Act);

"subordinate legislation" has the same meaning as in the Interpretation Act 1978

27

An offence under regulation 86 of the Money Laundering, Terrorist Financing and Transfer of Funds (Information on the Payer) Regulations 2007.

27A

An offence under regulation 49 of the Sanctions and Anti-Money Laundering Act 2018 (money laundering and terrorist financing etc).

Ancillary offences

28

Any ancillary offence relating to an offence specified in this Part.

Interpretation of this Part

29

'Ancillary offence', in relation to an offence, means—

(a) aiding, abetting, counselling or procuring the commission of the offence;

(b) an offence under Part 2 of the Serious Crime Act 2007 (encouraging or assisting crime) in relation to the offence;

(c) attempting or conspiring to commit the offence.

30

This Schedule applies in relation to conduct occurring before the commencement of this Schedule as if an offence specified in this Part included any corresponding offence under the law in force at the time of the conduct (and for the purposes of this paragraph, the common law offence of inciting the commission of another offence is to be treated as an offence corresponding to an offence under Part 2 of the Serious Crime Act 2007).

Power to amend this Part

31

The Secretary of State may by order amend this Part by—

(a) adding an offence of financial or economic crime;

(b) removing an offence.

Part 3 Consequential and transitional provision

Consequential amendments

32

In section 2 of the Administration of Justice (Miscellaneous Provisions) Act 1933 (procedure for indictment of offenders), in subsection (2) after paragraph (b) insert—

> '(ba) the bill is preferred with the consent of a judge of the Crown Court following a declaration by the court under paragraph 8(1) of Schedule 17 to the Crime and Courts Act 2013 (court approval of deferred prosecution agreement); or'.

33

In section 2 of the Criminal Procedure (Attendance of Witnesses) Act 1965 (issue of witness summons on application to the Crown Court), after subsection (6) insert—

'(6A) Where the proceedings concerned relate to an offence that is the subject of a deferred prosecution agreement within the meaning of Schedule 17 to the Crime and Courts Act 2013, an application must be made as soon as is reasonably practicable after the suspension of the proceedings is lifted under paragraph 2(3) of that Schedule.'

34

In Schedule 1 to the Contempt of Court Act 1981 (times when proceedings are active for purposes of strict liability rule for contempt of court), in paragraph 7, after paragraph (aa) insert—

> '(ab) in England and Wales, if they are discontinued by virtue of paragraph 11 of Schedule 17 to the Crime and Courts Act 2013 (deferred prosecution agreements);'.

35

In section 15 of the Prosecution of Offences Act 1985 (interpretation), in subsection (2)(d) after '(b)' insert 'or (ba)'.

36

In section 51 of the Criminal Justice and Public Order Act 1994 (intimidation etc of witnesses, jurors and others), in subsection 10(a)(iii) after '2(2)(b)' insert 'or (ba)'.

37

(1) The Criminal Procedure and Investigations Act 1996 is amended as follows.

(2) In section 1 (application of Part 1: disclosure), in subsection (2), after paragraph (f) insert ', or

(g) following the preferment of a bill of indictment charging a person with an indictable offence under the authority of section 2(2)(ba) of the Administration of Justice (Miscellaneous Provisions) Act 1933 (bill of indictment preferred with consent of Crown Court judge following approval of deferred prosecution agreement), the suspension of the proceedings against the person under paragraph 2(2) of Schedule 17 to the Crime and Courts Act 2013 is lifted under paragraph 2(3) of that Schedule.'

(3) In section 28 (application of Part 3: preparatory hearings), in subsection (1)(c) after '2(2)(b)' insert 'or (ba)'.

(4) In section 39 (meaning of pre-trial hearing), in subsection (2)(a) after '2(2)(b)' insert 'or (ba)'.

(5) In Schedule 3 (fraud), in paragraph 8(1)(c) after '2(2)(b)' insert 'or (ba)'.

38

In section 85 of the Proceeds of Crime Act 2002 (proceedings), in subsection (1)(c) at the end insert 'or subsection (2)(ba) of that section (preferment by Crown Court judge following approval of deferred prosecution agreement)'.

Transitional provision

39

(1) Conduct constituting an alleged offence that occurred before the relevant commencement day may be taken into account for the purposes of this Schedule.

(2) In this paragraph, the 'relevant commencement day' means—

(a) in a case where the alleged offence is an offence that is specified in Part 2 when this Schedule comes into force, the day on which this Schedule comes into force;

(b) in a case where the alleged offence is an offence that is subsequently added to Part 2 (whether by order under paragraph 31 or otherwise), the day when the enactment adding that offence to Part 2 comes into force.

Appendix 6: Criminal Procedure Rules Part 11: Deferred Prosecution Agreements

When this part applies

11.1.

(1) This Part applies to proceedings in the Crown Court under Schedule 17 to the Crime and Courts Act 2013[1].

(2) In this Part—

(a) 'agreement' means a deferred prosecution agreement under paragraph 1 of that Schedule;

(b) 'prosecutor' means a prosecutor designated by or under paragraph 3 of that Schedule; and

(c) 'defendant' means the corporation, partnership or association with whom the prosecutor proposes to enter, or enters, an agreement.

[Note. Under Schedule 17 to the Crime and Courts Act 2013, a designated prosecutor may make a deferred prosecution agreement with a defendant, other than an individual, whom the prosecutor is considering prosecuting for an offences or offences listed in that Schedule. Under such an agreement, the defendant agrees to comply with its terms and the prosecutor agrees that, if the Crown Court approves those terms, then paragraph 2 of the Schedule will apply and —

(a) the prosecutor will serve a draft indictment charging the defendant with the offence or offences the subject of the agreement;

(b) the prosecution will be suspended under that paragraph, and the suspension may not be lifted while the agreement is in force; and

(c) no-one may prosecute the defendant for the offence or offences charged while the agreement is in force, or after it expires if the defendant complies with it.

1 2013 c. 22; Schedule 17 comes into force on a date to be appointed.

The Code for prosecutors issued under paragraph 6 of that Schedule contains guidance on the exercise of prosecution functions in relation to a deferred prosecution agreement.]

Exercise of court's powers

11.2.

(1) The court must determine an application to which this Part applies at a hearing, which—

(a) must be in private, under rule 11.3 (Application to approve a proposal to enter an agreement);

(b) may be in public or private, under rule 11.4 (Application to approve the terms of an agreement), rule 11.6 (Application to approve a variation of the terms of an agreement) or rule 11.9 (Application to postpone the publication of information by the prosecutor);

(c) must be in public, under rule 11.5 (Application on breach of agreement) or rule 11.7 (Application to lift suspension of prosecution), unless the court otherwise directs.

(2) If at a hearing in private to which rule 11.4 or rule 11.6 applies the court approves the agreement or the variation proposed, the court must announce its decision and reasons at a hearing in public.

(3) The court must not determine an application under rule 11.3, rule 11.4 or rule 11.6 unless—

(a) both parties are present;

(b) the prosecutor provides the court with a written declaration that, for the purposes of the application—

(i) the investigator enquiring into the alleged offence or offences has certified that no information has been supplied which the investigator knows to be inaccurate, misleading or incomplete, and

(ii) the prosecutor has complied with the prosecution obligation to disclose material to the defendant; and

(c) the defendant provides the court with a written declaration that, for the purposes of the application—

(i) the defendant has not supplied any information which the defendant knows to be inaccurate, misleading or incomplete, and

(ii) the individual through whom the defendant makes the declaration has made reasonable enquiries and believes the defendant's declaration to be true.

(4) The court must not determine an application under rule 11.5 or rule 11.7—

(a) in the prosecutor's absence; or

(b) in the absence of the defendant, unless the defendant has had at least 28 days in which to make representations.

(5) If the court approves a proposal to enter an agreement—

(a) the general rule is that any further application to which this Part applies must be made to the same judge; but

(b) the court may direct other arrangements.

(6) The court may adjourn a hearing—

(a) if either party asks, or on its own initiative;

(b) in particular, if the court requires more information about—

(i) the facts of an alleged offence,

(ii) the terms of a proposal to enter an agreement, or of a proposed agreement or variation of an agreement, or

(iii) the circumstances in which the prosecutor wants the court to decide whether the defendant has failed to comply with the terms of an agreement.

(7) The court may—

(a) hear an application under rule 11.4 immediately after an application under rule 11.3, if the court approves a proposal to enter an agreement;

(b) hear an application under rule 11.7 immediately after an application under rule 11.5, if the court terminates an agreement.

[Note. See paragraphs 7(4), 8(5), (6) and 10(5), (6) of Schedule 17 to the Crime and Courts Act 2013.

The Code for prosecutors issued under paragraph 6 of that Schedule contains guidance on fulfilling the prosecution duty of disclosure.]

Application to approve a proposal to enter an agreement

11.3.

(1) This rule applies where a prosecutor wants the court to approve a proposal to enter an agreement.

(2) the prosecutor must—

(a) apply in writing after the commencement of negotiations between the parties but before the terms of agreement have been settled; and

(b) serve the application on—

(i) the court officer, and

(ii) the defendant.

(3) The application must—

(a) identify the parties to the proposed agreement;

(b) attach a proposed indictment setting out such of the offences listed in Part 2 of Schedule 17 to the Crime and Courts Act 2013 as the prosecutor is considering;

(c) include or attach a statement of facts proposed for inclusion in the agreement, which must give full particulars of each alleged offence, including details of any alleged financial gain or loss;

(d) include any information about the defendant that would be relevant to sentence in the event of conviction for the offence or offences;

(e) specify the proposed expiry date of the agreement;

(f) describe the proposed terms of the agreement, including details of any—

(i) monetary penalty to be paid by the defendant, and the time within which any such penalty is to be paid,

(ii) compensation, reparation or donation to be made by the defendant, the identity of the recipient of any such payment and the time within which any such payment is to be made,

(iii) surrender of profits or other financial benefit by the defendant, and the time within which any such sum is to be surrendered,

(iv) arrangement to be made in relation to the management or conduct of the defendant's business,

(v) co-operation required of the defendant in any investigation related to the offence or offences,

(vi) other action required of the defendant,

(vii) arrangement to monitor the defendant's compliance with a term,

(viii) consequence of the defendant's failure to comply with a term, and

(ix) prosecution costs to be paid by the defendant, and the time within which any such costs are to be paid;

(g) in relation to those terms, explain how they comply with—

(i) the requirements of the code issued under paragraph 6 of Schedule 17 to the Crime and Courts Act 2013, and

(ii) any sentencing guidelines or guideline cases which apply;

(h) contain or attach the defendant's written consent to the proposal; and

(i) explain why—

(i) entering into an agreement is likely to be in the interests of justice, and

(ii) the proposed terms of the agreement are fair, reasonable and proportionate.

(4) If the proposed statement of facts includes assertions that the defendant does not admit, the application must—

(a) specify the facts that are not admitted; and

(b) explain why that is immaterial for the purposes of the proposal to enter an agreement.

[Note. See paragraphs 5 and 7 of Schedule 17 to the Crime and Courts Act 2013.]

Application to approve the terms of an agreement

11.4.

(1) This rule applies where—

(a) the court has approved a proposal to enter an agreement on an application under rule 11.3; and

(b) the prosecutor wants the court to approve the terms of the agreement.

(2) The prosecutor must—

(a) apply in writing as soon as practicable after the parties have settled the terms; and

(b) serve the application on—

(i) the court officer, and

(ii) the defendant.

(3) The application must—

(a) attach the agreement;

(b) indicate in what respect, if any, the terms of the agreement differ from those proposed in the application under rule 11.3;

(c) contain or attach the defendant's written consent to the agreement;
(d) explain why—

(i) the agreement is in the interests of justice, and

(ii) the terms of the agreement are fair, reasonable and proportionate;

(e) attach a draft indictment, charging the defendant with the offence or offences the subject of the agreement; and

(f) include any application for the hearing to be in private.

(4) If the court approves the agreement and the draft indictment, the court officer must—

(a) endorse any paper copy of the indictment made for the court with—

(i) a note to identify it as the indictment approved by the court, and

(ii) the date of the court's approval; and

(b) treat the case as if it had been suspended by order of the court.

[Note. See paragraph 8 of Schedule 17 to the Crime and Courts Act 2013. See also rule 11.9 (Application to postpone the publication of information by the prosecutor).

Under paragraph 2(1) of Schedule 17 to the 2013 Act and section 2 of the Administration of Justice (Miscellaneous Provisions) Act 1933[2]*, the draft indictment to which this rule applies becomes an indictment when the court approves the agreement and consents to the service of that draft. Part 14 contains rules about indictments.*

Under paragraph 2(2) of Schedule 17 to the 2013 Act, on approval of the draft indictment the proceedings are automatically suspended.

Under paragraph 13(2) of Schedule 17 to the 2013 Act, where the court approves an agreement the statement of facts contained in that agreement is to be treated as an admission by the defendant under section 10 of the Criminal Justice Act 1967[3] *(proof by formal admission) in any criminal proceedings against the defendant for the alleged offence.]*

---

2 1933 c. 36; section 2 was amended by Part IV of Schedule 11 to, the Courts Act 1971 (c. 23), Schedule 5 to, the Senior Courts Act 1981 (c. 54), Schedule 2 to the Prosecution of Offences Act 1985 (c. 23), paragraph 1 of Schedule 2 to the Criminal Justice Act 1987 (c. 38), paragraph 10 of Schedule 15 to the Criminal Justice Act 1988 (c. 33), paragraph 8 of Schedule 6 to the Criminal Justice Act 1991 (c. 53), Schedule 1 to the Statute Law (Repeals) Act 1993, paragraph 17 of Schedule 1 to the Criminal Procedure and Investigations Act 1996 (c. 25), paragraph 5 of Schedule 8 to the Crime and Disorder Act 1998 (c. 37), paragraph 1 of the Schedule to S.I. 2004/2035, paragraph 34 of Schedule 3 and Part 4 of Schedule 37 to the Criminal Justice Act 2003 (c. 44) and sections 116 and 178 of, and Part 3 of Schedule 23 to, the Coroners and Justice Act 2009 (c. 25). It is further amended by paragraph 32 of Schedule 17 to the Crime and Courts Act 2013 (c. 22), with effect from a date to be appointed.

3 1967 c. 80.

Application on breach of agreement

11.5.

(1) This rule applies where—

(a) the prosecutor believes that the defendant has failed to comply with the terms of an agreement; and

(b) the prosecutor wants the court to decide—

(i) whether the defendant has failed to comply, and

(ii) if so, whether to terminate the agreement, or to invite the parties to agree proposals to remedy that failure.

(2) The prosecutor must—

(a) apply in writing, as soon as practicable after becoming aware of the grounds for doing so; and

(b) serve the application on—

(i) the court officer, and

(ii) the defendant.

(3) The application must—

(a) specify each respect in which the prosecutor believes the defendant has failed to comply with the terms of the agreement, and explain the reasons for the prosecutor's belief; and

(b) attach a copy of any document containing evidence on which the prosecutor relies.

(4) A defendant who wants to make representations in response to the application must serve the representations on—

(a) the court officer; and

(b) the prosecutor,

not more than 28 days after service of the application.

[Note. See paragraph 9 of Schedule 17 to the Crime and Courts Act 2013. See also rule 11.9 (Application to postpone the publication of information by the prosecutor).]

Application to approve a variation of the terms of an agreement

11.6.

(1) This rule applies where the parties have agreed to vary the terms of an agreement because—

(a) on an application under rule 11.5 (Application on breach of agreement), the court has invited them to do so; or

(b) variation of the agreement is necessary to avoid a failure by the defendant to comply with its terms in circumstances that were not, and could not have been, foreseen by either party at the time the agreement was made.

(2) The prosecutor must—

(a) apply in writing, as soon as practicable after the parties have settled the terms of the variation; and

(b) serve the application on—

(i) the court officer, and

(ii) the defendant.

(3) The application must—

(a) specify each variation proposed;

(b) contain or attach the defendant's written consent to the variation;

(c) explain why—

(i) the variation is in the interests of justice, and

(ii) the terms of the agreement as varied are fair, reasonable and proportionate; and

(d) include any application for the hearing to be in private.

[Note. See paragraph 10 of Schedule 17 to the Crime and Courts Act 2013. See also rule 11.9 (Application to postpone the publication of information by the prosecutor).]

Application to lift suspension of prosecution

11.7.

(1) This rule applies where—

(a) the court terminates an agreement before its expiry date; and

(b) the prosecutor wants the court to lift the suspension of the prosecution that applied when the court approved the terms of the agreement.

(2) The prosecutor must—

(a) apply in writing, as soon as practicable after the termination of the agreement; and

(b) serve the application on—

(i) the court officer, and

(ii) the defendant.

(3) A defendant who wants to make representations in response to the application must serve the representations on—

(a) the court officer; and

(b) the prosecutor,

not more than 28 days after service of the application.

[Note. See paragraphs 2(3) and 9 of Schedule 17 to the Crime and Courts Act 2013.]

Notice to discontinue prosecution

11.8.

(1) This rule applies where an agreement expires—

(a) on its expiry date, or on a date treated as its expiry date; and

(b) without having been terminated by the court.

(2) The prosecutor must—

(a) as soon as practicable give notice in writing discontinuing the prosecution on the indictment approved by the court under rule 11.4 (Application to approve the terms of an agreement); and

(b) serve the notice on—

(i) the court officer, and

(ii) the defendant.

[Note. See paragraph 11 of Schedule 17 to the Crime and Courts Act 2013.]

Application to postpone the publication of information by the prosecutor

11.9.

(1) This rule applies where the prosecutor—

(a) makes an application under rule 11.4 (Application to approve the terms of an agreement), rule 11.5 (Application on breach of agreement) or rule 11.6 (Application to approve a variation of the terms of an agreement);

(b) decides not to make an application under rule 11.5, despite believing that the defendant has failed to comply with the terms of the agreement; or

(c) gives a notice under rule 11.8 (Notice to discontinue prosecution).

(2) A party who wants the court to order that the publication of information by the prosecutor about the court's or the prosecutor's decision should be postponed must—

(a) apply in writing, as soon as practicable and in any event before such publication occurs;

(b) serve the application on—

(i) the court officer, and

(ii) the other party; and

(c) in the application—

(i) specify the proposed terms of the order, and for how long it should last, and

(ii) explain why an order in the terms proposed is necessary.

[Note. See paragraph 12 of Schedule 17 to the Crime and Courts Act 2013.

Part 6 of these Rules contains rules about applications for a restriction on reporting what takes place at a public hearing, or public access to what otherwise would be a public hearing.]

Duty of court officer, etc.

11.10.

(1) Unless the court otherwise directs, the court officer must—

(a) arrange for the recording of proceedings on an application to which this Part applies;

(b) arrange for the transcription of such a recording if—

(i) a party wants such a transcript, or

(ii) anyone else wants such a transcript (but that is subject to the restrictions in paragraph (2)).

(2) Unless the court otherwise directs, a person who transcribes a recording of proceedings under such arrangements—

(a) must not supply anyone other than a party with a transcript of a recording of—

(i) a hearing in private, or

(ii) a hearing in public to which reporting restrictions apply;

(b) subject to that, must supply any person with any transcript for which that person asks—

(i) in accordance with the transcription arrangements made by the court officer, and

(ii) on payment by that person of any fee prescribed.

(3) The court officer must not identify either party to a hearing in private under rule 11.3 (Application to approve a proposal to enter an agreement) or rule 11.4 (Application to approve the terms of an agreement)—

(a) in any notice displayed in the vicinity of the courtroom; or

(b) in any other information published by the court officer.

Court's power to vary requirements under this Part

11.11.

(1) The court may—

(a) shorten or extend (even after it has expired) a time limit under this Part;

(b) allow there to be made orally—

(i) an application under rule 11.4 (Application to approve the terms of an agreement), or

(ii) an application under rule 11.7 (Application to lift suspension of prosecution)

where the court exercises its power under rule 11.2(7) to hear one application immediately after another.

(2) A party who wants an extension of time must—

(a) apply when serving the application or notice for which it is needed; and

(b) explain the delay.

Appendix 7: Deferred Prosecution Agreements Code of Practice

Crime and Courts Act 2013

Introduction

This Deferred Prosecution Agreement Code of Practice ("DPA Code") is issued by the Director of Public Prosecutions and Director of the Serious Fraud Office pursuant to paragraph 6(1) of Schedule 17 to the Crime and Courts Act 2013 ("the Act").

Prosecutors should have regard to this DPA Code when:

i. Negotiating Deferred Prosecution Agreements ("DPAs") with an organisation ("P") whom the prosecutor is considering prosecuting for an offence specified in the Act;

ii. Applying to the court for the approval of a DPA; and

iii. Overseeing DPAs after their approval by the court, in particular in relation to variation, breach, termination and completion.

1. Whether a Deferred Prosecution Agreement is a possible disposal of alleged criminal conduct

1.1. A DPA is a discretionary tool created by the Act to provide a way of responding to alleged criminal conduct. The prosecutor may invite P to enter into negotiations to agree a DPA as an alternative to prosecution.

1.2. In order to enter a DPA the prosecutor is to apply the following two stage test. Prosecutors must be satisfied and record that:

Evidential stage

i. Either:

  a) the evidential stage of the Full Code Test in the Code for Crown Prosecutors is satisfied or, if this is not met, that

b) there is at least a reasonable suspicion based upon some admissible evidence that P has committed the offence, and there are reasonable grounds for believing that a continued investigation would provide further admissible evidence within a reasonable period of time, so that all the evidence together would be capable of establishing a realistic prospect of conviction in accordance with the Full Code Test.

And

Public interest stage

ii. The public interest would be properly served by the prosecutor not prosecuting but instead entering into a DPA with P in accordance with the criteria set out below.

1.3 The Prosecutor should first consider whether the test in paragraph 1.2 i a) is met. If it is not met consideration may be given to the test under paragraph 1.2 i b).

1.4 For the purposes of 1.2 i b) a reasonable time period will depend on all the facts and circumstances of the case, including its size, type and complexity.

1.5 If a DPA is considered appropriate by the relevant Director, having determined that either limb of the evidential stage is met, and that the public interest is best served by entering into a DPA, the prosecutor will (where the court approves the DPA) prefer an indictment. The indictment will however then immediately be suspended pending the satisfactory performance, or otherwise, of the DPA.

1.6 In cases where neither limb of the evidential stage can be met by the conclusion of any DPA negotiations and it is not considered appropriate to continue the criminal investigation, the prosecutor should consider whether a Civil Recovery Order is appropriate. Attention is drawn to the Attorney General's guidance to prosecuting bodies on their asset recovery powers under the Proceeds of Crime Act 2002, issued 5 November 2009.

2. Factors that the prosecutor may take into account when deciding whether to enter into a DPA

Negotiations

2.1 An invitation to negotiate a DPA is a matter for the prosecutor's discretion. P has no right to be invited to negotiate a DPA. The SFO and the CPS are first and foremost prosecutors and it will only be in specific circumstances deemed by their Directors to be appropriate that they will decide to offer a DPA instead of pursuing the full prosecution of the alleged conduct. In many cases, criminal prosecution will continue to be the appropriate course of action. An invitation to enter DPA discussions is not a guarantee that a DPA will be offered at the conclusion of the discussions.

2.2 Where the prosecutor is satisfied that:

i. either the evidential stage of the Full Code Test in the Code for Crown Prosecutors is met, or there is a reasonable suspicion based upon some admissible evidence that P has committed an offence;

ii. the full extent of the alleged offending has been identified; and

iii. the public interest would likely be met by a DPA,

then the prosecutor may initiate DPA negotiations with any P who is being investigated with a view to prosecution in connection with an offence specified in the Act.

2.3 When considering whether a DPA may be appropriate the prosecutor will have regard to existing Codes of Practice and Guidance, in particular:

i. The Code for Crown Prosecutors;

ii. The Joint Prosecution Guidance on Corporate Prosecutions ("the Corporate Prosecution Guidance");

iii. Bribery Act 2010: Joint Prosecution Guidance ("the Bribery Act Guidance");

iv. The DPA Code.

2.4 Where either limb of the evidential stage is passed, the prosecutor must consider whether or not a prosecution is in the public interest. The more serious the offence, the more likely it is that prosecution will be required in the public interest. Indicators of seriousness include not just the value of any gain or loss, but also the risk of harm to the public, to unidentified victims, shareholders, employees and creditors and to the stability and integrity of financial markets and international trade. The impact of the offending in other countries, and not just the consequences in the UK, should be taken into account.

2.5 Prosecutors must balance factors for and against prosecution carefully and fairly. Public interest factors that can affect the decision to prosecute usually depend on the seriousness of the offence, which includes the culpability of P and the harm to the victim. A prosecution will usually take place unless there are public interest factors against prosecution which clearly outweigh those tending in favour of prosecution.

2.6 In applying the public interest factors when considering whether to charge, seek to enter a DPA or take no further criminal action the prosecutor undertakes a balancing exercise of the factors that tend to support prosecution and those that do not. This is an exercise of discretion. Which factors are considered relevant and what weight is given to each are matters for the individual prosecutor. It is quite possible that one public interest factor alone may outweigh a number of other factors which tend in the opposite direction. Decisions will be made on an individual case by case basis.

2.7 Prosecutors should have regard when considering the public interest stage to the UK's commitment to abide by the OECD Convention on "Combating Bribery of Foreign Public Officials in International Business Transactions" in particular Article 5. Investigation and prosecution of the bribery of a foreign public official should not be influenced by considerations of national economic interest, the potential effect upon relations with another State or the identity of the natural or legal persons involved.

2.8 The prosecutor should have regard to the public interest factors set out in the Code for Crown Prosecutors. In addition the following non-exhaustive factors will be of relevance in deciding whether a prosecution is appropriate or not in order to satisfy the public interest:

2.8.1 Additional public interest factors in favour of prosecution

i. A history of similar conduct (including prior criminal, civil and regulatory enforcement actions against P and/or its directors/partners and/or majority shareholders). Failing to prosecute in circumstances where there have been repeated or serious breaches of the law may not be a proportionate response and may not provide adequate deterrent effects.

ii. The conduct alleged is part of the established business practices of P.

iii. The offence was committed at a time when P had no or an ineffective corporate compliance programme and it has not been able to demonstrate a significant improvement in its compliance programme since then.

iv. P has been previously subject to warning, sanctions or criminal charges and had nonetheless failed to take adequate action to prevent future unlawful conduct, or had continued to engage in the conduct.

v. Failure to notify the wrongdoing within reasonable time of the offending conduct[1] coming to light.

vi. Reporting the wrongdoing but failing to verify it, or reporting it knowing or believing it to be inaccurate, misleading or incomplete.

vii. Significant level of harm caused directly or indirectly to the victims of the wrongdoing or a substantial adverse impact to the integrity or confidence of markets, local or national governments.

2.8.2 Additional public interest factors against prosecution

i. Co-operation: Considerable weight may be given to a genuinely proactive approach adopted by P's management team when the offending is brought to their notice, involving within a reasonable time of the offending coming to light reporting P's offending otherwise unknown to

1 For what is reasonable see paragraph 2.9 below

the prosecutor and taking remedial actions including, where appropriate, compensating victims. In applying this factor the prosecutor needs to establish whether sufficient information about the operation and conduct of P has been supplied in order to assess whether P has been co-operative. Co-operation will include identifying relevant witnesses, disclosing their accounts and the documents shown to them. Where practicable it will involve making the witnesses available for interview when requested. It will further include providing a report in respect of any internal investigation including source documents.

ii. A lack of a history of similar conduct involving prior criminal, civil and regulatory enforcement actions against P and/or its directors/partners and/or majority shareholders; The prosecutor should contact relevant regulatory departments (including where applicable those overseas) to ascertain whether there are existing investigations in relation to P and/or its directors/partners and/or majority shareholders;

iii. The existence of a proactive corporate compliance programme[2] both at the time of offending and at the time of reporting but which failed to be effective in this instance;

iv. The offending represents isolated actions by individuals, for example by a rogue director;

v. The offending is not recent and P in its current form is effectively a different entity from

that which committed the offences – for example it has been taken over by another organisation, it no longer operates in the relevant industry or market, P's management team has completely changed, disciplinary action has been taken against all of the culpable individuals, including dismissal where appropriate, or corporate structures or processes have been changed to minimise the risk of a repetition of offending;

vi. A conviction is likely to have disproportionate consequences for P, under domestic law, the law of another jurisdiction including but not limited to that of the European Union, always bearing in mind the seriousness of the offence and any other relevant public interest factors;[33]

vii. A conviction is likely to have collateral effects on the public, P's employees and shareholders or P's and/or institutional pension holders.

2 The prosecutor may choose to bring in external resource to assist in the assessment of P's compliance culture and programme for example as described in any self-report.

3 Any candidate or tenderer (including company directors and any person having powers of representation, decision or control) who has been convicted of fraud relating to the protection of the financial interests of the European Communities, corruption, or a money laundering offence is mandatorily excluded from participation in public contracts within the EU. Discretionary exclusion may follow in respect of a conviction for a criminal offence.

2.9 With respect to the "Additional public interest factors against prosecution", at paragraph 2.8.2 i. above:

2.9.1 The prosecutor in giving weight to P's self- report will consider the totality of information that P provides to the prosecutor. It must be remembered that when P self-reports it will have been incriminated by the actions of individuals. It will ordinarily be appropriate that those individuals be investigated and where appropriate prosecuted. P must ensure in its provision of material as part of the self-report that it does not withhold material that would jeopardise an effective investigation and where appropriate prosecution of those individuals. To do so would be a strong factor in favour of prosecution.

2.9.2 The prosecutor will also consider how early P self-reports, the extent that P involves the prosecutor in the early stages of an investigation (for example, in order to discuss work plans, timetabling, or to provide the opportunity to the prosecutor to give direction and where appropriate commence an early criminal investigation where it can use statutory powers in particular against individuals).

2.9.3 The prosecutor will consider whether any actions taken by P by not self-reporting earlier may have prejudiced the investigation into P or the individuals that incriminate P. In particular the prosecutor will critically assess the manner of any internal investigation to determine whether its conduct could have led to material being destroyed or the gathering of first accounts from suspects being delayed to the extent that the opportunity for fabrication has been afforded. Internal investigations which lead to such adverse consequences may militate against the use of DPAs.

2.10 The Bribery Act Guidance provides factors tending in favour of or against prosecution in respect of each offence under the Bribery Act 2010. In doing so it refers to the Code for Crown Prosecutors, the Corporate Prosecution Guidance and unique considerations appropriate to the particular bribery offence being considered. A prosecutor in considering the public interest under the Code for Crown Prosecutors in respect of a bribery offence must therefore also consider the current Bribery Act Guidance offered in respect of the particular offence under consideration.

3. Process for invitation to enter into negotiations

3.1 If the prosecutor decides to offer P the opportunity to enter into DPA negotiations, it will do so by way of a formal letter of invitation outlining the basis on which any negotiations will proceed.

3.2 That letter will constitute the beginning of the DPA negotiation period, which period will end on either the withdrawal of one or both parties from the process, or the approval/ refusal by the court of a DPA at a final hearing. Neither party will be obliged to give reasons for withdrawal from negotiations. However in the event of withdrawal from negotiations by the prosecutor it will ordinarily be appropriate to provide P with the gist of the reasons for doing so. In some instances this may not be possible without prejudicing the investigation.

3.3 All parties should keep in mind that DPAs are entirely voluntary agreements. The prosecutor is under no obligation to invite P to negotiate a DPA and P is under no obligation to accept that invitation should it be made. The terms of a DPA are similarly voluntary, and neither party is obliged to agree any particular term therein. The Act does not, and this DPA Code cannot, alter the law on legal professional privilege.

3.4 DPA negotiations must be transparent.

The prosecutor must:

i. Ensure that a full and accurate record of negotiations is prepared and retained. It is essential that a full written record is kept of every key action and event in the discussion process, including details of every offer or concession made by each party, and the reasons for every decision taken by the prosecutor. Meetings between the parties should be minuted and the minutes agreed and signed;

ii. Ensure that the prosecution and P have obtained sufficient information from each other so each can play an informed part in the negotiations;

iii. Ensure that documentation and any other material relevant to the matters the prosecutor is considering prosecuting is retained by P for any future prosecution;

iv. Ensure that the proposed DPA placed before the court fully and fairly reflects P's alleged offending; and

v. The prosecutor must not agree additional matters with P which are not recorded in the DPA and not made known to the court.

The letter of invitation

3.5 In order to initiate the DPA negotiations, the prosecutor will first send P a letter containing:

i. Confirmation of the prosecutor's decision to offer P the opportunity to enter into DPA negotiations;

ii. A request for confirmation of whether P wishes to enter into negotiations in accordance with the Act and this DPA Code; and

iii. A timeframe within which P must notify the prosecutor whether it accepts the invitation to enter into DPA negotiations.

Undertakings

3.6 Where P agrees to engage in DPA negotiations, the prosecutor should send P a letter setting out the way in which the discussions will be conducted. This letter should make undertakings in respect of:

i. the confidentiality of the fact that DPA negotiations are taking place;

ii. the confidentiality of information provided by the prosecutor and P in the course of the DPA negotiations.

3.7 In doing so the undertaking will make clear:

i. the use which may be made by the prosecutor of information provided by P pursuant to paragraph 13 of Schedule 17 to the Act;

ii. that the law in relation to the disclosure of unused material may require the prosecutor to provide information received during the course of DPA negotiations to a defendant in criminal proceedings; and

iii. that the information may be disclosed as permitted by law.

3.8 The letter should also include:

i. a statement of the prosecutor's responsibility for disclosure of material pursuant to this DPA Code;

ii. a warning that the provision by P of inaccurate, misleading or incomplete information where P knew or ought to have known that the information was inaccurate, misleading or incomplete may lead to a prosecution of P:

   a. for an offence consisting of the provision of such inaccurate, misleading or incomplete information, and/or

   b. for an offence or offences which are the subject of an agreed DPA; and

iii. the practical means by which the discussions will be conducted including appropriate time limits.

3.9 The prosecutor will require P to provide an undertaking:

i. that information provided by the prosecutor in the course of DPA negotiations will be treated as confidential and will not be disclosed to any other party, other than for the purposes of the DPA negotiations or as required by law; and

ii. all documentation or other material relevant to the matters the prosecutor is considering prosecuting is retained until P is released from the obligation to do so by the prosecutor.

3.10 In exceptional circumstances and where permitted by law the prosecutor may agree in writing to different terms regarding the confidentiality of information. Ordinarily the decision to vary confidentiality terms will be dealt with on a case by case basis at the point that the disclosure is considered. In deciding whether to make such an exceptional variation, for example in relation to a disclosure of information to third parties, the prosecutor will take into account that statutory and common law safeguards already exist in respect of disclosure of information to third parties.

3.11 Until the issues of confidentiality, use of and retention of information have been agreed to the satisfaction of both parties, and the agreement reflected in signed undertakings, the prosecutor must not continue with the substantive DPA negotiations.

4. Subsequent use of information obtained by a prosecutor during the DPA negotiation period

4.1 The use to which information obtained by a prosecutor during the DPA negotiation period may subsequently be put is dealt with at paragraph 13 of Schedule 17 to the Act. The use of any particular item is therefore governed by that legislation.

4.2 It is recognised that there is a balance to be struck between encouraging all parties to be able to negotiate freely, and the risk that P may seek knowingly (or when it should have known) to induce the prosecutor to enter into a DPA on an inaccurate, misleading or incomplete basis.

4.3 If P provides inaccurate, misleading or incomplete information where P knew or ought to have known that the information was inaccurate, misleading or incomplete, the prosecutor may instigate fresh proceedings against P for the same alleged offence in accordance with paragraph 11 of Schedule 17 to the Act notwithstanding any DPA that may have been approved.

4.4 There are two contexts within which information obtained by the prosecutor during the DPA negotiation period may subsequently be used.

i. Where a DPA is approved by the court under paragraph 8 of Schedule 17 to the Act the legislation provides (at paragraph 13 (1) and (2) of Schedule 17) that the statement of facts contained in the DPA may be used in subsequent criminal proceedings as an admission in accordance with section 10 of the Criminal Justice Act 1967.

ii. Where a DPA has not been concluded and the prosecutor chooses to pursue criminal proceedings against P, the material described in paragraph 13(6) of Schedule 17 to the Act may only be used in the limited circumstances described in paragraphs 13 (4) and (5) of Schedule 17 to the Act.

4.5 Apart from the material described at paragraph 13(6) of Schedule 17 to the Act, there is no limitation on the use to which other information obtained by a prosecutor during the DPA negotiation period may subsequently be put during criminal proceedings brought against P, or against anyone else (so far as the rules of evidence permit).

4.6 By way of non-exhaustive example, if the DPA negotiations fail the following types of document provided to a prosecutor in those negotiations would be available to be used by the prosecutor subject to the rules of evidence in a subsequent prosecution of P:

i. pre-existing contemporary key documentation such as contracts, accountancy records including payments of any kind, any records evidencing the transfer of money, emails or other communications etc. provided to the prosecutor by P;

ii. any internal or independent investigation report carried out by P and disclosed to the prosecutor prior to the DPA negotiation period commencing;

iii. any interview note or witness statement obtained from an employee of P and disclosed to the prosecutor prior to the DPA negotiation period commencing;

iv. any document obtained by the prosecutor at any time obtained from any source other than P; and

v. any information obtained by the prosecutor as a result of enquiries made as a result of information provided by P at any time.

5. Unused Material and Disclosure

5.1. Negotiations to enter into a DPA will necessarily take place prior to the institution of proceedings and the statutory disclosure rules will therefore not be engaged at this early stage.

5.2. P should have sufficient information to play an informed part in the negotiations. The purpose of disclosure here is to ensure that negotiations are fair and that P is not misled as to the strength of the prosecution case. The prosecutor must always be alive to the potential need to disclose material in the interests of justice and fairness in the particular circumstances of any case. For instance, disclosure ought to be made of information that might undermine the factual basis of conclusions drawn by P from material disclosed by P. A statement of the prosecutor's duty of disclosure will be included in the terms and conditions letter provided to P at the outset of the negotiations.

5.3. Consideration should be given to reasonable and specific requests for disclosure by P. Where the need for such disclosure is not apparent to the prosecutor, any disclosure may depend on what P chooses to reveal to the prosecutor about its case in order to justify the request.

5.4. The investigator's duty to pursue reasonable lines of inquiry in accordance with the CPIA 1996 Code of Practice is not affected by the introduction of DPAs or the application of this Code. What is reasonable in each case will depend upon the particular circumstances.

5.5. Before the final DPA hearing the prosecutor must obtain from the investigator enquiring into the alleged offence or offences information that will enable the prosecutor to make a written declaration to the court, as required by Criminal Procedure Rule 12.2 (3) (b), namely that:

i. the investigator enquiring into the offence or alleged offences has certified that no information has been supplied which the investigator knows to be inaccurate, misleading or incomplete; and

ii. the prosecutor has complied with the prosecution obligation to disclose material to the defendant.

5.6. To satisfy (ii) above, the prosecutor should request that the investigator provide written certification to the prosecutor that any material retained by the investigator which may satisfy the test for prosecution disclosure as outlined in this DPA Code has been drawn to the attention of the prosecutor.

5.7 Where a DPA is approved by the court and a bill of indictment is preferred upon entering into a DPA, the CPIA will apply. However, the immediate suspension of the indictment will have the effect of immediately suspending with it the disclosure obligations imposed. The statutory disclosure obligations and standard directions providing time limits for compliance will only apply if the suspension is lifted in the event of termination of the DPA and the prosecution of P.

5.8 The disclosure duty of the prosecutor as outlined in this DPA Code is a continuing one and the prosecutor must disclose to P any material that comes to light after the DPA has been agreed which satisfies the test for disclosure above.

6. Statement of facts

6.1. The application must include a statement of facts which must:

i. give particulars relating to each alleged offence;

ii. include details where possible of any financial gain or loss, with reference to key documents that must be attached.

6.2. The parties should resolve any factual issues necessary to allow the court to agree terms of the DPA on a clear, fair and accurate basis. The court does not have the power to adjudicate upon factual differences in DPA proceedings.

6.3. There is no requirement for formal admissions of guilt in respect of the offences charged by the indictment though it will be necessary for P to admit the contents and meaning of key documents referred to in the statement of facts.

6.4. In the event that P is prosecuted for the alleged offence addressed by a court approved DPA, the statement of facts would be admissible against P in accordance with section 10 of the Criminal Justice Act 1967 in any subsequent criminal proceedings.

7. Terms

7.1. A DPA may include a broad range of terms, some of which are detailed in a non- exhaustive list in paragraph 5(3) of Schedule 17 to the Act.

7.2. The prosecutor and P are required to agree the terms of a DPA[4] which are fair, reasonable and proportionate. What terms are fair, reasonable and proportionate, including the length of the DPA, will be determined on a case by case basis. The terms may consist of a combination of requirements and it will normally be fair, reasonable and proportionate for there to be a financial penalty. It is particularly desirable that measures should be included that achieve redress for victims, such as payment of compensation. Paragraph 5 of Schedule 17 to the Act suggests that a possible term of a DPA is the recovery of the reasonable costs of the prosecutor in relation to the alleged offence or the DPA. The prosecutor should ordinarily seek to recover these costs, including the costs of the investigation where they have been incurred by the prosecutor.

7.3. The basis of the DPA and its terms will be explained in an agreed written application to the court.

7.4. The terms must set out clearly the measures with which P must comply. Clarity is important so P understands what is required. Further, in the event of breach of a term drafting ambiguity will complicate breach proceedings.

7.5. The terms must be proportionate to the offence and tailored to the specific facts of the case.

7.6. The DPA must specify the end date.

7.7. The following will normally be requirements of the DPA:

i. that the DPA relates only to the offences particularised in the counts of the draft indictment;[5]

ii. a warranty provided by both P and with P's consent, its legal advisers[6] that the information provided to the prosecutor throughout the DPA

---

4 The length of a DPA will need to be sufficient to be capable of permitting compliance with other terms such as financial penalties paid in instalments, monitoring and co-operation with the investigations and trials into individuals.

5 Prosecutors should not agree to a term that would prevent P from being prosecuted for conduct not included in the indictment even where the conduct has been disclosed during the course of DPA negotiations but not charged.

6 The SRA Code of Conduct sets out in Chapter 5 the duties of a solicitor when conducting litigation or acting as an advocate. There are obligations on a solicitor:

a. Not to attempt to deceive or knowingly or recklessly mislead the court [O5.1],
b. Not to be complicit in any other person deceiving or misleading the court [O5.2], and
c. Where relevant to inform their client of circumstances in which their duties to the court outweigh their obligations to their client [O5.4].

negotiations and upon which the DPA is based does not knowingly, contain inaccurate, misleading or incomplete information relevant to the conduct P has disclosed to the prosecutor.

iii. a requirement on P to notify the prosecutor and to provide where requested any documentation or other material that it becomes aware of whilst the DPA is in force which P knows or suspects would have been relevant to the offences particularised in the draft indictment.

7.8. The following will normally be terms of a DPA:

i. A financial order;

ii. The payment of the reasonable costs of the prosecutor;

iii. Co-operation with an investigation related to the alleged offence(s)[7].

7.9. The suggested financial terms may include but are not confined to: compensating victims; payment of a financial penalty; payment of the prosecutor's costs; donations to charities which support the victims of the offending; disgorgement of profits. There is no requirement to include all or any of these terms all of which are a matter of negotiation with P and subject to judicial oversight. The following should be noted:

i. A late payment may constitute a breach of the DPA leading to breach and termination. It may however be appropriate to make provision for short delays pursuant to paragraph 5 (5) of Schedule 17 to the Act requiring the payment of interest on any payment(s) not paid by the date agreed and specify the rate that applies[8].

ii. Where payment of a donation, compensation, financial penalty and/or costs is an agreed term of the DPA, the starting point should be that monies are ordered to be paid within seven days of the final hearing and this should be a standard term unless not fair, reasonable or proportionate.

iii. Where a financial penalty is to be imposed, the figure agreed must approximate to what would have been imposed had P pleaded guilty (see section 8).

iv. There should be a transparent and consistent approach to the setting of a financial penalty that is analogous to the sentencing framework for setting fines so the parties and the court will know before they enter into the process what the appropriate starting point is.

v. Financial penalties and disgorgements of profits will be paid to the prosecutor and then passed to the Consolidated Fund. Charitable donations and compensation will be paid by P directly or through an

7 For example in respect of individuals. The obligation would include the provision of material to be used in evidence and for the purposes of disclosure.

8 The rate should ordinarily be not less than the rate of interest payable on post judgment debts at the date when the DPA is approved

intermediary agreed by the parties and approved by the court as part of the DPA. P will provide confirmation and supporting evidence to the prosecutor of this as required.

7.10 Other terms that may be agreed might include:

i. prohibiting P from engaging in certain activities.

ii. financial reporting obligations.

iii. putting in place a robust compliance and/or monitoring programme.

iv. co-operation with sector wide investigations.

Monitors

7.11 An important consideration for entering into a DPA is whether P already has a genuinely proactive and effective corporate compliance programme. The use of monitors should therefore be approached with care. The appointment of a monitor will depend upon the factual circumstances of each case and must always be fair, reasonable and proportionate.

7.12 A monitor's primary responsibility is to assess and monitor P's internal controls, advise of necessary compliance improvements that will reduce the risk of future recurrence of the conduct subject to the DPA and report specified misconduct to the prosecutor.

7.13 Where the terms require a monitor to be appointed it is the responsibility of P to pay all the costs of the selection, appointment, remuneration of the monitor, and reasonable costs of the prosecutor associated with the monitorship during the monitoring period. In assessing whether a term of monitoring may satisfy the statutory test the prosecutor should give consideration to the costs of such a term as these may be relevant.

7.14 P shall afford to the monitor complete access to all relevant aspects of its business during the course of the monitoring period as requested by the monitor. Any legal professional privilege that may exist in respect of investigating compliance issues that arise during the monitorship is unaffected by the Act, this DPA Code or a DPA.

7.15 As part of the DPA negotiations P should provide the prosecutor and the court with details of three potential monitors, including relevant qualifications, specialist knowledge and experience; any associations the monitor has or has had with P and/or associated companies and/or person(s) or any named companies or person(s) that feature in the DPA to avoid any conflict of interest; and an estimate of costs of the monitorship.

7.16 P should indicate their preferred monitor with reasons for the preference.

7.17 The prosecutor should ordinarily accept P's preferred monitor. However where the prosecutor considers there to be a conflict of interest or that the monitor is inappropriate, or does not have the requisite experience and authority, they may reject the proposed appointment. Similarly the court may register its dissatisfaction with the selection by not approving the proposed term.

7.18 Where monitorship is proposed to be a term of a DPA, before the DPA is approved the monitor will be selected, provisionally appointed, the terms of the monitorship agreed by the parties to the DPA, a detailed work plan for the first year (to include the method of review and frequency of reporting to the prosecutor) and an outline work plan for the remainder of the monitoring period agreed with the monitor including provisions or limits as to costs. The monitor's report should include a breakdown of his proposed costs, and on what matters costs are incurred.

7.19 Terms of the DPA should include the length of time the monitors should be appointed. Provision should however be made in the DPA that if the monitor is satisfied that P's policies are functioning properly such that there is no need for further monitoring, the monitor may inform the prosecutor who will, subject to being satisfied through discussion with the monitor that the monitor's views are reasonable, agree to the termination or suspension of the monitor's appointment. Conversely the DPA should provide that, if the monitor and the prosecutor agree that P has not, or it appears will not by the end of the monitoring period have successfully satisfied its obligations with respect to the monitor's mandate, the term of the monitorship will be extended provided that no extension exceeds the length of the DPA.

7.20 Monitors' reports and associated correspondence shall be designated confidential with disclosure restricted to the prosecutor, P and the court, save as otherwise permitted by law.

7.21 No two monitoring programmes will be the same, given the varying facts and circumstances of each case including the nature and size of P. Terms included in the monitor's agreement may include, but are not limited to, ensuring that P has in place[9]:

i. a code of conduct;

ii. an appropriate training and education programme;

iii. internal procedures for reporting conduct issues which enable officers and employees to report issues in a safe and confidential manner;

iv. processes for identifying key strategic risk areas;

v. reasonable safeguards to approve the appointment of representatives and payment of commissions;

vi. a gifts and hospitality policy;

9 These policies and procedures are not intended to provide an indication of what can amount to adequate procedures under s. 7 Bribery Act 2010.

vii. reasonable procedures for undertaking due diligence on potential projects, acquisitions, business partners, agents, representatives, distributors, sub-contractors and suppliers;

viii. procurement procedures which minimise the opportunity of misconduct;

ix. contract terms between P and its business partners, subcontractors, distributors, and suppliers include express contractual obligations and remedies in relation to misconduct;

x. internal management and audit processes which include reasonable controls against misconduct where appropriate;

xi. policies and processes in all of its subsidiaries and operating businesses, and joint ventures in which it has management control, and that P uses reasonable endeavours to ensure that the joint ventures in which it does not have management control, together with key subcontractors and representatives, are familiar with and are required to abide by its code of conduct to the extent possible;.

xii. procedures compatible with money laundering regulations;

xiii. policies regarding charitable and political donations;

xiv. terms related to external controls, e.g. procedures for selection of appropriate charities;

xv. policies relating to internal investigative resources, employee disciplinary procedures; and compliance screening of prospective employees;

xvi. policies relating to the extent to which senior management takes responsibility for implementing relevant practices and procedures;

xvii. mechanisms for review of the effectiveness of relevant policies and procedures across business and jurisdictions in which P operates;

xviii. compensation structures that remove incentives for unethical behaviour.

7.22 In designing a monitoring programme regard should be had to contemporary external guidance on compliance programmes[10].

8. Financial Penalty

8.1. The prosecutor represents the public interest, and should assist with the identification of appropriate terms by drawing the judge's attention where possible and relevant to the following information:

10 At the time of publishing guidance can be found in the Ministry of Justice Bribery Act 2010: Guidance to help commercial organisations prevent bribery, the OECD Good Practice Guide on Internal Controls, Ethics and Compliance, the BS 10500 Anti-Bribery System Standard, the US Sentencing Commission's Federal Sentencing Guidelines Manual, in particular its guidance on effective compliance and ethics programmes, and the guidance on corporate compliance programmes in the US Department of Justice's Principles of Federal Prosecution of Business.

i. any victim statement or other information available to the prosecutor as to the impact of the alleged offence on the victim;

ii. any statutory provisions relevant to the offender and the offences under consideration;

iii. any relevant Sentencing Council Guidelines and guideline cases; and

iv. the aggravating and mitigating factors of the alleged offence under consideration.

8.2. Such information where available and relevant should form part of the agreed written application to be provided to the court at the final hearing.

8.3. Any financial penalty is to be broadly comparable to a fine that the court would have imposed upon P following a guilty plea.[11] This is intended to enable the parties and courts to have regard to relevant pre-existing sentencing principles and guidelines in order to determine the appropriate level for a financial penalty in an individual case. This should include consideration of P's means and where compensation is appropriate, this should be given priority over a penalty.

8.4. The extent of the discretion available when considering a financial penalty is broad. The discount for a guilty plea is applied by the sentencing court after it has taken into account all relevant considerations, including any assistance given by P. The level of the discount to reflect P's assistance would depend on the circumstances and the level of assistance given, and the parties should be guided by sentencing practice, statute and pre-existing case law on this matter. A financial penalty must provide for a discount equivalent to that which would be afforded by an early guilty plea. Current guidelines provide for a one third discount for a plea at the earliest opportunity.

8.5. To be considered as voluntary and therefore mitigating, co-operation should be over and above mere compliance with any coercive[12] measures.

9. Preliminary hearing(s)

9.1. The Criminal Procedure Rules make provision for the contents of the application[13].

9.2. The prosecutor should contact a court designated to approve DPAs in order to request a listing and in doing so provide a realistic time estimate for a preliminary hearing.

9.3. The draft proposed application and any supporting documents must be submitted on a confidential basis to the court before the preliminary hearing.

11 Schedule 17, Paragraph 5 (4).

12 Such as notices under s.2 (1) Criminal Justice Act 1987 issued by the Serious Fraud Office

13 Crim PR 12

9.4. The application must explain why the agreement is in the interests of justice and fair, reasonable and proportionate. In so explaining the prosecutor must address issues such as concurrent jurisdiction, on-going and/or subsequent ancillary proceedings, any conduct outwith the scope of the DPA which P has disclosed to the prosecutor but which does not form part of the draft indictment on account of the test at paragraph 1.2 above not having been satisfied.

9.5. Consideration should be given at the preliminary hearing to additional relevant issues such as timing of subsequent hearings.

9.6. The appropriate manner and timing of a preliminary hearing will vary on a case by case basis, and the court may adjourn a preliminary hearing if it requires more information about the facts or terms of a proposed DPA before it can make the full declaration under paragraph 7(1) of Schedule 17 to the Act.

10. Application for Approval

10.1. The Criminal Procedure Rules make provision for the contents of the application for final approval[14]. They further provide that an application for final approval should be sought as soon as practicable once the court has made a declaration under paragraph 7(1) of Schedule 17 to the Act and the parties have settled the terms of the DPA.

10.2. The basis of the DPA and its terms will be explained in an agreed written application accompanied by the proposed final terms of the DPA, agreed case statement with any supporting documents and the prosecutor's confirmation of which evidential test has been met. These documents must be submitted to the court on a confidential basis before the application for approval.

10.3. Issues germane to whether the DPA is in the interests of justice and its terms being fair, reasonable and proportionate such as concurrent jurisdiction, on-going and/or subsequent ancillary proceedings, must also be addressed by the prosecutor in the application for approval.

10.4. The application for approval of the DPA may be in private. This is likely to be almost always necessary as the prosecutor and P will be uncertain as to whether the court will grant a declaration under paragraph 8 (1). For the parties to make an application in open court which was refused might lead to the uncertainties and destabilisation that private preliminary hearings are designed to avoid.

10.5. The court may adjourn an application for approval if it requires more information about the facts or terms of a proposed DPA before it can make the declaration under paragraph 8(1) of Schedule 17 to the Act.

---

14 Ibid

11. Declaration in Open Court

11.1. If a DPA is approved, the court must make a declaration to that effect along with reasons in an open hearing[15].

11.2. Once the declaration has been made in open court the prosecutor will, unless prevented from doing so by an enactment or by an order from the Court, publish on its website:

i. the DPA;

ii. the declaration of the court pursuant to paragraph 8 (1) of Schedule 17 to the Act with the reasons for making such a declaration;

iii. the declaration of the court pursuant to paragraph 7 (1) of Schedule 17 to the Act with the reasons for making such a declaration; and

iv. if appropriate, any initial refusal to make such a declaration with reasons for declining.

11.3. Immediate publication may be prevented by any enactment or order that postponement is necessary to avoid a substantial risk of prejudice to the administration of justice in any legal proceedings. P's offence and the sanctions provided for in the DPA will be made public as soon as it is safe to do so.

12. Breach of a DPA

12.1. Paragraph 9 of Schedule 17 to the Act deals with the situation where P is, or is believed by the prosecutor to be, in breach of a term of a DPA that has been approved at a final hearing.

Alleging and proving breach of a DPA

12.2. If, prior to the expiry of the DPA, it is believed that P is in breach of it, where possible the prosecutor should ask P to rectify the alleged breach immediately. In cases of minor breaches, it may be possible for a solution to be reached efficiently in this way, without the need for either an application under paragraph 9 of Schedule 17 to the Act or a variation of the DPA under paragraph 10 of Schedule 17 to the Act. The prosecutor will nevertheless still be required to publish details of the breach pursuant to paragraph 9 (8) of Schedule 17 to the Act. The prosecutor should also notify the court of any such developments.

12.3. If the prosecutor is unable to secure a satisfactory outcome in this way, it may apply to the court seeking a finding that P is in breach of the term as alleged, and explaining the remedy it seeks as a result. The question of whether or not there has been a breach of a term is to be judged on the balance of

15 See paragraph 15.4 in respect of listing

probabilities. The successful party may seek its costs of an application under paragraph 9 of Schedule 17[16].

12.4. If the court finds that P is in breach of a term of the DPA it may invite the parties to agree a suitable proposed remedy. If agreement can be reached, that proposed remedy must then be presented to the court by way of an application in accordance with paragraph 10 of Schedule 17 to the Act. The court will approve the variation only if that variation is in the interests of justice and the terms of the DPA as varied are fair, reasonable and proportionate. It is anticipated that this mechanism should generally be used to rectify relatively minor breaches of a DPA where the parties have been unable to agree a remedy without the involvement of the court.

Termination following breach of a DPA

12.5. Where the alleged breach is more material or the parties are unable to agree a suitable remedy or the court does not approve a proposed remedy, the court may order that the DPA be terminated. If the court makes such an order the DPA shall cease to take effect from that point onwards, and the prosecutor may apply to have the suspension of the indictment covered by the DPA lifted in accordance with paragraph 2 of Schedule 17 to the Act.

12.6. Where a DPA has been terminated in this way, P is not entitled to the return of any monies paid under the DPA prior to its termination, or to any other relief for detriment arising from its compliance with the DPA up to that point (for example the costs of a monitoring programme). The prosecutor may seek from P the costs of an application under paragraph 9 of schedule 17 to the Act[17].

Post termination process

12.7. Should the DPA be terminated it will be usual for the prosecutor to apply for the suspension of the indictment to be lifted and P to be prosecuted. The application to lift the suspension need not be made at the time that the DPA is terminated.

12.8. The lifting of the suspension would reinstitute criminal proceedings. Given the manner in which the earlier investigation was concluded and/or the passage of time since the DPA was concluded the prosecutor may not be in a position to commence criminal proceedings immediately. Further investigation and preparation may be needed in order for the prosecutor to be trial ready.

12.9. Before re-opening proceedings, the prosecutor must be satisfied that the Full Code Test under the Code for Crown Prosecutors is met in relation to each charge. The court will have been informed at the final hearing if the original

16 Crim PR 76.1 (c)
17 Ibid

charge was pursuant to the second limb of the evidential stage at paragraph 1.2 i b) above, in which case the prosecutor will now need to be satisfied that the more stringent evidential stage of the Full Code Test is met. Furthermore the public interest position will need reassessing in light of the breach.

12.10. If the prosecutor requires time before being in a position to re-open proceedings the court should be informed of the prosecutor's proposed course of action and then kept informed of progress.

13. Variation of a DPA

13.1. Paragraph 10 of Schedule 17 to the Act deals with the situation where it becomes necessary to vary the terms of a DPA that has been approved.

13.2. There are two possible situations in which variation may be necessary.

i. The first is where a breach has occurred in respect of which the prosecutor has applied under paragraph 9 of Schedule 17, and the court has invited the parties to agree a solution to that breach, which the court then has to consider whether to approve.

ii. The second situation is where a breach has not yet occurred, but, absent the variation, is likely to. A variation in this category will only be approved by the court if it arises from circumstances that were not, and could not have been, foreseen by the prosecutor or P at the time that the DPA was agreed[18]. What circumstances a court considers to be adequate in these types of cases will have to be decided on a case by case basis. Variation of a DPA is not a mechanism that exists for mere convenience or efficiency. A DPA is a serious sanction for criminal conduct and will have been approved by the court on that basis. In the vast majority of cases the terms of a DPA that are approved at a final hearing should be strictly complied with in their entirety, failing which P risks prosecution.

13.3. In both situations, it is the prosecutor that must apply to the court to seek a declaration that a variation is acceptable. P does not have a right to apply to the court for a variation; it may only ask the prosecutor for a variation.

13.4. If a variation is approved, the court must give its declaration to that effect in an open hearing. Costs of an application under paragraph 10 of Schedule 17 to the Act may be sought[19].

14. Discontinuance

14.1. On expiry of the DPA, the prosecutor should give notice to the court that it does not want proceedings to continue, in accordance with paragraph 11(1) of Schedule 17 to the Act.

18 Paragraph 10(1)(b) of Schedule 17 to the Act
19 Crim PR 76.1 (c)

14.2. Where considered necessary, consultation with the investigator and any monitor should take place prior to discontinuance.

14.3. Discontinuance notices should be sent to the court as soon as practicable after the decision to discontinue, and copies should be sent to P and the investigator.

14.4. The notice should state:

i. The effective date of discontinuance;

ii. The offences to be discontinued;

iii. Confirmation that the DPA has expired.

14.5. A DPA will ordinarily expire on the date specified in the agreement. However, this will not always be the case, and prosecutors should be aware of the various circumstances under paragraph 11 of Schedule 17 to the Act in which a DPA is to be treated as having or not having expired.

14.6. No notice of discontinuance is needed where the court terminates the DPA: see paragraph 11(5)(b) of Schedule 17 to the Act.

14.7. In contrast to discontinuance under the section 23A of the Prosecutions of Offences Act 1985, once proceedings are discontinued under paragraph 11(1), fresh proceedings against P for the same offence may not be instituted unless the conditions specified in paragraph 11(3) of Schedule 17 to the Act (provision of inaccurate, misleading or incomplete information by P) are satisfied.

15. Applications in Private

15.1. Where an application in private is contemplated all parties should consider whether the hearing can be heard in public as a starting point and if not, whether as much as possible of the hearing can be heard in public.

15.2. An application for a private hearing might be made for example where it is necessary to avoid a substantial risk of prejudice to the administration of justice in any legal proceedings.

15.3. The court will not identify the parties to a private application.

15.4. Where the application to approve the DPA is in private it would be normally appropriate for reasons of transparency and open justice for the parties to request the court to delay the making of a declaration approving a DPA in open court so that a listing might be publicised in the normal manner.

15.5. All communications with the court in respect of a DPA will be confidential and the use of secure email should be the preferred means to maintain confidentiality.

16. Publishing decisions and postponement

16.1. Transparency remains a key aspect of the success and proper operation of DPAs, and accordingly Schedule 17 of the Act requires in prescribed circumstances the prosecutor to publish on its website orders made by the court or decisions made by the prosecutor.

16.2. All requirements to publish under this section are subject to any enactment or order of the court under paragraph 12 of Schedule 17 to the Act preventing such publication from being made.

16.3. There is no requirement to publish a conclusion reached by a prosecutor alone that no breach has in fact occurred so that no application to the court has been made.

Appendix 8: Transparency International Corruption Perception Index 2020

The following figures are reproduced from the Corruption Perceptions Index 2020 by kind permission of Transparency International. The full report and analysis are available from the Transparency International website at www.transparency.org/en/cpi/2020.

This table shows the perceived levels of public sector corruption in 180 countries/territories around the world. They are scored from 0 to 100, where 0 is Highly Corrupt and 100 is Very Clean.

Transparency International Corruption Perception Index 2020

RANK	COUNTRY/ TERRITORY	SCORE
1	New Zealand	88
1	Denmark	88
3	Finland	85
3	Switzerland	85
3	Singapore	85
3	Sweden	85
7	Norway	84
8	Netherlands	82
9	Luxembourg	80
9	Germany	80
11	Canada	77
11	United Kingdom	77
11	Australia	77
11	Hong Kong	77
15	Austria	76
15	Belgium	76
17	Iceland	75
17	Estonia	75
19	Japan	74
20	Ireland	72
21	United Arab Emirates	71
21	Uruguay	71
23	France	69
24	Bhutan	68
25	United States of America	67
25	Chile	67
27	Seychelles	66
28	Taiwan	65
29	Barbados	64
30	Bahamas	63
30	Qatar	63
32	Spain	62
33	Portugal	61
33	Korea, South	61
35	Botswana	60
35	Brunel Darussalam	60
35	Israel	60
35	Slovenia	60
35	Lithuania	60
40	Saint Vincent and the Grenadines	59
41	Cabo Verde	59
42	Cyprus	57
42	Costa Rica	57
42	Latvia	57
45	Poland	56
45	Georgia	56
45	Saint Lucia	56
48	Dominica	55

RANK	COUNTRY/ TERRITORY	SCORE
49	Czech Republic	54
49	Rwanda	54
49	Oman	54
49	Latvia	54
49	Rwanda	54
52	Malta	53
52	Grenada	53
52	Italy	53
52	Saudi Arabia	53
52	Mauritius	53
57	Malaysia	51
57	Namibia	51
59	Greece	50
60	Slovakia	49
60	Jordan	49
60	Armenia	49
63	Cuba	47
63	Croatia	47
63	Sao Tome and Principe	47
63	Belarus	47
67	Montenegro	45
69	Romania	44
69	Hungary	44
69	South Africa	44
69	Jamaica	44
69	Bulgaria	44
69	Tunisia	44
75	Vanuatu	43
75	Ghana	43
75	Maldives	43
78	Argentina	42
78	Solomon Islands	42
78	Bahrain	42
78	China	42
78	Kuwait	42
83	Benin	41
83	Lesotho	41
83	Guyana	41
86	Morocco	40
86	India	40
86	Burkina Faso	40
86	Trinidad and Tobago	40
86	Turkey	40
86	Timor-Leste	40
92	Ecuador	39

RANK	COUNTRY/ TERRITORY	SCORE
92	Colombia	39
94	Suriname	38
94	Serbia	38
94	Sri Lanka	38
94	Tanzania	38
94	Ethiopia	38
94	Peru	38
94	Brazil	38
94	Kazakhstan	38
102	Indonesia	37
102	Gambia	37
115	Moldova	34
117	Egypt	33
117	Eswatini	33
117	Zambia	33
117	Nepal	33
117	Sierra Leone	33
123	Ukraine	33
124	Pakistan	31
124	Bolivia	31
124	Kyrgyzstan	31
124	Mexico	31
124	Kenya	31
104	Vietnam	36
104	Kosovo	36
104	Thailand	36
104	Albania	36
104	Cote d'Ivoire	36
104	Algeria	36
104	El Salvador	36
111	Bosnia and Herzegovina	35
111	Panama	35
111	Mongolia	35
111	North Macedonia	35
115	Philippines	34
129	Gabon	30
129	Malawi	30
129	Azerbaijan	30
129	Mali	30
129	Russia	30
134	Togo	29
134	Laos	29
134	Mauritania	29
137	Myanmar	28
137	Guinea	28
137	Liberia	28

RANK	COUNTRY/ TERRITORY	SCORE
137	Dominican Republic	28
137	Paraguay	28
142	Djibouti	27
142	Papua New Guinea	27
142	Uganda	27
142	Angola	27
146	Bangladesh	26
146	Central African Republic	26
146	Uzbekistan	26
149	Lebanon	25
149	Iran	25
149	Guatemala	25
149	Nigeria	25
149	Mozambique	25
149	Cameroon	25
149	Tajikistan	25
149	Madagascar	25
157	Zimbabwe	24
159	Nicaragua	22
160	Comoros	21
160	Eritrea	21
160	Cambodia	21
160	Chad	21
160	Iraq	21
165	Burundi	19
165	Congo	19
165	Turkmenistan	19
165	Guinea-Bissau	19
165	Afghanistan	19
170	Haiti	18
170	Democratic Republic of the Congo	18
170	Korea, North	18
173	Libya	17
174	Equatorial Guinea	16
174	Sudan	16
176	Venezuela	15
176	Yemen	15
178	Syria	14
179	South Sudan	12
179	Somalia	12

Every effort has been made to verify the accuracy of the information contained in this report. All information was believed to be correct as of January 2021. Nevertheless, Transparency International cannot accept responsibility for the consequences of its use for other purposes or in other contexts.

Index

All references are to paragraph number